HANDBOOK OF MANAGEMENT CONSULTING

The Contemporary Consultant

Insights from World Experts

Contributors

Larry Bennigson
Arvind Bhambri
Anthony Buono
Richard Chase
Tom Cummings
Fiona Czerniawska
Tom Davenport
Robert Duboff
Alan Glassman
Larry Greiner
Philip Kotler
Ravi Kumar
Edward Lawler
Jay Lorsch

David Maister
James Malernee
Susan Mohrman
David Nadler
Richard Nolan
Robert Quinn
Shawn Quinn
Flemming Poulfelt
Larry Prusac
Stephen Rhinesmith
Adrian J. Slywotzky
Robert Spekman
Morley Winograd

Larry Greiner
and
Flemming Poulfelt
Editors

THOMSON

™

SOUTH-WESTERN

Australia • Canada • Mexico • Singapore • Spain • United Kingdom • United States

THOMSON
SOUTH-WESTERN

Handbook of Management Consulting – The Contemporary Consultant
Insights from World Experts

Larry Greiner and Flemming Poulfelt, Editors

VP/Editorial Director:
Jack W. Calhoun

Production Editor:
Starratt E. Alexander

Production House:
OffCenter Concept House

VP/Editor-in-Chief:
Michael P. Roche

Manufacturing Coordinator:
Rhonda Utley

Internal Designer:
Justin Klefeker

Publisher:
Melissa S. Acuña

Technology Project Editor:
Kristen Meere

Cover Designer:
Justin Klefeker and Chris Miller

Executive Editor:
John Szilagyi

Media Editor:
Karen L. Schaffer

Cover Images:
©Corbis

**Senior Developmental
Editor:**
Mardell Toomey

Design Project Manager:
Justin Klefeker

Printer:
Transcontinental Printing, Inc.
Louiseville, QC

Marketing Manager:
Jacquelyn Carrillo

Table of Contents

Preface

The consulting industry and the profession itself are undergoing rapid and dramatic change where neither will be the same again. Most of the old fundamentals about how to consult and what to consult about are now in a state of question and transformation. These radical changes are being produced by a myriad of new forces in the consulting environment, including especially the Internet, information technology, and globalization. Client demands are moving toward higher and different expectations, and the consultant's job is being revolutionized.

To be an effective consultant in this rapidly changing world, one must be "out front" in both specialized knowledge and in perspective for the wider world of the consulting industry as well as the competitive issues facing increasingly sophisticated clients. This book contributes not only the "big picture" for viewing the leading edge in the consulting industry today, but it takes the reader into the changing specifics of the major practice areas, new contexts for consulting, emerging issues now facing clients, modern change concepts and intervention methods, and the multiple challenges of managing growth and performance in consulting firms.

Foremost, the book is about the "mindset" of the contemporary consultant—his or her ways of thinking, attitudes, skills, and capabilities in identifying and resolving complex issues within unique client situations. Readers should include long experienced consultants, beginning consultants, aspiring consultants, teachers of consultants, leaders of consulting firms, solo practitioners, students of consulting, researchers on consultants, and clients who want to become more savvy about the use of consultants.

But this is not a "how to do it" book. Many such specialized texts are already on the market, covering everything from proposal writing to selling projects; these books are useful but understandably narrow in their focus and standard solutions. Rather, the goal of this book is to provide both breadth and depth about today's rapidly changing face of management consulting—where the industry is today, where it has been, and where it is going. The profession is rich, complex, and changing and needs understanding from many angles.

To evaluate this evolving picture, we have called on twenty-five authors, all leading experts and highly experienced in consulting, to describe and explore each of their special areas, from past to future. These authors provide the reader with the heightened awareness and deeper knowledge needed to prepare for success in the changing consulting environment.

Transformation best characterizes what is happening to the industry of management consulting. Its traditional focus on the consultant performing the role of specialist diagnostician is being supplemented and often times replaced by one of facilitator and increasingly as a seller of hardware and software while serving as an employee of a mega corporation that owns other businesses outside consulting. Much of this revolution is being caused by the impact of information technology, which has lead to new opportunities ranging from e-business to outsourcing to the automation of corporate staff functions and the use of online consulting tools. All of which gives rise to changing definitions and debate about what is and is not management consulting.

The genesis of this book began with the editors' passion for the consulting field and their concern that management consulting was lacking in its intellectual foundation. New consultants were entering the field without sufficient preparation and perspective about what consulting was really about. And many advanced consultants had been narrowly trained by spending their entire careers in one firm where they were beholden only to their particular firm's approach to consulting.

When we first went about laying out the book, we identified six major sections with several chapters within each section. The sections ranged from the industry to knowledge management to the consulting change process and to the management of consulting firms. However, it rapidly became clear to us that no single author could write a book of such breadth and depth. So we turned to several leading experts from around the world who possessed wide knowledge and consulting experience in each of the particular chapters we had in mind.

As a way of attracting the authors, we invited them to a two-day conference where they presented outlines of their proposed chapters. The other authors sat in the audience and reacted with valuable feedback. After the conference, the authors drafted their chapters and went on to draft three or four revisions as we, the editors, made suggestions back to them. Several authors even went outside for critique by other consultants and scholars. Amazingly, everyone stayed with the project and gave their best effort.

The result is a book about consulting issues, current trends, analytical frameworks, different situations, substantive knowledge, intervention approaches, potential pitfalls, and future predictions—all of which are essential for the consultant to be readily aware of before diving in and applying one's favorite approach to consulting to a particular client. Without this broader perspective, a consultant's personally preferred approach, or any "how to do it" method, can easily be applied blindly and wrongly, causing client resistance or even missing the mark completely.

We want to express our admiration and appreciation to our authors who joined us in this stimulating but uncertain venture, and were willing to share their knowledge, wisdom and experience in an open way with everyone who reads this book. Our publisher constantly went the extra mile for us, including especially Executive Editor John Szilagyi for his thoughtful and friendly support, ideas, and consideration from the beginning to end, as well as his high performing editorial and production team of Mardell Toomey and Starratt Alexander. Sheryl Nelson did a superb job of editing. We also want to thank Bill Hicks and Alan Harvey, friends and early supporters who liked the idea of this book and encouraged us.Our families also constantly reminded us about the joys of life beyond sitting in front of a computer screen. Books of this type are clearly a team effort, from authors to loved ones to publishers, and we are very grateful to all of them.

Larry Greiner and Flemming Poulfelt

Author Biographies

Lawrence A. Bennigson is a senior fellow and senior vice president of Harvard Business School Interactive. He oversees development, design, and delivery of the school's custom executive development programs for individual companies. He has been president of the Scandinavian Institutes for Administrative Research in the United States, a Managing Partner of The MAC Group, and senior vice president of Gemini Consulting. He is a board member of public companies and serves on the Advisory Board of Toffler Associates, founded by Alvin and Heidi Toffler, the futurists.

Arvind Bhambri is Associate Professor of Management and Organization at the Marshall School, University of Southern California, where he specializes in strategic change, competitive strategy, global business development, and leadership. He is co-author of three books and more than thirty articles and cases.

Anthony F. Buono is a Professor of Management and Sociology at Bentley College. He has written and edited seven books and is editor of the *Research in Management Consulting* book series. Dr. Buono is past Chair of the Academy of Management's Management Consulting Division. His research and consulting interests include the management consulting industry, organizational change, and mergers and acquisitions.

Richard B. Chase is Professor of Operations Management at the Marshall School, University of Southern California. He has written and lectured extensively on the subject of service design. His textbook, *Operations Management for Competitive Advantage* (with R. Jacobs and N. Aquilano) ninth edition, has been among the most widely adopted textbooks in the field for over twenty-five years.

Thomas Cummings is Professor and Chair of the Department of Management and Organization at the Marshall School of Business, University of Southern California. He has authored/co-authored nineteen books and is currently vice president/Program Chair Elect of the Academy of Management. His major research and consulting interests include designing high-performing organizations and strategic change management.

Fiona Czerniawska is the founder and managing director of Arkimeda, a research firm focusing on strategic issues in the consulting industry. She is also the Director of the UK Management Consultancies Association's Think Tank. Dr. Czerniawska is the author of numerous books and articles on the consulting industry, including *Management Consulting: What Next?*, *Value-Based Consulting*, and *The Intelligent Client.*

Tom Davenport is Director of the Accenture Institute for Strategic Change and the President's Distinguished Professor of Information Technology and Management at Babson College. He has also led research centers at McKinsey and Company, Ernst & Young, and CSC Index. Dr. Davenport has co-authored or edited ten books, including books on business process reengineering, knowledge management, and enterprise systems.

Robert Duboff is a lecturer and Executive-in-Residence at The Carroll School of Management at Boston College. He was a line consultant for over two decades with Mercer Management Consulting, serving a client base that featured professional service firms. He then served as Director of Marketing for Ernst & Young.

Alan M. Glassman is Professor of Management and Director of the Center for Management and Organization Development, California State University, Northridge. He has served as Chair of the Managerial Consultation Division of the Academy of Management and editor of *Consultation: An International Journal.* He consults actively with municipal governments, the criminal justice system, and social services.

Larry Greiner is Professor of Management and Organization in the Marshall School at the University of Southern California. Dr. Greiner has served as Chair of Managerial Consultation Division of the Academy of Management. He is the author of numerous books and articles on organization growth, management consulting, and strategic change, including *Consulting to Management,* with Robert Metzger.

Philip Kotler is the S.C. Johnson Distinguished Professor of International Marketing at the J.L. Kellogg Graduate School of Management. He has been honored as one of the world's leading marketing thinkers. Dr. Kotler is the author of over 100 articles and twenty-five books, including *Marketing Management, Principles of Marketing, Social Marketing, and The Marketing of Nations.* His research covers strategic marketing, consumer marketing, professional services marketing, and e-marketing.

Ravi Kumar is Professor of Information and Operations Management in the Marshall School at the University of Southern California. He is the author or co-author of many articles on operations management. Dr. Kumar teaches courses on Operations Consulting and has consulted with many global Fortune 100 companies in the United States, Europe, and Asia.

Edward E. Lawler III is Distinguished Professor of Business and Director of the Center for Effective Organizations in the Marshall School at the University of Southern California. His most recent books include: *Corporate Boards: New Strategies for Adding Value at the Top, Organizing for High Performance, Treat People Right,* and *Creating a Strategic Human Resources Organization.*

Jay Lorsch is the Louis Kirstein Professor of Human Relations at the Harvard Business School. He is the author of many articles and over a dozen books, including *Aligning the Stars,* and *Pawns or Potentates: The Reality of America's Corporate Boards.* Dr. Lorsch has been a consultant to many companies in the United States and abroad and is currently a director of three companies.

David Maister consults to professional firms worldwide. He is the author of numerous articles and books on professional service firms, including *Managing the Professional Service Firm, True Professionalism, The Trusted Advisor, Practice What You Preach,* and *First Among Equals.*

James Malernee, co-founded Cornerstone Research, a litigation research and consulting firm, in 1989. Dr. Malernee is CEO of the firm and heads its New York City office. Prior to that, Dr. Malernee was a senior vice president of The MAC Group, a general management consulting firm. He has taught finance at the University of Texas at Austin and business strategy at the Stanford Graduate School of Business.

Susan A. Mohrman is senior research scientist at the Center for Effective Organizations in the Marshall School at the University of Southern California. She researches and writes in the areas of organizational design and effectiveness, knowledge and technology management, and the human resources function. She is the co-author of three books and several articles, and consults to a number of organizations on team-based management.

David A. Nadler is Chairman of Mercer Delta Consulting, a management consulting firm. Dr. Nadler consults at the CEO level, specializing in the areas of large-scale organization change, executive leadership, and corporate governance. He has written numerous articles and book chapters and has authored and/or edited fourteen books. He is a member of the Academy of Management and was elected a Fellow of the American Psychological Association.

Richard Nolan is the William Barclay Harding Professor of Management of Technology, at the Harvard Business School. Previously, he was Chairman of Nolan, Norton & Co. from 1977 to 1992. His research and consulting interests include business transformation and information technology. His latest book is *Dot Vertigo,* which reports his case-based research on management lessons from both dot com companies and industrial age companies when incorporating the Internet into their operations.

Flemming Poulfelt is Professor of Management and Strategy and Vice Dean at Copenhagen Business School in Denmark. His research and consulting focuses on strategic management, knowledge management, and management consulting. He is the author of numerous books and articles on professional services firms and management consulting. He is a past Chair of the Management Consulting Division of the Academy of Management and has served on various corporate boards.

Larry Prusak is a researcher and consultant living in Lexington, Massachusetts. Over the past twenty-five years, he has worked for five major management consulting firms in a variety of roles. His most recent books include: *What's the Big Idea,* co-authored with Tom Davenport, and *In Good Company,* co-authored with Don Cohen.

Robert E. Quinn holds the Margaret Elliot Tracy Collegiate Professorship at the University of Michigan. Dr. Quinn's research and teaching interests focus on organization effectiveness and leadership. Quinn has written several articles and books, including *Letters to Garrett, A Company of Leaders,* and *Change the World.* He has consulted with nearly 100 of the Fortune 500.

Shawn E. Quinn is a full-time consultant and project manager at Creativity-at-Work. He specializes in designing and facilitating organizational change processes, with particular emphasis on aligning vision, strategy, technology and human systems. He holds a Masters degree in Organizational Psychology from Columbia University.

Stephen H. Rhinesmith is a partner in CDR International and focuses on global business strategy implementation and human resource development.

Dr. Rhinesmith has served as a consultant to many Fortune 100 corporations on the development of global competencies and corporate cultures. His recent book, *A Manager's Guide to Globalization,* is used in management and leadership development programs throughout the world.

Adrian J. Slywotzky is vice president and member of the Board of Directors of Mercer Management Consulting, Inc., where his responsibilities include leading the development of the firm's intellectual capital. Mr. Slywotzky is the co-author of *How to Grow When Markets Don't, How Digital Is Your Business, Profit Patterns,* and *The Profit Zone.*

Robert E. Spekman is the Tayloe Murphy Professor of Business Administration at The Darden School. He is a recognized authority on business-to-business marketing and strategic alliances. He has edited/written seven books and has authored (co-authored) over eighty articles and papers. Among his consulting clients are many Fortune 100 companies.

Morley A. Winograd is a managing principal of Governmentum Partners, L.L.C. and Executive Director of the Center for Telecommunications Management and Associate Professor of Clinical at the Marshall School of Business at the University of Southern California. He served as Senior Policy Advisor to Vice President Gore and Director of the National Partnership for Reinventing Government. He is the co-author, with Dudley Buffa, of *Taking Control: Politics in the Information Age.*

Part 1

Consulting Industry, Skills and Professionalism

INTRODUCTION

Management consulting has long been in the fast lane of an expansive and straight track that has never seemed to circle back on itself. In Chapter 1, "The Changing Global Consulting Industry," it makes clear that the business of consulting has grown faster than most other businesses, not only from increased demand by clients, but also from the innovative capabilities of numerous consulting firms as they developed new services. At the end of the last century, the world economy was booming. Everything was moving fast and upwards, seemingly unstoppable. An economic tailwind was apparent as the consulting business rode its tidal wave of success.

However, trees rarely grow into the sky—not even for the consulting industry. In late 2001, a sudden downturn for the industry occurred when a number of negative forces, beginning with the 9/11 tragedy and the Enron debacle, deeply impacted the economies of the world. Chapter 1 describes these changes and how the industry responded with cost cutting, layoffs, and deficits. But beneath these quick fixes, the chapter also points out that a number of transformational forces are still deeply at work within the industry, producing new challenges for firms and for consultants. The industry itself will be transformed over the coming decade.

Major changes stemming from the Internet and information technology are likely to significantly alter the face of consulting for the long term. The outsourcing of IT services is changing the economic and strategic face of many consulting firms. In addition, clients have become more sophisticated, now expecting their consultants to collaborate rather than to stand apart as lone objective evaluators. Strategic responses from consulting firms and their consultants to these many changes will determine their mutual fate in the years ahead.

But changes in services, economics, and skills will likely not be enough. The improprieties in its audit and consulting divisions that lead to the demise of Arthur Andersen has brought to the forefront the importance of professionalism and ethical conduct in management consulting. Chapter 2's focus, "Professionalism in Consulting," recognizes that the lack of professionalism by a few consultants is able to bring down a whole firm and place a taint on the entire industry. This chapter attempts to define professionalism and how it should be inculcated by firms into the psyches of consultants. The concept of professionalism, in the author's view, is an ambiguous one that refers to a wide range of skills, attitudes, values, and behavior. He points out that professionalism is a state of mind embedded in the consultant's individual behavior, and thus is not easily regulated by codes of ethics and industry rules.

The key message of Chapter 2 is that professionalism is nothing a consultant can claim for himself or herself; rather, it's an adjective that one hopes that clients and colleagues will apply to each other's behavior. Professionalism, in essence, has to be earned through one's daily behavior by taking the "high road" to results.

The marketing and competitive positioning of a consulting firm affects not only the success of the firm but its degree of professionalism and even the future of the industry. In Chapter 3, "The Marketing and Selling of Consulting Services," the author makes clear that without successful marketing, no consulting revenue is forthcoming. The chapter emphasizes that successful consulting requires both effective marketing and exceptional sales skills; one cannot exist without the other. Consulting is a subjective service that is purchased by wary clients who need both persuasion and reassurance when making large expenditures for consulting projects in the millions of dollars. The ethics of consulting marketing require that clients be lead to expect a service that can be delivered as promised. Chapter 3 discusses various other issues in marketing and sales, such as the role of market research, compensation and rewards, relationship marketing, public relations, sponsorship, and ethical marketing. Although consulting has become more mature as a business, the underlying theme of the chapter is that professional marketing and sales are still in their youth searching for maturity.

Taken together, these three chapters provide an important orientation to a dynamic industry, the complex issues facing it and the required skills that consultants, both neophytes and those with long experience, will need to acquire if they are to succeed. While there are many problems to overcome, the opportunities remain bright. Consulting is an industry making a significant impact far beyond its size, not only for improving the performance of clients but also in developing new knowledge about business and in improving the state of the global economy.

CHAPTER 1

The Changing Global Consulting Industry
Flemming Poulfelt, Larry Greiner, and Arvind Bhambri

For over four decades leading up to 2000 and the new millennium, the management consulting industry experienced explosive and continuous growth, approximating an increase of 15 to 20 percent per year. Profit margins also increased dramatically, due to larger projects, better leverage ratios between partners and staff, and diversification into new services, such as outsourcing. Total revenues of the global industry are now moving toward $150 billion, and the worldwide number of consultants is close to one million, including both those who work in large and small firms, as well as solo practitioners. Few other industries in history have experienced such sustained growth and financial success for so long a period of time.

This impressive record of growth and financial success is only an indication of the consulting industry's deeper and wider impact around the world. Over the years, the industry's many firms and consultants have made significant worldwide contributions to management know-how and, in so doing, have greatly advanced the cause of professionalism in management. They have also improved the performance of thousands of companies and public agencies, leading to significant economic growth in many industrialized countries. In addition, management consulting has helped greatly to advance the quality of education in business schools, and it has become a major employer for graduating MBAs and an elite training ground for many of today's CEOs and senior executives.

Yet, despite all its success, the consulting industry is today in a state of continuing economic transformation, insecurity, and heightened uncertainty about its future. This is a troubling but challenging condition that, as it evolves, will likely serve to redefine future winners and losers and eventually the industry's overall structure and direction.

The Big Shock

The year 2000 began with a major wakeup call for the consulting industry, beginning noticeably in the second half of 2000 and, in all likelihood, continuing well into 2004. First, there was the dot.com bust, followed by the fall of the telecom industry. Then came the 9/11 disaster, continued terrorism threats, and economic recession, all of which took a big toll on sales and morale within consulting firms. Occurring almost simultaneously was the Enron debacle and the self-inflicted demise of Arthur Andersen, leading to broader negative consequences for many accounting firms and their consulting operations. The net fallout from these events, many of which were uncontrollable, resulted in a big slowdown in growth for many consulting firms. Numerous potential clients hesitated to buy consulting services, and began requesting lower fees. Clearly, the rapid growth era of the 1990s was over.

Notwithstanding the downturn in the early 2000s, several bright spots have either survived or recently emerged. Most notable are new projects in customer relationship management (CRM), systems integration and massive information systems for government, cost-saving HR technologies, plus expanding overseas markets in Asia, as well as a heavy demand for outsourcing solutions to help clients reduce their costs.

Still, if we eliminate outsourcing from most of the revenue calculations (we consider it to be a service but not actual management consulting), the growth rate for the industry throughout the early 2000s is likely less than 10 percent and for many firms possibly even negative.

Signs of Industry Transformation

How have consulting firms responded to these serious threats and challenges brought in by the new millennium, and which are still continuing? There is obviously no single uniform response, but the main pattern has been one of shake-up, downsizing, consolidation, layoffs, hiring freezes, and even the bankruptcy of the once-venerable Arthur D. Little. Many of the large firms, whether in information technology or general management, have suffered because of their dependence on large contracts to cover expensive global infrastructures and armies of highly paid consultants.

In 2002, Deloitte Consulting asked senior executives to take a 10 percent pay cut. Even the blue chip general management firms, such as McKinsey and BCG, were forced to make capital calls on partners, while Bain borrowed from a private investor, and Booz Allen Hamilton reduced its partners by one-fourth in its private sector consulting division. Divestments have also occurred at BCG and Bain, which shed their venture businesses. Several large firms are for sale at valuations less than one-third of their value during the 1990s.

At this point in history, the industry is facing a single overriding question: Is it undergoing a significant transformation and long-term directional shift or just a mid-course correction and then back to business as usual? If we believe the former to be true, then the current cost reductions and temporary downsizings by firms will not suffice. Under the transformation scenario, consulting firms will have to change their existing strategies and restructure their practices in order to survive. No doubt one can argue both sides of this question, but we believe the odds are clearly on the side of fundamental and transformational change.

Deeper Re-Structuring Direction

The future is usually revealed in underlying historical trends rather than superficial symptoms, and to us the underlying trends emerging in client needs and industry economics point toward major transformative changes in the industry. SEC pressures have prompted the divestment of consulting divisions from the accounting firms. The computer hardware firms, notably IBM and HP, as well as information technology services companies like EDS and Cap Gemini are building substantial consulting practices, and nonconsulting companies are acquiring consulting firms. Witness Marsh-McLennan's earlier successful acquisition strategy, which began over a decade ago with William M. Mercer, followed by Temple, Barker & Sloane, Delta Consulting, National Economic Research Associates (NERA), and Lippincott and Margulies. In Europe, Atos recently acquired KPMG's UK and Netherlands consulting groups (now known as Atos KPMG) focusing on IT-related activities. Just what cash-rich Microsoft is likely to do is uncertain, but we predict it will eventually diversify out of lower margin software into higher margin IT consulting and outsourcing.

In our opinion, the future competitive life for the consulting industry will not only become different but highly challenging, especially for large consulting firms and their consultants. At the same time, we think that small and medium-sized firms will be less affected by the competitive wars occurring among the "big boys," provided these small firms are able to niche their specialized services and give highly personalized attention to local clients.

Consulting Insights	**Trianz, Inc.—Succeeding in the New Era**

During this discontinuous shift in the consulting industry, Trianz is a consulting firm that has achieved triple digit growth to become a respected player in its information technology niche. Trianz helps clients to reinvent business processes across the entire value chain using the Internet as the medium for achieving leverage in the chain. Trianz provides a full-service outsourcing infrastructure in the United States and India, supported by a team of professional consultants capable in strategic and value chain analysis.

To begin our assessment of the industry's future, we must first establish an historical perspective for the industry. In doing so, we will identify earlier trends and issues that still face firms and consultants today. As we move along, we will point out what are likely to be the changing needs of clients, and how consulting firms will have to change their strategies to meet these needs. Without this broadened perspective, consulting firms can easily misjudge where they are in the unfolding dynamics of the industry. Hanging on to past practices and strategies will likely become a recipe for future disaster.

HISTORY IN BRIEF

In a 1998 article in the *Journal of Management Consulting*, Staffan Canback made an interesting observation with reference to the experience curve in consulting services. He wrote, "If the experience curve applies in consulting services, then it may be noteworthy that approximately 80 percent of all consulting experience was generated in the last seventeen years, and only 20 percent in the period from 1886 (when Arthur D. Little started the first consulting firm) to 1980."[1] With further accumulated experience since Canback's article, we can reasonably conclude that, in this 115+ year-old industry, more than 90 percent of all experience has been generated in the last 20 years.

What are the factors that stimulated growth in the 1980s and 1990s and made the industry fundamentally different in both quantity and quality from the preceding years? What can we conclude about this growth that may influence client needs and consulting practices over the next few decades? As Exhibit 1.1 shows, changing business issues and opportunities facing clients

Exhibit 1.1	The Historical Developmentz of Consulting

Phases	Time	Firms	Management Issues
1. Origins of consulting	Before 1900	Fayol, Taylor	Birth of scientific management
2. The engineering epoch	1900–1925	Arthur D. Little	Scientific management, work design
3. Birth of personnel and HR	1925–	Hay, Towers Perrin	Human relations, compensation
4. Emergence of the generalist approach	1930	McKinsey, Booz Allen, PA	General management
5. Internationalization/ reentrance of engineering	1950	Cresap	Operations management (OR, OM)
6. Rise of computer consultants, conglomerates	1960	The Big 8 Accounting Firms	Performance measurement, electronic data processing, portfolio management
7. Business strategy	1970	BCG, Bain	Planning, organization structure, marketing, competitive advantage
8. Restructuring and effectiveness	1980	March & McLennan, Saatchi & Saatchi, KPMG, Ernst & Young	Excellence, culture, M&A, globalization
9. Information technology and reengineering	1990	Accenture, PwC, Monitor, IBM Consulting Services	Internet, leadership, change, Y2K, BPR, ERP
10. E-Business and value chain	2000	Cap Gemini/E&Y, IBM Global Services	Outsourcing, transformation, networks, alliances

have led to new management techniques and concepts, which in turn have changed the offerings of consulting firms.

Before 1950

Prior to 1950, most consulting firms focused on efficiency and technical issues in manufacturing. The first consulting firm was Arthur D. Little (ADL) founded in 1886 (and filed for bankruptcy protection in 2002). ADL grew out of a research laboratory, and it continued to maintain links with its technical roots for several decades, long after its management consulting accounted for a majority of its revenues. ADL's ascendancy occurred in the maturing period of scientific management, whose origins go back to Frederick Taylor[2] and Henri Fayol[3] in the early 1900s.

In the first half of the 20th century, most of the consulting firms were founded either with specific customer opportunities in hand, such as Booz Allen Hamilton with the U.S. government, or with a specific functional specialization, such as Towers Perrin in compensation and human resources. For the most part, this early imprinting led to a lasting impact on both firms. Thus, even today Booz Allen continues to retain significant federal business, and Towers Perrin is still known for its major presence in human resources consulting.

Following World War II, the focus of management consulting turned to designing, improving, and systematizing the internal functioning of client organizations and the marketing of products. Specific emphasis was given to designing divisional structures, formal budgeting, performance evaluation, strategic planning systems, goal setting, compensation schemes, and other such performance improvement techniques. Advertising and sales force management were major issues in marketing. Most consulting firms chose to specialize only in a narrow range of needs as expressed by clients.

In the 1960s, a dramatic and discontinuous shift occurred in the scope and complexity of management consulting. Client companies were growing rapidly through diversification and creating the first conglomerates, and the novelty of international competition was fast becoming a reality. In this changing environment, companies asked consultants for help on pressing strategic questions about which business they should be in and how they should internationalize themselves. This was the stage where the elite strategy consulting firms, such as BCG, became household names.

1960–1980

McKinsey & Co. had existed as a generalist firm for almost four decades (since 1925) when Bruce Henderson founded the Boston Consulting Group (BCG) in 1963. Henderson pioneered the marketable idea of strategy consulting based on expert analysis of a client's competitive situation. BCG differentiated itself through promoting new strategy concepts, notably the Experience Curve and the Growth/Share Matrix. The accelerating popularity of these concepts began to establish the credibility of consulting firms as developers of intellectual capital and lead to a two-way, synergistic relationship between business schools and consulting firms. The top strategy consulting firms became the first job choice of MBAs, an advantageous recruiting position that certain elite firms like McKinsey and BCG continue to maintain to this day.

During the 1960s nontraditional players began to enter the consulting industry, but often with mixed results. A negative example was Citibank acquiring Cresap, McCormack & Paget, and then divesting it to preserve the consulting firm's independence. Eventually, Towers Perrin acquired Cresap. The high visibility of top strategy consulting firms in the 1960s also attracted attention from the Big 8 accounting firms, which had long established auditing and tax relationships with many large Fortune 500 companies. Without exception, these accounting firms all launched management consulting services, which promised higher fees and margins than yielded by their auditing services. For the most part, the consulting divisions of the accounting firms were not able to penetrate the elite strategy market. However, with a larger employee base and lower fees than the strategy boutiques, they gravitated toward operations consulting and information technology.

1980–2000

By the end of 1980, the stage was set for the golden era of management consulting, which evolved around information technology and global expansion. Consulting firms grew in the 1980s and 1990s through both organic means by developing new practices in-house and also rapidly by mergers and acquisitions. This was also the era of global growth for U.S. consulting firms as they moved out around the world to capture over 80 percent of the world consulting market.

At the same time, the accounting firms made many mergers and acquisitions in order to achieve greater scale and leverage in their auditing and consulting practices. Thus, we saw PMI (Peat Marwick International) merge with KMG (Klynveld Main Goerdeler) in 1987 to become KPMG; Deloitte merged with Touche Ross in 1989 and turned into Deloitte & Touche; Ernst & Whiney with Arthur Young in 1989 to become Ernst & Young; and Price Waterhouse with Coopers & Lybrand in 1998 turning into PricewaterhouseCoopers. In addition, numerous small- and medium-sized consultancies were acquired by larger firms during this same period, such as the French company Sogetti in 1991 acquiring both the MAC Group, which was founded as a faculty-based general management consulting firm, and United Research, an operations consulting firm. These latter acquisitions were merged to form the core of Gemini Consulting.

Attracted by the consulting industry's growth and high profitability, several nontraditional companies also attempted to enter the industry through high profile acquisitions. Saatchi & Saatchi was one of the first companies to articulate the concept of "one-stop-shopping" for professional services. Their acquisitions included Petersen in litigation consulting and Hay in human resources and compensation consulting, along with other companies in market research and financial services. The results of Saatchi's acquisition strategy proved disastrous; most of the acquired consulting firms were later sold back to their original sellers for a fraction of the price paid just a few years earlier. Marsh & McLennan, from insurance, was more successful in moving into consulting with the acquisition of Mercer and several other professional services firms.

By the 1990s, the main driver for acquisitions appeared to shift toward providing integrated IT solutions under one roof, which in turn led to EDS acquiring A. T. Kearney and to CSC acquiring Index. These combinations were not deterred even though some consulting acquisitions by nonconsulting firms resulted in serious incompatibilities. By far the largest growth during this period occurred among the information system providers. Driven by the increasing interdependence of information technology and strategy, these firms helped clients to formulate an information strategy, and then to design and install the appropriate IT infrastructure; all of which is further discussed in Chapter 4, *Information Technology Consulting*.

During the late 1990s, many of the IT consultancies diversified into outsourcing, which subsequently became a major growth driver. As clients began outsourcing their entire IT departments to consultants, it attracted hardware and software firms like IBM and EDS. In the marketing of outsourcing, the consultant's value-added proposition is that of shifting assets to the consultant so the client's balance sheet is improved, and the client can focus on its core business.

Firms in the IT segment included IBM Global Services, which is now the largest consulting firm in the world, Electronic Data Systems (EDS), Accenture, Deloitte Consulting, and Cap Gemini Ernst & Young (CGE&Y). Their primary consulting focus, other than outsourcing, is on providing a wide range of IT services, including: 1) the assessment of a client's IT infrastructure; 2) the development of appropriate systems and software; 3) the integration of incompatible technology; 4) the redesign of business processes; 5) the purchase and installation of appropriate hardware; and 6) change management and training of employees. Among the many services provided by these firms, strategy analysis is a relatively small segment, and even it is usually conducted with an IT emphasis.

2000 into the Storm

As Exhibit 1.2 shows, in 2001–2002, the ten largest consulting firms recorded approximately $52 billion in revenues (about 42 percent of the total market), up from less than $2 billion in 1980. This suggests an industry that is increasingly dominated by a few large firms, primarily IT-oriented firms. Only two generalist firms, McKinsey and Mercer Consulting, appear in the top ten in revenues. The IT firms remain at the top even if we discount their revenues by 20 to 40 percent derived from outsourcing.

Exhibit 1.2	The 10 Largest Global Management Consulting Firms, 2001–2002		
	Revenues (US$/b)	Number of Consultants	Estimated Market Share (%)
IBM	$10.8	50,000	8.6
Accenture	9.5	63,000	7.6
Cap Gemini Ernst & Young	5.9	31,500	4.7
Deloitte Consulting	5.6	26,000	4.5
PricewaterhouseCoopers Consulting	5.5	32,000	4.4
CSC	3.6	15,500	2.9
McKinsey & Co.	3.3	8,400	2.6
EDS (incl. A. T. Kearny)	2.9	8,900	2.3
KPMG Consulting	2.7	7,500	2.1
Mercer Consulting Group	2.2	11,700	1.8
Total	$52.0	254,500	41.5

Source: Management Consultant International, June 2002

If we break down total revenues into separate practice areas, Exhibit 1.3 reveals that, in 2001–2002, the ten largest consulting firms accounted for approximately $9.8 billion in revenue for the strategy practice area; the ten largest information technology practices for $27.6 billion; the ten largest human resources consulting practices for $9.2 billion; and the ten largest operations consulting practices for $9.9 billion. As one can see, the IT segment is about three times larger than each of the remaining services, all of which are at about the same level.

Interestingly, in Exhibit 1.3, twenty-two different firms compose the top ten across the four practice areas, which indicates some degree of cross-specialization, since the table would require forty firms if it was "pure" specialization

Exhibit 1.3		The Top Ten Revenue Firms in Four Practice Areas					
Strategy	2001	IT	2001	HR	2001	Operations	2001
1. Deloitte Consulting	$1.7	IBM	$8.6	Mercer Consulting Group	$1.9	Accenture	$2.5
2. McKinsey & Co.	1.6	PwC	3.2	Accenture	1.2	CGE&Y	1.4
3. Accenture	1.4	Deloitte	2.8	D&T - Human Capital	1.2	PwC	1.1
4. BCG	0.9	Accenture	2.6	Towers Perrin	1.1	IBM	1.1
5. CGE&Y	0.9	EDS	2.6	Watson Wyatt	1.0	McKinsey & Co.	0.9
6. CSC	0.8	CSC	2.1	Aon Consulting	0.9	Deloitte Consulting	0.8
7. PwC	0.7	KPMG	1.8	PwC	0.5	CSC	0.7
8. Bain & Co.	0.7	CGE&Y	1.6	Hewitt Associates	0.5	EDS/A. T. Kearney	0.6
9. Booz Allen Hamilton	0.6	Atos	1.2	Buck Consultants	0.5	Booz Allen Hamilton	0.5
10. EDS/A. T. Kearney	0.5	T-Systems	1.1	Andersen	0.4	Getronics	0.3
TOTAL	$9.8		$27.6		$9.2		$9.9

All numbers are in billion dollars
Source: *Consultant News,* 2002

with no overlap across practice areas. However, only two firms, Accenture and PwC (now IBM) have been successful in broadly diversifying themselves across all four categories, although we suspect that much of this coverage is closely related to IT activities.

As for profitability, the economics clearly favor the strategy consulting firms over the IT consultants. The top strategy consulting firms average about $450,000 in revenues per consultant per year, which compares to approximately $200,000 in IT-based consultancies. The profits per strategy consultant are considerably higher than in IT firms. Although Accenture is approximately eight times bigger than McKinsey in total number of employees, it is only three times larger in total revenues. However, the IT firms clearly lead in total revenues and total profits because of their much greater size.

Exhibit 1.3 also suggests that human resources consulting is a highly specialized field where the IT firms are not so dominating. However, this practice area is also more IT-focused in its development (see Chapter 8 on *Human Resources Consulting*). Apparently, the fastest growing part of human resources consulting lies not in its historical work on HR strategy and compensation but in arranging for the outsourcing of a client's back-office HR functions. In these arrangements, some or all of a client's entire payroll, benefits, and training programs are transferred to an outsourcing partner.

ENDURING TRENDS AND CLIENT NEEDS

The current period of industry turmoil provides an opportunity for consulting firms to examine the underlying forces shaping the future needs of clients. Being able to meet these needs will determine the consulting winners in the future. Firms need to avoid the easy assumption that their growth is assured by client growth. Today, many clients aren't growing, or they are turning away from consultants to rely on their own staff professionals for help. So it is important to begin with prospective clients to see what is on their minds—this is where all consulting firms should their start analyses as they reexamine their future business strategies.

We detect five major trends affecting client needs, all of which arose over the past decade and are likely to continue into the future. Consulting firms must tune their service offerings to these trends.

1. Keeping up with the pace of change. All industries have increasingly had to cope with ever shortening product life cycles. Although some industries, such as personal computers and consumer electronics, have long operated with cycles of less than a year, even traditional, long life-cycle companies like aircraft engines and airplane manufacturers are now greatly reducing their cycle times for competitive reasons. In addition, many potential clients are facing other threatening shifts that limit long-term thinking, such as new nontraditional competitors, deregulation, and technological shifts—all of which create uncertainty and cause companies to rethink their strategic positions and reinvent themselves more frequently.

Discontinuous change requires new strategic concepts, which is the province of strategy consultants. Not surprisingly, new and proprietary strategy concepts and tools have become a major basis for achieving differentiation among the offerings of consulting firms (see Chapter 5, *Strategy and Organization Consulting*). In the future, consulting firms that focus their strategies and skills on helping clients with issues of speed to market, whether it is in operations or in marketing, will likely receive a favorable audience.

2. Continuously reducing costs. Operational efficiency and cost containment have become necessary for corporate survival (see Chapter 7, *Operations Management Consulting*). As a result, companies are seriously reevaluating their mix of operating activities, and many are deciding to outsource activities that are not part of their core competency. For the most part, these outsourced functions include back-office departments concerned with logistics, data processing, human resources transactions, and sometimes even the complete manufacturing of products.

This trend toward reconfiguring a company's value chain is leading to considerable growth in consulting. Consultants are undertaking large projects to help companies assess and reengineer their activity mix, assisting them in deciding what their core competencies are, and what activities should be outsourced. In addition, consulting firms are becoming primary outsourcing and infrastructure providers to their clients. This is opening up an entirely new and sizeable revenue stream with a reliable cash flow, in contrast to a tradition of sporadic payments by clients.

3. Accelerating product and market development. As companies face maturing markets and intense competition in their home bases, they are actively seeking new products and redesigning old ones. In this effort, tradition-bound companies often lack creativity within their organization cultures, and so they look to consultants for outside help. This requires consultants to study customers' needs and competing products and to work closely with a client's R&D, marketing and product designers, as illustrated in Chapter 6, *The Marketing Consultant.*

In addition, there are now major international openings in nontraditional markets, including China, India, and Eastern Europe. With limited experience in these markets and abundant horror stories of failed ventures, client companies are seeking assistance from consultants with offices abroad. Not surprisingly, McKinsey's office in India became its fastest growing, most profitable office in the late 1990s.

4. Coping with discontinuous technology shifts. Many experts argue that science and technology are driving the economics of business and product development. Moving from central mainframes to client-servers and distributed computing, from intra-networks to EDI and then to Web-based collaboration, many companies have found that information technology is not just an implementation tool but a key driver of business strategy. Most companies have learned painfully that the impact of information technology has been pervasive throughout society, causing them to rethink strategically the state of their product lines, asset utilization, and likely future markets.

This need has in turn reopened debates such as "What should be owned versus outsourced?" and "Where in the value chain should we add value?" Indeed, companies like Dell have become industry leaders because of their ability to outsource almost their entire value chain, and thereby construct a new business model based on tight coordination with outsiders. On the other hand, Nokia outsources very little of its operations relative to its competition, and yet it remains successful through the extensive use of IT for coordinating internal production and logistics.

The emergence of industry leaders with nontraditional business models, such as Dell, has made it a business imperative for companies to reexamine the fundamentals of their business models. For example, entrenched competitors like General Motors and Ford have come together to form a joint venture, Covisint, to create and manage common e-commerce platforms for procurement. Similarly, the largest consumer packaged goods companies have joined to form Transora. In both cases, a major portion of the initial budget of these new ventures went to consulting firms who helped to set up the joint venture.

5. Meeting the global imperative. As we shall see in Chapter 10, *Globalization Consulting,* consulting firms of all sizes, in order to prosper in the future, are positioning themselves to handle the globalization of industries and companies. Large consulting firms will need to locate themselves overseas at many sites, and smaller ones will have to join with larger consulting firms to assist clients in addressing issues of globalization. Consultants have long recognized that their clients will require at some point a global presence and perspective. However, many consulting firms choose to globalize only after following an existing client overseas. More proactive consulting firms have decided to internationalize before their clients so as to exploit new markets abroad. For example, a U.S. firm choosing Japan can begin to serve back-home clients but also local companies in Japan. Research also supports a commonly held belief among large potential clients that consulting firms must be international in order to qualify as a leading-edge player.

Moving abroad may also be a matter of survival. In a 1990 report from ACME, it was noted that North American consulting firms had experienced a continuing drop in revenues attributable to domestic operations to 81 percent of total revenues, with predictions of a further drop to 67 percent in 2000.[4] Similar shifts have been observed in Europe. According to *Consultants News* in 2002, the breakdown of total worldwide consulting revenues is as follows: 56.6 percent North America, 34.5 percent Europe, Latin America 1.4 percent, Asia Pacific 5.6 percent and rest of world 2 percent.[5] These numbers indicate that, although consulting is popularly regarded as a global industry, 90 percent of the market remains concentrated in North America and Europe. Interestingly, Asia trails far behind with only 5.6 percent, which not only indicates an opportunity, but also a difficult challenge to penetrate.

All fifty leading global consultancies now occupy offices spread around the world. A majority have expanded abroad through mergers, acquisitions, joint ventures, and alliances. Today, many firms are focusing on Asia, especially China (see Consulting Firms in China). However, some have also closed offices or operations during this same period due to the recession and an inability to manage operations in a different culture. For example, both CSC Index and Gemini closed down in Japan after several years of frustration and lack of success.

RESPONSES OF CONSULTING FIRMS TO MARKET TRENDS

In this section, we give our opinions about how consulting firms are adjusting to the new competitive world facing them. These adjustments represent the transformation currently taking place in the consulting industry.

Consulting Insights | **Consulting Firms in China**

Is China the next big growth market? In 2002, BearingPoint was the largest international consulting practice in China with about 350 consultants in four offices, and two more soon to open. Its main clients include Beijing Airport Group, China Construction Bank, Samsung, BMW, and China Mobile. The consulting market in China is growing about 50 percent per year. Other firms present include: McKinsey with 180 consultants and $20 million revenue, A. T. Kearney with 70 consultants and $6 million, and Accenture with 160 consultants and $4 million. Also present are Mercer, Monitor, BCG and Roland Berger. The largest domestic firm is HANPU (51 percent owned by China's Legend Computers) in IT consulting with 400 consultants. Clients of these firms include multinationals trying to become profitable in China, large SOEs (state-owned enterprises) required by government and WTO entry to restructure to become private and profitable (telecom, aerospace, energy, banking), and government ministries attempting to become more effective and less bureaucratic. Key issues include strategy (planning, implementation, change), marketing (branding, advertising, channels), and operations management (organization, goal setting, incentives, control systems). Barriers include a lack of understanding among Chinese managers about value and use of consultants. International consulting firms face difficulty in understanding Chinese enterprises and government and being price competitive. Local Chinese consulting firms, numbering only three over ninety consultants, lack sophistication and credibility but possess strong local knowledge.

From detached experts to involved partner. Traditionally, consulting firms have promoted themselves as experts who possess superior analytic capabilities and tools. Thus, a BCG consultant would apply its Growth-Share Matrix in a way that a client company's staff could not do. Moreover, the client's competitors were at a presumed disadvantage because they did not have access to the consultant's model and talent in using it. Over time, however, clients have gradually become disillusioned with the difficulties, if not impossibility, of implementing many of their consultant's abstract conclusions and recommendations. In response, more and more consultants are becoming involved in implementation and change management. These topics will be further explored in Chapters 12, 13, and 14 (*Intervention Strategies in Management Consulting, Consulting to Integrate Mergers and Acquisitions,* and *Becoming a Transformational Change Agent*).

The value of a consulting engagement has moved from an emphasis on expert analysis to greater involvement in a client's operations, so as to directly influence the results. Consequently, the role of the consultant is changing from one that relies on expert knowledge to one of collaborating with clients to implement action plans. Some consulting firms even stake their fees and advertising on promised results. Bain, for example, tracks the increase in the share prices of its clients and is known to proclaim, "Our clients outperform the market 3 to 1." Several large IT firms measure their success on the basis of successful implementation of new information systems. And McKinsey now considers itself successful if it has built in-house client capabilities to solve its own problems the next time around. It remains a moot question as to how far firms should go with the depth of their involvement and promises to clients before possibly losing their objectivity. Clearly, safeguards have to be built, and the litigious consequences also weighed.

From advisory services to outsourcing revenues. A press release from *Top-Consultant.com* on October 20, 2002, highlights where the growth opportunities are in today's consulting environment when they state:

> The thousands of consultants that have faced redundancy in the last 12 months would be bemused to hear the industry fared well in 2001. The reality is that traditional consulting suffered while a strategic push into outsourcing has allowed consultancies to cushion the fall."

In the same report, *Top-Consultant* notes:

> . . . the U.K. consulting sector enjoyed revenue growth of 17% in 2001, according to figures released this week by the Management Consultancies Association (MCA). However, this favorable picture was largely thanks to 50% growth in outsourcing revenues. . . .

This last quote highlights the fact that underlying the recent growth of the consulting industry is the outsourcing market. In 2001–2002, the six largest consulting firms in terms of total revenues were all firms with strong positions in outsourcing, e.g., IBM, Accenture, PwC, Deloitte Consulting, EDS, and CSC. All types of noncore activities are being considered by clients for outsourcing, from supplier management to routine human resources transactions such as signing up for benefit plans. Many efficiencies can be achieved, as well as self-service through Web-enabled systems.

However, this growth in outsourcing is not without its issues of concern. Clients can lose control over certain operations, leaving themselves vulnerable to the quality of the outsourcing firm. For the consulting firms, there is the potential conflict of interest question: How can IT consulting firms provide objective consulting at the same time it is actively managing major business functions for the same clients? Some industry critics have recommended that once a client becomes an outsourcing client, all consulting should cease for that client.

From conservative professionals to aggressive marketers. As consulting firms move to increase their competitiveness, they are making big investments in marketing to differentiate themselves, including branding efforts, increased advertising, dedicated sales forces, innovative incentive contracts, books with gurus, free seminars, and even low priced consulting as a loss leader (see Chapter 3, *The Marketing and Selling of Consulting Services*). Direct advertising, once a "no-no," is now fairly commonplace; Accenture, for example, spends in excess of $50 million on advertising.

Consulting firms are also turning to indirect forms of marketing, using investments in intellectual capital as a strategic differentiator. Many of the leading firms have funded so-called centers of excellence, as well as research in collaboration with academic scholars to produce books and frameworks to enhance the firm's reputation for intellectual leadership. Large firms now offer their own quarterly journals, electronic newsletters, newsy Web sites and other publications.

From go-it-alone firms to networks. The management consulting industry is slowly developing from stand-alone firms to new organizational forms involving the combination of firms into networks and alliances. The most serious are the alliances between IT consulting firms and their vendors. Accenture with Hewlett-Packard, and SAP with several big IT consultancies are just two examples. All outsourcing contracts clearly involve outside partners where control and commitment remain somewhat tenuous.

Another type of nonoutsourcing network is a "loose" one representing various combinations of partners such as locally owned franchises operating under one brand name, while others promote themselves as a large "alliance" in order to appear bigger in the eyes of potential clients. Most networks are unstable over the long term, so some firms have moved to acquire their former partners, such as IBM Global Services buying PwC Consulting in 2002. Learning how to manage oneself and the other partners in an alliance is a new challenge where a collaborative give and take attitude must be the norm.

From private firms to public ownership. The question of what legal form is the most suitable ownership structure—private partnership or public ownership—has been on the agenda of firms for many years. Mostly, consulting firms, especially the general management ones, have long believed in the partnership model. Some earlier attempts to go public have been failures. For example, Booz Allen endured a disastrous period as a publicly owned company in the 1970s. PA Consulting Group went public in the late 1970s, but in the early 1990s, they were close to bankruptcy. Also the Swedish firm, Indevo, in its public offering during the 1980s fell short of its expected outcome from being listed.

One explanation for these negative experiences is offered by Rodenhauser in his newsletter *Inside Consulting:* "The bottom line of going public is that it only works with good management, sustainable business enterprise systems and scalable pricing models for those systems. Very few firms can measure up to all three factors."[6]

Today, several publicly listed consulting firms are selling well below their offering prices. Ernst & Young has sold its consulting business to CAP Gemini, which is quoted on the Paris Stock Exchange, but not fairing well in market value. KPMG Consulting in the U.S. is now listed on the New York Stock Exchange and has changed its name to BearingPoint, Inc., but it is also down by more than half from its opening IPO price.

Just what will happen in the future is problematic, with much depending on the stock market. Consulting firms would like access to capital that a public listing can bring; it also provides a way to put a clear valuation on the firm, enabling them to reward partners and eventually cash them out. A significant deterrent, though, is the potential for an erratic stock market, as well as continuous pressure from financial analysts for quarterly improvement.

We doubt that the large private general management firms will eventually go public, but most of the IT firms will, if not already, because their capital requirements for outsourcing equipment are much larger than private partnerships can provide. Small- and medium-sized firms don't have the same option of going public unless they are acquired by larger, publicly owned companies.

As for the effects on the firms that go public, many questions remain unanswered. There will be governance questions, conflict-of-interest questions, and public scrutiny questions. We do believe that those firms that go public will be driven by market pressure to grow faster in revenues and profits and to expand their operations further into nonconsulting services. And what will be the effects on the "partnership mentality" and traditional spirit of collegiality when the stock market drops precipitously and a partner's net worth is depleted?

From single projects to long-term relationships. In the 1960s and 1970s, consulting was typically thought of as a single, discrete project where the consultants arrived, performed their study, made their recommendations and left, moving on to the next interesting client. It was Bain that pioneered the art of relationship consulting when they promised exclusivity to a client, rejecting projects from other companies in the same industry. Then the IT companies, with their very large multi-million dollar projects, began to set up offices within clients, staying as long as five years and perhaps longer if they assumed an outsourcing contract.

Today, the general norm in many consulting firms is to strive for long-term relationships with clients—estimates are that at least 60 percent of current consulting revenues originate from existing or former clients. The benefits for the consultant are that it reduces marketing costs and startup time in getting acquainted, and the benefits for the client are that they are dealing with a known quantity. The essential elements of trust and credibility are already established.

Despite the potential for conflicts of interest and even litigation if projects go wrong, we believe that consulting firms will continue to pursue long-term relationships with clients, and they will develop new services and products to assure the continuation of this relationship.

From "loose" confederations to "tight" professional leadership. Given the current market slowdown and the intensity of competition, consulting firms are increasingly being challenged to manage themselves more effectively and professionally. In particular, those firms that are publicly listed are also feeling strong pressure from analysts and boards to increase their performance. Previously, many consulting firms were managed more as a loose confederation of partners, led by a Managing Partner who was often elected, either formally or informally by popularity and political power. Many of the "best practice" attributes that these firms recommended to clients— clear focused strategy, well-aligned organization structure, pay for performance, etc.—were frequently lacking within the consulting firm itself.

For the many Managing Partners with "laissez-faire" styles, it was rather easy to manage loosely, so long as growth was abundant, thereby providing for high compensation, while hiding lots of mistakes. As a close observer, J. A. Moynihan of PA Consulting commented, "Most consulting firms are very badly managed. They wouldn't survive a day if they had to compete with GE or whomever."[7]

Today we find more firms carefully scrutinizing the selection of their future CEOs. They want "take charge" leaders who are well-schooled in professional management and who know how to motivate and move firms in a coherent strategic direction. For these new leaders, difficult choices await them on their strategic agenda, including making acquisitions, developing innovative marketing programs, going public, forming alliances, creating Web opportunities, and developing the intellectual capital of the firm. In addition, performance standards need to become clearer and rewards more closely tied to performance. These new leaders must come out of their offices to articulate the firm's future strategy and encourage a unified effort in implementation, which is further discussed in Chapter 15, *High-Performance Consulting Firms* and in Chapter 16, *Managing Growth Stages in Consulting Firms.*

INDUSTRY RESTRUCTURING

The emerging profile among consulting firms is one of large, multi-service businesses using aggressive consumer marketing techniques, forming alliances, and displaying a willingness to enter nonconsulting businesses. Most of these firms' new services, such as outsourcing, require large infusions of capital investment and substantial sales volume in order to achieve scale and efficient operations. This trend, therefore, suggests fundamental implications for the emerging structure of the industry, which in many ways is witnessing the creation of mega-enterprises where management consulting may only become a subsidiary division of a multi-service holding company.

In a provocative book titled *The Rule of Three,* Sheth and Sisodia propose an intriguing thesis on industry maturity, supported by case studies from many industries, arguing that "naturally occurring competitive forces, if allowed to operate without excessive government intervention, will create consistent structures across nearly all mature markets."[8] They conclude that every industry will inevitably form a core, or inner circle, of three major players who are full-line generalists, surrounded by niche companies that are product or market specialists. They also caution that professional services firms have been slow to reach a level of structural maturity because the combination of ownership and management in professional services creates "emotional attachment and inhibits purely efficiency-driven economic decision-making."

We believe that the time is coming when the "Rule of Three" will likely emerge in the consulting industry, composed most probably of IBM, Accenture, and one of either CGE&Y or Deloitte Consulting. The big gorilla here is IBM after its recent growth in Global Services and its acquisition of PWC for only $3.5 billion. The goals of these firms are directed toward achieving large scale market dominance, and already they are the biggest in total revenues.

Other technology hardware firms, such as HP, Cisco, and Oracle, are likely to increase their acquisitions of smaller consulting firms once their stock prices recover and they are able to use their market value for acquisitions. The equipment makers and software providers, like HP and Microsoft, realize that consulting services are a necessary complement to the sales of their other products. For these firms, consulting might be used as a "loss leader" in hopes of landing bigger dollar contracts in hardware and outsourcing.

We suspect that the general management consulting firms, though far behind in the acquisition game, will also consolidate, with McKinsey, Mercer Consulting Group, and Booz Allen likely becoming the major players, swallowing up the likes of BCG, Monitor, Bain, and Towers Perrin.

The net result over the next ten years may be an industry that divides itself into two different industries composed of "infrastructure providers," such as IBM and Accenture, and "problem solvers," such as McKinsey and Mercer. Each segment might have three dominant players surrounded by a number of market and/or product specialists.

Thinking further out, will General Management merge with IT? The increasing trend among clients is toward internalizing their intellectual value-added activities while outsourcing back-end systems, and assets suggest that the consulting industry may become one large market with three core IT/Infrastructure companies in the center and all other firms acting as specialists around the periphery.

For the future, there are not only emerging opportunities but also profound questions to be raised about the current direction of the consulting industry. Clearly, a major transformation is occurring, not only in the industry but within firms. This will result in major changes that create not only challenging identity questions for firms but perhaps a split in the industry between firms that are problem solvers and those that are service providers.

ROLE RESTRUCTURING

Until recently, the use of knowledge and tools for advanced analysis was very much the captive domain of consulting firms and business schools. Thus, it was assumed that BCG understood the experience curve better than others; that Monitor understood the value chain more than others; and that Strategos led in their understanding of core competencies. However, experienced MBAs and former consultants now permeate all levels and functions of client organizations. Thus, management knowledge and techniques are widely disseminated and available, especially analytical concepts, techniques, and best practices.

These changes have altered the relative balance of expertise and power between consultants and clients. Increasingly, clients are using consultants to supplement their own thinking rather than to supplant it. We believe that clients will do less intellectual outsourcing (i.e., strategic planning) while continuing to increase operations outsourcing (i.e., infrastructure and back-office) over the next decade. This bodes well for the IT folks, but not so well for the general management consultants. Many clients will increasingly become reluctant to turn over intellectual control to consultants; instead, they will want to stay heavily involved in the analytical and implementation process, to the point where the consultant needs to become more a facilitator than an expert diagnostician.

Another role change is occurring in the traditional definition of a professional consultant as a specialist observer giving independent and expert advice. Deviating from this definition are the IT-oriented firms, which are developing a broad array of nonconsulting services, such as outsourcing, facilities management, interim turnaround management, and IT software and hardware tools. Because of profit pressures, many consulting firms seem willing to take on new services, products, and ventures that may or may not have much to do with consulting.

As a result, industry critics are asking if consulting firms have forgotten their heritage as independent observers who restrain themselves from over involvement in those management situations where there can be conflicts of interest. This concern obviously applies to the IT-oriented consulting firms; however, we note this retort by a senior executive at IBM Global Services, "We are not independent—but we are objective. What we do is in our customer's best interest."

Thus, today's consultants are taking on a broad set of diverse roles and agendas—acting as sparring partners in connection with strategic development, as recruiters of new CEOs, as advisors in merger cases, as facilitators in management development, as arbitrators in settling alliance conflicts, as consultants to government, and as managers and operators of IT outsourcing operations. Some of these specialized roles and issues are discussed in Chapter 9, *Consulting to CEOs and Boards,* and Chapter 11, *Public Sector Consultation.*

MORE QUESTIONS THAN ANSWERS

Historically, the consulting industry has been an influential player in shaping the evolution of a variety of industries and public agencies. In doing so, it has provided useful intellectual frameworks for rethinking business strategies; it has helped to design innovative organizations, systems, and processes; and it has been a translator of academic concepts into techniques for industries to use. Now, it is becoming a partner in streamlining its value-chains through the design and management of outsourced functions, information infrastructure, and physical assets. As consultants provide these new services, the consulting industry is being transformed into a business of enormous size and global scale with a wide array of services.

This transformation process raises many serious questions for reflection and debate within consulting firms and the profession at large.

Consulting vs. Nonconsulting

We need to ask what constitutes and should be defined as management consulting in the future? For example, is outsourcing a consulting function? On the surface, it is not, but one might argue that it is a form of implementation resulting from an earlier consulting study. We prefer the more traditional definition that consulting involves the independent study of a client issue, and often times with assistance in implementation, but not with taking over the managerial function. We do not object to consulting firms building other divisions that do outsourcing and other businesses, but the "firewall" needs to be stronger than what existed previously in accounting firms between auditing and consulting.

We predict this issue of potential conflict will gain considerable public scrutiny and attention in the future, and that consulting firms will have to do more to indicate separation of their problem solving and infrastructure support services, such as legally setting up separate companies, probably under different boards and perhaps with restrictions on the amount of combined consulting and nonconsulting services that can be performed for a single client. If firms don't make headway on this issue, there is likely to be legislation.

This brings us to a related issue concerning the tendency of many consulting firms to aggregate their nonconsulting revenues into their total consulting revenues. We believe this practice misleads the public, competitors, and potential clients. Professional associations and trade publications concerned with the consulting industry, as well as financial analysts and FASB, can perform a valuable service by asking for financial reports that make a clear distinction between consulting and nonconsulting revenues and profits.

Ethics vs. Pressure for Results

Consulting firms in the future are likely to face public challenges to their credibility, ethics, and governance. We, therefore, need to ask what are the appropriate standards of professionalism that consultants should adhere to in their relationships with clients? This is a difficult challenge considering that consulting is a highly competitive industry with little or no barriers to entry. Most industry-wide attempts at certifying consultants have been weak at best. We prefer that firms themselves take charge of this issue through their selection and training methods. A few firms already do an outstanding job of extensive training in ethics, but this training should be mandatory for all consultants across all firms. Clear written policies are necessary, and performance reviews should include the degree of professionalism exhibited by consultants on projects. In addition, responsibility for monitoring a firm's professionalism should be assigned to a key partner at the highest level of the organization. Any signs of an individual breaching firm policies should result in immediate termination.

Education vs. On the Job

Most consultants really learn to be consultants on the job, which is not saying much for a profession that earns its living from being on the leading edge. Despite business schools being the spawning ground for most consultants, few schools provide explicit training in consultant skills, and they continually overlook issues of professionalism and ethics (see Chapter 2, *Professionalism in Consulting*). These schools need first to understand that training managers in the functional disciplines is not by itself sufficient preparation for consulting, which requires many other skills ranging from proposal writing to interviewing methods, to reducing complex analyses to communicable insights, and to persuading reluctant clients to make difficult changes. Every MBA program should sponsor at least one course on consulting, and hopefully consulting firms will be supportive and involved in this effort. Also, business schools (and even consulting firms) have been slow to support research on consulting and consultants. We still know very little about the actual behavior of "good" consultants on the job and why certain projects succeed or fail; these issues are further discussed in Chapter 19, *Research on Management Consulting*.

Links between universities and consulting firms will no doubt intensify as consultants search for new frameworks for viewing client problems, and for new techniques that facilitate change and implementation. There will also be extensive contact on the computing science side as information technology advances. In addition, some firms will develop exclusive agreements with "gurus" from the universities to advise them internally, as well as showing them off in their marketing and before clients. More books and articles are likely to be written by consultants and internal staff working in well-funded R&D departments, as illustrated in Chapter 17, *Creating and Managing Knowledge in Consulting*.

Analysis vs. Facilitation Billing

The essence of consulting firms rests in their intellectual capital, which is reflected in their branded conceptual frameworks, proprietary software, and skills of their consultants. However, many clients have become much more sophisticated in their management knowledge and skills, making them competitive with their consultants, if not resistant to consulting help. It is, therefore, likely that consulting firms will need to develop new skills at facilitating behavioral processes where the consultants act more as a facilitators than as expert problem solvers.

Because these facilitative efforts will involve less consultant time, this will change the traditional billing formula based on hours and days. A strategic planning engagement that previously took hundreds of hours might now take only one hundred hours in holding a series of retreats. Another example that is already reducing time as a billing factor is online forms of consulting, as discussed in Chapter 18, *Will Consulting Go Online?* Clearly, new billing concepts will have to evolve, and we predict these will be based on some subjective judgment of the value of results to be derived for the client.

Diversity vs. Homogeneity

To date, many large consulting firms are international in their operations, yet they still retain much of their home-country character in their internal cultures. Given that many pundits predict that this current century will be the Asia/China/India century and not the American or Western century, what will this mean for consulting firms and their consultant skills? A much more diverse consulting workforce will be needed.

Perhaps in conflict with this future market direction toward the Far East is the movement of many large Western consulting firms, especially the IT-oriented ones, toward standardized services. How can they strike a balance between standardized versus customized services in order to meet the needs of diverse clients? This question raises the issue of whether *Fordism (assembly line consulting)* will take over or will the industry develop new concepts that allow for individualized types of services with a personal consulting touch? Our hunch is that the business strategies of IT-oriented firms will focus on selling to large multinationals with homogeneous needs across all their operations; global general management firms with greater flexibility will opt to establish relationships with or acquire local or regional specialty firms that can tailor-make strategies to regional clients. Small "boutique" consulting firms with specialized practices limited to single countries will likely become acquisition targets by larger firms acting to diversify their services. Small local and regional consulting firms will continue to take on smaller clients nearby, and they will emphasize personal service and lower fees.

These complex and potentially divisive issues will preoccupy tomorrow's consulting firm managements, if not already today's leadership. Their strategic responses will determine who will survive in the new millennium. As Charles Darwin pointed out about 150 years ago, "It is not the strongest of the species that survives, not the most intelligent, but the one most responsive to change." This book addresses many of the key change issues facing these firms.

Notes to the Chapter

[1]Staffan Canback, "The Logic of Management Consulting (Part One)," *Journal of Management Consulting*, 10, no. 2 (1998): 1–8.

[2]Frederick W. Taylor, *Principles of Scientific Management* (New York: Harper & Brothers, 1911).

[3]Henri Fayol, *Administration Industrielle et Générale* (Paris: Dunod, 1916), translated in *General and Industrial Management* (London: Pitman, 1949).

[4]J. E. Kielly, *Global Outreach in Management Consulting 1990: The State of the Profession* (Kennedy Publications, 1990).

[5]Consultant News (2002). Personal communication with Professor Poulfelt.

[6]T. Rodenhouser, *Inside Consulting* Newsletter (2000).

[7]M. Skapinker, "Counting the Cost of Going Public," *Financial Times* (UK), (July 5, 2000).

[8]Jagdish Sheth and Rajendra Sisodia, *The Rule of Three: Surviving and Thriving in Competitive Markets* (New York: Free Press, 2002).

CHAPTER 2

Professionalism in Consulting
David H. Maister

ABOUT THE AUTHOR

David Maister

David Maister consults to professional firms worldwide. He is the author of numerous articles and books on professional service firms, including *Managing the Professional Service Firm* (1993), *True Professionalism* (1997), *The Trusted Advisor* (2000), *Practice What You Preach* (2001), and *First Among Equals* (2002).

Like many profound ideas, "professionalism" is an ambiguous concept used to refer to a wide range of attitudes, skills, values, and behaviors. For example, if one asks people what it means to refer to a consultant as "really professional," one hears a variety of replies. A really professional consultant, I am told:

- gets involved
- doesn't just stick to the assigned role
- reaches out for responsibility
- does whatever it takes to get the job done
- is a team player
- is observant
- is honest
- is loyal
- really listens to the clients' needs
- takes pride in his or her work
- shows a commitment to quality
- shows initiative

This list indicates some of the differences between a "really professional" consultant and an ordinary consultant. It reveals that a high level of professionalism doesn't stop with a foundation of technical qualifications and analytical skills. In addition to these basic attributes, the right *attitudes* and *behavior* must also be in place, and these become the distinguishing factors for achieving real professionalism. My former business manager, Julie MacDonald O'Leary, said it best: "Professional is not a title you claim for yourself; it's an adjective you hope other people will apply to you. You have to earn it."[1]

"You have to earn it" may not be a bad way to summarize what professionalism is really all about. It means deserving the rewards you wish to gain from others by being dedicated to serving their interests, as part of an implied bargain. Professionalism implies that you do not focus only on the immediate transaction, but you care about your relationship with the person with whom you are working. It means you can be trusted to put your clients' interests first, can be depended upon to do what you say you will do, and will not consistently act for short-term personal gain. Professionals make decisions using principles of appropriate behavior, not just short-term expediency.

Significant efforts have been made, and continue to be made, to "professionalize" consulting by promoting the use of the CMC—Certified Management Consultant—qualification. However, professionalism is not about qualifications and certification. Having an MBA from a name school or official recognition from a trade association or certifying body might say something about your *knowledge,* but these pieces of paper are unlikely to be predictive of your *attitudes* and *behaviors,* and maybe not even your *skills.* No formal qualification will ever provide complete assurance to the buyer that the provider will act appropriately, even if equipped with the required skills.

FORGING ATTITUDES

The B-School Problem

It is not clear how consciously business schools, even those with special programs on consulting, set out to forge the appropriate attitudes for consulting. Through oversight or neglect, they may even sometimes create inappropriate behaviors. For example, many professional schools, whether in law, business, or medicine, work hard to create a sense in their students that they are an elite, the "best and the brightest." This can breed an arrogance that later shows up (no matter how unintentionally) as pompous, patronizing, condescending behavior when dealing with clients. "You are the person with the problem; I am the trained expert, so shut up and do what I say." Only in recent years have medical schools begun to provide programs to fight this socialization, and few business or law schools have anything substantive in this area.

Some schools have attempted to tackle the difference between knowledge and skill by building real or simulated consulting projects into the curriculum, but few, if any, are consciously designed to provide a critical examination of the consulting experience, by debriefing and exploring issues such as (a) what does it feel like to be a client?; (b) what is the difference between being an expert (providing answers) and being a skilled advisor (helping the client solve his or her own problem)?; (c) what is the clients' role when members of the client organization are at odds or in disagreement?

Yet the need is readily apparent to each of us whenever we contemplate our own experiences as buyers of professional services. In working with professionals, I frequently ask them to tell me what they dislike about having to deal, as a client, with other professionals such as doctors, accountants, lawyers, interior designers, and, yes, management consultants. The list I am given of how people are treated as clients by these professionals is remarkably similar, regardless of the profession being discussed. Professionals ("those guys") I am told:

- Are pompous, patronizing, condescending, and arrogant
- Don't listen
- Treat me like a job, not a person
- Don't explain what they're doing and why
- Don't like to be asked questions or challenged
- Leave me out of the loop and take over my issue
- Tell me what they think I must do, instead of giving me options
- Are more interested in my money than me
- Ignore my feelings and treat the issues as purely technical
- Apply standard solutions and approaches; don't make me feel as if they are customizing to my needs
- Don't act as if they care about me

Test this list against your own experience as a patient or client with professionals. Does it sound familiar? What should be obvious about this list is that many, if not all, of the behaviors reported as missing are the very ones we would use to describe someone as a real professional. Note, however, that none are technical in nature, and all relate, one way or the other, to the provider's attitude toward dealing with the client.

A business-school education does little to help students distinguish between the "consultant as expert" (I can solve your problem) and consultant as helpful advisor (I can facilitate your decision-making process, and help you make your decisions).[2] Successfully conveying an attitude of trying to *help* (as opposed to being *right*) is a prerequisite for all consulting work. Without the ability to earn a client's trust, clients will not listen to content expertise.

Few consultants report that they have been trained in these human interactive skills. Their entire education in schools and in firms has been about logic, rationality, and intellect; little, if any, experiential learning was provided to them on how to earn trust, win influence, and establish relationships. Many do not want to engage in the interpersonal, social, and emotional activities that being a "trusted advisor" requires. Many consultants consciously avoid anything that smacks of intimacy with their clients, and rush to return to the "high ground" of detached, logical analysis where they feel most comfortable.

Further attitude problems, perhaps unconsciously, can be formed from the educational experience itself. In case study intensive programs, the student is invited to stand as the "outsider" and form judgments on the solution of business problems. This can breed an attitude of detachment or disengagement, a view that logical, rational, intellectual analysis is the primary virtue, and that emotions, passions and interpersonal dynamics are relevant only as subject matter to be studied and likely of secondary importance in consulting unless one is a "behavioral" consultant. At no time does the student receive the message that immersing oneself in the messy human dynamics of a business situation is a requirement to find constructive solutions.

This problem is accentuated by other social conditioning absorbed in business schools about what business is about and what management involves. In one school of my acquaintance, hardly a single case study was examined without someone saying something like, "This company is not in business to make widgets, it's in business to make money," thereby dismissing any need to feel passionately involved in the product, the customers, or the employees. For better or for worse, such attitudes will influence the future consultant's view of what is important in his or her profession and inevitably send the wrong signals to clients.

Firm Weaknesses

The socialization that takes place in consulting firms varies immensely. Firms often develop their own cultures of what they think is "professionalism" and consciously or unconsciously socialize their employees into their specific definition of the term. They use the term constantly in their hiring and in proposals to prospective clients.

These varying definitions of professionalism differ immensely from firm to firm. For example, some firms emphasize "implementation" as the key to their professionalism, while others stress that their value is added by providing a "big picture" review. Is one of these strategies more "professional" than the other? Clearly not. It would be wrong to conclude that, for example, one must be involved in implementation or to give the big picture to be deemed fully professional. The underlying issue is really one of integrity. Is the firm consistent in what it claims to be and do? Does it deliver on what it claims to provide? In essence, the issue is whether or not the firm has (and lives by) a clear ideology of high standards.

Some firms with a clear ideology, such as McKinsey, go out of their way to indoctrinate new hires into their value system (their way of doing things): concrete positions on the role of the consultant, the appropriate way to work with clients, and the attitudes expected of all consultants. Of course, what makes this formal indoctrination "stick" is whether or not the attitudes preached are, in fact, the ones that the young consultant sees modeled every day by the more experienced people in the firm.

Other firms such as the Boston Consulting Group and Bain also have a reputation for articulating clear, consistent, firm-wide positions on what they consider the role of a consultant to be (an ideology) to which all members of the firm are expected to adhere. Naturally, these definitions are not identical, firm-to-firm, but all serve the role of communication and forming a set of attitudes that are *required* by the firm. Whether or not the firm provides formal training or documentation is of lesser importance than the fact that there is a clear role model that all recruits are expected to emulate, and that the culture is strong enough to rein in instances of noncompliance.

However, many firms, particularly those that provide widely varying services to widely different marketplaces, experience a harder time in conveying a clear, unambiguous view of the consultant's role. In addition, many firms do not have a firm-wide ideology on this point. For these firms, which are probably in the majority, there is no enforced, common approach to working with clients. Individuals are socialized not through formal indoctrination, but informally and randomly by the specific individuals they happen to work with. Little or no attempt is made to discuss formally the consultant's role, and the attitudes it requires. As a consequence, the concept of professionalism is left ambiguous and, almost certainly, randomly implemented.

SKILLS WITH CLIENTS

An effective consultant who wishes to become "fully professional" must develop a long list of skills. While many firms train their people in such things as presentations, written communications, proposal writing, and selling, a much smaller percentage actually teach their people about how to work with a client. Client service training, where it exists, is spotty and is usually an afterthought. Almost none of it is taught in business schools.

Again, there are singular exceptions. Not surprisingly, McKinsey, with its reputation for making a heavy investment in training, is one of the shining examples. Formal programs of "influence skills," taught by psychologists, are required, and reinforced by a second or third consultant sitting in on client meetings to observe and debrief the interactions. Such activities take place in other firms, but few have such an organized approach that is clearly signaled and is mandatory for skill development, rather than one that is optional and idiosyncratic.

Other skills are required as a consultant develops. Paul Glen, in his book *Leading Geeks*[3], lists, among others, the following competencies needed by an IT professional:

- Ability to manage client relationships
- Ability to manage technical teams
- Ability to play positive politics
- Ability to help expand client relationships
- Ability to work through others and make them productive
- Ability to manage ambiguity
- Ability to manage time horizons
- Ability to manage client relationships

To this fairly familiar list one could add a number of skills that most consultants wish they had mastered earlier in their careers:

- How to earn other people's trust and confidence
- How to earn, deserve, and thereby nurture a relationship with a client
- How to give advice without being assertive or patronizing
- How to deal with conflicts among client personnel
- How to manage meetings
- How to supervise others so they want to work for you again
- How to get the best out of those in support or administrative roles
- How to get someone in a more senior role to want to help you
- How to receive work delegated to you so you know what you're supposed to be doing
- If, when, and how to say "no" to a senior person or client
- Getting feedback from others, inside and outside, in a timely manner and form you can use

All of these are learnable skills (some are even teachable), and all are components of what I mean by the term "a fully skilled professional." Some of these are commonly contained in the typical firm's training program; a remarkable number of these skills are not.

INTEGRITY AT THE CORE

Integrity is usually taken to be central to the idea of professionalism. But what, precisely, does integrity mean? Consider the following list of statements, each taken from the mission or values statement of a real consulting firm:

- We always put the clients' interests first, ahead of our own.
- If a client wants to pay us to do things that we think aren't in his or her best interests, we'll turn the work down.
- If we have even the smallest doubt that we can't do this work to excellence, we'll turn the work away.
- We never lie, misrepresent, or exaggerate, in any way, to anyone, under any circumstances.
- We stand by our work. If clients don't like our work, we refuse to take their money.
- If a client treats our people badly, or with a lack of respect, we'll walk away from that client.
- We will fire any employee who fails to treat others (at any level) with respect and dignity. -

How many firms do you know that could meet all these standards? If you think the standards are too tough to be realistic, how would you change them? Do you think a firm that lived by these rules would flourish financially or die? What else do you think belongs on the integrity rules list? Every firm (and individual consultant) should reflect on the above questions.

The key point is that integrity cannot be judged by what you advocate, only by that which you always do. A claim to integrity is only meaningful if it includes this follow-up statement:

> We treat our espoused values as nonnegotiable minimum standards, and counsel anyone who is not in compliance with them. If, after counseling, the person does not or cannot get into compliance with our values, we will help them find alternative employment.

One of the readers of my Web site, where I first posted this statement, responded as follows:

> No firm meets all these tests. Putting the clients' interests first, ahead of our own is difficult to rationalize in public corporations. The commonly held guideline for behavior (maximize shareholder value) inevitably leads to a violation in spirit of this principle. Leaders are willing to deceive (if not outright lie) to anyone producing a "drag coefficient" on revenue, including customers. Can (should) this change? I don't think that adherence to strict integrity rules would actively constrain a firm's performance. However, the traits that lead to violations may lead to disadvantages down the road (e.g., lying can work in the short term, but not the long term.)

Another reader of my Web site posed the following question:

> *Do you think many professional firms are compromising their integrity in favor of money? The more competitive their environment and the larger their firm, it seems the pressure to maintain or increase revenue is just too great. Are professionals in such firms, just high-paid technicians, if the driving force from the firm is to make money even if this means risking its reputation?*

As these cynical comments show, there clearly are those firms out there that send a clear message to their people: "It's about the money, stupid: do whatever it takes." I have experienced firsthand those consulting clients who create such pressure to meet short-term financial goals that their people are led into faking orders, padding bills, neglecting client service, and psychologically beating their staff to a pulp. In fact, if you read the gossipy bulletin boards on the Internet about consulting firms, you can easily conclude that such behavior is more common than not.

Integrity Pays Off

It is difficult to prove with hard science, but my twenty years of watching consulting firms leads me to believe that, in consulting, you can't get away with a lack of integrity or ethics for long. I'd risk the generalization that those consulting firms that have, over the years, vigorously enforced values, standards, and principles will also have achieved the best brand names and the highest profits.

In my book *Practice What You Preach*,[4] I surveyed 5,500 people in 139 professional firm offices in thirteen countries, posing seventy-four culture questions, as well as obtaining three years' worth of financial performance data. Using both stepwise regression and structural equation modeling (path analysis), I discovered that the answers to only *nine* questions accounted for more than 50 percent of all financial performance differences between and among these 139 businesses.

- Client satisfaction is a top priority at our company.
- We have no room for those who put their personal agenda ahead of the interests of the clients or the office.
- Those who contribute the most to the overall success of the office are the most highly rewarded.
- Management gets the best work out of everybody in the office.
- Around here you are required, not just encouraged, to learn and develop new skills.
- We invest a significant amount of time in things that will pay off in the future.
- People within our office always treat others with respect.
- The quality of supervision on client projects is uniformly high.
- The quality of the professionals in our office is as high as can be expected.

The firms that succeeded financially were not those that preached these standards (nearly every firm does) but those whose staff, top to bottom, agreed that they were the principles on which their firm actually operated. What's notable about this list is how familiar it is. All it says is that the firms making the most money are those who are actually living up to familiar standards that everyone preaches. The message is that you can make more money when you behave and enforce standards, not when you superficially advocate them or merely post them on a bulletin board or company Web site.

Whether or not a consulting firm actually has the necessary standards of professionalism is proven by whether or not there are consequences for non-compliance. If a firm has a partner who does not treat others with respect, that partner must be counseled, and if the counseling doesn't work, then that partner must be fired. If the firm is prepared to go that far, it can, in my opinion, be called truly professional and will likely make more money.

Origins of Failure

If all this evidence is valid, why then is excessively risky short-term behavior reported to be so common in business in general, and even in many consulting firms? Why do we keep hearing of managers "forcing" their people into behaviors that, at its kindest, can be described as "cutting corners," and at its worst, as unethical?

The most important point to make is that you don't have to be unethical to be dumb. As my questioner put it, consulting firms are doing things to make short-term profits that put their reputation at risk. That's not necessarily a lack of integrity; it's just stupidity. And, at some level, it's even understandable stupidity. A slightly compromised reputation might hurt you tomorrow, or the day after that, but, hey, that's the future, and you wouldn't believe the discount rate we apply to profits in the future compared to today! (And we'll have a year or two to make up for it, won't we? And maybe the clients will forget that we weren't that great two years ago!) Call this the *short-termism* excuse.

There are others too. I have sat in strategy meetings where firm leaders acknowledge the future cost of compromising reputation, but argue that, by the time it hurts the firm, they will have made their pile and cashed out. These people aren't really short termers; they're just *selfish* and *greedy*.

Then there are consulting firm leaders who don't really believe their own mission statements, vision, values, and strategy. They say that they believe a reputation for excellence is worth its weight in gold, but they are not willing to actually put the proposition to the test. For example, how many firms that preach dedication to outstanding client service are also willing to give an unconditional client satisfaction guarantee? Not many! These people are not being excessively short-term thinkers: They are cynics and unbelievers. They don't really think that building or sustaining a reputation is worth sacrificing any amount of short-term cash.

Another pathology that occurs among a firm's leaders who are not short-term thinkers, greedy, or cynical, is that they are scared and lack courage. They would really like to stick with the firm's strategy and standards and not accept a short-term hit, but they are frightened to take such a risk, either because they think their partners will rise up and revolt, which is actually quite possible, or, if they are publicly held, that Wall Street will take out a substantial chunk of their market value.

A final group of consulting firms with low standards engages in short-term compromises and acts of expediency because they actually don't have ambition. To accept a short-term adverse consequence, you've got to have a passionately held ambition to get somewhere. Otherwise, why would you make sacrifices? Yet many firm leaders are more concerned about "not messing up" than they are about "going for the gold."

So what have you got to be as a person to "do the right thing?" You have to have integrity, *and* really believe in your strategy, mission, and values, *and* have a dream, fervently desired, *and* have the patience and courage to bet on the long term, and resist palpable pressure from the constituencies you serve *and* be willing to accept the short-term consequences of your actions. This all takes a level of self-discipline that few of us measure up to in our everyday behavior. I guess that's why it's not common. And I guess that's why they call it professionalism.

PROBLEMS OF ENFORCEMENT

If you really want to obtain the commercial benefits from any strategy, you must put in a system that forces you to execute that strategy. The tragedy of many consulting firms, and the source of their lack of professionalism, is that they have not put in place systems to enforce accountability for standards.

As an example of one that has, consider EDS, the computer services giant. They have a Web-based project management system that records everything about the project—when the next due dates are, what has been done, what's on time, what's delayed, and how much of the budget has been spent and accumulated. Here is the key point: This information is entirely accessible to the client! At any time, the client can log in and see where his or her project stands, with budget, due dates, deliveries, etc. They ask their clients to log in every two weeks to indicate on a simple scale of one to four their level of satisfaction with the client project so far. The chairman of this multi-billion dollar company logs in every day and can see client feedback from every client for the entire company, and that is the first thing he does every day.

What's impressive about EDS is not the technology but the willingness to be held inescapably accountable to high standards. Many consulting firms haven't even got a decent internal project management system, let alone one to which they would give access to clients. Most firms have a mission statement that declares a commitment to client satisfaction and client service. But how many have a feedback system where they regularly ask clients, at the end of every transaction, how happy they are with the work? Only a few! How many publish those results with the names of the relevant partner to everybody in the firm? Even fewer! Instead, what exists in most firms is a frequently espoused belief that client service is very important, yet a refusal in their actual behavior to accept accountability for it.

Firms typically leave it up to the individual and his or her self-discipline to accomplish high standards of professionalism, but that usually doesn't do the job. If there is no system that keeps people honest about performing up to standard, you don't get the benefits. The key, if you really want to make something happen, is don't leave it to self-discipline. If you really want to make something happen, create an external discipline. And if you don't want to try that hard, and if you don't want to be held strictly accountable, then fine, move on to something else. But if you can't find anything you're prepared to actually commit to, then recognize that you're probably never going to be anything other than no worse than anybody else.

The Upside

Imagine a world where every junior member of the firm says, "In this firm, one thing you can bank on is that you will be superbly supervised on every transaction. It is a matter of professional principle with us. We don't do work unless we supervise it superbly." (Note that this was one of the nine profit predictors in my statistical study). What commercial benefits would come to that consulting firm if it were true that supervision was always done superbly?

First, from the firm's point of view, there would be less wasted time and rework, and the firm would experience lower write-offs and higher realization. You could obtain better economic leverage because people would feel more confident delegating work to trained people. Second, the firm would spread skills faster and the firm would do a better job of retaining people.

Clients, on the other hand, will notice a higher level of quality and therefore might feel less fee sensitive, knowing that they had found someone who always supervised the work well. This is terribly scary, because maybe that might mean they also notice when the work is not supervised superbly.

If, as a senior partner, I knew that every junior consultant had been supervised superbly since the day they joined the firm, I might actually trust these young people and delegate more to them. Whereas, if I am living in a normal consulting firm where excellence in supervision happens only sporadically, then it's quite logical never to delegate because the juniors are untrained, unguided missiles.

This list of benefits for both firms and clients can be obtained by diligent, enforced adherence to a high standard of project supervision. But here is the issue: Why are many consulting firms not getting these benefits despite everything they promise to new recruits about the importance of quality, professional pride, and great work environments? Why does the average consulting firm not enforce this standard? Because they can get away without doing it!

Many consulting firms fail to meet the high standards of professionalism, not because they do not believe in them and advocate them, but because they fail to enforce them. It's not an issue of being "unprofessional" or unethical. It's simply a matter of the difference between the true pursuit of excellence and the acceptance of mere competence. They have wonderful standards of quality that are preached. But they will forgive any partner who does not do this, as long as he does not go to the opposite extreme and do something ugly—sexual harassment or get us sued. Competence ("Don't mess up") is not the same as professionalism ("uncompromisingly high standards").

Partners' Failed Leadership

If you go to the typical consulting firm today and ask, "What percentage of your partners would put hand-on-heart to say they regularly read every issue of their main client's trade magazine? Not all your clients, just your main client?" I can report from experience that, around the world, the answer is sadly in single digits. Yet we all know that clients like for their consultants to show an interest in their business. So let me ask again: "Do you act as if you care about your clients?" In the typical consulting firm, the honest answer is, "We believe that we should care, but we frequently don't act that way."

I often talk about meeting three kinds of partners in consulting firms: *dynamos, cruisers,* and *losers.* This, by the way, is not different people; rather it is all of us at different stages in our lives. A *dynamo* is somebody who is always acting like they have a career. In addition to taking care of this year, every year they are doing something to bring about their personal future. Every year they're always saying, "Where do I want to go next, and what do I do today to make that happen?"

The *cruisers* (by definition, not *losers*) are a very important category that includes the majority of partners. They are good, solid citizens, coming in each week to make the sausages. They come in next month and they make the sausages. They come in next year and they make the sausages. And everybody knows those sausages are fabulous. The quality is there. The hard work is there, but that person isn't actually going anywhere. He's acting like he's got a job, but if you said, "Where do you want to go next with your career? What kind of transactions do you want to be doing three years from now?" he'd say, "Sausages!" He has no particular desire to advance his professional career.

At some stage in your life, you're probably a *loser.* The usual reasons: divorce, alcoholism, cocaine, manic depression, the kids have been arrested again. Things happen. If you're lucky, you deal with it and recover; if you're unlucky, you get stuck.

In the typical consulting firm, I am told by firms around the world, the percentage of partners in those three categories is about 15 percent *dynamos,* 75 percent *cruisers,* 10 percent *losers.* If that's the makeup of the typical partnership in the typical consulting firm, only 15 percent of the partners are trying to get somewhere, but the large majority is just coasting along while making sausages day after day. Is that professionalism?

If my estimate is accurate, firms should not waste their time doing strategic planning. Because strategic planning in that environment is like trying to figure out which way shall we point the thundering herd when the herd isn't thundering. The issue is not direction or strategy. The issue is do they or do they not have the appetite to go somewhere, and to accomplish it with high standards of professionalism?

We, therefore, come to the key choice if you're considering a firm to join as a partner: Which gang do you want to belong to? The tolerant firm says, "If you want to cruise, that's okay. Not only is it acceptable, but it's actually the overwhelming norm here," just like in many consulting firms. Or you might want to join a firm where they say, "The rule here is you've got to be learning and growing, or otherwise you're not meeting your requirements as a partner. It's something we have a right to expect of each other, that we are all continually learning and growing." Notice there's an option here for firm leaders to confront and decide. The choice is do you want to set forth and enforce a high standard in your partnership agreement?

THE REAL BOTTOM LINE

The lessons should be clear. You get the benefit of that which you actually do, not that which you encourage. Ultimately, professionalism goes beyond, attitudes, knowledge, and skills and is about dependable, reliable, consistent behavior. You may believe in something, know how to do it, and be skilled at doing it. But unless you can be relied upon to actually do it (unfailingly), then you cannot hope to develop a reputation for professionalism.

The way you make money in consulting is not to be good at managing the money. The way you get money is to decide how you want to compete—whether it be quick delivery at McDonald's or fabulous cooking for some cuisine connoisseur—and then enforce the standards appropriately for that choice though superb leadership. The money is an outcome of how high your standards are and what you do about them. He or she who lives to the highest standards—in other words, is most professional—wins.

Notes to Chapter

[1]David H. Maister, *True Professionalism* (New York: Free Press, 1997).

[2]David H. Maister, Charles H. Green, Robert M. Galford, *The Trusted Advisor* (New York: Free Press, 2000).

[3]Paul Glen, *Leading Geeks* (San Francisco, CA: Jossey-Bass, 2002).

[4]David H. Maister, *Practice What You Preach* (New York: Free Press, 2001).

CHAPTER 3

The Marketing and Selling of Consulting Services
Robert Duboff, Boston College

ABOUT THE AUTHOR

Robert Duboff

Robert Duboff is a Lecturer and Executive-in-Residence at The Carroll School of Management at Boston College. He was a line consultant for over two decades with Mercer Management Consulting, serving a client base that featured professional service firms. He later served as Director of Marketing for Ernst & Young.

Successful consulting businesses require both effective marketing and exceptional sales, each of which must be closely aligned and made consistent with actual delivery to expectant clients. Good marketing matched with poorly executed sales dooms a firm to revenues too low to justify added investments in marketing. Good sales efforts backed by poor marketing leads to an exhausted sales force and, again, wasted money spent on marketing. Delivered services that don't measure up to prior expectations set by marketing or sales result in disaffected clients usually lost forever.

Beyond the need for consistency between marketing and sales, there is the danger of overlap and confusion between these two key functions. The demarcation between them, always blurry, is often indistinct in many consulting firms, compounded by the fact that most consultants want to avoid looking like salesmen. After all, consultants want to consult, not sell. They use euphemisms such as "business development" or "thought leadership" instead of acknowledging the need to really do marketing and selling. Consulting carries the heritage that consultants should be able to produce revenues without ever asking for the business, and certainly without committing such unseemly acts as advertising.

My definition of marketing for consulting includes all indirect activities aimed at attracting a broad market segment composed of many potential buyers, such as the "financial services industry," while sales are direct activities designed for winning over a single, specific client. Nevertheless, firms often debate about which activities are marketing and which are sales. More important is to reach strategic agreement within a firm so that all marketing and sales tactics are made consistent and set correctly for the target market and client.

Typically, marketing is the province of a small group of staff people, often augmented by outsiders, using market research, advertising, public relations, speeches, and publications. Sales are frequently the exclusive domain of senior line consultants, the most successful of whom, the "rainmakers," are highly rewarded and promoted to partners. Sales techniques are numerous—and are no different in consulting from other service enterprises. In between marketing and sales lie the murky waters of employees working in sales support and proposal development. These practitioners are better thought of as part of the sales process than as marketers.

Solo practitioners, of course, must play all marketing and sales roles, although some use outsiders for marketing assistance.

THE ELUSIVE CHALLENGE

Consulting is one of the most intangible of all services, depending on humans engaged mainly in words and ideas. Furthermore, although consultants like to call the business a "profession," anyone can play. No set training or expertise certifies one as a qualified consultant or firm. All of this makes differentiation difficult, if not impossible for any firm or individual consultant to assert a true difference from all other firms or individuals.

To make marketing and selling even more difficult, the important tool of pricing frequently remains outside the control of those directly engaged in marketing and selling. While consulting marketers often are given leeway to create positioning, ad themes, brochures, and the like, they are rarely involved in pricing. The CFO, the CEO, or the whole management team annually produce daily rates or hourly fees that then become the building blocks of bids.

Most consultants rely on a model of pricing based on estimates of hours or days multiplied by a rate per consultant. However, during the dot.com and stock market boom, many senior consultants responsible for pricing grew envious of "get rich quick" clients and shifted to other models (e.g., stock in lieu of dollars or agreements in which the consultants shared in future returns or in savings created, etc.). These incentive arrangements, in my opinion, are highly problematic because they alter the consultant-client relationship by threatening the independence, if not the objectivity, of the consultant. A better alternative for establishing a fee, if one is needed, is to assess the value to be created by the consultant's work, and use this as the basis for a price, instead of simply the number of projected hours.

WHERE TO START?

What are marketers and salespeople to say when asked why a potential client should hire their firm? This largely depends on the stage of a potential engagement, which exists along a continuum. Exhibit 3.1 describes the process of converting nonclients into clients, and then extending the existing relationship through additional work.

Using this perspective, the early stage objectives (target selection, awareness building, and establishing qualifications) are the marketers' domains. Sales begin to coalesce with marketing at the point where trying to demonstrate qualifications turns toward setting specific expectations about what the firm is qualified to perform for that target. Note, too, that after an initial sale and completed project, marketing has a role in working to develop and

Exhibit 3.1	Stages in Marketing and Sales
Objective	Sales and Marketing Focus
Selection	Marketing: Market sizing, competitive analysis, profitability analysis (for clients)
Awareness	Marketing: Name recognition
Qualifications	Marketing: Positioning Sales and marketing: Setting expectations
Selection	Sales
Building a long-term relationship	Marketing: Information dissemination (e.g., newsletter); thought leadership Sales: Customizing and personalization

maintain a long-term relationship with the client through various media, some tailored to the specific client and others broadly distributed to many clients, such as a newsletter.

In my experience, the first stage, selection, is the most important and, along with establishing differentiation, the most difficult. Selection requires the combination of economic foresight as to which types of clients can be served profitably and competitive insight as to which types of clients can be sold successfully. Even when this is done well, consultants need great discipline to avoid the temptation to sell to prospective clients who do not fit the desired profile. They also need even more discipline to drop a client that has proven unprofitable. I have helped firms analyze their client base, and typically at least one-third of all client relationships are unprofitable. Yet, senior partners still find it hard to weed out clients in the vain hope that over time unprofitable clients will become profitable, or because partners serving those clients want to retain their own revenue base.

ACHIEVING THE RIGHT BALANCE

While the marketing and sales functions each have a distinct role, consulting firms struggle with their relative priorities, budgets, and allocation of scarce resources. Typically, rather crude judgments are made, such as marketing budgets being set as a percent of last year's revenues. Marketing is a forward-looking function where the objective is to build future revenues. So, logically, if revenues are declining, more marketing fuel is needed for the firm to fly higher. Unfortunately, the prevalent percent-of-past-revenues decision allocates fewer funds when revenues are declining.

A helpful way to approach these trade-off decisions is to use what I call the Sales and Marketing Matrix, depicted in Exhibit 3.2.

The first step is to compute or estimate the raw numbers in each of the four boxes. It may be necessary to find these numbers through marketing research or interviews with line consultants. Focus should be on boxes A and C, while rapidly discontinuing any expenditures directed primarily at B and D. A key number for determining a marketing emphasis can be found in

Exhibit 3.2	Sales and Marketing Matrix

	Know the Consultant/Firm	**Don't Know the Consultant/Firm**
Desirable Client	A	C
Not Desirable Client	B	D

quadrant C—how many desirable clients are there who don't really know the firm? Sometimes, this is a small number such as when the consulting firm is targeting CEOs in a specific industry. The number doesn't dictate the marketing strategy, but a comparison of box C to box A can help inform the firm about whom to target and in what way. The issue for box A is to employ sales techniques focused on and customized to the individual target. On the other hand, box C requires marketing's tools, whether designed for name awareness or to present the firm's qualifications for consulting to clients in certain industries. Box C's marketing number could be in the hundreds, and, therefore, an efficient allocation of marketing money and effort will be required. In this case, advertising in a business magazine or industry trade journal is a potential alternative. If a small number, advertising would not be a good choice; perhaps a better choice would be to pursue a personal email campaign including an attachment describing the firm's intellectual capital.

KEYS TO EFFECTIVENESS

Even the most rational priority setting and budgeting does not ensure successful marketing and sales. There are five underlying and essential keys to achieving effectiveness.

Key 1: Marketing and Sales Must Link to the Firm's Strategy

Years ago, David Maister sagely suggested that there are two main types of professional service firms—hunters and farmers.[1] The hunter is characterized by a sales driven culture where each professional acts as a separate entrepreneur out selling and defining the work to be performed. These firms are usually not bound together by any cohesive set of principles proscribed to guide all the firm's consultants; central discipline is lacking. Farmers, and here McKinsey is a striking example, are characterized more by a core philosophy that is enforced across all geographies and all practices; it is the collective image, reputation, and team effort of the firm that attracts clients to it. There are numerous examples at McKinsey where adhering to principle overrode short-term revenue opportunities. Although both hunting and farming can work, they can't work well together in the same firm since the hunting ethos would undermine the discipline that defines a farmer type firm.

Too often today, companies try to market their way to success. Frequently, businesses launch or change advertising campaigns, logos, and the like in a new "branding initiative," but at its core, these approaches will not work if they are not based on the firm's underlying business model and business strategy. The dot.com ads during the 2000 Super Bowl were a visible example of this phenomenon, but even these ill-fated attempts to market oneself to success have done little to discourage others from making the same mistake. *Launching a Marketing Initiative within the Firm* gives an example of how one should go about developing a new marketing initiative within the firm.

No one is quite sure how branding started. Historically, artisans and ranch owners had two purposes for brands: to signify ownership/authorship and to emphasize quality, or at least, consistency. Over time, the meanings have become blurred and even confused. "Brand" is often used when "brand name" or "name" is what is meant, and the term "brand equity" is associated with financial concepts so as to convey an impression that having a brand automatically adds value. Branding has also been used by proponents of advertising to suggest that this marketing technique is best, if not unique, at building name

---

Consulting Insights **Launching a Marketing Initiative within the Firm**

The key to launching an effective campaign is making a connection between what the firm's consultants can deliver with what potential and current clients want. The best first step is to develop a fact base about the current market (clients, prospects, employees and competitors), then to line them up with how prospects fit with hot trends in the market. Next, review this information with the firm's leaders and plan to hold an offsite meeting to sift through the key data and discuss implications for new marketing strategies. It is advisable to have an outsider present to facilitate the discussion and give objective counsel. A typical agenda for this offsite meeting includes:

- Pre-read research on the market (e.g., market research, articles, etc.), firm and competitor data (e.g., market share, key clients), and client information (e.g., profitability, satisfaction, retention)
- Kick-off dinner with speaker (a visionary or commentator on the industry) and call-to-action by firm leaders

Day 1
- Small group activity to determine likely trends and shifts in market relevant to the firm's future
- Panel of senior clients and/or prospects to give their perspective
- Diagnosis of recent client defections
- Plenary session to propose a few alternative marketing scenarios
- Discuss scenarios to consider if the firm can deliver on what is needed
- Proposed actions to close gaps between delivery capability and what's wanted in the marketplace
- Working dinner

Day 2
- Presentation from teams on specific action steps
- Debate/discussion/next steps
- Adjourn

recognition over time, such that customers will be willing to be loyal to that brand and even pay a premium price.

Promoting a brand not linked to an underlying strategy translates into meaningless marketing. Promoting a brand promise that is not delivered translates into a marketing mismatch. Marketing and strategy are like love and marriage in the old song, yet without solid execution, the venture will fail.

A brand only has a meaning if there is consistency. Every Coke tastes like Coke, every Snickers like Snickers. Branding is relatively easy for products but more problematic for services. Hotels strive to bring a consistent meaning to their properties, and those who have problems doing this have the weakest brands and businesses. Southwest is the most consistent airline by far with its branding strategy, signifying low price and frequent departures. The other airlines all struggle with the consistency issue because of their diverse offerings.

Brand strength requires consistency in both delivery and execution. Consulting firms should not market a brand unless they can deliver on it. A firm that is a hunter should likely avoid branding and attempt to market itself in other ways (e.g., build up the reputation of individual senior consultants and/or invest in sales support), while farmers can more easily use branding tactics to promote the firm's reputation.

Key 2: Link Internal and External Communications

Internal communications to consultants and staff are just as important as external communications for implementing effective marketing and sales. This is true for any service where the delivery depends so heavily on human motivation and skill, and where every client must be treated as unique. If communications about the link between the firm's strategy, marketing and sales are not in alignment, prospective clients are likely to question the firm's credibility and lose interest in making a purchase. Over time, repeated poor links in communication lead to damaged credibility and lost reputation.

Internal marketing is not only vital to keep employees informed about the firm's current strategies and policies, but also, if done skillfully, to help employees feel included in and aware of the "big picture" of the firm. As with any business, employees' views of the enterprise are shaped by the information they receive. Effective internal marketing, which includes newsletters, emails, events, training, and visits by senior partners, can augment pay and other tangible benefits to create greater loyalty among staff members. One best practice, for example, is Ernst & Young's *The Daily Connection,* a cleverly written set of two to three daily news blurbs of relevance emailed daily to thousands of employees. Those that want more information on a topic (e.g., a new voluntary benefit or particular E&Y report) can click for elaboration. Employees can opt out of *The Daily Connection,* although less than 1 percent have done so.

Close linkage between internal and external communications creates a positive effect on potential recruits who can tap Web sites to learn more about what is going on inside the firm. On the other hand, when linkage is poor or mixed signals are given, these same recruits will perceive the firm as not having its act together. Unfortunately, many firms do not coordinate their external recruiting messages with their internal messages to employees. Different departments go their separate ways. Certain issues, of course, are salient only to potential new employees, but there is little justification for sending a plethora of separate messages from different departments about the firm to employees, recruits, and alumni. In today's Internet world, client personnel, college and MBA students, and employees can all readily gain access to the same information. Ours is now a transparent world that requires consistent messaging and brand meaning.

A disastrous example of poor linkage occurred several years ago when an ad produced by Saatchi & Saatchi bragged to its investors about its rapid growth through acquisitions and soaring profits. Current and prospective clients gained access to this ad and complained both privately and publicly, demanding lower fees because, in their view, Saatchi's profits seemed exorbitant. The agency soon experienced a decline in revenue.

The point is to focus on the internal market and be sure that messages are consistent both inside and outside the firm. In this regard, while the firm's ads designed for clients may or may not gain public attention, employees will definitely see them and react. If the messages do not ring true to employees, they will lose confidence in their firm's leadership. In fact, the best communicators will test all potential external communications on people within the firm first. After external testing as well, all employees are notified about the communication before the ad appears or sent as a mass email to current and prospective clients.

Today's employee is tomorrow's alumni and potential client. Good communications build credibility—the key and necessary ingredient to effective marketing and sales. If recipients don't believe what you say, it doesn't matter how often, how cleverly, or how loudly you say it.

Key 3: Understand Buyer Values

Any consulting firm needs to know the buying criteria that clients will use to select or reject its proposals. The term "buyer values" comes from Michael Porter's work where, as many readers know, he describes two viable ways to compete within any industry.[2] You can be a "low cost" leader, which affords the luxury of being the lowest priced and still having a good chance while still achieving sales and profits through volume. Price will always be a factor with most, if not all, buyers. However, the second option is to differentiate, but you must differentiate on a dimension that buyers will value sufficiently to pay a premium. This allows the consultant to sell for a price above the low cost provider.

In spite of its usefulness, many marketers frequently ignore Porter's theory and seem willing to assert almost anything that appears to have been generally attractive to clients in the past. They forget about whether the proclaimed virtue holds real value to the particular buyer. Finding out about buyer values is not easy, but it is necessary. While sales and marketing are arts, it is foolish not to use whatever information is available or can be secured. The best way is through marketing research, and Exhibit 3.3 gives a brief summary of a solid research process.

It is critical that the results of market research be discussed at the highest levels of the firm so that resulting recommendations are accepted across the firm. While it would be nice to identify a single universal buyer value on which the firm has a leading reputation, this rarely happens. More typical is to locate a set of attributes that is valued by many clients (current and potential), and

Exhibit 3.3	Marketing Research Steps

Step 1:   Encapsulate what is currently known about the relevant buyers.

Step 2:   Through discussions with line partners, generate hypotheses about buyer values.

Step 3:   Set up a Steering Committee to oversee the research, which, with Step 2, will help ensure that the results will be used.

Step 4:   Conduct qualitative research (such as focus groups) with buyers to explore hypotheses and develop new ones.

Step 5:   Conduct a survey of buyers. This will require at least 100 interviews with any given target level (e.g., CFOs, IT Directors, entrepreneurs, etc.). Once the questionnaire is developed and tested, it can be administered by telephone or through the Internet.

Step 6:   Conduct analysis guided by the hypotheses that pinpoints in rank order, those buyer values that can drive selection/retention. The research must also detail current perceptions among those who know the firm about its credibility for delivering on the dimension that is valued.

supported by people within the firm, too. Then, assuming the marketplace does not currently disbelieve the firm's ability in this area, the firm can emphasize the attributes internally and communicate them externally. It is folly to simply begin asserting attributes if the firm's line consultants are not able or willing to deliver them.

Many consulting firms underutilize market research despite its use in one of the most successful strategies in the history of consulting. In the early 1980s, Victor E. Millar, a former senior partner of Arthur Andersen & Co., launched research into buyer values for all three of the firm's divisions (audit, tax, and consulting) of the then Big 8 firms. Up to that point, Millar had helped drive Andersen's consulting business to a leadership position. His research revealed how buyer values were distinctly different in selecting an audit firm compared to hiring a consulting firm. This insight (and his instinctive understanding of Key 1 above) led to the strategic split of Andersen Consulting (a new brand name) from Arthur Andersen.

The power of research extends to other arenas as well. Firms can survey their employees to develop strategies to engender loyalty. There are also advanced techniques (with enticing descriptions such as "Lead User" and "Delphi") to aid in identifying trends and coming changes in the market.

It is also imperative to use research techniques to garner objective feedback from clients about past marketing campaigns and each sales effort. Too often firms spend thousands of dollars and hours on a proposal but make no systematic inquiry into why the job was won or lost. If the consultants who are directly involved also make the inquiry, the potential client will invariably and politely reply that the proposed fees were "too high." When a less personal and independently hired research firm makes the same inquiry, far more useful insights are likely to be gained. It may come down to seemingly minor points such as some clients prefer to receive materials in advance of a presentation and others don't. Some like to know the key points before hearing details; others prefer the reverse order. In a similar vein, "blind" follow-up satisfaction surveys are needed to learn if delivered performance matches the marketing and sales claims made earlier in garnering a client. The book *Market Research Matters*[3] contains many useful points for those interested.

Key 4: Match Expectations and Performance

Again, David Maister's work provides a useful framework, depicted in Exhibit 3.4, for discussing various types of consulting that can be delivered to meet a client's needs and expectations. On the vertical dimension of the matrix is the range from "muscle" (pharmacy and nursing ward) to "brainpower" (surgery and psychotherapy). For "muscle" work, the client knows how to do the work but prefers to outsource the labor. Sometimes, the need is more intellectual where the client is looking for expertise or insight or even skills not available within the client's organization. On the horizontal dimension, there is the process dimension ranging from "out front" frequent with intensive personal contact with clients to "back office" support involving little client contact.

It is important in staffing and pricing that client and consultant agree about what is being sought. In fact, most unsuccessful projects probably were doomed by lack of mutual understanding as to what the client really wanted from the consultant. Consultants like to believe the clients want their brainpower and don't really care about how the job is staffed, akin to brain surgery. However, it may be that the client merely wants some temporary help (muscle) to gather some information to which they will later apply their own brainpower in analyzing the data. This kind of mismatch helps to explain a variety of client misunderstandings and complaints about overpriced consulting or off-target reports.

The matrix is also helpful in explaining why consulting is so hard to market and sell. Each firm has a variety of services and sometimes even some products to sell. At the "product" end, it might be proprietary software or a canned

Exhibit 3.4	Types of Consulting Practices

		Degree of Customization	
		Standardized Process —Execution Emphasis	Customized Process —Diagnosis Emphasis
Amount of Client Contact	High Degree of Client Contact— the "Front Room"	**Nurse**	**Psychotherapist**
	Low Degree of Client Contact— the "Back Room"	**Pharmacist**	**Brain Surgeon**

training program, while at the other end it could be the design of a unique business strategy requiring extensive data gathering and analysis. Fees can range from a few thousand to millions of dollars.

To prevent serious misunderstandings, consultants need to perform a good deal of upfront work interviewing the client about its needs and expectations. Then some basic fundamentals take over as a written proposal becomes essential for clearly stating the client's needs from the consultant's viewpoint, as well as laying out in concrete terms the consultant's views on deliverables, benefits, fees, and schedule. The consultant also needs to review this proposal carefully with the client before work begins, and then return to it frequently in meetings with the client to assess progress. It may be that the original agreement will have to be renegotiated, but this should happen before a project goes too far in the wrong direction. These are simple fundamentals, but often a determining factor in client satisfaction.

Key 5: Monitor and Measure

The only way to deal with the variety of challenges and complexity in the marketing and selling of consulting is to relentlessly monitor and measure each of the many tactics used. Isolating the impact of any single tactic or even any single strategy is difficult. The key is to follow the admonition of Len Lodish in his classic book, *The Advertising and Promotion Challenge* where he opts for being "generally right" instead of "precisely wrong."[4] At a minimum, sales should conduct a win/loss analysis based on an objective third-party debriefing after each major sales pursuit. Marketing should also conduct a survey each year, both internally and externally, to assess progress on major objectives (e.g., current client satisfaction or prospective client awareness for the firm's services).

At the firm-wide level, the firm's leadership should accept and agree upon key measures of marketing and sales accomplishment. If surveys are not credible to senior management, then other measures should be planned and used; for example, the firm's CEO might contact people he or she respects who have been previous targets of the firm's marketers. However, even if the CEO doesn't respect the existing measures, the marketers and sales leaders can still use this information for themselves as self-guidance for improvement. It is difficult to improve at bowling or golf if you don't know the result of each roll or shot.

While the measurement of sales results can be fairly straightforward in terms of wins and losses, the assessment of marketing programs is far more complicated and usually more qualitative in its measurement. Some possible approaches include:

- How many new clients were attracted by marketing (won/lost interviews can show the impact of positioning, marketing events, etc.), and what is their projected lifetime value,
- How many current clients were positively influenced by a marketing campaign, and what is their (increased) lifetime value to the firm,
- Growth in customer/client total lifetime value that might be attributed to marketing due to more positive attitudes toward the firm,
- Changes in how clients/recruits/alumni feel about the firm consistent with marketing campaigns, etc.

It is important to keep trying and adjusting measures that are tailored to the firm's specific activities. Remember, though, not to fall into the trap of measuring marketing progress in terms of sales results alone. That unitary measure can be very misleading about marketing's success or failure because the real purpose of marketing should be to focus on a longer time horizon and to create broader effects on the market in general.

COMPENSATION AND REWARDS

Different consulting firms handle this issue differently. Firms with a hunter orientation recognize partners who produce the most business. If a hunter identifies a poor seller within the firm, even if a good deliverer, they will probably fire that partner or never promote him or her. The farmer orientation will reverse the emphasis and be willing to let go of a poor consultant or disruptive citizen regardless of selling ability.

Of course, in a large firm, an underlying issue is whether or not the management can accurately identify which people are skilled at either marketing or selling. Scorekeeping on revenue generation is a thorny subject, and even the most sophisticated systems can be misleading if the only basis is annual gross revenue produced while overlooking profit for each client. A troubling issue is the potential trade-off of work sold versus quality of work delivered. "Quality" is very difficult to assess because the delivered service is intangible, depending on client perception and other factors outside the control of the consultants.

A second difficulty lies in ascertaining who really sold what. Sales are usually a team activity, and the most senior partner is not always the deal closer. Win/loss analyses and client satisfaction surveys can help management assess performance in general, but allocating specific rewards to individuals is a subjective process and does not always recognize or produce the best consultancy.

My preference is to emphasize both individual and team rewards, while placing more emphasis on the latter. The criteria used should include multiple measures, such as revenues, profitability, quality, and client satisfaction. Ethics should also be a component. Has the consultant done the work professionally and in accord with the firm's values? Too often, firms ignore this issue. Overlooking ethical violations can be debilitating and alienating to junior people who are more likely to witness violations of ethical policy. The best companies do what GE does: plot both ethical and economic performance.

RELATIONSHIP MARKETING

Generally, consultants rarely practice relationship marketing well. This is especially disturbing in the case of current clients who are usually the easiest to sell. Instead, in many firms, rewards and budgets tend to emphasize "fresh meat." Somehow, conquering a brand new client is regarded as a more noteworthy sign of sales success than reselling to an old client.

For those few wise firms that succeed at deepening relationships with current clients, a number of strategies are employed. Incentives are carefully designed to reward retaining a client and increasing revenues. Sales forces and rainmakers are assigned to existing clients instead of aligning them only against new prospects. It also means entertaining and visiting clients when there is no new project on the table. Intellectual capital is developed for existing client issues, not just designed to attract new clients.

Consultants who are best at building relationships follow a process based on their understanding of how they have previously succeeded in developing long-term, profitable relationships. They are able to identify clients with this potential and then know how best to serve them. Those firms that have implemented effective client relationships follow a process with steps like these:

- Designate the clients to target
- Profitable now (and likely to be so in the future)
- Solid chemistry
- Client culture open to loyalty to consultants
- Focus on building loyalty, not simply trying to maintain the relationship
- Strategize what the client needs and which individual consultants might work well with the client
- Ensure that the client knows you are qualified to deliver the services needed
- Reward loyalty by providing intellectual capital (if not entertainment)
- Visit often, especially when no new work is in the offering
- Develop an ongoing communications plan
- Systematically prioritize efforts and continuously measure effectiveness

Loyalty is also built at the interpersonal level through "chemistry" between consultant and client. David Maister and Jag Sheth have separately written extensively on how individual consultants can best become "trusted advisors" and cultivate lasting relationships. It may be "old school" ties that gain an introduction, but the relationship continues only if the client finds it easy to talk with the consultant and, more importantly, values the consultant's advice and ability to serve as a wise sounding board. Years of experience and lack of ego create these kinds of skillful consultants.

ADVERTISING, PUBLIC RELATIONS, AND MEDIA MANAGEMENT

Over the past decade, Andersen Consulting (now Accenture) has demonstrated that consistent advertising, while spending more than competitors year-in and year-out, can significantly help a firm establish a strong brand image. Andersen embarked on its program in the early 1990s and has stuck with its campaign, designed initially to differentiate Andersen from the other consulting arms. But its real goal was to be compared with IBM, not with other accounting firms. And they succeeded, eventually separating completely from the accounting business and becoming the largest consulting firm in the world.

Andersen's success at brand building stood the firm well when it changed its name to Accenture. Teresa Poggenpohl is an author as well as partner and Director for Global Advertising and Brand Management at Accenture, and one of the few Accenture marketing professionals to have been involved with the firm's advertising since its inception. In a personal interview she credited several factors for Accenture's long-term success: [5]

1. Each stage "informed the next." All the learning from Andersen Consulting's decade plus of advertising was applied to the launch of Accenture. Amazingly, the company was able to design a new name and initiate successful advertising within 147 days of learning they would need to change.

2. Accenture has taken a "consumer marketing approach to professional services." It was the first in its category to use advertising, as well as to use market research, to understand buyers and measure results. Perhaps most importantly, they have "employed the strategy of continuous investment" in the brand. Poggenpohl notes that often competitors will use a burst of advertising to create "a spike in results" and then "spend the next eighteen months doing nothing, completely eliminating any gains they had made." Accenture invests in advertising every year in more than thirty countries across the world.

3. There is also strong "commitment from incredible leadership partners" willing to make the necessary investment in advertising, even though image advertising is difficult to link directly to sales. We "measure literally everything," but Poggenpohl acknowledges that image advertising cannot really be proven.

Advertising does not work for all firms, particularly where discipline and strategy to give meaning to brand image, is lacking and/or when senior management has little commitment to advertising. The rewards are there, since numerous research studies across industries show that the larger spenders over time are granted a perception of leadership. Interestingly, few firms beyond Accenture and IBM Consulting have pursued advertising with a long-term goal of building their reputations and brand names.

An alternative route to marketing that is less expensive and more in keeping with what consultants like to do is through promoting their intellectual capital. One of the PR masters in the industry is Pat Pollino of Mercer Management Consulting. Pollino relies heavily on the use of media to publish articles about the firm and by partners. He has said that "media relations are an essential way of bringing a firm's leading-edge thinking to the global marketplace." He and Mercer have a three-prong strategy:

- "Source" articles in which Mercer experts are quoted,

- Placing articles written by Mercer professions, and

- Prominent mentions in articles about the strategy consulting industry.

This is the path taken by McKinsey as it publishes its own journal. The *McKinsey Quarterly* supports speech-making opportunities for its consultants and sponsors an annual prize for the best article in the *Harvard Business Review*. McKinsey's emphasis on its intellectual capital allows the firm to establish itself on the leading edge in management thought, which is appealing to many clients.

Other firms, smaller in scope and scale, use techniques like consultant-authored books on important issues to attract clients. These can be highly effective in establishing the author's point-of-view, and many books have launched consulting growth. It is clear that a best seller with a strong message, such as Champy and Hammer's *Reengineering the Corporation*[6] or Slywotsky's *Value Migration,*[7] helped greatly to increase their respective firms' revenues. It is unclear whether books have the same impact on large consultancies, particularly those with hunter orientations.

OTHER APPROACHES

Another popular marketing technique is sponsorships, which straddle marketing and sales. Often the decision to sponsor an event or a team or individuals such as golfers is as much to entertain clients and recruits as it is to gain brand recognition or differentiation.

Some firms also rely on pro bono work to garner positive press for their citizenship and, not incidentally, make connections at a senior level to produce leads for gaining future business. For example, as Bain expanded geographically years ago, they offered "free" studies to a few mayors of large cities, knowing this would lead to interviews with CEOs on the projects.

A relatively new strategy is to hire a "professional" sales force to overcome the frequent problem of good consultants not being good salespeople. Only a few firms have done this with the scale necessary to allow sales people to feel comfortable within the firm and to give them enough staff to be successful. Ernst & Young, for example, and Mercer HR have both gained revenue growth from a sales group, mostly hiring IBM (or like businesses) trained sales people. The cultures in both of these firms are rather self-effacing, sufficiently so that line partners readily accept the possibility that sales professionals are able to market and sell a service even when these sales people have not been consultants themselves.

SOLO PRACTITIONERS AND SMALL FIRMS

Much of the advice in this chapter applies to all consultants. However, the size of a firm does make a difference in marketing and selling. If a rainmaker at a large firm has a bad year or two, success of the other partners can keep the firm growing. But when there are only one or a few partners, this luxury does not exist. The solo consultant is constantly caught in the "do-sell" cycle, alternating back and forth between consulting and selling—a cycle that can be highly inefficient and exhausting. This requires added discipline from the solo consultant to ensure making a certain number of calls/emails/visits each week to prospects for future work. Careful monitoring of progress through the steps in Exhibit 3.3 is also critical, in order to make sure there are sufficient numbers at each stage to produce sufficient numbers of clients in the future.

It is also vital for solo practitioners to recognize their own strengths and weaknesses. If they are strong closers, able to sell well, but weak at marketing, they should consider hiring others to help produce leads (through advertising, PR, ghost writing, and/or telemarketing/prospecting). In the reverse instance of being weak at sales, they might hire a sales representative or join an alliance with other solos who are good at selling projects where they need help. Finally, solo or small firms should measure and monitor their marketing and sales efforts just like the big firms to allow for self-analysis and improvement.

FUTURE NEEDS AND CHALLENGES

The marketing and sales functions in consulting firms have clearly become more diverse and complicated in their approaches. Some have started to advertise; others have hired a sales force. In addition, the economics of book publishing have changed to make it possible for many consultants to publish books such that most large firms have multiple authors on staff. The advent of the Internet and advanced computer programs has also made available new marketing and sales techniques.

On another challenging front, ethical concerns will continue to preoccupy senior leaders of most firms, including their marketing staffs. They need to ask if their firm's marketing and sales are accurately and candidly describing what the firm is able to deliver. In an era where neither marketers nor consultants are above reproach, this is a serious challenge. The firm's marketing leaders must think twice before exaggerating benefits that can't be delivered. In my mind, it is unethical to promise what one can't deliver, but even if this remains a moot question, a mismatch on "Maister's matrix" will be created that will inevitably cause lower credibility and a short-lived "one and done" relationship.

As more consulting firms go public, they will need to become highly sophisticated in communicating to a new set of audiences (analysts, shareholders, etc.). Historically, consultants have remained largely "invisible" and not worried about their communications to legislators or to the general public. Certainly, publicly traded firms will have to focus their communications on multiple stakeholders. In the wake of Enron and Andersen, even privately owned consultants will need to watch their public image.

At the same time, the diffusion of interactivity on the Internet will require new skills allowing firms to disseminate intellectual capital in highly efficient and more customized ways than in the recent past. McKinsey, for example, provides access to its Quarterly journal online to anyone who registers. Users can then order updates on whatever topics they select. At some point, firms like McKinsey will use the Internet to accommodate real-time questions and answers combining instant messages and chat lines.

All of these occurrences have made marketing and sales a far more vibrant part of the consulting industry, while establishing these functions in the front lines of an industry struggling amid unsettling economic conditions. For the foreseeable future, it will take strong and creative marketing and sales efforts for firms to remain competitive.

Notes to the Chapter

[1] David Maister, *Managing the Professional Service Firm* (New York: Free Press, 1993).

[2] Michael Porter actually lists alternatives but focus (e.g., on an industry) can be viewed as an aspect of differentiation. *Competitive Strategy* (New York: Free Press, 1980).

[3]Robert Duboff and James Spaeth, *Market Research Matters* (Wiley, 1999).

[4]Leonard Lodish, *The Advertising and Promotion Challenge* (Oxford: Oxford University Press, 1986).

[5]Interview with Teresa Poggenpohl, July 9, 2002.

[6]Michael Hammer and James A. Champy, *Reengineering the Corporation* (New York: HarperBusiness, 1993).

[7]Adrian J. Slywotsky, *Value Migration* (Boston: Harvard Business School Press, 1996).

Additional Bibliography on Marketing Consulting

On Marketing ROI:

Ambler, Jim. Marketing and the Bottom Line *(Financial Times/Prentice Hall, 2000)*.

Kotler, Philip, Thomas Hayes, Paul Bloom. Marketing Professional Services, *Second Edition (Peramus, NJ: Prentice Hall Press, 2002)*.

Jensen, Bill. Simplicity *(Cambridge, MA: Perseus Books, 2000)*.

Schiemann, William, and John H. Lingle. Bullseye *(New York: Free Press, 1999)*.

On becoming a trusted advisor:

Sheth, Jagdish, and Andrew Sobel. Clients for Life *(New York: Simon & Shuster, 2000)*.

Maister, David H., Charles H. Green, Robert M. Galford. The Trusted Advisor *(New York: Free Press, 2000)*.

Part 2

Major Practice Areas in Consulting

INTRODUCTION

This section focuses on the five major practice areas of consulting that are dominant today and likely will be into the future: 1) IT consulting, 2) strategy and organization consulting, 3) marketing consulting, 4) operations management consulting, and 4) human resources consulting. These five areas comprise approximately 90 percent of the total consulting market, with 46 percent in the IT area, 12 percent in strategy, 10 percent in marketing consulting, 12 percent in operations management, and 10 percent in human resources.

Clients hire consultants for their leading-edge knowledge and ability to solve problems within each of the five major practice areas. Knowledge within each area is constantly changing, as are the issues that clients face. The beginning consultant is usually challenged to become an expert in only one of these four areas. But as one gains consulting experience and rises to senior levels, it is important to become more aware of all five fields because each greatly affects the other in the client's situation. Clients expect a breadth of awareness from their senior consultants in determining how specific recommendations will fit with the rest of their business.

Information technology consulting is the largest and most expansive area within the industry today. In Chapter 4, "Information Technology Consulting," the authors provide a roadmap of IT consulting and its development over time and into the future. The remarkable growth of IT consulting has passed from an era of information systems used for simple financial reporting to today's conduct of e-business. As a result, IT has become a source of competitive advantage for the firm, as well as an efficiency tool. It has also become a basis for outsourcing, which is now a major generator of revenues for consulting firms. The competitive dynamics have also changed as large computer hardware and software firms, e.g., IBM and HP, have moved in on the consulting industry to become major players. We see in this chapter how this IT evolution and revolution is taking place, and what it portends for the future with the introduction of Internet2 and other upcoming opportunities.

Another major practice area of consulting is concerned with "Strategy and Organization Consulting," which is covered in Chapter 5. Here the authors examine the evolving relationship between these two disciplines over the years. In the early writings of Peter Drucker, these fields were indistinguishable, but they separated in the 1960s with the advent of new economic models for strategic planning, such as BCG's Growth Share Matrix. In contrast, the organizational discipline became dominated by psychologists with motivational models and sociologists with structural models. Only recently, according to the authors, have the two areas been rejoined as an integrated response for coping with fast-moving markets and the dynamics of hyper-competition.

While marketing has been a classic discipline in consulting for years, it is now changing significantly with the introduction of new media technology and electronic channels of distribution and communication to customers. In Chapter 6, "The Marketing Consultant," the extent of change caused by IT and the Web are discussed in depth. For example, many new client opportunities exist for selling over the Internet, conducting marketing research via the Web, and using CRM software to serve customers better. These opportunities give the marketing consultant powerful new tools and problem-solving services to bring to clients. In addition, the chapter highlights various types of marketing consulting firms, from specialist marketing research to general management. It concludes by identifying a number of trends lasting into the future that will affect the marketing consultant, ranging from micro-segmentation to the nurturing of lifetime customers.

Operations consulting is the oldest practice area, going back to Frederick Taylor and the advent of the stopwatch in measuring worker productivity. Although often overlooked, operations management remains a thriving domain for consultants. Clients are continually concerned about the efficiency and quality of their production processes. Chapter 7, "Operations Management Consulting," discusses how OM consultants go about their jobs, attacking major operational issues in a variety of contexts that make each project different, such as in companies with multiple plant versus those with only one plant. The effective OM consultant needs to understand these varying contexts because they often require unique solutions, not cookie-cutter programs that advocate best practices derived from entirely different situations. The chapter also covers major concepts used in OM consulting, from supply chain management to mass customization. It concludes with predictions about the future issues facing tomorrow's OM consultants.

Chapter 8 on "Human Resources Management" takes a provocative stance in arguing that HR consulting is going through a major transformation caused by information technology. Much of the HR function in companies has for years been involved in routine transactions involving benefits, payroll, and policy communication. Now, much of these routine operations can be performed through the company intranet or even completely outsourced to a consulting firm. The chapter discusses several alternative approaches to automation, from "do it yourself" to complete outsourcing. The chapter predicts a variety of different roles emerging for HR consultants, ranging from acting as HR strategy consultants to outsourcing managers. Consulting firms are also being challenged as to whether they should specialize in a narrow HR niche or adopt a broader range of "one stop" HR services. All of these challenges offer significant opportunities, though HR consulting must be prepared to embrace the new IT reality.

CHAPTER 4

Information Technology Consulting

Richard Nolan, Harvard Business School and Larry Bennigson, Harvard Business School

ABOUT THE AUTHORS

Richard Nolan

Richard Nolan is the William Barclay Harding Professor of Management of Technology, at the Harvard Business School. Previously, he was Chairman of Nolan, Norton & Co. from 1977 to 1992. His research and consulting interests include business transformation and information technology. His latest book is *Dot Vertigo* (Wiley and Sons, 2001), which reports his case-based research on management lessons from both dot.com companies and industrial-age companies when incorporating the Internet into their operations.

Lawrence A. Bennigson

Lawrence A. Bennigson is Senior Fellow and Senior Vice-President of Harvard Business School Interactive. He oversees development, design, and delivery of the school's custom executive development programs for individual companies. He has been President of the Scandinavian Institutes for Administrative Research in the United States, a Managing Partner of The MAC Group, and Senior Vice President of Gemini Consulting. He is a board member of public companies and serves on the Advisory Board of Toffler Associates, founded by Alvin and Heidi Toffler, the futurists.

Between 1996 and 2000, more than $1.7 trillion was spent in the United States on information technology (IT). Today, IT spending in the United States accounts for more than half of all companies' capital spending. No recent development has impacted management consulting more than IT, and nothing on the horizon will impact management consulting more. Today, IT consulting accounts for more than 45 percent of all management consulting revenue in the world.

All management consulting presumes some degree of knowledge and use of IT in the various functions of a client's business. The primary focus of IT consulting is IT-oriented expertise (e.g., computers, software, Internet, e-business, and outsourcing) versus functional-oriented expertise (e.g., marketing, organization, finance, and accounting). IT is also a major tool in many aspects of management consulting, playing a central role in such activities as scenario analysis in strategic planning consulting, customer data-mining in marketing consulting, and assembly line load-balancing in operations consulting.

In 2000, after the consulting industry had experienced many years of explosive growth, a traumatic shakeout began, resulting in the restructuring of the IT consulting industry and a repositioning among all the major firms. The

Internet frenzy had run its course and the "Y2K" investments had ground to a halt. The dot.com bubble burst, rapidly plunging most of the dot.com companies into bankruptcy and sending IT consulting into a tailspin, seriously stagnating growth. The number of potential U.S. client companies with 5 percent revenue growth, 10 percent earnings growth, and a market capitalization in excess of $1 billion, dropped from 156 in 2000 to 71 in 2001. Hyper-growth has clearly turned to negative growth for many IT consulting firms, and a significant number of IT consulting firms with revenues in the hundreds of millions have simply disappeared: Zefer, Viant, and MarchFirst.

This change continues today and will for the foreseeable future. Just how all this turmoil sorts itself out will determine the future of the IT consulting industry, as well as the future careers of IT consultants, and even portends broader implications for all of management consulting. To better understand how and why this transformation is taking place and where it is leading, we will discuss the growth of IT consulting, address the current transformation and its many new developments, and then look at the future of IT consulting.

THE DEVELOPMENT OF IT CONSULTING

Over the last forty years, the growth of IT consulting has closely paralleled the growth of management as a profession. Throughout this period, a remarkable transition has taken place from the Industrial Economy to the Information Economy, which in turn has required companies to transform their internal operations from manual to computer-based.

Initially, the development of the accounting field with its financial auditing requirements provided a need for assistance from professional services firms with expertise in accounting principles. These firms, led by the Big Eight, helped clients to apply accounting principles to the reporting of information about financial performance. Later, this reporting function was greatly facilitated by the development of computer technology. At this point, the IT consulting business was born, most of which was originally housed within the major accounting firms.

Eras and Stages of Growth

We view the growth of IT consulting as occurring over three broad eras leading up to the present, with each era being determined by major innovations in computer technology and software. Exhibit 4.1 presents the three eras: 1960–1980, the Data Processing (DP) Era; 1975–2000, the Micro Era; and 1995–2010, the Network Era. The DP Era centered on the mainframe and its batch processing with paper print-out, which was typically performed and maintained by a centralized IT organization within any given company. The Micro Era was initiated by microcomputers and the personal computer, which resulted in the decentralization of the IT function, thereby placing more control in the hands of individual employees. The Network Era is now upon us with the phenomenal growth of the Internet and e-business, making possible rapid communication and transactions that extend beyond the corporation to include the entire value chain and value network.

Richard Nolan has identified four stages of implementation that occurred within each of the major eras, also depicted in Exhibit 4.1. These four stages consisted of initiation, contagion, control, and integration. They occurred in

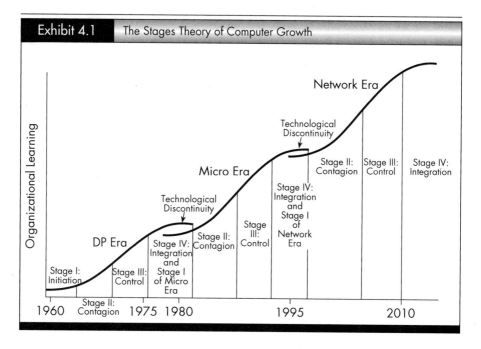

Exhibit 4.1   The Stages Theory of Computer Growth

order as a new technology matured and was replaced by another new technology. This process is based on the idea that the complicated nature of newly introduced computer technology produces a constantly evolving body of learning and knowledge about the effective management of IT within organizations. In turn, this developing body of knowledge becomes institutionalized, forming an "S-shaped" curve, which reflects how an initial trial-and-error learning process gradually leads to a higher level of sophistication in managing information technology.

We should also note that the transition from one major era to another is not automatic or easy for most firms. The S-shaped curves within each era tend to overlap to cause a transformational period of "technological discontinuity between the major eras."[1] History has shown that every industry experiences a few years of lead or lag time in learning new technologies. The senior levels of management in each organization directly influence the pace of change.[2] During this transition period, further efforts by management and technicians to develop the old technology's mature dominant design often conflict with the vigorous growth of a new technology's emerging design. Those who mastered the old design struggle to retain their knowledge and power against those who propose replacing it with a new technology. With the rapid expansion of the IT industry and its innovative technology, most management and IT workers have faced "a diet of continual change."[3]

This broad context of IT change and transformation has provided fertile ground for the growth of IT consulting services. The first major stimulus for consulting assistance is clearly traceable to the advent of the PC and its open standards in the 1980s, followed by the development of greatly increased computer capacity and sophisticated software, and then at the end of the 1990s with the commercialization of the Internet.

1990s Explosion of IT Consulting

By the 1990s, IT consulting activities had developed into a significant source of growth and profits. The consulting industry's large IT players continued to adapt and grow with the changing IT environment. For clients, IT became a way of providing competitive advantage, as evidenced by a surge of reengineering-led IT projects and Enterprise Resource Planning (ERP) installations.

However, few firms were prepared for the impact of so much change. Arthur Andersen experienced a painful separation of its accounting and IT consulting activities. And the chaos continued in the restructuring of the professional services industry through several acquisitions, including the IT product firms acquiring consulting firms and grafting them onto their product structures. Even McKinsey suffered a trying experience in attempting to assimilate a rogue group of Arthur Andersen IT consultants.

Recently, the Internet has ushered in a new era, in which IT has developed into an effective way for companies to communicate with customers, suppliers, and partners. A new term has entered the business vocabulary: e-business. Building e-business capability often means reworking much of a company's business model. Among these clients, the key decision-making responsibility for considering and implementing e-business projects has migrated away from IT professionals to senior line managers.

TODAY'S IT CONSULTING FIRMS

The IT consulting market is currently composed of several segments, including both full-service firms and highly specialized boutiques. In Exhibit 4.2, we identify six types of IT consulting companies, which are differentiated by type and scope of consulting services. As one can see, there are many competitors and many services, with some firms marketing a broad range of consulting combined with hardware and software, while others are narrowly focused on software or research for clients.

Up to now, the industry has been highly fragmented with hundreds of firms competing for a share of a rapidly expanding market. The two top players in 2002 (Accenture Consulting and IBM Global Services) together account for 38.4 percent of industry revenues. The strongest IT consulting firms are using the current shakeout to make strategic acquisitions, such as IBM's acquisition of PricewaterhouseCoopers Consulting.

Today, IBM is by far the largest IT consulting firm in the world with revenues exceeding $10.8 billion, more than twice its hardware sales. In its earlier years, IBM's focus was on hardware and maintaining close control over its software applications. However, the IT environment significantly changed in the 1980s with the advent of the PC and open standards. IBM stumbled and experienced billion dollar losses in the early 1990s. Under Lou Gerstner, IBM reversed strategy, unbundled its services, embraced open standards, and has now reestablished itself as the dominant IT consulting firm, while also providing hardware and outsourcing services.

Hundreds of small consulting firms have also arisen to help clients with new e-business opportunities. These startups, typically built by young entrepreneurs with relatively little consulting experience, compete in specialized niches. They

Exhibit 4.2	Types of IT Consulting Firms
Type/Examples	**Primary Focus**
Full Product/Service Firms: IBM, Microsoft, Cisco, Novell	Large full product/service firms have moved into IT consulting as (1) a major source of high margins and (2) to reinforce their product businesses. IBM and Novell have acquired major IT consulting firms to facilitate their strategic IT consulting initiatives.
Full IT Consulting Service Firms: Accenture, Bearing Point (formerly KPMG), Cap Gemini	Large full IT consulting firms generally operate independently of IT product and software connections enabling them to present a position of vendor objectivity. These firms have also focused on the tricky process of managing highly talented professional consultants.
ERP, CRM, and ASP Providers: SAP, Peoplesoft, Seibel Systems, Oracle, ADP	ERP, CRM, and ASP providers are relatively recent additions to IT consulting. These firms have addressed the problem of integration of legacy systems in companies. They provide packages that integrate across functions and tasks. The ASP firms generally specialize in providing full functional and IT consulting for a particular business process, including the operation for the client.
Outsourcers and Web Services Firms: EDS, CSC, TPI, Ajilon, Comsys, Offshore (Indian companies offering Systems Development services and HELP desk services)	Outsourcing IT operations has been around almost as long as IT consulting. Pioneered by EDS and IBM, outsourcing has become a very large business, and the trend continues as the complexity of IT increases in the Network Era.
IT Research Firms: Gartner Group, Meta Group, Compass, Forrester	IT Research firms help both companies and IT vendors understand the trends in IT products and management.
e-Business and Web Services: e-Business and Web services are emerging lines of business in all the IT Consulting firm types—e.g., Microsoft .NET, IBM—Websphere, Novell—OneNet.	e-Business and Web Services are the fastest growing segments in IT consulting. With the continued increase in companies building complex IT networks, and integrating with the Internet/Web, these services represent very large revenue segments in IT consulting over the next 10 years.

rarely possess the scale to take on big clients, which are mainly pursued by the large IT consulting firms. Yet, collectively these small consulting firms represent a major force in IT consulting.

An important aspect of the new e-business consulting environment includes helping clients to understand the strategic aspects of the Internet. Strategic consulting involves rethinking the client's business model, helping to design a new organization, and planning the rollout of various e-business segments. Strategy consulting work provides higher margins and allows these firms to build relationships at the highest levels of a clients' organization.

Although some consulting firms have touted their ability to assist clients with both business strategy and IT implementation, the reality is that most firms are focused on one or the other. What many implementation-oriented firms have called strategy consulting actually amounts to designing system requirements or reengineering particular business processes. On the other hand, what strategy-oriented firms have called *implementation* often appears as acting more like a general contractor who subcontracts out specialized IT skills needed for delivery capability.

Among the larger consulting firms, there is some movement and increasing interest in diversification toward MDPs (Multi-Disciplinary Practices), which offer legal, consulting, and accounting services under one roof. In November 1999, Ernst & Young began a strategic relationship with a Washington, D.C. law firm, McKee Nelson, to "use an alliance platform to leverage the knowledge, infrastructure, and client base of a world-class professional-service firm"—in other words, to act as an MDP whenever possible. In Britain, the Law Society has approved MDPs, and legislation is being proposed that would make them a reality. Big accounting firms like KPMG are also setting up their own independent legal arms overseas; KPMG's law firm in France, Fidal, is the biggest law firm in France, currently employing 1,200 lawyers.

While professional service firms insist that they want to diversify because their corporate clients demand it, we do not see corporations clamoring for MDPs yet. A 2001 survey determined that more than three-quarters of a large global business sample used different consulting firms from the ones that they used for electronic business-services, even when they might have purchased all services from the same vendor. An ongoing debate exists regarding the attractiveness of one-stop shopping versus a client's comfort level in being held captive by one provider. Clients recognize the potential conflicts of interest that can arise in such an arrangement. Furthermore, it is questionable whether one firm can provide clients with a full range of services, each at the level of best-in-class quality. And, in the United States, the Sarbanes-Oxley Act will significantly limit the variety of services that auditing firms can provide.

"Scar Tissue" from the Implosion

IT consulting leaders and entrepreneurs rode a roller coaster through the late 1990s. Fortunes were made rapidly and lost just as rapidly. Partners learned the age-old lessons about over-expanding staff and fixed costs. Partners have had calls on cash, and partner ranks have thinned. These are the same professionals who are now rebuilding for the future. And they will bring these recent experiences with them to decisions about investment, staffing levels, and staff performance demands. Partners and Practice Leaders will face painful trade-offs as they assess the attraction of new opportunities while still smarting from the excess risk-taking of the past. And consultants will have to rise to the higher standards of quality and billability that these leaders will demand.

IT consulting embraces a paradox: All management consulting requires both IT knowledge and functional domain knowledge, but all management consultants cannot be both IT experts and functional experts. The crux of this paradox is the breadth and depth inherent to the many knowledge domains of both IT and the functional areas of business. IT has penetrated deeply into every functional area of business and has enabled new capabilities in most functional areas not before possible, such as real-time logistics and self-help services. Accounting has become increasingly sophisticated, extending beyond financial accounting into managerial control involving real-time interactive control systems.

Effectively coping with this paradox of breadth versus depth continues to plague the execution of successful management consulting initiatives. We believe its resolution will require complex collaborative consulting arrangements among a combination of IT consultants, functional consultants, and employees of organizations.

IT AND CLIENT TRANSFORMATION

IT consulting has always followed the impact of IT on the structure and strategy of the client firm. By the early 2000s, IT became an integral part of the infrastructure of the firm, linking together networks of customers and partners and enabling the firm to operate in a global environment.

Stages of Organizational Evolution

Exhibit 4.3 illustrates the long and gradual evolution of organizations as IT has been integrated into the structure and decision-making processes of many companies. The DP Era of the last century corresponded with a period when organizations typically did not challenge the M-Form (Multi-level) functional hierarchy and the Industrial Age management model. However, as the computer became more omnipresent in organizations, companies began to use them in more ways to promote efficient transaction processing. This automation of manual and clerical functions eliminated the need for many blue collar and clerical jobs. Layoffs and downsizing started mutating the traditional pyramid organization structure, as shown in Exhibit 4.3, beginning with reduced numbers of workers at the base of the pyramid.

The PCs of the Micro Era have enabled workers to rapidly obtain and manipulate figures, previously available to only select individuals in the firm. As illustrated in the middle of Exhibit 4.3, the incremental business model showed more erratic business performance than the incremental EPS "march to the northeast corner" of the earlier model. (The "march to the northeast corner" is popular accounting slang for the direction of charts in annual reports showing EPS, profit, revenue growing from left to right and bottom to top.)

As we begin this new century, many large client companies have integrated IT into their organizations to the point that the speed and form of their organizations are more like IT-enabled networks than the slower functional hierarchies of the past. The development of Intranets during the current Network

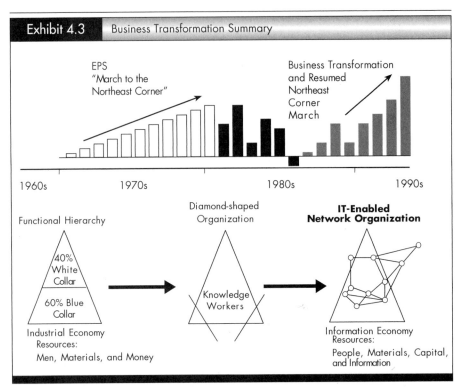

Exhibit 4.3 Business Transformation Summary

Era requires more coordination and promulgation of open standards than the traditional use of controls and long-range plans. Organizations maintain focus by basing key IT decisions on delivering value to customers.

Today's CIO faces the challenge of building an IT architecture that consists of many partners, strategic alliances, and outsourcers. Informal shadow networks are taking form and floating over the formal hierarchies to speed up the pace of performing work. In the Network Era of this century, the CIO is managing a formal but highly permeable network organization, which is constantly changing, and characterized by its "extended organization" involving many suppliers and customer groups.

The New IT Infrastructure

Case studies of organizations with leading-edge IT infrastructures like IBM, Cisco, Schwab, H.E. Butt Grocery Company, and Amazon.com allow us to see the form of the new network IT infrastructures being built. These new IT infrastructures go well beyond the automation of back-office transactions to provide real-time network collaborative capabilities, thereby enabling the company to "sense and respond" rapidly to customers.

Whereas early mainframes and databases were hierarchical, like the Industrial Age organizations that assimilated them, the new Information Age organizations are increasingly modeled on IT network architectures. The popular children's building block, Lego, serves as an analogy for the latest trend in information technology architecture—the notion that you can "snap together" software components, or *objects*, to build more complex objects (e.g., enterprise applications built from Java software components).

These new combinations allow organizations to acquire functionalities uniquely suited to market demands. Beyond partnerships, analogous to the disassembly/manipulation/reassembly of atoms or molecules, temporary-consortia are a form of flexibility that goes further than the nimble and flexible firm. Ubiquitous, open systems are a significant enabler.

A notion rapidly losing currency is that of fixed line and staff functions. Today's typical company is more usefully construed as a set of business processes supported by databases and object-oriented software. A defined process, together with supporting data and software, constitutes the integration of organizational and technological components. Some components may be outsourced while others remain under company control.

There are both organizational components and technology components. The organizational components serve to make the company more permeable on a real-time basis to suppliers, employees, and customers. The technology components provide the software features that enable this permeability. Each of these components represents a niche opportunity for small, specialized consultants, while the larger consulting firms are more likely to pursue clients who want an integrated approach.

Organizational Components

Information Transparency. The emerging policy for the network age is information transparency, whereby information is made freely available to all who might act on it. Although information transparency enables instant access, companies do not want to saturate their workforce or partners with irrelevant information. Cisco, for example, releases financial data 24/7, but only to those who need to act on the information. However, attempting to maintain secrecy in some parts of the system and not in others can prove antithetical to the idea of the permeable organization in the network economy.

The Extended Enterprise. This component is central to the permeable organization by stretching it beyond the fixed, physical boundaries of a traditional organization. Companies that use the Internet to open their Intranets to suppliers and customers are extended enterprises. Providing access to the I-Net's databases creates information transparency throughout the supply chain and enables various players to act on information instantly. Suppliers are able to schedule and order materials more efficiently; manufacturers to reduce order-to-delivery cycle times; and customers to receive products faster. Vendors manage customer relationships and even bid on corporate contracts electronically, making the entire supply chain—including the selection process—a more expedient one.

Strategic Alliances. These arrangements are often an essential part of today's corporate strategies and are inherently opportunistic. As such, they need to be arranged and formalized expeditiously, exploited for as long as they make sense, and disbanded when they are no longer relevant to the business. An effective I-Net ensures strategic alliances become an integral part of a company's business. To truly benefit the organization, alliances must maintain constant and frequent interactions. Working with alliance partners in an environment that operates in zero time enables a dynamic relationship. For example, Akamai supplies cache services that allow its partner organizations to use one of Akamai's servers to speed up the responsiveness of an organization's

Web site. Drugstore.com uses Akamai so that when a customer orders from anywhere in the United States fast-loading graphics speed the transaction.

Outsourcing. Today's savvy organizations are acting to outsource the necessary, but potentially resource-heavy, business functions such as payroll processing (e.g., to Automatic Data Processing, Inc. [ADP]), logistics (e.g., to Federal Express), and catering (e.g., to Marriott Corporation). The Internet facilitates such relationships by providing a common platform capable of improving communications, coordination, and supporting electronic transactions (i.e., purchase orders, invoicing, and payments) with outsourcing partners.

Knowledge Management. Knowledge management consists of capturing, storing, combining, analyzing, mining, and distributing information resources and then translating this information into forms and formats that create value. I-Nets provide the essential means for enabling effective knowledge management. Management needs to learn from the pioneers who use both I-Nets and knowledge management. For example, Drugstore.com employs knowledge management to continuously improve the design of their virtual store for personalized shopping. Each time a customer visits the virtual store, the way the customer shops the store is watched. The information is carefully mined and used as a basis for more conveniently laying out the store for the customer's next visit.

Self-Directed Work. Self-directed work transfers the tasks once performed by others to the person who most benefits from it. Individual employees can participate in self-service or self-directed work in everything from corporate tasks (such as corporate communications, payroll, and employee benefits programs) to activities that help execute the company's strategic intent, which include interacting with customers, product delivery, supply procurement, order processing, and data management. At Cisco, for example, electronically monitoring a product's performance enables employees to sense problems and take corrective action before product outages bring down a customer's network.

Technology Components

Real-Time Messaging. In the pre-Internet economy, the often-used monthly, quarterly, and twelve-month time frame for measuring business performance was deeply institutionalized into the pace of business. This process reviewed and established revenue and expense goals based on a calendar. However, the technology component of real-time messaging enables the dissemination of company data at all times. Instant access to information is critical if companies are to remain sensitive and responsive to market fluctuations, changes in customer buying patterns, emerging technology trends, and competitive activity.

Data Warehousing. The data warehouse literally retrieves and stores data gathered from a variety of sources and facilitates the management of this information. Data warehousing is among the first steps toward developing corporate knowledge used by a strategic I-Net. The data warehouse and real-time messaging go hand-in-hand. Data transaction processing techniques update and time-stamp the data so managers always work with the most current information. The degree of simplification realized by tracking customer orders, supplier shipments, and financial status instantaneously allows employees to spend more time on value-added activities. Amazon's sophisticated data storage and retrieval techniques allow the company to track customer purchases and then develop a customer profile and make product recommendations.

Direct Access for Everybody. Networked companies must commit to putting all the relevant people involved in networked processes online and then supporting them while ensuring that the total cost of ownership (TCO) remains at appropriate levels. Companies that adopt this mandate must support it with a disciplined, network-oriented program that updates and maintains their staff's PCs. They also should equip their workforce with technology that ties them to the I-Net, whether by PC, notebook, or personal appliance (i.e., Palm Pilot) that workers may need.

The Browser. The browser was among the first of the Internet's "killer apps" because its immediate and dramatic use helped foster the Internet explosion. The browser is intuitive and, once learned, can be applied in a wide variety of applications—and therein lays its power. Adopting a browser as a standard user interface renders a company's entire portfolio of applications accessible across the enterprise and allows easy access to most of the Internet's applications.

Directory Technology. An internal user directory specifies levels of access to and interaction with an I-Net. Novell, the leading provider of directory technology, characterizes the directory as providing the "digital personas" of the network's users. These personas govern individuals' entry to specific network layers and access to specific resources. Security is incorporated into digital personas, developed not only for employees, but also for suppliers and existing and prospective customers. Increasingly, sophisticated directory technologies enable tailored reporting and priority services to individual users and can also provide preferred paths to specific Web sites and databases that contain information of interest to particular employees or managers.

The Company's Web Site. A company's Web site is the "front door receptionist," acting as the portal through which those who interact with the company enter—that is, everybody in one way or another. Client computers that access the company's Web site display a version of the company's I-Net homepage. Outsiders, such as customers or suppliers, possess digital personas that determine what information appears via their browsers when they access the company's Web site.

IT CLIENTS AND THEIR CURRENT NEEDS

CIOs and their IT organizations play a central role in determining the demand for IT consulting. In our discussions with a number of leading CIOs about their impact on the shape of the IT industry, seven themes emerge:

IT is now an established function in the structure of most organizations. For many years, the IT function was the "new kid on the administrative block." In that tenuous capacity as a newcomer, it was necessary and appropriate to use resources and expertise from outside the company. It was natural for companies to rely on outside sources for guidance on key design and investment decisions and for resource capacity itself. This reliance helped fuel the growth of IT consulting services. Now, a strong IT function is accepted as central to a healthy company, just as are the HR, finance, or purchasing functions. As a result, the degree of IT's reliance on outside consulting support is both sharpened and diminished, especially among large and experienced companies.

The roles of IT in some companies are being redefined by the move to outsource many aspects of the IT operation. While there are efficiencies to be gained, not everyone is convinced that arriving at a skeleton IT function by "default" is a good thing. For example, one CIO we interviewed sees establishing the "information backbone" of the company as about all that is left after it has outsourced maintenance of the data-center, running of the network, and programming. However, this CIO will not outsource the ownership of design or maintenance of the so-called information backbone because he believes it is central to the competitiveness of the company.

As an established function, IT in the company now has more degrees of freedom to source services for highly specific purposes and value. One CIO describes the IT organization of the future as consisting of the following:

- Business analysis to understand the needs of the businesses and to be able to translate business terms into technical specifications.

- Technical architecting to oversee the system landscape and interfaces and to ensure that the business requirements are solved by the IT system.

- Project management to implement change consistent with the practices of the company.

- Management of the above mentioned IT critical competencies and the relations with integrators, software suppliers, and the internal clients.

For each of these four capabilities, this CIO easily identifies the IT consulting outsiders who currently provide that service to his corporation. And, he states that his strategy aims to steadily bring in more capability on the first three into his own organization. He prefers that these capabilities reside in his organization and then, by default, go to the outside if he has no alternative.

CIOs have migrated from being mainly IT technical experts to participating in high-level dialogue about the strategic direction of the company. For example, the views of the CIO may be central to design or redesign of the business model or significant in assessing the viability and future value of a major acquisition. One CIO told us that, "If you have good people in the IT organization, they are good partners with the businesses." In the past, consultants helped bridge the needs of the businesses and the capabilities of IT. As an established strategy partner with business and corporate executives, the CIO and staff replace many of the IT-related strategy needs that IT consultants satisfied in the past.

Many CIOs say they will do less outsourcing in the future. This is driven by several factors, including a decrease in the number of new, "gorilla" ERP and CRM initiatives and the increasing need for rapid and flexible modifications to existing systems. What they do outsource will be the "body shop" activity when they need more capacity, but they plan to keep the deeper expertise within their companies.

Offshore suppliers are providing an increasing share of IT services for activities such as coding. These are companies like Infosys, Syntel, and WiPro. They market and deliver services online and are viewed as providing rapid response, high quality, and low cost service. One CIO told us that ". . . typically the outsource company will have 60 percent of their people on a project offshore and the other 40 percent at our location." These offshore providers were 50 percent of the cost of the large U.S. IT consultants during 2001–2002.

The applications portfolio conundrum is bothering many IT managers as they make decisions about future needs. Previously, the applications portfolio concept had gained wide acceptance among CIOs as a proven and effective way to plan for IT costs and benefits as well as a tool to manage a company's IT technical and functional quality. However, with the Internet-driven move to real-time networks, the job of managing a company's IT through the applications portfolio concept now poses some real difficulties.

The first difficulty lies with directly associating IT benefits with individual applications. New IT benefits generally involve either the whole applications portfolio or major parts of it, and this requires greater depth and breadth in implementation skills. Examples include real-time messaging, single sign-on to the network, and security. Implementing these new capabilities requires not only skills to work at the top level applications layer of the IT architecture, but also the more technical layers through the Application Protocal Interfaces (APIs), Operating System, and, perhaps, the hardware. Both functional breadth skills and technical depth skills are necessary.

A second difficulty concerns the overall benefits that the new IT capabilities are supposed to provide. Realizing full benefits often requires experimentation and continuous redesign. For example, real-time messaging and an integrated database are IT technologies that must be implemented throughout the applications portfolio to achieve IT-based customer service similar to the type of customer service developed at Cisco (and being pursued by many other companies in diverse industries).

DRIVERS AND ENABLERS OF FUTURE IT CONSULTING GROWTH

As illustrated in Exhibit 4.4, the IT consulting industry is shaped by the convergence of the forces that drive business growth and the enablers of structural change. On the driver side, the IT consulting industry grows during strong economic periods and contracts when economic conditions soften. Competitive pressures for adoption of new IT initiatives create IT consulting demand. The expansion phase for IT consulting delivery comes after a new concept has been proven and becomes a competitive "imperative" among players. At later stages in the life cycle of initiatives, IT consulting firms may contract, disappear, or move on to other applications, depending on their positions and capabilities.

The change management capabilities of the adopting client organizations are also a critical driver in affecting demand for consulting. Companies and industries with little experience and capability in handling the required organizational and management process changes will typically turn to outsiders for help. The growth of business process improvement consulting emerged partly

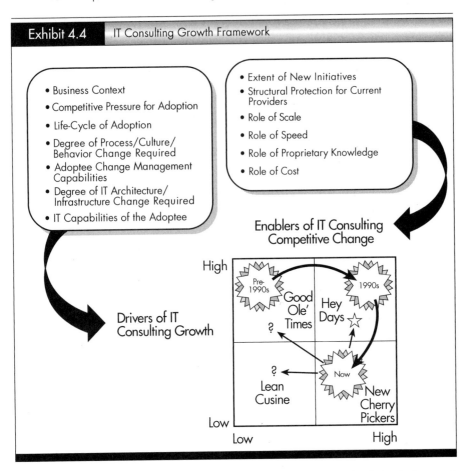

Exhibit 4.4   IT Consulting Growth Framework

- Business Context
- Competitive Pressure for Adoption
- Life-Cycle of Adoption
- Degree of Process/Culture/Behavior Change Required
- Adoptee Change Management Capabilities
- Degree of IT Architecture/Infrastructure Change Required
- IT Capabilities of the Adoptee

- Extent of New Initiatives
- Structural Protection for Current Providers
- Role of Scale
- Role of Speed
- Role of Proprietary Knowledge
- Role of Cost

Enablers of IT Consulting Competitive Change

Drivers of IT Consulting Growth

High

Pre-1990s   Good Ole' Times   Hey Days   1990s

?   Lean Cusine   ?   Now   New Cherry Pickers

Low

Low   High

because of the lack of client capability to do this kind of analysis, design, and implementation. IT initiatives differ in the degree of IT architecture/infrastructure changes required. The extent of these technology and process changes clearly emerge when an IT paradigm shift occurs, such as the changes from mainframe transaction to distributed processing and then to network centric operations.

Among the enablers shown in Exhibit 4.4, there is a mix of scale, speed, proprietary knowledge, and cost. For example, early in IT's consulting history, when scale and proprietary knowledge were critical, IBM held the lion's share of the IT consulting market. At a later time, speed of customization and open standards became more important. This new condition invited newer and smaller service providers into the market. Still later when reducing client costs became the opportunity, the consulting firm turned to outsourcing and partnering with offshore service providers.

Predictions for Future Growth

As depicted in Exhibit 4.4, we expect the IT consulting industry to recover and move toward a "heyday" period of growth, but this growth will not be as explosive or dramatic as experienced in the late 1990s. Potential clients have already acquired considerable talent and experience that was not available to them during the early heydays, so this will ease their dependence on outside service providers.

Many factors will continue to drive consulting demand for IT services. Most of the current issues within clients will continue: (1) ERP or similar aggressive programs are needed to replace legacy application portfolios, which are ticking time bombs; (2) IT strategic applications are moving from back-office applications to front office capabilities and realizing real-time "sense and respond" strategies for customers; and (3) outsourcing continues its momentum even though it has slowed due to the economy.

Other new developments portend changes in the structure of the IT consulting industry. Considerable IT action outside the United States is being ignored by many U.S. companies (such as Internet growth in Asia and Europe). Security remains a perplexing issue, and even though not much is being done right now, there will be a lot of action and investment around this issue in the future. Applications will become more diverse as new segments, such as telematics and bioinformatics, develop. Internet2 is on the horizon. And companies competing globally in a world of intense rivalry and constantly accelerating change will demand rapidly delivered services that provide them with the ability to respond quickly and nimbly.

With advances in related fields, new limbs of the IT services tree will emerge: IT + genomics, IT + biotechnology (bioinformatics), IT + automobiles (telematics). A "two-way" impact exists. IT enables biotechnology, which, in turn, reshapes IT by illuminating biological models of information processing. This suggests that a convergence of IT as a larger development exists within certain fields so that it will become increasingly difficult to draw a boundary between them. To the extent that is valid, we should expect to discover new generations of "IT-like" consulting firms formed at the leading edges of those convergences.

A high degree of industry adaptation in the IT consulting industry will be required in the future. IT consulting, as much as any product or service, creates its own demand. By introducing innovations and educating the market about the competitive benefits of those innovations, IT consulting invents and "earns" its opportunities for growth. This ability of IT consulting to lead and to adapt is a key to its robust development.

WHO WILL BE THE FUTURE WINNERS?

We indicated earlier with the help of Exhibit 4.4 that we see a return to less robust "heydays" in the future of the industry. But this does not answer the question of which firms may prevail. With this question in mind, we see three possible scenarios that suggest the repositioning of IT consulting firms in the 2000s.

1. Giants Prevail

IT services giants like IBM, Microsoft, and Cisco have developed products and services to earn significant positions, if not partnerships, with their customers. Today, each giant firm is highly oriented toward moving their company's products into their customers' IT architectures and strategic I-Nets, but they have also adjusted to the multiple vendor environment. IBM's Websphere strategy, the most product agnostic of the giants, revolves around helping companies build strategic I-Nets and realizing global e-business advantages with the most appropriate set of IT products available.

Microsoft's I-Net based product/service strategy called dot-net (.NET) appears more directed to Microsoft products through its concept of "embrace and extend." Embrace and extend assumes that Microsoft will monitor the IT product/service environment and ensure that everything integrates into its overall architecture. Cisco wants to be perceived as the "Internet Leader" who fully focuses its strategy on the Internet. Cisco continually brings customers to the company to experience its methodologies for building a strategic I-Net. These three companies (IBM, Microsoft, and Cisco) enjoy the benefits of both scope and scale, and they are well positioned to prevail, provided they avoid the ever-present temptation of complacency.

A "counter-scenario" of "giants prevail" is that the big product companies like IBM and Microsoft will not be successful in integrating consulting professionals into their product-oriented firms. If this is the case, the more traditional IT consultants, such as Accenture and EDS, may be the new giants that prevail.

Either way, the entire consulting industry is likely to be dominated by very large IT firms, surrounded by smaller specialty players.

2. New "Emerging Edge" Players

As we indicated earlier, the IT consulting industry is highly diverse and very fragmented. This condition makes it possible for new "emerging edge" players who specialize in leading-edge technology and software to grow into large, multi-billion dollar competitors. In much the same way that Cisco exploded onto the marketplace and dominated Internet equipment, similar neophyte firms may emerge out of important niches such as ASP, security, or bioinformatics.

3. New Non-U.S. Players

IT is a great equalizer. For example, it has enabled companies like drugstore.com to enter the $160 billion U.S. retail drugstore industry in less than a year and become a $150 million competitor within a couple of years.

About 300 million people currently use the Internet worldwide. The United States boasts about 150 million Internet users, and nearly half of U.S. homes have an Internet connection. The U.S. population is about 280 million. Consider that there are about 40 million Chinese Internet users this year (even more as you read this book). There were about 20 million users last year and China's population is about 1.3 billion. With rapid growth in demand, and the relatively low Internet penetration, it is not hard to imagine large IT consulting players emerging in China and India.

This possibility gains more plausibility in light of the attention given to high-speed networks associated with Internet2 outside the United States, while, within the United States, a prevailing sense of "dot vertigo" and cautious IT spending lingers.

OUR ADVICE TO FUTURE IT CONSULTING FIRMS

The history of IT consulting is short, tumultuous, and characterized by continuous change. Only recently have IT consulting firms evolved from the dominant partnership form to the corporate form, giving them access to equity markets. The rash of mergers and acquisitions in the IT consulting industry has helped some firms to prosper, but left many in disarray, and caused still others to disappear. Now the big boys from the hardware and software side, especially those with deep financial pockets, are building consulting practices, notably IBM, HP, and Microsoft. The ultimate outcome of this development is still being played out—although with more than $10 billion in consulting revenues, IBM is already looking highly successful.

At present, much of the consulting industry is demoralized, and marginal players have been eliminated. Those IT consulting firms still standing represent a core group able to craft virtual, integrated client delivery capabilities. This is an opportunity to reposition firms for high-speed Internet2 networks that may spawn further growth. Internet2 currently exists as primarily an academic initiative to determine important applications for a high-speed network many times faster than the existing Internet. While the existing Internet2 initiative is being spearheaded by the National Science Foundation, it is rapidly becoming a global phenomenon as Asia, Europe, and Central/South America build out high-speed networks based on optical switching.

Lucrative opportunities continue to appear as the industry enters into the second stage of the Internet era, but the outcomes are not obvious. We should approach the future carefully and with a high degree of organizational flexibility. The good news is that today's IT affords us flexibility never before possible: We can monitor the marketplace in real time to sense direction and opportunities; we can pounce on opportunities faster; we can cast off mistakes rapidly; we can gain access to resources at previously unheard of speeds; and we can redirect these resources more appropriately and much faster than in the past.

If we were building an IT consulting firm for the future, we would keep in mind the above perspective, and then we would act in accordance with the following assumptions. These six assumptions take the form of admonitions that will help to determine our firm's core competencies for success.

1. Be strong at change management. We believe that IT consulting will return to healthy growth but not repeat its earlier, explosive aberration. We believe that clients are still absorbing IT into their structures and cultures and that significant benefits for them are yet to be realized. We have learned that we must calibrate IT absorption with the ability of the organization to assimilate the changes required. It is the long-term nature of change management that will govern the rate of IT consulting industry growth, and the winners will invest in knowing more about change management than any of their competitors.

2. Manage and develop intellectual assets. IT consulting is basically a people business where it is essential to acquire, motivate, and retain a highly educated and creative group of professionals. Virtually all of a consulting firm's assets are contained in its professional consulting staff. It is a very difficult business to manage, requiring leadership and management principles radically different from those used in managing physical assets. For example, consulting firms must nurture egos and diversity among professional consultants, but this approach would be anathema in manufacturing firms that depend on uniformity and standardization. Because of the importance of innovation in the creation of intellectual assets, successful consulting firms must excel at managing a diverse core of talent.

The probable losers in the IT consulting industry talent war will include those that graft consulting onto existing product/software oriented organizations without fully understanding the unique people management aspects of the consulting business. Many of the IT consulting companies that arose in the late 1990s were more oriented to their financial pro-forma than to the management of their consultants and customers. The emerging giant firms will be especially vulnerable to loss of talent because of pressures for conformity from bureaucratic approaches. People management knowledge, skill, and effectiveness will have to be recognized and rewarded in the IT consulting organization of tomorrow.

3. Access part-time specialized talent. As in the legal profession, there are times when an IT consulting company requires access to the best-of-the-best talent in a narrow area. For example, when lawsuits escalate to millions of dollars in potential damages, the best and most capable lawyers are sought. Few companies possess the necessary resources to retain a group of expensive, specialized lawyers on their permanent staffs. Similarly, consulting firms will not have the resources to retain enough IT gurus who can solve highly specialized problems. Therefore, IT consulting firms must have a means to attract and deliver highly skilled professionals to clients when their expertise is needed. Fortunately, IT consulting firms are generally open to operating "virtual" organizations, enabling efficient tapping of scarce talent within the global marketplace for brief periods of time.

4. Develop niche opportunities. We believe the difficulties of scaling professional consulting firms will constrain the ultimate size of the IT consulting players. Accordingly, we believe there will be lucrative niches for widely diverse players who enter the industry. IT consulting firms will have to take a portfolio management approach to the diversity of specializations and niches in their firms. Niche capabilities can be included in the portfolio where the right professionals can be obtained to meet a sustained demand. Strategies will be required for accessing other niche capabilities only when needed. Consulting firms will need to rapidly create temporary partnerships with individuals and organizations on a highly opportunistic basis.

5. Establish strong network organization. The successful IT consulting firm will be highly networked, global, and virtually integrated. Both personal and IT-enabled networks will be nurtured and continued with clients upon completion of engagements. Clients will become important parts of the extended organization so that the IT consulting firm can effectively "sense and respond" to needs and opportunities when they arise, as well as to forge high degrees of mutual trust.

6. Accept bi-modal capabilities within the firm. Many IT consulting firms will have two dramatically different kinds of capabilities. One of these will be highly intellectual, creative, technologically advanced, and sophisticated, in order to handle the client's technical challenges and change processes. This will be a leading-edge capability that will open new applications markets and provide direction to existing application services. The work of the second advanced capability will be more tactical and transactional, such as in code-writing and project administration. The firm will utilize very different kinds of people, cultures, strategies, and processes to maintain each of these capabilities and will be adept at maintaining two different cultures at the same time.

CAUTIOUSLY AND SWIFTLY RACING TO THE FUTURE

If we, Nolan and Bennigson, ran our own consulting firm today, we would remember that the past tells us that IT consulting became one of the fastest growing industries in the world. It also tells us that the industry remains quite new and immature. A lot of mistakes have been made and money wasted by both clients and consultants. In the present, we still see many opportunities to reevaluate ourselves and to prepare our consulting capabilities to meet the next generation of opportunities. And in the future, there will be numerous challenges, meaning both opportunities and problems, characterized by change, innovation, excitement, and risk. The future will belong to those consultants who appreciate the past but are not bound to it and to those who sense emerging changes and who can run faster and work more flexibly than their competitors. It will be quite a run.

Notes to the Chapter

[1]See Louis A Girifalco, "The Dynamics of Technological Change," *The Wharton Magazine 7* (Fall 1982): 31–37. Also, Edwin Mansfield, *Economics of Technological Change* (New York: W. W. Norton, 1968); Richard N. Foster, *Innovation: The Attacker's Advantage* (New York: Summit Books, 1986); Clayton M. Christenson, *The Innovator's Dilemma: When New Technologies Cause Great Firms to Fail (Management of Innovation and Change Series)* (Boston: Harvard Business School Press, 1997); and Philip Anderson and Michael L. Tushman, "Technological Discontinuities and Dominant Designs: A Cyclical Model of Technological Change," *Administrative Science Quarterly* 35 (1990): 604–633.

[2]Richard L. Nolan "Managing the Advanced Stages of Computer Technology: Key Research Issues," in Warren F. McFarlan (ed.), *The Information Systems Research Challenge: Proceedings* (Boston: Harvard Business School Press, 1984): 195–216. The article lists various corporations that have applied the stages theories to their information systems. Several Harvard Business School cases have applied the stages theory to a particular industry or company. These include: Linda M. Applegate, "Frito-Lay: The Early Years (A)," 9-193-154 *Harvard Business School Case* (1993); Linda M. Applegate and Donna B. Stoddard, "Xerox Corp.: Leadership of the Information Technology Function (A)," 9-188-113 *Harvard Business School Case* (1988); Linda M. Applegate, "Xerox Corp.: Leadership of the Information Technology Function (B)," 9-191-024 *Harvard Business School Case* (1990); Linda M. Applegate and Ramiro Montealegre, "Eastman Kodak Co.: Managing Information Systems Through Strategic Alliances," 9-192-030 *Harvard Business School Case* (1991).

[3]Anonymous, "Institutionalizing Change," *Crossborder Monitor* (April 1, 1998): 1.

CHAPTER 5

Strategy and Organization Consulting

David A. Nadler, Mercer Delta Consulting and Adrian J. Slywotzky, Mercer Management Consulting

ABOUT THE AUTHORS

David A. Nadler

David A. Nadler is Chairman of Mercer Delta Consulting, a management consulting firm. Dr. Nadler consults at the CEO level, specializing in the areas of large-scale organization change, executive leadership, and corporate governance. He has written numerous articles and book chapters, and has authored and/or edited fourteen books. He is a member of the Academy of Management and was elected a Fellow of the American Psychological Association.

Adrian J. Slywotzky

Adrian J. Slywotzky is Vice President and a member of the Board of Directors of Mercer Management Consulting, Inc., where his responsibilities include leading the development of the firm's intellectual capital. Mr. Slywotzky is the coauthor of *How to Grow When Markets Don't* (2003), *How Digital Is Your Business?* (2000), *Profit Patterns* (1999), and *The Profit Zone* (1998).

The authors would like to thank Mark Nadler and David Morrison for their contributions to this chapter. Some of the ideas discussed here build on an earlier paper by Jay Galbraith.

Since its earliest days, management consulting has rested squarely on the twin pillars of strategy and organization. In the beginning, the two concepts were practically indivisible; the same practitioners consulted in both areas. Those were simpler times. Over the past four decades, the increasing complexity of business organizations has given rise to two very different—and very separate—consulting disciplines, each rooted in very different methodologies, knowledge bases, and delivery models, and each achieving a remarkable level of sophistication. But nothing stays the same.

For a host of reasons—the increasingly global nature of business, massively accelerated product life cycles, the growing frequency of major discontinuities in the marketplace—we are witnessing a fundamental shift in the way many clients require consulting services about strategy and organization. Despite its intellectual elegance, the consulting model we've all come to accept—a highly compartmentalized process of strategy development followed by organization design followed by implementation—is quickly losing its relevance and value.

Companies no longer have the luxury of dealing with issues of strategy and organization either separately or sequentially. They need to understand that strategy and organization consulting work happens in parallel and have a reciprocal influence on each other; they must deal with the fact that strategic change begins the moment one starts discussing a new strategy or organization structure, and it has to happen faster than ever before.

Our goal in this chapter is to describe how we got where we are today, where we believe we're headed, and what this implies for the profession of management consulting. We will trace through history how current concepts about strategy and organization have evolved. Many of the older concepts are still useful when supplemented with current thinking. On the other hand, too many consultants are still using outdated concepts that they learned years ago. Most important, the client context under which these concepts are used is dramatically different today.

BEFORE 1960: THE PRIMACY OF INTUITION AND JUDGMENT

Management consulting has always mirrored and been shaped by the way managers think about their jobs and their organizations. The real roots of modern consulting were planted in a much simpler time, when the prevailing model of industrial companies basically involved figuring out how to systematize a process for churning out the highest possible volume of products at the lowest possible cost.

The early consulting pioneers (for example, Marvin Bower, 1966, and Peter Drucker, 1946) generally thought of strategy and organization as almost indistinguishable. From the 1930s through the early 1960s, their consulting model consisted of experienced practitioners incrementally adding to the intuition and judgment of senior managers. Consultants would begin by helping clients think about their business, both in terms of planning the strategy and organizing the work. Then consultants would turn their focus to execution, advising on staffing, and methods of controlling and directing the work, all with the goal of improved performance.

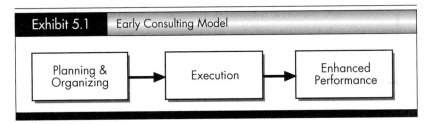

Exhibit 5.1   Early Consulting Model

Planning & Organizing → Execution → Enhanced Performance

As one looks at this early model of consulting through a modern lens (see Exhibit 5.1), three deficiencies are worth pointing out. First, it's startling to note the absence of focus on the influence of the external environment. In contemporary terms, it was a "closed system." The emphasis was on the internal workings of each organization, rather than on its interaction with the larger business environment. In part, that reflected the comparatively stable times in which this model was used.

That leads to the second issue: This was not a model built for speed. Compared with today, product life cycles in the first half of the 20th century were nearly generational. You could easily get by producing essentially the same products in basically the same ways, with only occasional incremental improvements, for ten or fifteen years.

The final issue speaks to the nature of the value consultants brought to their assignments. The best that consultants had to offer was their experience, insight, and analytical abilities. Generally speaking, consultants on strategy and organization brought little in the way of formalized concepts, conceptual models, transferable tools, or a body of knowledge that we would describe today as intellectual capital. Instead, it was a model that relied on the wisdom and judgment of each individual consultant, backed up by the analysis of more junior associates.

1960–2000: SEQUENTIAL CONSULTING, DIVERGENT DISCIPLINES

The modern era of strategy and organization consulting really began in the 1960s and 70s, when the extended post-war era finally came to an end. During that turbulent era, U.S. companies confronted a new set of challenges: foreign competition, domestic deregulation, market fragmentation, and the inevitable exhaustion of pent-up consumer demand that had for so long made it so easy to sell so much to so many.

As time went on, good managers realized they needed new and sophisticated strategies involving technology, distribution, and marketing—a whole host of specialized approaches that hadn't been necessary in the past. So the search was on for consultants who could help managers attack each specific issue with a scientific, disciplined, and specialized approach. This was a dramatic departure from the days of the intuitive wise men who would consult on everything. Managers wanted strategy consultants to help them with strategy. At the next stage, there was a widely accepted assumption that "strategy dictated structure," so for the next phase of work, they turned to the organization design consultants. And when they were finished, it was time for the change management consultants. The result: a steadfastly sequential, highly compartmentalized approach to consulting (see Exhibit 5.2). The same process might be repeated every five years or so, as senior managers came and went, and the environment experienced periodic change.

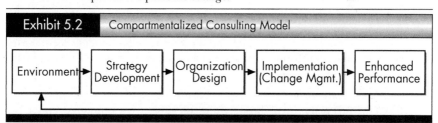

Exhibit 5.2   Compartmentalized Consulting Model

Environment → Strategy Development → Organization Design → Implementation (Change Mgmt.) → Enhanced Performance

This model of executive behavior—and of management consulting—became and still remains pervasive today. To a great extent, it was fueled not just by the needs of companies but by an explosion of research and writing within each discipline at major business schools. As a result, the major consulting firms capitalized on this trend toward specialization and built separate practice areas in each discipline. The result was a historic shift from the early model of general, intuitive management consulting into three distinct, scientifically rigorous consulting disciplines, each with its own tools, methodologies, models, and vocabularies.

Broadly speaking—and we'll describe this evolution shortly in more detail—the general management consultants migrated toward strategy.

Thanks in large part to the work of such thought leaders as Bruce Henderson, founder of the Boston Consulting Group (BCG), and Igor Ansoff at Carnegie, the 1960s brought a series of conceptual breakthroughs, an unprecedented degree of intellectual rigor, and a whole new set of methodologies. During this same period, a burst of creative activity at the nation's top business schools laid the groundwork for an emerging discipline in organizational consulting that focused on integrating the formal structures and processes of the organization with the human side of the enterprise.

As the consulting disciplines diverged along very different paths, it became increasingly difficult for the strategy and organization types to integrate their work. They came from different academic roots and viewed the organization from very different vantage points. Modern strategy consulting emerged from economics, while organization consulting found its roots in psychology —two inherently uncongenial disciplines. Moreover, strategists viewed their work as a "top-down" proposition centering on senior leaders who put their stamp on the strategy and announced it to the organization. Conversely, organization work, with its initial focus on individual and small group behavior, started with group dynamics and then looked upward at the organization. It was virtually impossible to connect strategy and organization consulting until both began seeing potential in joint activity at the top of the enterprise—something that didn't happen until the 1990s.

Those are the broad outlines of the consulting model that has prevailed for the past two decades. In order to understand the threats to this model's continued viability, it's important to step back and fully understand the specific ways in which strategy, organization, and change management consulting developed.

FROM BUSINESS POLICY TO VALUE CREATION MODELS

Up until the 1960s, only a few companies—most notably, the General Motors of Alfred P. Sloan—practiced what would today be called "strategy." Even when practiced, the word itself was rarely used; executives spoke instead of "business policy" or "planning," and most firms made strategic decisions on an *ad hoc* basis, guided more by instinct and tradition than by empirically-driven, methodology-based analysis.

In the 1960s, Bruce Henderson (Boston Consulting Group, 1968) produced the first major breakthrough in the field of business strategy. Trained as an engineer, Henderson became intrigued by the question of why the unit cost of products varied so greatly among suppliers, even those using seemingly identical equipment and processes. His work uncovered what is now a familiar notion: the concept of the "price experience curve." Later, quantitative research and modeling under the rubric of the Profit Impact of Market Strategy, or PIMS, showed that Henderson's E-Curve was virtually a universal phenomenon and that higher market share meant higher profits.

Henderson's work also led to a method of strategic resource allocation called the Growth Share Matrix. In the 1970s, state-of-the-art strategic thinking was based on the economic logic of "get as big as you can as fast as you can." Increased market share would let you build bigger factories, reduce your costs, improve your products, and open up an ever-widening advantage over your competition. During the 1980s, GE's success with its formula of participating only in businesses where it was number one or number two in market share illustrated the logic of this low-cost-producer class of strategies.

The Porter Breakthroughs

The next major breakthrough was Michael Porter's work at the Harvard Business School. In his book *Competitive Strategy* (1980), Porter broadened the focus from market share by describing the so-called Five Forces that determined any company's strategic effectiveness (supplier power, barriers to entry, threat of substitutes, buyer power, and degree of rivalry). For Porter, strategic thinking demanded awareness of the threats and opportunities posed by each of the five forces, and a winning strategy had to take all of them into account.

In his book *Competitive Advantage* (1986), Porter popularized another key concept (one that was already being used within a number of strategy firms) with his description of the *value chain.* Porter showed that any business can be modeled as a chain of value-creating activities, beginning with inbound logistics and including operations, outbound logistics, marketing and sales, and service. By analyzing how this generic value chain operates in a specific business, managers can discover a range of strategic options involving how to optimize the process flows, determine which steps to outsource or eliminate, and how to streamline linkages among the remaining steps.

As a result of Porter's work, there were now three different competitive strategic alternatives for managers to consider. First, the Hendersonian low-cost, market-share strategy still was relevant. Second, Porter added the differentiation strategy (maximizing the relevant differences between a firm and its immediate competitors); and third, the niche strategy (identifying a defensible niche market relatively immune to external cost and competitive pressures). This three-alternative system may be considered the classic formulation of strategy. And for a while it worked.

The Classic Models Falter

But changes in the business environment gradually forced practitioners and theorists to reconsider the simplicity of the Henderson-Porter models. During the late 1980s and early 1990s, market value was increasingly seen as a crucial determinant of company success. As the decade progressed, market value and sales volume were seen to diverge more and more. The implication was that the rules of business were changing—that such widely accepted corollaries as, "Get market share and the profit will follow," were no longer as reliable as they had been.

At the heart of this new strategic problem was the emergence of so-called "no-profit zones": businesses in which companies were apparently *unable* to earn a profit, no matter the size of the market share they controlled. The concept of no-profit zones emerged in the early 1990s because of a variety of changes in the business environment. These included:

- Global over-capacity in many product categories;
- An increase in customer power, thanks to broader global competition among suppliers and increased availability of information about alternatives;

- Improved capabilities for imitating any product or service offering, including an expansion of global manufacturing capacities and reduced transportation costs;
- Venture capital funding of new competitors unburdened by old business models and assets.

Due to these and other pressures, more and more businesses, from airlines and D-RAMS to consumer banking and electronics, were unfortunately transformed into no-profit zones.

Business Design Innovation

As a result, the 1990s caused management practitioners and thinkers to consider a new range of strategic issues. A company's products, technology, quality, and efficiency all remained important, but even more important was its business model. In response, a new strategic discipline known as *business design innovation* emerged.

In our view, a company's business design includes five strategic elements:

- Customer selection—Who are my customers, and why do I choose to serve them rather than any others?
- Unique value proposition—Why do my customers buy from me?
- Value capture—How do I retain, as profit, a portion of the value I deliver to customers?
- Strategic control—How do I protect my profits from competitor imitation and customer power?
- Scope—What activities in the value chain must I engage in to remain customer-relevant, to generate high profits, and to create strategic control?

During the 1990s, business design innovation increasingly became the key to strategic effectiveness. Businesses with traditional designs became less relevant and lost value, while companies that developed new business designs better suited to changing conditions captured growing shares of profit. This phenomenon, whereby value shifted from firms like Sears, American Airlines, Compaq, U.S. Steel, and IBM to firms like Wal-Mart, Southwest Airlines, Dell, Nucor, and Microsoft, became known as value migration (Slywotzky and Morrison 1998; Slywotzky 1996).

Value-Driven Business Design—The Current Framework

Strategy consultants have developed a variety of models to assist clients' pursuit of value, which is the theme of much strategy consulting today. As an illustration, we'll briefly describe our own consulting approach, which we call Value-Driven Business Design (see Exhibit 5.3).

Value-Driven Business Design is about strategic choices. It involves understanding the opportunities to create value in the marketplace and then making the choices that enable a business to address the customer's most important priorities and capture a return for shareholders. The choices must be aligned with where customers and competitors are going to be in the future. And the choices must be internally consistent and mutually reinforcing. Typically, the Value-Driven Business Design process consists of six phases.

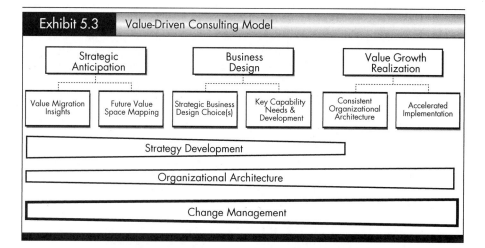

Exhibit 5.3   Value-Driven Consulting Model

1. Value Migration Insights. Most companies that create significant growth in shareholder value do so by acting on insights that change the rules of competitive advantage in their industry. So the first step in the process is to help clients break through the barrier of incremental thinking by engaging in exercises that help them redefine their competition, anticipate where future value will emerge, and consider which business designs might best exploit that value opportunity.

2. Future Value Space Mapping. The next step is to use sophisticated interview and analysis methodologies to determine how customers and competitors are likely to react to a client's innovative value growth initiatives, which, in turn, makes it possible to determine where potential revenue and profit opportunities might exist in the future.

3. Strategic Business Design Choices. The next step is to define one or more business designs that will create high utility for customers and high value for shareholders. It is often possible to identify multiple opportunities and business design options; and from those, they need to select the best.

4. Key Capability Needs and Development. New business design choices often create the most value when they are driven by an understanding of a future value space, rather than by an organization's current competencies. So the next phase is to identify and start filling the gaps between the organization's existing capabilities and those required by the new business design.

5. Consistent Organizational Systems. By an overwhelming margin, senior managers believe that internal barriers are the primary cause of strategy failures. To pave the way for successful strategy implementation, it is essential to develop a plan to redesign those aspects of the organization that are inconsistent with the new direction.

6. Accelerated Implementation. To create high value growth, new business designs must be implemented rapidly. A year's delay in launching a new business design can easily have a serious negative impact on value. In the current environment of hyper-competition and technological change, accelerated implementation of the business design is crucial.

Looking Ahead

One final thought regarding strategy consulting. In the model we just described, you will see a forewarning of our previously stated premise that strategy, organization, and change management consulting are now converging, both for dynamic competitive reasons and in part because they were neither as distinct nor as sequential as we have portrayed them in the past.

The last three of the six steps in the Value-Driven Business Design model, involving organizational capabilities, organizational "systems," and the process of implementation, mark a clear move from pure "strategy" work into both organizational consulting and change management. Now, as we move into our discussion of these other fields of consulting, we'll see that the boundaries delineating all three have become increasingly porous in today's business environment.

ORGANIZATION CONSULTING: FROM THE INDIVIDUAL TO THE ENTERPRISE

In contrast with strategy consulting, organization consulting's historical roots were primarily academic. With foundations in behavioral science—the confluence of psychology, social psychology, and sociology—organization consulting was largely divorced from the work of the large management consulting firms, which were firmly rooted in the disciplines of engineering and economics. More specifically, organization consulting can trace its intellectual roots to four sources.

The first source stems from the famous Hawthorne studies (Roethlisberger and Dickson 1939; Homans 1941). Their work, for the first time, applied rigorous methodologies to the study of human behavior in organizations and formed the basis of the hugely influential organizational behavior group at the Harvard Business School. Ultimately, this work proved to be the source of entirely new perspectives about systems in organizations.

The second source involved work in the new area of small group dynamics. Beginning with the work of Kurt Lewin at the Massachusetts Institute of Technology, then later at the University of Michigan and the National Training Laboratories (NTL), this area of study led to the development of the concept of organization development. Building on the pioneering work of Chris Argyris (1962), Ed Schein (1973), Douglas MacGregor (1960), and Warren Bennis (1966), among other notable figures, this work focused on issues of leadership, culture, and team behavior and grew aggressively during the 1960s and 1970s.

The third important source was "organization design." Rooted in the work of Lawrence and Lorsch (1967), it formed the basis of work in the 1970s and 1980s by Jay Galbraith (1973), David Nadler, and Michael Tushman (1987, 1998). Organization design involved a systematic and behavioral-based approach to designing an organization's formal structures, systems, and processes.

The final ingredient was open systems theory, drawing off biological theory and finding its industrial roots in the Hawthorne work of Henderson and his colleagues. By the 1960s, researchers at Harvard and Michigan were beginning to explore the similarities between naturally occurring systems and human organizations. However, it wasn't until the mid-1970s that systems theory found wide acceptance among students of organizations. Its first published appearance was Harold Leavitt's *Star Diagram* (1964), and further refined by Jay Galbraith at MIT. At Columbia, Nadler and Tushman (1979, 1980), building on the work of earlier theorists (Katz and Kahn 1966; Lorsch and Sheldon 1972; Seiler 1967), were developing their own model based on systems theory. This outpouring of work in the early and mid-1970s marked a major milestone in the development of organization design, focusing on the integration of technical systems with social dynamics —the organization's "hardware" and "software."

By the early 1990s, there was a convergence of thought around the notion of "fit models," which integrated the various emerging views of organization design:

Open systems. In sharp contrast with early models, the new models emphasized the organization as an interactive entity, influencing and influenced by environmental factors;

Organizational dynamics. Traditional models were static, involving a snapshot in time of formal structures and systems. They failed to reflect the reality that organizations change over time or to demonstrate the ways in which those changes are triggered or the impact they have;

Integration of hardware and software. An emerging view that neither formal structures nor social interactions exist in a vacuum;

Organizational diagnosis. Reflecting increasing scientific rigor, the models underscored the need to collect and analyze valid data as a precursor to diagnosing organizational problems;

Concepts of change management. These models also embraced the emerging approaches to managing large-scale change, touching upon the implementation phase that had long been considered beyond the purview of traditional organization design.

As we said, a variety of useful models was developed and came into wide use in the 1980s and 1990s. As an illustration, we'll describe the Congruence Model of Organizational Behavior (Nadler & Tushman 1980, 1998), which we and others continue to use as a core organizational consulting tool (see Exhibit 5.4).

The Congruence Model describes the organization as a system that draws input from both internal and external sources, employs a strategy to translate its vision into a set of decisions about where and how to compete, and provides a transformation process that combines the technical and social components of the organization to convert input into output. The model's power lies in its ability to help clients understand the components of their organization and the relationship of one component to another.

From Input to Output

The three sources of input for the organizational system each affect the organization in different ways.

1. **Environment:** Every organization exists within—and is influenced by—a larger environment involving conditions (political, economic,

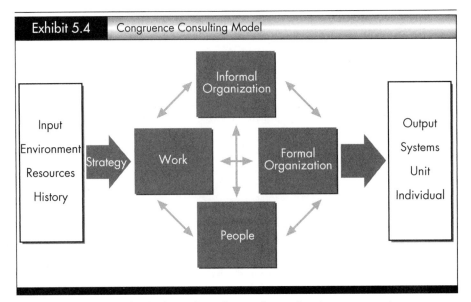

Exhibit 5.4   Congruence Consulting Model

technological, etc.) and constituencies (customers, investors, lenders, regulators, etc.). The environment creates demands and opportunities while imposing constraints on the organization's ability to meet both.

2. **Resources:** The full range of accessible assets—employees, technology, capital, and information.

3. **History:** Landmark events in an organization's past strongly influence its current behavior in terms of strategic decisions, culture, values, and responses to crises.

Like other contemporary models, the congruence model acknowledges the importance of strategy. Every organization must select the optimal alternatives for creating and sustaining value by deciding which business to be in and how to configure their resources in response to opportunities, threats, and constraints in the external environment. The goal is to produce the optimal "output." In this context, the term output describes not only the organization's ability to create products and services but also to achieve certain levels of individual and group performance.

The Organizational Transformation Process

The heart of the model is the transformation process, which draws upon the input implicit in the environment, resources, and history to produce a set of outputs. This process is shaped by four key components that make up each organization:

1. **The work:** The inherent activity engaged in by the organization and its people. Any analysis from a design perspective must focus first on the nature of the tasks to be performed and the inherent requirements of those tasks in the context of strategy.

2. **The people:** What knowledge and skills do they bring to their work? What are their preferences, perceptions, and expectations about their relationship with the organization?

3. **The formal organizational arrangements:** The pattern of structures, systems, and processes that define and coordinate how roles are defined and work gets done.

4. **The informal organization:** The unwritten processes, practices, and political relationships that embody the organization's values, beliefs, and behavioral norms.

The Concept of "Fit" and Resulting Output

So far, we've been describing the components of an organizational system. But the model is more than a list or a chart; its real value is that it helps us understand how the components interact to produce a result. The underlying hypothesis is that tighter alignment leads to greater congruence and better performance. Indeed, the congruence model suggests that the interaction between each set of organizational components is more important than the components themselves.

For years, the field of organization design attempted to align all of these elements by using formal organization structure as the linking mechanism. As a result, we saw the growth of different structural forms—functional, product, geographic, and matrix—each intended to link the major elements under different conditions faced by a company in its markets and with its given technology and business strategy.

In normal times, the job of managers was that of constantly fine-tuning the formal structure and systems to maintain alignment of the key elements. However, when the environment shifted substantially, organizations were required to undergo radical change. During these periods, simply maintaining the alignment of the organizational components through the formal structure is not only insufficient, but likely dangerous. These situations call for discontinuous change, which sometimes involves the profound overhaul of most, if not all, of the organizational components (Nadler 1998; Nadler, Shaw, and Walton 1994).

For example, the Internet and the alternative of outsourcing has caused major disturbances in how organizations should be designed and managed. We now see the birth of "virtual" organizations where major functions, such as information technology and manufacturing, are being outsourced (see Exhibit 5.5). This change has required management to manage in a more "horizontal" way through alliances and partnerships, often connected together through the Internet and software systems—and personal relationships. In these situations, decisions have to be negotiated with partners, not simply announced to subordinates, as in prior models.

Formal structure obviously has serious limitations in a world where change is a constant phenomenon. Organizations must now seek new internal arrangements that are more flexible and resilient, thereby shifting emphasis from structure to the informal culture and the quality of leadership and employees throughout the organization. In the Internet world, many employees are working out of sight from their supervisors, thereby requiring new forms of leadership, motivation, and control. Autonomous work teams are being formed and empowered to react quickly. Spans of control are widening, placing a premium on self-management, the selection of self-starting employees, and the use of online knowledge sharing in place of formal training.

Exhibit 5.5	Virtual Network Structure

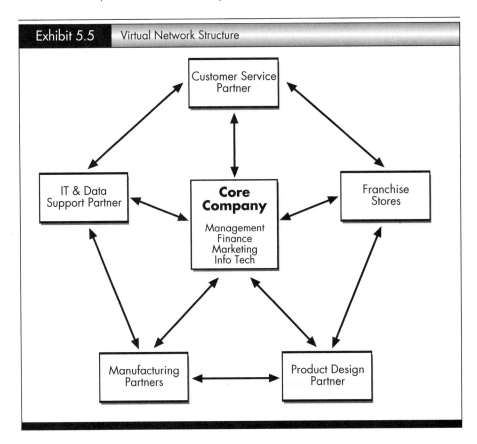

REQUIREMENTS FOR ORGANIZATION CONSULTANTS

As organization consulting developed to embrace concepts such as the congruence model, the skills and strategies required to successfully consult in this area have evolved as well.

First, while early practitioners tended to be psychologists largely concerned with individual and small group behavior, today's consultants must understand the organization as a complex system, including both technical systems and social dynamics, and one that both influences and is influenced by the strategy. It is no longer sufficient to think about business strategy and human behavior as separate, isolated, and unrelated phenomena.

Second, rigorous diagnosis has become a mandatory prelude to organization consulting. However, in contrast with the initial market research that often sets the stage for strategy consulting, much of the essential information about how an organization functions can only be found within the client organization itself. So consultants need to understand how to use the diagnostic process as a lever for engaging the client and, hopefully, increasing the client's understanding of the issues at hand and its ownership of results incurred under its management.

Third, consultants who think of organizational performance in terms of "fit" understand that the solutions will take a variety of forms involving both the organizational hardware (e.g., structure and systems) and software (e.g., culture and leadership). It is insufficient for a seasoned practitioner to deal exclusively with one side of the organization or the other.

Finally, significant and sustainable organizational change succeeds only if critical groups and individuals feel genuine commitment to, and ownership of, the changes about to take place. For consultants, that places a premium not on passive recommendations, but on engaging interventions that actively involve clients in their own design process.

CHANGE MANAGEMENT CONSULTING

The origins of change management consulting were closely associated with the development organization consulting. Because organization consulting involved a broad range of changes involving both the technical and social dimensions of the organization, its implementation required special attention to the human dynamics of change. Strategy consulting did not move toward change management issues until much later, since early strategy projects focused mainly on a very small group of very senior leaders.

The discipline of change management had its earliest roots in academic experiments on changing individual behavior, and later, on group behavior. By the 1960s, academics were also serving as consultants focusing on changing organizational behavior in companies, largely through the medium of training programs, such as the *Managerial Grid* (Blake and Mouton 1964) and sensitivity training. Early on, these efforts became known as "organization development programs," a term that later gave way to "change management" in the late 1980s. The watershed work in this area was Dick Beckhard's book, *Organizational Transitions* (1977), in which he proposed the simple but powerful idea that successful change requires a set of deliberate actions that move an organization from its *Current State* through a turbulent and often perilous *Transition State* in order to reach the desired *Future State.*

Many similar models of change have been developed over the years, which propose a series of phases beginning with the arousal of the need for change, through introducing the required changes via formal and informal means, and finally reinforcing these changes to assure a lasting result. More recently, models of change focused on CEOs and their attempts at strategic change have been offered, which again involve a series of specific phases but with additional attention to surrounding conditions in the organization and environment that facilitate or impede the change sequence (Greiner, Cummings, and Bhambri 2003).

Building on the Beckhard approach of phases, we have developed in our practice a set of concepts about change and intervention that has formed the basis for our consulting over the past two decades (Nadler 1982; Nadler, Shaw, and Walton 1994; Nadler 1998). In our experience, successful change requires leaders to address certain issues:

Power: Major change raises concerns about a significant redistribution of power within the organization, leading to an upsurge in unproductive and often harmful political activity;

Anxiety: The uncertainty and lack of information that often accompany major change fuel anxiety which, in turn, diminishes individual and organizational performance; and

Control: The very prospect of impending change loosens management's control, as widespread uncertainty dulls both the fear of punishment and the hope of reward.

Consequently, any successful change strategy must address those issues by:

Shaping the political dynamics in ways that generate support;

Motivating constructive behavior and providing ways for people to participate in planning their future; and

Managing the transition with the structures, processes, and resources needed to maintain performance during the interim period.

Over time, we have also developed our own list of "best practices" (see Exhibit 5.6) for managing successful transitions.

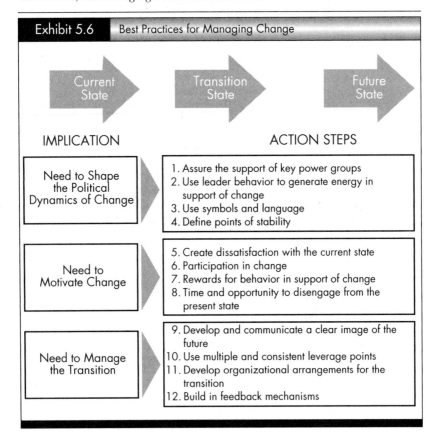

| Exhibit 5.6 | Best Practices for Managing Change |

Current State → Transition State → Future State

IMPLICATION

ACTION STEPS

| Need to Shape the Political Dynamics of Change | 1. Assure the support of key power groups
2. Use leader behavior to generate energy in support of change
3. Use symbols and language
4. Define points of stability |

| Need to Motivate Change | 5. Create dissatisfaction with the current state
6. Participation in change
7. Rewards for behavior in support of change
8. Time and opportunity to disengage from the present state |

| Need to Manage the Transition | 9. Develop and communicate a clear image of the future
10. Use multiple and consistent leverage points
11. Develop organizational arrangements for the transition
12. Build in feedback mechanisms |

AN AGING MODEL

The sequential consulting model that reflected the evolution of strategy, organization, and change management as highly compartmentalized disciplines firmly took hold in the 1980s and 1990s. To a large extent, it worked—and in many situations, still does.

But as the 1990s drew to a close, we started to see some cracks in the model. We're not suggesting that the current model is bad; in fact, it's intellectually right, and in a perfect world, would point the way to successful consulting. But it has two major flaws: It is ill suited to the pace and intensity of change in the modern marketplace, and it fails to recognize the inherently messy ways in which consulting plays out in real-life situations.

Adapting to the Changing Marketplace

To be successful, consulting must enable companies to keep pace with the demands of the marketplace—and ideally, to stay one step ahead. The early consulting model that had its roots in the years following World War I worked just fine in an era when product life cycles were measured in decades. Similarly, the current model was ideally suited for a world of five-to-ten-year product life cycles. For example, companies might easily take six to ten months to work out a reasonably complex strategy. Once that was done, they'd start working with their consultants on redesigning the organization—and that would typically take anywhere from six months to a year. Then came the implementation phase, and by the time that kicked in, you might have been at this for close to three years. And that was all right, because you still had seven years remaining of a ten-year cycle in which to reap the benefits of all your hard work.

In a growing number of industries, that same arithmetic doesn't work any more. On average, product life cycles last less than six years; in some cases, especially high technology products, the cycle is closer to one to two years.

The second issue is the nature of change. You could pursue a more leisurely pace in a world of incremental change. Your competitors might figure out how to make a product faster or cheaper, but the fundamental basis of competition really hadn't changed. Discontinuous change—a sharp, dramatic change in the marketplace or the nature of competition—was rare. In the 1950s, you might find a Sears, General Motors, or IBM introducing new technology or a new business model that changed the rules of the game, but it didn't happen often. In the past decade, in contrast, more than two dozen companies created that kind of seismic impact (e.g., Dell and eBay). A drawn-out process for shifting strategy, organization, and performance, rather than costing some business while catching up, could actually cost the entire business.

Fallacy of Sequential Processes

The second problem with the current consulting model is that it still embraces the traditional wisdom that "structure follows strategy." That might have been true at a time when most changes in strategy were really nothing more than refinements of an existing business model; you tinkered with the strategy, then you tinkered with the organization to make it fit the strategy.

Today, strategy and organization are interdependent. Strategic work starts with a lot of "what if" questions. A company's existing organization—who is sitting around the table, in what roles, and bringing which skills, experience, knowledge, and perspectives to the discussion—will inevitably shape the conversation and influence the company's ability to assess a broad range of strategic alternatives. For example, if you happen to be a slide rule company trying to figure out if it's time to make the big leap into calculators, and if everybody sitting around the table is a life-long slide-rule expert who doesn't know the first thing about electrons or circuit boards, the discussion will inevitably turn to how to build a better slide rule.

By the same token, we've seen CEOs come up with brilliant strategies—visionary, far-reaching plans that were just what the company needed—but they quickly realized that they had neither the right people nor the right structures and processes nor the right culture to begin implementing it right away. So even though, in a pure sense, Strategy A might be the right way to go, the CEO had to settle for Strategy B or C as an interim option while getting on with the work of building an organization capable of executing Strategy A.

In other words, strategy and organization are inseparable; no matter what the model suggests. In the real world, it's impossible to work on one without talking about the other. The realities of the organization will lead to a set of rational or irrational strategic choices and will probably have an even greater influence than the realities of the marketplace on a company's future direction.

Finally, just as strategy and organization happen in parallel, rather than in sequence, the reality is that change management doesn't fit neatly into a separate, nearly delineated third step in the model. For better or worse, as soon as you begin working on strategy, the process of change is underway. The moment you begin talking about the strategy and what kind of organization will be required to achieve it, you inevitably start asking, "How are we going to make this happen? How do we get from here to there?"

If we're honest, we have to acknowledge that the iterative nature of strategy, organization, and change was always true, even if it didn't fit the neat model used by consultants and expected by clients. Handled sequentially, the process ignored the fact that the dynamics of change had already been triggered by the initial strategy and organization work.

CONCURRENT AND INTEGRATED ENTERPRISE DESIGN

In light of the inherent and increasingly serious weaknesses in the sequential consulting model, which unfortunately is still quite popular, we believe a new model is imperative (see Exhibit 5.7). What we have in mind is actually a new version of the earliest model, combining our now-rigorous disciplines of strategy, organization, and change management consulting into a concurrent, reciprocal consulting process.

This new approach, which we call concurrent, dynamic enterprise design, is like the shift from batch to parallel processing. Rather than continuing to impose the intellectual straightjacket of a sequential, compartmentalized model, it acknowledges that consulting on strategy, organization, and change management is like trying to solve a set of simultaneous equations. The moment you solve for one variable, you change all the other equations. Here's how we envision the new model:

| Exhibit 5.7 | Concurrent Design Consulting Model |

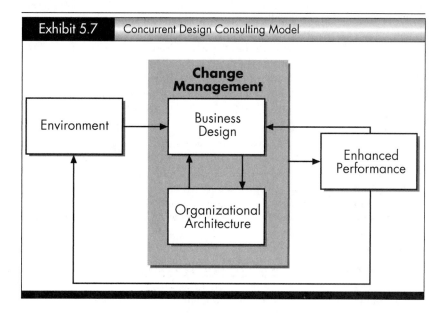

It begins with an aggressive, proactive approach to the environment. Companies frequently put off developing a new strategy until developments in the outside environment are absolutely clear; however, this approach can prove fatal in today's fast moving world. Therefore, they need concepts such as strategic anticipation and value migration to help them understand proactively what's happening in the marketplace and its implications for their value proposition.

It involves an integrated, iterative approach to strategy and organization. It recognizes that the earlier assumption of "strategy drives structure" is only half the equation, because the shape of the organization also drives critical thinking about strategic alternatives. Neither issue can be worked in isolation; instead, both must be considered inside the envelope of change management, because how you get "from here to there" will shape, and is shaped by, both strategic objectives and organizational capabilities.

This is a model in which the feedback loops are more pronounced and immediate than in the past. Within the organization, the impact of strategy, organization, and change upon one another is significant and swift, which is why we talk about the iterative nature of the model. Interestingly, greatly enhanced performance resulting from this model can also have a sudden and major impact on the external environment, causing major disruptions in the nature of competition.

We believe this new approach—concurrent, dynamic enterprise design—is an appropriate response to a business environment that is more complex, less forgiving, and faster moving than anything we have experienced before. The cost of doing too little, too late has never been higher, and the markets have never been quicker to punish failure.

It also recognizes and incorporates the various consulting disciplines that have developed along separate but not entirely different paths. Strategists such as Ghoshal and Bartlett (1997) have reached beyond the traditional boundaries of their discipline to recognize the importance of the human side of the organization. Organization consultants such as Nadler and Tushman (1997) have made a strong case for incorporating strategy into any discussion of organizational issues. And organization design's relatively recent shift in focus from individuals and small groups to change driven from the top has created a shared perspective with strategists regarding enterprise-level consulting.

In essence, the disciplines have begun talking to each other, making it easier and more efficient to solve issues iteratively rather than proceeding all the way down one road before starting on the next. And it is the iterative, concurrent nature of consulting that is really the key to this model. If we can employ it successfully, we can make it possible for clients to successfully design and deploy complex, discontinuous change in a fraction of the time previously consumed in sequential consulting assignments while engaging in incremental change. In short, this is all about enabling organizations to move at least as fast as their markets.

IMPLICATIONS FOR CONSULTING

The ability to understand the environment, anticipate change, select business models that capture value, to design and create organizations capable of implementing those models—and to do all of that quickly, concurrently, and continuously—is the task of management in the modern era. That's simply the way it is. So, regardless of the consulting models each of us might hold dear, our job is to accommodate to our clients' needs.

The clear imperative is a faster, fully integrated approach to consulting. That's easier said than done; if it were simple, more of us would be doing it already. Nevertheless, just as our clients must periodically revamp a long-cherished business model, so must we.

This new mode of consulting is still in its earliest stages. More experience will give us a clearer idea of how best to deliver it and what obstacles stand in our way. But we have some preliminary thoughts on the implications—some troubling, some exciting, and all of them challenging for consulting firms and practitioners.

1. Increasingly, clients will be looking to consultants for help in the form of fully integrated, multi-disciplinary teams than can help them work their range of strategic and organizational issues concurrently. The Holy Grail for consulting firms will be the true integration of the consulting disciplines, starting with intellectual capital and tools specifically designed to weave together the various processes and continuing through the coordinated delivery of various consultative services. Thus far, no one has truly cracked the code of how to accomplish all of that, given the inherently different delivery models.

2. Although we envision a need for increased integration of consulting capabilities, we are not suggesting a return to the original model of the consultant as generalist. To the contrary, there's a growing need for people who bring deep knowledge in the areas of strategy, organization, and change management. What we will need, however, are consultants who are conversant in all three disciplines so they can work seamlessly with consultants from other disciplines.

3. As strategy work becomes more closely integrated into organization design and change management, it will be necessary to involve more people in the client organization in order to build broader participation and ownership. The shift from imparting expertise to building ownership might well require a fundamental shift in delivery models from strategy consulting's traditional "study/recommend" mode toward the "teach and facilitate" mode more common among organization consultants (to use the appropriate terminology discussed by Tom Cummings in Chapter 12). Indeed, we may need to rethink the highly leveraged, case team approach favored by strategy consulting firms and move instead toward a more dynamic model that features senior consultants collaborating and interacting closely with their clients as they work together as peers to solve complex strategy and organization issues simultaneously. The previous model of lengthy data gathering and analysis controlled completely by the consultant, which resulted in high fees, is likely on the wane. And so would be the formula of charging by the hour.

4. Organization consultants, for their part, will have to develop much more streamlined processes for designing organizations to suit particular strategies. The best consulting firms, for years, have eschewed the idea of off-the-shelf designs, and rightly so. But if they're to work concurrently with the strategy consultants in a fast-moving process, they can't start with a blank sheet each time; it simply takes too long. It might well become necessary to start thinking more in terms of a limited set of design alternatives that might be optimal for certain business models—an approach that will require considerable research and analysis in the very near future. Similarly, change management consultants will have to find ways to build understanding and buy-in faster than ever before. They'll have to employ new participative approaches—smarter use of large group interventions, for instance, or more creative use of information technology to involve people—in order to accelerate the speed of change.

5. If our view is correct—that many organizations now experience almost constant change—then we should reevaluate exactly how we provide value to clients and what we charge for it, because it's hard to imagine any of them wanting us to endlessly hang around gathering data and working on new strategies and organization designs. Instead, we need to arm our clients with the tools and methodologies to handle incremental change on their own, while providing more intense, specialized support during periods of discontinuous change.

6. At the end of the day, we must be ready to sell our services in whatever configuration our clients want to buy them. For the foreseeable future, some clients will be hesitant to buy a fully integrated package of consulting services from a single firm. So it's essential that we continue to maintain the modularity of our offerings even as we pursue our efforts to integrate our expertise.

As we said at the outset, we seem to be coming full circle with the convergence of strategy and organization consulting. But this time, there are profound differences. We're looking at the reintegration of disciplines based on science and experience rather than intuition. We're operating in a very different time, and with the benefit of decades of experience and highly sophisticated concepts and tools. The question now is whether we can successfully apply some of these tools to our own businesses and recreate our consulting models to help our clients meet their own compelling challenges.

References

Ansoff, I. 1965. *Corporate Strategy.* New York: McGraw-Hill.

Argyris, C. 1962. *Interpersonal Competence and Organizational Effectiveness.* Homewood, Ill.: Dow-Jones-Irwin.

Beckhard, R. 1977. *Organizational Transitions: Managing Complex Change.* 2d ed., Reading, MA: Addison-Wesley.

Bennis, W. 1966. *Changing Organizations.* New York: McGraw-Hill.

Blake, R., and J. Mouton. 1964. *The Managerial Grid.* Houston, TX: Gulf Publishing.

Bower, M. 1966. *The Will to Manage: Corporate Success Through Programmed Management.* New York: McGraw-Hill.

Boston Consulting Group. 1968. *Perspectives on Experience.* Boston: The Boston Consulting Group.

Drucker, P. 1946. *Concept of the Corporation.* New York: John Day.

Galbraith, J. R. 1973. *Designing Complex Organizations.* Reading, MA: Addison-Wesley.

Ghoshal, S., and C. A. Bartlett. 1997. *The Individualized Corporation: A Fundamentally New Approach to Management.* New York: HarperCollins.

Greiner, L., T. Cummings, and A. Bhambri. 2003. *4-D Theory of Strategic Transformation: When New CEOs Succeed and Fail.* Organization Dynamics, 32 (1): 1–16.

Homans, G. C. 1941. *The Western Electric Researchers.* National Research Council Report. New York: Reinhold.

Katz, D., and R. L. Khan. 1978. *The Social Psychology of Organizations.* 2d ed. New York: Wiley.

Lawrence, P. R. and J. W. Lorsch. 1967. *Organization and Environment: Managing Differentiation and Integration.* Homewood, IL: Richard D. Irwin.

Lorsch, J. W. and A. Sheldon. 1972. *The Individual in the Organization: A Systems View,* in J. W. Lorsch, and P. R. Lawrence, eds. *Managing Group and Intergroup Relations.* Homewood, Ill.: Irwin-Dorsey.

Leavitt, H. 1964. *Managerial Psychology: An Introduction to Individuals, Pairs, and Groups in Organizations,* 2d ed. Chicago: University of Chicago Press.

MacGregor, D. 1960. *The Human Side of Enterprise.* New York: McGraw-Hill.

Nadler, D. A., and M. L. Tushman. 1979. *A Congruence Model for Diagnosing Organizational Behavior,* in D. Kolb, I. Rubin, and J. McIntyre *Organizational Psychology: A Book of Readings,* 3d ed. Englewood Cliffs, NJ: Prentice Hall.

Nadler, D. A., and M. L. Tushman. 1980. Frameworks for Organization Behavior. *Organizational Dynamics,* Autumn.

Nadler, D.A. 1982. *Implementing Organizational Change,* in D.A. Nadler, M. L. Tushman, and N. G. Hatvan, eds. *Managing Organizations.* Boston: Little, Brown.

Nadler, D. A. and M. L. Tushman. 1987. *Strategic Organizational Design.* New York: Scott Foresman.

Nadler, D. A., R. B. Shaw, and E. A. Walton. 1994. *Discontinuous Change: Leading Organizational Transformation.* San Francisco: Jossey-Bass Publishers.

Nadler, D. A., and M. L. Tushman. 1997. *Competing by Design: The Power of Organizational Architecture.* New York: Oxford University Press.

Nadler, D. A. 1998. *Champions of Change: How CEOs and Their Companies Are Mastering the Skills of Radical Change.* San Francisco: Jossey-Bass Publishers.

Porter, M. E. 1980. *Competitive Strategy.* New York: Free Press.

Porter, M. E. 1986. *Competitive Advantage.* New York: Free Press.

Roethlisberger F., and W. Dickson 1939. *Management and the Worker.* Cambridge: Cambridge University Press.

Schein, E. H. 1973. *Process Consultation.* Reading, MA: Addison-Wesley.

Seiler, J. A. 1967. *Systems Analysis in Organizational Behavior.* Homewood, Ill.: Irwin-Dorsey.

Slywotzky, A. J. 1996. *Value Migration.* Boston: Harvard Business School Press.

Slywotzky, A. J., and D J. Morrison. 1998. *The Profit Zone: How Strategic Business Design Will Lead You to Tomorrow's Profits.* New York: Three Rivers Press.

CHAPTER 6

The Marketing Consultant
Robert Spekman, University of Virginia and Philip Kotler, Northwestern University

ABOUT THE AUTHORS

Philip Kotler

Philip Kotler is the S. C. Johnson Distinguished Professor of International Marketing at the J. L. Kellogg Graduate School of Management. He has been honored as one of the world's leading marketing thinkers. Dr. Kotler is the author of over one hundred articles and twenty-five books, including *Marketing Management, Principles of Marketing, Social Marketing,* and *The Marketing of Nations.* His research covers strategic marketing, consumer marketing, professional services marketing, and e-marketing.

Robert E. Spekman

Robert E. Spekman is the Tayloe Murphy Professor of Business Administration at The Darden School. He is a recognized authority on business-to-business marketing and strategic alliances. He has edited/written seven books and has authored (co-authored) over eighty articles and papers. Among his consulting clients are many Fortune 100 companies.

There are growing opportunities for marketing consultants as new forms of media and channels open up to cause a reallocation of corporate marketing budgets. In 2000, companies in the United States spent $5.9 billion on marketing research while firms in the UK, Germany, Japan, and France together spent approximately $5.1 billion.[1] Also, in the same year, U.S. TV advertising revenue equaled $40.8 billion and B2B e-commerce figures were estimated to exceed $255.0 billion. Hambrecht and Quist predict that by 2005, global Internet consulting (not just marketing) will exceed $50 billion.[2] Kevin Clancy, CEO of Copernicus, estimates that $7 billion is spent globally in "general marketing consulting," exclusive of marketing research expenditures.[3] These figures reflect only a portion of the total amount of marketing and sales budgets spent by companies in pursuit of a competitive advantage. In fact, the dollars at stake are quite remarkable.

The drive to the digital age will force a number of changes in how marketing consultants build their skills and market their services. Over the coming decade, traditional marketing skills, as practiced by marketing consultants, may become outmoded by the need to retool for the Internet. The Web now affords access to global markets; the ability to evaluate a marketing program's success in real-time; and the ability to tailor instantaneously a variety of messages, product offerings, and prices to different customer segments. In fact, all this can happen the second a company's Web site goes live.

Exhibit 6.1	Illustration of Marketing Problems Across Marketing Planning Process

Stage of Marketing Plan
    Sub-Area of Plan

Illustrative Strategic Problems	Illustrative Tactical Problems

Goals/Objectives

What business are we in?
What is the competitive space?
How will we compete?
What are our objectives, short- and long-term?
Where is value created and captured?

Situational Analysis
    Threat and Opportunities

What is the size and growth of the market?
Where is value created and captured in this market?
What does the external/macro environment present for the future?
Are there government, regulatory concerns?
What is the state of technological change/innovation?
How do firms compete?
Where does the power lie among suppliers, buyers, and customers?

    Strengths and Weaknesses

What do we do well or badly?	How to gain cost efficiencies?
Core competencies?	Benchmarking studies
What is our cost position relative to others?	Perceptual mapping studies
Do we have a differential advantage? Is it sustainable?	
Where is the business today?	

Strategy Development
    Segmentation

Are there priority customers? Now and in the future?	What attributes are important and how can we better position ourselves?
What do they look like?	Where is the ideal point and where should we be?
How are we perceived?	What is our image? Relative to competition?
How is the competition perceived?	How should we decide to allocate resources to these segments?
Are customers' needs being met?	Understanding consumer behavior?
Which segments are key to us?	Evaluating segments?
What is our unique selling point?	
Do our segments align with business objectives?	

Strategy Execution
    Marketing Strategy—Price

What is objective for pricing? Margin? Penetration?	Pricing discounts? Dating?
Price/Performance relative to competition	Margins plus incentives to the trade?
Product line pricing to maximize profits? Other goals?	Pricing to Stimulate consumer demand?

Exhibit 6.1	continued

Stage of Marketing Plan
    Sub-Area of Plan

Illustrative Strategic Problems	Illustrative Tactical Problems
Marketing Strategy—Channels Channel Design to meet needs of customers? Partnering with the channel? Use of the Internet, Intermediaries, etc.? Improve channel performance? Avoiding/resolving channel conflict Dealing with questions of logistics and the movement of goods from supplier to end users?	Supporting the channel? Incenting the channel? Training and lead generation? Understanding bases of power, areas of disagreement, etc?
Marketing Strategy—Promotion Developing an integrated promotional/communications strategy How to allocate $s over elements? Sales response issues for all aspects of strategy Advertising's role in the process Sales force management Other elements of the mix	Deciding on media and trading off among the options? Sales promotion efforts? Motivating sales force? Slotting allowances, etc. Special events?
Marketing Strategy—Products Product design, innovation, etc.? Managing over the life cycle? Managing a portfolio of products Understanding value in use	Branding, packaging, and labeling decisions Service as part of the product? Trade-off analysis/conjoint analysis
Implement/Control Setting performance expectations within the firm and among partners? Output control versus behavioral control Staffing and organizational issues Marketing's relationship with other departments?	Compensation plans—metrics and criteria Benchmarking and best practices Profitability? Market share?
Evaluation Balanced Score Card Marketing Audits Social/environmental responsibility Capturing the voice of the customer	Questions of efficiency

We are now witnessing a revolution in the role played by marketing consultants as technology advances at an unparalleled pace. Not only are we on the cusp of changes affecting the role of the marketing consultant, we are also witnessing major changes in both client expectations and consultant capabilities, with both parties anticipating the requirements of the digital age.

Many of these same clients are currently selling over both the Internet and through their own bricks and mortars. Consultants will have to advise clients who appear bipolar as they pursue different paths to their markets. There are many challenges posed by these changes, as well as numerous opportunities for those who remain flexible and adjust to sometimes conflicting demands. Recall that Darwin actually said that those who can adapt are most likely to survive!

In this chapter, we focus on the marketing consultant, who plays a unique role among all consultants because, although he or she is often sought after for a specialized set of skills, his or her recommendations can affect the entire firm. If the job is done effectively, marketing consultants are responsible for incorporating the voice of customers into a broad range of corporate strategic and tactical decisions. We will discuss the different roles played by marketing consultants, the kinds of problems they address, the challenges they face, and what the future holds for them. Our objective is to understand better the evolving landscape of marketing consulting and to indicate better its place within the larger context of this book.

WHAT KINDS OF PROBLEMS CALL FOR MARKETING CONSULTANTS?

Marketing can no longer be seen as relevant to selling only. Consultants are involved in all phases of the marketing planning process. In addition, their input can be useful in managing the interface across functions and departments, as well as across the boundaries of the firm to include interactions with other network members, such as alliances.

Exhibit 6.1 illustrates the common types of problems that consultants are likely to address in the marketing planning process. Some of these problems are clearly strategic in nature and others are more tactical. Each problem can affect the entire organization and each of its network partners. Any solution chosen must integrate the various parts into a comprehensive, unified, and mutually supportive set of actions. Inconsistent messages, mixed quality in execution, and other mal-aligned aspects can easily undermine the client's ability to achieve his or her goals. Marketing consultants must now, in a real sense, become information networkers and knowledge brokers working across many institutional boundaries.

Marketing consultants are likely to be commissioned to conduct a wide variety of studies: market analysis, segmentation analysis, positioning analysis, channel studies, pricing analysis, marketing audits, and so on. We cannot find any data on the relative frequency of these studies, and, in addition, they will probably vary over time depending on the economic climate and on the surge of "hot" topics. But we would guess that marketing strategy represents the lion's share of marketing consulting. The varying cost levels of different studies also affect the frequency. Conjoint studies and other sophisticated statistical techniques in which the samples tend to be large are relatively expensive. While these studies are quite useful, many firms might shy away because of the price tag. Marketing audits, competitive analysis, projects to adapt/change a channels design, and the like are often very time intensive and carry a high price tag as well.

It is increasingly easy for companies to undertake less expensive studies on their own instead of farming them out to consultants. There are a number of Web sites (e.g., the American Marketing Association) that post diagnostics and other self-help checklists and processes for conducting any number of studies. Exhibit 6.2 shows a page from the AMA's toolkit section. These templates and surveys can be used to help the marketing manager gain skills and begin to solve problems without the assistance of a consultant.

Exhibit 6.2	Consulting Tools Offered by American Marketing Association

Marketing

Templates for ROI Analysis, Marketing Plans, New Product Processes, Price Modeling, and more.

Sales

Templates for Sales Forecasting, Account Business Plans, Sales Reviews, Commission Policies, Profitability Analyses, and more.

Customer Service

Templates for Customer Satisfaction Surveys, Customer Service Questionnaires, Evaluating Help Desk Software, and more.

Business Development

Templates for Non-Compete Agreements, Account Tracking, Determining Corporate Value, Due Diligence, and more.

International

Templates for Integrating Remote Offices, Customs Management, International Shipping, and more.

Training

Templates for Strategic Planning Training, Developing Certification Programs, Retail Training, Management Training, and more.

Human Resources

Templates for Interview Checklist, Performance Review Forms, Career Planning, Employee Manuals, and more.

Other Topics

Templates for Legal, Finance, Administration, Supply Chain Management, Engineering, Manufacturing, and more.

Firms continue to need the help of outside consultants, however, in a number of areas. Segmentation studies are popular as firms acknowledge the need to focus their efforts on key customer groups and key customers. These efforts are supplemented by technology, especially the Internet, which does permit very targeted messages in search of the "segment of one." Intimately tied to segmentation are both positioning and targeting questions. These questions drive the entire marketing mix and the range of projects that examine the *Four Ps.*

Pricing decisions have become more complex in light of the Internet. Previously, trade-off analysis or other methods were employed to show price sensitivity and customer utility functions. The seller offered a price and it was either accepted or rejected. Through net-based tools, buyers can now search for the lowest price, can aggregate demand through intermediaries, or can rely on auctions to set the price. These changes raise new strategic questions for the marketer.[4]

Go-to-market studies are popular for similar reasons. Channels should be designed around how the customer wants to be met in the marketplace. Given the expense of face-to-face selling and the rise of telemarketing and the Internet, managers are challenged as to how to best utilize and integrate the growing number of channels. As a company adds more channels to satisfy the preferences of different customers, channel conflict inevitably emerges. Just note the difficulty faced by manufacturers who sell through established retailers while also wanting to add online sales channels.

Time-to-market remains a critical issue for many companies since delays have an immediate impact on current sales and long-term profitability. Drug companies acknowledge that delays on new product introductions can mean millions of dollars in lost profits over the life of the product. Marketing consultants engage in different kinds of project engagements depending on how the time-to-market question is handled. If the firm is thinking about outsourcing its new product development, decisions must be made about finding the right partner, what skills are needed, and what the relationship should be. If the firm manages the new product development process internally, projects typically involve streamlining the process, gaining greater cooperation/synergy among the functional areas who participate in the process, and incorporating better the voice of the customer. These studies might be accompanied by other engagements to forecast the size and composition of the market, to gather competitive intelligence, and to better gain market entry.

Of late, customer relationship management (CRM) has become a critical topic for banks, credit card companies, telecommunications companies, and many others. In the case of financial services, companies are using CRM to improve customer retention and share of wallet. In 2001, financial institutions spent $6.8 billion in search of closer relationships with customers.[5] A key challenge has been how to measure the return on these expenditures. While the core objective of CRM is to build a dialogue with customers, continuing debate still centers on determining whether you have been successful. For banks, what is the right metric: new deposits, cross-selling, greater share of wallet, or customer satisfaction? To complicate the measurement issue further, CRM is usually linked to other systems for managing the customer relationship, such as with Internet banking, telemarketing, and front-line interaction.

It should be apparent that companies do not have the luxury of only solving one set of marketing-related issues through a single technique, since all elements of the marketing process are interrelated. Such interrelationships raise the question again about the relative value of generalists versus specialist consultants. One study in the telecom industry showed that the effectiveness of a firm's CRM performance accounted for only 50 percent of the variance in its return on sales,[6] meaning that CRM projects are ultimately linked to a number of other marketing issues and that to treat them in isolation is going to suboptimize the firm's performance. The requisite capabilities to effectively use CRM are obviously not developed over night and require the support of the entire enterprise.

WHO ARE THE MARKETING CONSULTANTS?

Clearly, many consulting firms have emerged to help clients with their marketing issues. From a large population of firms, we classify them into four types: (1) *specialist marketing consulting firms,* (2) *marketing research firms,* (3) *industry-oriented marketing consulting firms,* and (4) *general marketing consulting firms.* Many industry observers might consider some of these firms, especially the more specialized ones such as advertising and marketing research, not to be engaged in consulting. However, we place them in the consulting category because they are typically hired from the outside by clients to do independent thinking and analysis, which in itself we believe is a consulting function. If we include all of these firms, it makes the total consulting industry much larger than it is often assumed to be.

Specialist Marketing Consulting Firms

Common to these firms is the fact that they address a particular marketing problem area, such as advertising, sales promotion, public relations, marketing channels, and pricing. The Strategic Pricing Group specializes in helping firms set their prices. Kuczmarski & Associates, Inc. specializes in helping firms grow through new product development. Seurat specializes in helping firms build, manage, and exploit their customer information and direct communication opportunities. Other firms specialize in channel issues. Media buying consultancies compete for business with established advertising agencies. A large number of specialist consulting firms help companies to set up and operate Internet sites. We will undoubtedly witness a further growth in the number and types of these specialized marketing consulting firms.

Hiring such a firm has an upside and downside. The upside is that these firms have a highly developed expertise in solving certain types of marketing problems. They have worked with many companies on similar problems and have presumably developed a sense of "best-of-class practices." It is unlikely that a client could develop a similar understanding of the issues and alternatives that these marketing problem specialist firms have developed. The downside arises out of the fact that each marketing decision area has implications for the other marketing decision areas, as well as for R&D, production, purchasing, and supply chain management. A major tenet of the *marketing mix* is that the marketing elements must be internally consistent in supporting the firm's positioning and branding and, therefore, cannot be individually set without considering the other mix elements. Here are some illustrations where specialists can go astray:

- The advertising agency recommends a large budget to achieve higher brand awareness and preference. This could well result in the need to increase product prices in order to cover higher advertising costs. But the pricing people argue that the increased advertising won't be strong enough to make a higher price acceptable to the target market.

- The sales promotion agency recommends an increased budget for sales promotion, but the advertising people argue that sales promotion cheapens the image of the brand that advertising has worked so hard to establish.

The downside of specialist consulting firms raises the question of whether their advice can be as useful as the advice of general marketing consulting firms that are able to consider the whole marketing mix and strategy. Our own opinion is that problem-oriented consulting firms can be helpful in those situations that have more to do with efficiency issues (doing things right = tactics) rather than effectiveness issues (doing the right thing = strategy). The strength of a firm such as this is its weakness in that a specialized skill offers a focused solution that can easily overlook the wider implications of its recommendations.

Marketing Research Firms

It is important here to focus on one kind of specialist firm, marketing research, because of its size and importance in consulting. In 2001, it is estimated that U.S. firms spent nearly $6.2 billion for marketing, advertising, and opinion research.[7] At a fundamental level, marketing research tends to be highly tactical and data-oriented. Marketing research is defined as a problem-solving process in which data are collected with the express purpose of answering a specific marketing question.[8] Following a formal process, from defining the problem to reporting the results, marketing research encompasses the gamut of marketing decisions and a range of tools and techniques appropriate for the decision at hand. Marketing research often provides answers to questions that appear to be highly circumscribed and delineated. For example, a marketing research project might address questions such as:

- How large is the market?
- Are there different clusters of customers in a market, and what distinguishes one segment from another?
- What attributes are important to customers who buy X over Y, and what are they willing to pay for X?
- Which set of advertisements/promotional campaigns had greater impact? Is one media more cost effective than another?

These questions lead to a set of responses, collected from primary or secondary data. It is not uncommon for a research project to end at this stage, leaving the managers who commissioned the study to grapple with how to utilize the analysis and make the best use of the results. Here, the data must be converted to conclusions with practical impact.

Generalist marketing consultants often begin where the marketing researcher ends. Marketing consulting employs marketing research techniques and principles and carries the analysis farther on a number of dimensions. First, rather than just report findings and conduct the analysis of data, marketing consultants transform the data beyond information to knowledge based on their personal experiences, lessons learned from clients, and best practices. This is a key point of distinction. Marketing researchers tend to report that the survey interviewed 500 potential users and that they said this and that. Consultants will draw parallels to other studies, show how these results might track with conventional wisdom, or offer a novel approach. The consultant brings experience and insight to the findings and frames the results in a larger context, while the researcher tends to focus mainly on the results at hand. One analogy to describe this difference in roles is that both use a microscope in their work but look through different ends—researchers seek intense detail about the problem, and consultants place the problem in a larger context.

Industry-Oriented Marketing Consulting Firms

A number of marketing consulting firms can be found that specialize in an industry rather than on a particular problem. For example, Pharma Strategy Consulting AG out of Basel, Switzerland (http://www.pharma-strategy.com) focuses on helping pharmaceutical companies do successful product launches. Other marketing consulting firms can be found specializing in health care, transportation, banking, energy, consumer goods, and the like. These firms do not focus on specialized problems but rather address the marketing mix as a whole and the client's strategy within an industry.

At the same time, there are firms that specialize in an industry but with a narrow problem focus. An excellent example is ZS consultants of Evanston, Illinois (http://www.zsassociates.com), a firm that specializes in consulting to the pharmaceutical industry but only in the area of sales force optimization. This double nicheing has led the firm to grow from two professors and three graduate students in 1983 to over 400 employees who have consulted to almost every pharmaceutical company in the world.

General Marketing Consulting Firms

Some firms set themselves up with the capability to handle any marketing problem in any industry. They either have staff specialists in various marketing problem areas or industries, or they have built a network of consultants who can be hired on an as-needed basis to work on specific projects. Copernicus Marketing located in Auburndale, Massachusetts (http://www.copernicusmarketing.com) uses a large staff of consultants plus a network of academic and other consultants ready to help a company improve its marketing strategy. They apply a consulting cycle that goes from Situation Analysis through Strategy through Model-Based Planning, Systematic Implementation to Performance Evaluation. Copernicus not only offers general marketing consulting but also sells a set of trademarked services such as Copernican Media Optimizer, Copernican Strategic Pricer, and Copernican Service Designer.

General marketing consulting firms offer specific advantages as well as disadvantages. The positives are that these firms are able to offer both broad strategy consulting as well as marketing problem-oriented consulting. Even when they consult on a specific marketing problem area, they may take a broader view of how that problem fits into the firm's overall strategy. On the other hand, it would be hard for the general marketing consulting firm to claim a deep expertise and experience in a specific problem area or in a specific industry context. This means that a client firm may face a hard choice between hiring a specialist firm and a general firm, since they bring different advantages and disadvantages in the engagement.

Comparison of General Marketing vs. Specialist Consultants

Many types of specialist marketing consultants face a serious challenge regarding how the client perceives them. In recent years, ad agencies and other specialized marketing firms have attempted to reshape themselves into becoming full-service and generalist marketing consultants. In part, this effort has been motivated by higher profit margins derived from new services, as well as the desire to build stronger relationships with existing clients. However, it has not been an easy sell because these diversification strategies can easily fail in attempting to meet heightened client expectations. First, the specialists need to understand that the client relationship is different under a full-service strategy. Management expects that generalist consultants think longer term and have a deeper and more intimate understanding of a client's business. Second, it has been difficult for specialists to shed their tactician mentality and legitimately sit at the table to conduct high-level strategic discussions. In short, many of these specialized agencies have not demonstrated the necessary business acumen that management expects. Compounding their difficulty is client cynicism about the value of consultants in light of rising fees.

Second, general marketing consultants will usually work with clients to implement the changes either implied or suggested by the findings. Given the consolidation across all avenues of marketing consulting, consultants have acquired research firms, and research firms have bought consultancies. Nonetheless, general marketing consultants tend to think more expansively about the problem and solution implementation. On the other hand, market research consultants tend to treat the research question in isolation and are usually hired for that purpose only. General marketing consultants are seen as providing a more comprehensive set of tools, insights, and capabilities.

Third, general marketing consultants will typically help to develop processes and systems to monitor and evaluate the ongoing success of action programs that result. Once the action plan is implemented, how does the client know whether the consultant's recommendations and suggestions will work? Furthermore, general marketing consultants are usually better equipped with the vision to think beyond today's results and work with the client firm to ensure a longer-term solution to what might have been interpreted as a fairly straightforward marketing research problem.

It should be recognized that building great marketing programs requires an integration of several marketing functions, including marketing research, pricing, channel selection, and communication planning. Either the specialist marketing consulting firm has to offer some of these services in which they are less well versed or reach out to form alliances with general marketing consulting firms to deliver an integrated program. The general marketing consulting firm has the skills and experience to work out the entire program, although it may lack depth in some specific areas.

One thing to note is that all marketing consulting firms vary considerably in whom they relate to in client firms. Ad agencies and media companies normally report to marketing directors; marketing research companies report to mid-level marketing research directors; and marketing management consultants generally report to CMOs and/or CEOs.

WHAT IS THE RELATIONSHIP BETWEEN MARKETING CONSULTING FIRMS AND GENERAL MANAGEMENT CONSULTING FIRMS?

To further complicate the problem of choosing a consulting firm, the client firm also may consider hiring a general management consulting firm even when the issues are largely marketing-related. General management consulting firms, such as McKinsey, Booz-Allen, and A. T. Kearney, offer general strategy consulting along with functional consulting. These firms vary from a few hundred to several thousand consultants who cover virtually all the business areas, industries, and specialties. Given an engagement opportunity, they offer to put together the best team of consultants from their own ranks (and sometimes adding outside specialists) that can offer a superior solution (at usually a superior price). They not only review and recommend a strategy but also are skilled at recommending appropriate organizational and cultural changes required to implement the strategy. They stand ready to help the client implement the strategy rather than disappear after giving their advice.

Thus, it would seem that general management consulting firms have more to offer to clients than general marketing consulting firms. Many clients face a choice between hiring a general management consulting firm versus a general marketing consulting firm. For example, Copernicus, a general marketing consulting firm, is often bidding against Bain, BCG, McKinsey, and Monitor.[9] But while both emphasize strategic over tactical issues, they tend to approach problems with a different set of variables. Marketing consultants begin with the consumer and start their inquiry from the consumers' perspective. Management consultants begin with a competitive analysis of the firm's resources, cost positions, and other differences to determine relative advantage.[10] This analysis provides insight into the behavior of firms and the nature of rivalry among competitors in an industry. From our perspective, this analysis is necessary but not sufficient to understand the bases for a sustainable competitive advantage. Without insight into the customers' perceptions and how they evaluate competitive offerings, managers will lack an appreciation for what drives customer buying behavior, what shapes their needs, and what attributes become important in determining whether one competitive offering is chosen over another. Management consulting firms may have been historically weak in marketing but are now recognizing the growing importance of marketing and throwing more resources into it. But they need to move beyond consulting on strategy into assisting in implementation.

We hear a great deal of talk about the customer-centered enterprise and the importance of placing the customer first. However, many general management consultants take an inside-out approach to strategy development and often fail to acknowledge that a major key to competitive advantage is customer relationships. Quality and cost are important; speed to market and the ability to innovate are also critical to a firm's financial success; and more recently, supplier relationships have emerged as an important lever to improving a firm's competitive stance. Yet, if these efforts are not built around an in-depth understanding of the customer and what the critical factors to successfully providing value to the target segments or set of desired customers are, the firm will sub-optimize and fail to achieve a sustainable advantage. One simple test is to ask whether the target customer is featured in either the business mission or vision statement. If the answer is yes, it is likely that a marketing consultant helped shape corporate thinking and might have even assisted in the crafting of the verbiage.

Another area in which the differences between marketing consultants and general management consultants are profound lies in the practice area of supply-chain management. For general management consultants, whose background may be logistics or operations research, the focus of their work often centers on reducing the total costs of procurement either through achieving greater leverage over suppliers, improving internal operations to gain greater efficiency, and/or shedding certain activities along the value chain so the firm can focus on what it does best. A marketing consultant would engage in a similar analysis and additionally would bring a mindset that expands the inquiry to ask what array of suppliers are critical to help the firm better meet the needs of customers. That is, the decision process would encompass both managing the cost side of the equation and the revenue side.

From our perspective, the central marketing challenge is to build an enduring customer relationship. Many management consultants are ill-equipped to address this challenge adequately since it requires a blend of marketing and business knowledge, coupled with competence in technology infrastructure and fundamental marketing tactics. Marketing consultants have skills that encompass developing the appropriate marketing strategies and tactics within the broader business context in which the client operates. General management consultants have traditionally given less credence to marketing concepts and practice.[11] In the future, they need to work together more closely, or one should acquire the other.

WHAT DAILY CHALLENGES DO MARKETING CONSULTANTS FACE?

The *blurring of boundaries* in a consulting practice is common, and it presents challenges on two levels. At one level, it is becoming more difficult to know where one area of expertise ends and another begins. Consulting projects are complex and usually involve more than one element of the marketing mix, so to attempt to solve one problem in isolation becomes an exercise in futility. The challenge here is to integrate across marketing functions, responsibilities, and budgets. Sales management may hire the consultants but the effectiveness of the project is impacted by both channel management and marketing communications. Also, the budget is partly controlled by the IT department that must maintain the software.

On another level, this problem becomes more complicated as third parties become part of the success equation. Supply chain projects, channel design engagements, the implementation of co-marketing and co-branding strategies, and designing strategies using other forms of alliances are all affected by partner firms over which the consultant may hold little sway. Given the rise of networks of firms working together to achieve joint gains, the task of managing across inter-firm boundaries becomes more profound.

The converse of blurring boundaries is *silo* (i.e., narrow funnel). The challenge here is to foster enterprise-wide thinking. Most functions are protective of their turf and their budgets. While some of the misplaced behavior can be attributed to different perspectives of what is important, other explanations are less easily understood and suggest less than honorable motivations. Consultants might find that results are kept under wraps and important information is not shared because of parochial thinking about what is considered *mine*. In other instances, consultants, due to their own specialization, might not view the problem from an enterprise-wide perspective. The problem is that in large multi-division companies their business systems have often evolved into individual fiefdoms that result in higher costs, slower decision making, less adaptive structures, and less responsive action taken to changing market conditions. Herein lays the challenge. Marketing input and expertise should be tied to R&D, manufacturing, supply chain, and management. In fact, if any decision affects the end user, consumer marketing should play a role. Certainly, the examples of corporate failures and bad decisions can be tied to silo thinking where marketing input was either ignored or not sought.

Another challenge converges on *liability*. What happens when the sought after results are not forthcoming? The marketing consultants developed a plan, did the research, analyzed the data, recommended a course of action, and yet market share fell. Marketing consultants have been held responsible for their bad advice in a small number of legal cases. In one case, the consultant recommended a plan for a new product and, based on the data analysis, said the client should reach a 20 percent market share within a year. The result was much less and the client sued the consultant, even though the client had reviewed and accepted the data. The issues in fact are more complex than being accused of giving the wrong advice. Marketing is not a science, and even under the best conditions, unanticipated events can ruin the best recommendations. Markets change, competitive reactions cannot always be anticipated, consumers are more fickle than we are willing to acknowledge, network partners do not always do what they say they will do, and the list goes on. Compounding the problem is that the consultant ultimately does not own the solution, the client does. Plans are not always implemented as the consultant recommends—budgets get cut, managers protect their turf, and other factors intervene.

Related to the question of performance is the challenge of how should consulting *fees* be structured? The approaches range from a simple fee for service (x hours at y dollars per hour) to sharing the gain and the pain. In the fee for service model, the consultant gets paid by the hour and the client either uses the advice/expertise or not. There is no linkage to outcomes and consultants implicitly shoulder no liability/responsibility assuming they have acted in good faith. The opposite end of the continuum places the consultant in the shoes of the client where the consultant shares in the risk and the reward. Many of the early consulting engagements in supply chain management were sold on the basis of "pay us only if we achieve a certain percent savings." Consultants may offer this arrangement as an incentive to close the deal. The problem is that by tying the consultant to performance, clients encourage the same short-term thinking that might have gotten them into trouble to begin with. The challenge is how to achieve a balance between the two extremes. Should the advertising agency be compensated as a percentage of the cost of ads placed (as has been done traditionally) or should it receive a percentage of the gain in market share or revenue attributed to its efforts? The assumption being made here is that causality can be easily determined, when in reality many factors affect performance. This last point begs a discussion that converges on a much larger set of issues.

Another challenge concerns the *validity* of the research findings. Marketing researchers especially are confronted with consumers who have become more cynical and are less willing to respond to surveys or become members of panels. The challenge is to report accurate findings when the sample might not be as truthful as would be expected or when the sample consists of people who are less like the true population under scrutiny. Both response and non-response bias are issues to be addressed, as are issues concerning sample bias. A related problem is one of privacy and the researcher's ability to use all the consumer information that is available. The privacy issue has become the war cry of consumer rights groups especially as it relates to the Internet. Companies can track a person's browsing patterns across a number of Web sites and build a consumer profile based on search patterns. These profiles can be built without the consumers' knowledge and permission. Both the United States and the EU have taken a closer look at the use of cookies that registers the details of one's PC when logged on to a site. Tighter control over these data, coupled with a general tendency towards lower response rates, will result in higher costs for marketing research studies.

Finally, there is *timeliness*. Clients want results yesterday. Although Internet-based research allows faster data collection and information retrieval on a global basis, the expectation is that, with new and burgeoning technology, results should be available in real time. The challenge is really one of expectations management. Although the pace of change is fast, it is not possible to conduct primary research at the same pace. This challenge is particularly salient in the Internet space where time delays can mean the difference between success and failure. To be sure, the ability to respond to price changes and to make other tactical adjustments is critical when time is compressed and distance is irrelevant. Inventory models build on supply, and demand forecasts rely heavily on the accuracy of real time data. Dell Computer is a master of data management in real time.

WHAT IS THE FUTURE OF MARKETING CONSULTING?

Will the role of the marketing consultant change dramatically? Probably not. Specialists and generalists will remain, as will the tensions between them. Many of the challenges listed above will remain as well. It is hard to believe that these basic issues will be resolved, as they seem to be endemic to the consulting relationship. However, we anticipate that marketing consultants will devote more of their time to, and will develop greater expertise in tools and techniques that help clients, in the following areas:

Shifting from market share at any cost to managing profits and margins. Market share simply cannot be taken to the bank! The PIMS data reveal the importance of market share and the power it conveys, but the truth is that the blind pursuit of share is less important than managing profits. The old maxim about *making it up in volume* has not withstood the test of time.

De-emphasizing product sales in favor of share of wallet/cupboard. Cross-selling or any attempt to gain a greater percentage of a consumers' total purchases across a firm's portfolio will become more important. For SunTrust or P&G to gain a greater percentage of their customers' total category expenditures not only lowers the cost of customer retention, it raises the switching costs and builds loyalty. At the end of the day, it is customer loyalty that counts! For P&G, it is one thing to know a household buys Crest toothpaste; it is much more profitable when they discover that this same household also purchases P&G laundry detergent, cleaning supplies, cosmetics, and personal care products.

Managing the lifetime value of a customer. Not all customers are good customers. Good marketers know when to walk away from business and to pursue customers who will remain loyal over the long haul. Price buyers are not necessarily good customers. The challenge for the company is to know what kind of customers it has and the cost of customer acquisition and retention. These considerations will continue to be more important. In fact, although we advocate the importance of customer loyalty, we also caution against blindly believing that all loyal customers are highly profitable.

| *Consulting Insights* | **Are My Marketing Efforts Paying Off?** |

How do you know if your marketing programs are reaping the benefits for which they have been created? This question has haunted marketing consultants and their clients for years. Often the question is tied to productivity, and the issue becomes how many distributors, sales people, advertising exposures, etc. are enough? Sales response models often show diminishing returns at some level of marketing effort. Here, the implicit focus is on marketing activities as an expense. Why not view these marketing dollars as an investment? Instead of measuring expenses as a percentage of revenue, it might make more sense to begin defining marketing as an investment in customer satisfaction, retention, and loyalty. Now the question becomes what is the ROI on my marketing efforts? Marketing ROI measures the direct revenue from a specific marketing effort and also attempts to incorporate the longer-term effects that build over time, such as loyalty.

The use of Marketing ROI requires changes in mindset and metrics. Operationally, these changes mean tracking and measuring relevant inputs and outputs. With the advent of better data collection and analysis techniques and with the rise of customer relationship management tools, marketing ROI is replacing subjectivity in the allocation of marketing dollars. Strategically, it means working with senior management to define what is marketing's role, its effectiveness, and how its goals relate to the firm's larger business plan.

In essence, marketing is central to the bottom line of clients, and it will clearly remain high in the future priorities of top management and in the services provided by the many types of marketing consultants.

The transition from vertical integration to virtual integration. We have witnessed greater attention given to networks of firms competing with other networks. Such relationships force the managers of the various marketing activities to entertain different roles and capabilities. Similarly, the marketing consultant must develop additional skills for managing across networks, which require levels of specialization, integration, and coordination that have not been needed in the vertically integrated firm.

A shift from owning the customer to managing the customer experience. As firms work with third parties and networks to provide value to customers, there has initially been a question of "my customer" versus "your customer." Companies located at different levels in the distribution chain have historically been loath to share customer information for fear of disintermediation and loss of their relationship. We are now shifting to an explicit recognition of the need to share customers since no one firm can provide the full set of value added services required to compete. To a large degree, strategies that have been built on a command and control model are no longer viable, and other approaches must be developed.

Customer Relationship Management will continue to grow in importance. Not only will more clients demand this tool, the nature of the engagement will shift to managing the entire process from installation, to implementation, to integration of all the parts of the firm and, if relevant, its network members that are responsible for "touching" a customer. The system can have no flaws since each interaction is a moment of truth.

Segmentation will continue to be refined, and micro segments will take on greater importance. The data are clear that segmentation leads to greater profitability. While marketers will continue to look for better ways to segment, the emerging technology makes it possible to design very narrow, well-defined segments based on precise data about customer spending patterns, search behavior, and including detailed profiles. It is even possible to define segments down to one customer and, thus, to deliver mass customized products, services, and experiences that reflect the unique nature of subsets of consumers. Given the importance of the Internet, it is likely that segmentation consulting engagements will increase substantially.

Tailored marketing mix responses will complement broad-based strategies. The face of advertising and marketing communications will change to reflect the impact of the Internet. Again, as the technology permits very accurate profiling of customers, the marketer's response can mirror this precision both in the content of the message and the media through which it is delivered. The same holds for pricing decisions, channel selection, and product/service offerings. Pricing can be adjusted in real time to accommodate a range of decision variables. While price discrimination could be an issue, technology can assist in deriving individually bundled prices or prices based on individual benefits/constraints. Again, the ability to meet unique individual needs crosses each element of the marketing mix.

Managing across channels will accelerate in importance. Go-to-market strategies have become more complex, and the high cost of face-to-face sales has called into question the efficacy of direct channels. With the rise in the Internet and other lower cost direct marketing channels, telechannels, and hybrid channels, marketers have begun to rethink their entire channel strategies. It has been difficult to change mindsets and to appreciate that the issues are ones of integration and not one channel versus another. Related to the channels question and the use of the Internet is the problem of fulfillment. The weak link in the Internet is the delivery of goods. Regarding Internet sales, the current level of customer satisfaction is low, and the rates of problems with on-time and accurate delivery are high.

OUR PREDICTIONS

The role of the marketing consultant will remain important so long as firms continue to grapple with their marketing strategies and the accuracy of information they gather from the marketplace. Unlike the general management consultants, marketing consultants begin with the consumer and build from marketplace inward to the firm. Strategic issues are couched with recognition of the importance of understanding the perceptions of customers. While such a worldview sounds basic and almost intuitive, it is not. Consider the number of new product failures that can be attributed to not taking into account the needs of the marketplace, or the channel design failures that were driven by what is good for the firm.

Among marketing consultants, there will remain a healthy tension between the generalist and the specialist with respect to the level of expertise required to address different marketing problems and to apply competently new techniques and tools. One challenge concerns the ability of consultants to engage clients as strategic partners while demonstrating an understanding of the enterprise-wide impact of a proposed project. Also relevant here is the consultant's ability to coordinate specialists, each of whom must complete part of the larger puzzle. The question is whether the consultant is able to take on the role of "systems integrator" as well as subject matter expert. Those who can take on this role provide a much-valued service and, as a consequence, will receive a greater slice of the profits.

More attention will need to be paid to the types of problems faced when customer value is created through the use of networks of cooperating autonomous companies. These interdependencies create both structural and process-related problems in addition to understanding the substantive marketing issues. Thus, the skill set of most marketing consultants will have to adapt to the demands of network marketing. Many marketing consultants have not thought of themselves as change agents, but the complexities of a networked economy demand such thinking.

In addition to new skill sets, there are a number of challenges these marketing consultants face. Credibility, accountability, and liability issues should be of concern to all consultants. Given the recent reporting scandals and the resultant restating of SEC filings, consumers' faith in business is at an all time low. Unfortunately, consultants have taken a major share of the ill-will and notoriety. These feelings spill over to a skepticism that affects a researchers' ability to gather valid and reliable marketing data. Other challenges arise from changes in how business is conducted. Greater cross-functional and cross-boundary dependencies have forced consultants (and their clients) to think both enterprise and network wide. This change in perspective is not easily done since structural barriers and process-related obstacles encourage and sustain silo thinking.

We envision that marketing consultants have a positive future with many opportunities to grow their businesses in spite of the challenges and skepticism. Pressure will come from general management consulting as they develop more focused marketing practice areas. They currently are advantaged by virtue of their strategic orientation and the confidence given to them by senior managers. Certainly, with few seats at the strategy table, it is likely that specialized marketing consultants will lose their place to their more strategic brethren. The tension between general marketing and specialized marketing consultants will continue. In fact, this tension is healthy and both types will be forced to work together to solve complex enterprise-wide problems.

The range of topics addressed by consultants will expand to cover the impact of virtual integration, global competition, the Internet, and the pace of technological change. The problems and projects will require greater depth of knowledge. Use of simulation models to evaluate in advance the performance of proposed marketing programs will grow. Multi-channel solutions, greater share of wallet, consumer loyalty initiatives, consumer-centric strategies, will all be high on the agenda. At the core of the needed competencies is *knowledge management*. Marketing consultants will more and more become knowledge brokers who bring to a problem a knowledge base, a set of relationships, and an ability to think both strategically and act tactically simultaneously.

Notes to the Chapter

[1]"2002 Marketing Fact Book," *Marketing News*, July 8, 2002, 14–20.

[2]Michael Evamy, "Web Clients Pursue Design Strategies," *Marketing*, July 1, 1999, 38+.

[3]Private correspondence with Kevin Clancy of Copernicus.

[4]Gordon Wyner, "New Pricing Realities," *Marketing Research*, 13, no. 1 (2001): 34–35.

[5]Janet B. Bernstel, "Strained Relationship," *Bank Marketing*, 33, no. 10 (2001):⊠ 14–19.

[6]Dale Raaen and Mark Wolfe, "CRM Takes the Driver's Seat for Shareholder Value," *Telecommunications*, 33, no. 9 (1999): 60–65.

[7]*Marketing News*, June 10, 2002: This figure differs from the one in the first paragraph because it is a year later and might include sales measurement expenditures (IRI and Nielsen).

[8]Philip Kotler, *Marketing Management, Analysis Planning, and Control,* 11th ed. (New Jersey: Prentice Hall, 2003).

[9]Private correspondence with Kevin Clancy of Copernicus.

[10]Michael Porter, *Competitive Advantage* (New York: Free Press, 1985).

[11]Alan Weiss, "This Is Not the Consulting Business Any More," *Consulting to Management,* 11, no. 3 (2000): 9–14.

CHAPTER 7

Operations Management Consulting

Richard B. Chase, University of Southern California and K. Ravi Kumar, University of South California

ABOUT THE AUTHORS

Richard B. Chase

Richard B. Chase is Professor of Operations Management at the Marshall School, University of Southern California. He has written and lectured extensively on the subject of service design. His textbook, *Operations Management for Competitive Advantage* (with R. Jacobs and N. Aquilano), 9th edition, has been among the most widely adopted textbooks in the field for over twenty-five years.

K. Ravi Kumar

K. Ravi Kumar is Professor of Information and Operations Management in the Marshall School at the University of Southern California. He is the author or co-author of many articles on operations management. Dr. Kumar teaches courses on Operations Consulting and has consulted with many global Fortune 100 companies in the United States, Europe, and Asia.

Operations management (OM) consulting is often overlooked in today's discussions about what is "hot" in consulting; instead, more attention is paid in the media and at business schools to the romance and rewards of IT and strategy consulting. Yet in 2002–2003, operations consulting was the second largest generator of worldwide consulting revenues at 20.4 percent, second only to IT consulting with 51.1 percent, and trailed by strategy at 18.1 percent, and HR consulting at 10.4 percent.

Despite the current economic downturn for many consultants, operations consultants remain in high demand by clients. The reasons for this demand include: market and profit pressures on clients to reduce costs; a resulting need to reengineer core processes and eliminate noncore processes; globalization requiring advice on setting up operations in foreign markets; outsourcing decisions relative to current operations; and the need for real-time information to better guide global operations in satisfying customers worldwide.

What is OM Consulting?

Many people think OM consulting is only concerned with technical matters, machinery, and engineering. In other words, an OM consultant should have a Ph.D. in engineering in one hand and a stopwatch in the other. That assumption is a long way from reality. Far more MBAs than engineers are employed in operations consulting, and much of their work is performed in service-oriented companies that exist and thrive without plants and machinery.

Operations consulting deals with assisting clients in developing operations strategies and improving systems that affect the production, delivery, and after-service of a product or service. It can often play a central role in the formulation and implementation of a company's overall business strategy, especially where operations can be a source of competitive advantage or an efficient deliverer of goods and services—or both!

Treacy and Wiersema[1] suggest that market leadership can be attained in one of three ways: (1) product leadership, (2) operational excellence, or (3) customer intimacy. Each of these strategies may well call for different operations capabilities. The operations consultant must be able to assist management in understanding these requirements, and then be able to define the most effective combination of technology, systems, and people to execute the business strategy. See the sidebar for two examples of potential OM consulting issues.

Consulting Insights **Examples of OM Problems**

Waste reduction: It is said that the U.S. grocery industry, in the way it goes about conducting its business, has inherent wasteful practices that can account for over $30 billion. Such practices include overstocking of inventories of products that do not sell well and understocking products that do. They also include inefficient performance due to poor coordination of various partners in the value chain, namely, manufacturers, wholesalers, distributors, and logistics service providers. Operations consultants are called in to identify best practices and innovative ways in which remedies to such large-scale inefficiencies can be implemented.

Logistics: This area encompasses the various activities of freight transportation, inventories, warehousing, etc. The logistics industry in the United States makes up approximately 10 percent of the Gross Domestic Product, which amounts to a whopping $1 trillion annually. With the current focus on redefining and restructuring supply chains, which deal with end-to-end integration from suppliers to end customer, the scope for operations consulting in this area alone is enormous, and the task daunting for companies seeking competitive advantage. For example, Compaq (now, part of Hewlett-Packard) estimated that in 1995, it lost $500 million to over $1 billion in sales when it could not supply laptops when and where they were needed.

Historical Foundations

Modern OM grew out of industrial engineering, as pioneered by Fredrick W. Taylor, H. L. Gantt, and Frank and Lillian Gilbreth. It was Taylor, "the father of scientific management," who devised a philosophy and system of production management at the turn of the century. His book, *The Principles of Scientific Management* (1911),[2] converted what had been an art into a systematic, teachable approach to the study and design of work—Taylor's book was the *In Search of Excellence* [3] of its day, and Taylor's book became a best seller even in Japan). H. L. Gantt, the developer of the bar chart, worked with shipbuilders during World War I to improve the scheduling and refitting of liberty ships. Frank Gilbreth developed the principles of motion study, which became part of the consultant's tool kit, and his wife Lillian developed the application of basic psychology to work design.

The industrial model for operations processes was the assembly line design implemented by Henry Ford and his engineers. From the 1920s until the 1960s, OM became synonymous with factory management; for example, during WWII, we often associate the name of Henry Kaiser with applying factory production techniques to shipbuilding and after the war to producing home construction on a mass scale.

The 1970s and 1980s saw a broader and more holistic view emerge of operations management, mainly through the widespread application of Materials Requirements Planning (MRP), Just-in-Time (JIT), and Total Quality Management (TQM) systems. These approaches recognized the need to view all parts of a production system as being interrelated, much like a skein of cloth where pulling on one thread impacted all of the others.

WHO ARE THE OPERATIONS CONSULTANTS?

Operations consultants range from the neighbor down the street who used to work for General Electric to multi-billion dollar multinationals, like Accenture or Booz Allen Hamilton. Each, in their own way, supports the needs of clients in terms of improving operations efficiency and effectiveness.

Multi-Service Operations Consultants

Firms like Accenture and CGE&Y are large consulting businesses offering a wide-range of operations consulting services. Accenture's repertoire of operations and consulting skills includes operations strategy, manufacturing operations, logistics, sales-operations planning, channel management, configuration management, and service management. They also take on a large amount of outsourcing activities from clients in the area of logistics.

Specialized Operations Consultants

Here we find McKinsey, BCG, and Bain focusing on operations strategy, PRTM/Tomkins Associates for supply chain, Aon/Rath & Strong for Six Sigma, PROS Revenue Management for yield management, along with such industry-focused firms as SAIC for government and aviation, and Food Consultants Group for the food industry. Each of these consulting companies position themselves as best-in-class for a narrow set of skills that serve a particular need of clients.

Independent Operations Consultants

Many small consulting firms, sometimes just individuals, draw on their operating experience from large companies to service the needs of small and medium-size companies in their particular locale or region. These clients cannot afford the fees of large consulting firms; moreover, clients probably feel more comfortable working with a local consultant who can give them a lot of personal attention. These consultants usually seek to build a long-term relationship with the owner-manager, serving as a confidant and advisor on operations issues.

Internal Consulting Groups

Some large diversified companies have invested in their own internal staff to become consultants serving line managers in efforts to improve the operational effectiveness of various business units. The newly popular process view of business has created the need for cross-functional consulting teams to address and rationalize the effectiveness of large parts of the value chain, such as order-fulfillment and customer service. General Electric, Pfizer, and American Express are well known exponents of this approach. GE has developed a large cadre of internal consultants who work throughout various GE plants while using Six Sigma methods to improve quality.

THE FIVE Ps OF OPERATIONS MANAGEMENT

It is important for consultants to understand the objectives under which the operations function is measured against in most companies. Obviously, the most commonly known objectives are the cost and quality of producing products and services. But today, we see additional priorities assuming importance, such as speed (e.g., time-to-market in new product development and response to sales opportunities) and flexibility (e.g., responsiveness to customization requests, timing, and mode of delivery). For those companies that want to draw closer to customers in services, the quality of a company's services, such as field and sales support, call centers, and order status, have become a way to differentiate oneself in the marketplace.

With these objectives in mind, one needs to turn to the key building blocks of operational plans. Exhibit 7.1 provides a useful lens for considering five key focal areas in operations management, which overall is concerned with managing the inputs through transformation to outputs and including even the servicing of outputs. The five Ps represent five specific and interrelated concepts that consultants often address in their analyses and recommendations when attempting to create strong and integrated operations management systems and practices.

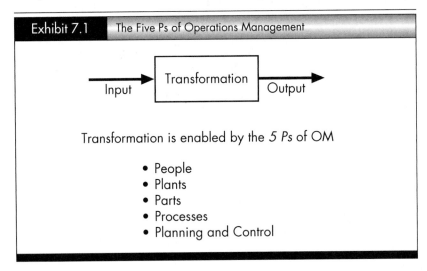

Exhibit 7.1   The Five Ps of Operations Management

Input → Transformation → Output

Transformation is enabled by the *5 Ps* of OM

- People
- Plants
- Parts
- Processes
- Planning and Control

- **Plant/Site:** Adding and locating new plants or service outlets; expanding, contracting, layout, or refocusing existing plants and service outlets/networks

- **People:** Quality improvement, setting/revising work or customer service standards, and learning curve analysis, and training

- **Parts:** Make or buy decisions, vendor selection decisions, materials inventories, and service supplies

- **Processes:** Manufacturing and service processes, purchasing, technology evaluation, process improvement, process reengineering, and after-market services

- **Planning and control systems:** Supply chain management, shop-floor control, warehousing, distribution, call centers and workforce scheduling, and customer reservation systems

Manufacturing Versus Services Operations

In operations consulting, the five Ps take on a different character depending on whether one is looking mainly at manufacturing products or delivering services. Manufacturing operations deals with transforming material inputs into physical product outputs. This transformation process can be described as a two-way interaction between technology and the production worker. In theory, the variability that enters the process is highly controllable as one standardizes the material inputs, rationalizes the worker's job, and automates the process. The focus is on inanimate objects, which means that much of manufacturing OM consulting is devoted to figuring out how to produce, move, store, and distribute physical objects in the most efficient manner. This challenge implies that the skill set of manufacturing consultants lies heavily in materials management and factory technologies.

For services OM, we must add a big C—for Customer—to the five Ps list. The addition of the customer creates a three-way interaction between the technology by which the service is carried out, the service provider, and the customer. The service process is thus both a production process and an experiential process. The experience element puts service quality in the eye of the beholder (the customer!), which also creates difficulties in measuring service performance. What works well in providing one kind of service may prove disastrous in another. For example, consuming a restaurant meal in less that half an hour may be exactly what you want at Jack-in-the-Box, but such brevity in eating would be totally unacceptable at an expensive French restaurant.

OM consultants need to understand that the quality of work is not the same as the quality of service. For example, an auto dealership may do good work on your car, but it may take a week too long to get the job done. Also, contributing to the variability issue is the service person's attitude and demeanor, which may vary from day-to-day or even minute-by-minute.[4] Additionally, services often take the form of cycles of encounters involving face-to-face, telephone, electronic, and mail interactions. Each of these encounters may call for different skills on the part of the services workforce. Finally, the service encounter is really just the tip of the iceberg—successful performance is also the result of "back-office" support functions (e.g., shipping and delivery). In total, these features mean that the service OM consultant's skill set will have to include an understanding of consumer behavior, as well as the blocking and tackling side of operations process design.

KEY CONCEPTS FOR OM CONSULTANTS

Today's operations consultants need to be armed with fundamental ideas that are the bedrock of sound practices in operations management. The following concepts are widely used to illuminate operational issues, be they in the United States or other parts of the world. In-depth knowledge about each concept can help the OM consultant deal with many of the problems encountered in operations management.

Total Quality Management

The general history of Total Quality Management is well known: Its renaissance began in Japan with the auto industry, and it spread to the United States at the urging of the quality gurus—Deming, Juran, and Crosby.[5] An integral part of TQM is the recognition that the organization's ability to provide high quality products is dependent on the quality of its management.

Operations executives (and consultants) need to be educated to view quality improvement as a continuous never-ending process, and that the goal should be one of preventing quality problems, rather than solving them later when customers complain. A strong management will implement sophisticated improvement approaches, such as Six Sigma[6] quality, which signifies a level of quality that allows for less than three to four defects per million operations.

Supply Chain Management

Since the mid-1990s, the concept of "supply chain management" has come to the forefront, connoting the fact that materials management extends beyond the four walls of the factory to include suppliers upstream and distributors and retailers downstream. This concept has also become central in the teaching of operations management in most universities. Its objective is to move goods and services as expeditiously as possible across the broad chain from supplier to customer. A thorough study by consultants is required of the entire chain, including identification of those processes that can best be performed by the client and those that should be performed by others. There is also a need for a supportive IT network system to support management of the overall process.

Lean Operations

A fundamental concept underlying much of the practice of OM is the philosophy of "lean" operations. With origins in JIT and TQM, this framework approaches operations with a view to eliminate "waste" and improve productivity. To do this, "waste" is identified as any nonvalue adding activity, with value typically being defined from the end-customer's perspective. Thus, the problems in moving a part from one place to another or in machine downtime (be it due to breakdown or for setup activities) need to be investigated and eliminated where possible. Ideas such as cellular workflows, setup time reduction, and preventative maintenance are standard ways to drive waste out of the system.

Theory of Constraints

A key construct that emerged at the same time as "lean" operations was one of prioritization, meaning all work areas and resources are not equally important! This viewpoint is articulated in the "theory of constraints,"[7] which focuses on managing one's way through both required and unnecessary bottlenecks (those barriers that constrict the outflow of goods and services). These bottlenecks affect volume throughput and lead-time of products in the queue; hence, there can be major effects on revenue and cash inflow to the company.

Focused Operations

A fundamental concept that relates to operations strategy is that of focusing the appropriate resources on the target market. The notion of focus is that operations processes should be chosen to fit the market conditions for the product in terms of specific volume and variety required. For example, assembly lines are more suited to high product volumes and low product variety, while those operations configurations based on flexible cells or machine functionality are more suited to low product volume and higher product diversity.

Prior to the 1970s, a common belief among non-operations senior management, particularly in discrete parts manufacturing companies, was that operations labor and machines should be used to produce whatever products, in whatever quantities, at whatever timeframes, in whatever quality, and at whatever cost was needed to satisfy customers! International competition, not just from the Japanese but from German manufacturers as well, demonstrated the importance of not trying to be all things to all people.

Mass Customization

Finally, the inexorable push towards getting the best of both worlds is achieved through mass customization, which couples higher price margins from custom products with standardized production. This typically occurs through the design of products or services where a few key attributes are chosen to be customized, usually occurring at the tail end of the production process. This gives the opportunity to produce the product in a very efficient cost-effective manner, while also achieving higher profit margins.

Furthermore, customization can be done through involving the customer, both spatially and temporally—thus, the addition of value is de-linked from typical factories, and labor costs are often reduced. As a simple example, a cafeteria prepares food in a standardized manner but places them out for customers to make their own selections as they pass through the line. Customers can also be involved before the production process begins, such as occurs when a new car purchaser orders a car in advance on a computer, indicating the desired options. In highly automated Audi plants, each car platform passing down the line includes a small box with a computer program representing the customer's chosen design features, and the robots at each station perform according to this program.

DIFFERENT CONTEXTS FOR OM CONSULTING

The set of operations problems facing clients today vary considerably by the context in which they occur. Exhibit 7.2 presents a useful framework for classifying four different contexts that raise different OM issues centering around two key dimensions: (1) the number of operations facilities involved from single to multiple and (2) the geographical scope covered from domestic to global. Clearly, the complexity of OM problems increases from single facility to multiple facilities, and from domestic to global spread. As the number of facilities increases, the coordination between them poses a significant problem, and similarly, the larger the spread in geography, the greater the communication difficulties involving language, culture, and local regulations/customs.

Exhibit 7.2	Classification of Operations Problems

	Domestic	Global
Single Facility	Configuration Issues (A)	Configuration and Communication Issues (B)
Multiple Facilities	Configuration and Coordination Issues (C)	Configuration, Coordination, and Communication Issues (D)

Single Facility/Domestic Issues

The typical problems facing consultants with clients in Quadrant A are generally concerned with productivity and quality improvements. One way that these companies get into operational trouble is that they become a victim of their own success. Their products/services do so well in the local marketplace that their managements have only one goal in mind—to expand existing capacity in the same plant as fast as possible to keep up with demand. When this happens, procedures are trampled on, recruiting is haphazard, quality becomes variable, and the entire operation is stressed. A myriad of problems get embedded into the operations, and these issues last even after demand slows down. Frequently, local demand is not as great as predicted to fill increased capacity; a better decision would have been to expand geographically to open a second factory in a new market.

Another issue that frequently arises in this rapid growth scenario is the resulting large increase in inventories of raw material, work-in-process, and finished goods. This asset intensity starts to hurt profit and cash-flow performance, and even worse, it starts to impede production throughput and worker efficiency. Wrong stuff in the wrong place in the wrong quantity! Operations consultants typically will benchmark the operations to highlight the gap in performance between this company and best-in-class performance. Then, they will identify the sources of the problems, focusing on supply-demand coordination and its alignment with the planning process. The consultants in this case may propose new planning methods that sometimes are pilot tested before moving to full implementation.

This is also a chance to apply the philosophy of just-in-time and total quality management to see if more improvements can be made in productivity and quality. The OM consultant can check to determine whether the level of vertical integration in the company is too high, compared to best-in-class, and if so, can then suggest outsourcing options. Finally, issues such as procurement and supplier management processes may also be audited to identify improvement potential.

Single Facility/Global Issues

For a company located in Quadrant B, all of the problem scenarios mentioned in Quadrant A are applicable, plus even more! When facilities are in a foreign location, a variety of new issues arises pertaining to language, culture, local customs, and government regulations. For example, consider a U.S. consumer household retailer who is expanding by opening additional retailing facilities in several Asian cities. The retailer's first instinct is to replicate its success in the United States by structuring its new facilities (layout, shelving, light fixtures, cash registers, parking lot, etc.) in exactly the same way. However, many problems can arise. Besides the issue of managing procurement of goods that cater to local taste, the retailer may run into trouble if it tries to implement a just-in-time delivery model for replenishment. The availability of reliable logistics service providers can be questionable, especially if the road infrastructure is bad and there is a lack of availability of large container-load trucks (as used in the United States). The company may also get into difficulty trying to outsource services such as cafeteria, housekeeping, information services, etc. Finally, the type of service culture needed in the United States may be impossible to implement given the nature and customs of the local people. Thus, the consultants will have to adjust their U.S.-based notions of TQM, JIT, outsourcing, and lean operations to fit these other cultures.

Multiple Facilities/Domestic Issues

As companies expand and grow their businesses geographically, the natural tendency is to launch more new facilities, even if they are just stocking points (the case of a company in Quadrant C). Sometimes when the business is not growing, there is a tendency for labor intensive companies to move elsewhere in search of low-cost labor. Yet another rationale is to escape tough environmental rules and regulations that some states proscribe. As soon as more facilities are added, the efficient configuration of the various facilities and their coordination becomes critically important.

Consider the case of a growing manufacturer who, due to pressures of customer service, decided to increase the number of regional distribution centers around the country. Clearly, while delivery was expected to improve, the inventory intensity also increased. As a result, as time went on, there was an increase in product variety, which greatly raised the amount of financial investment in inventory. Even worse, the delivery service performance began to decline!

Consultants are often called into situations like this to sort out the interfaces between manufacturing and the various distribution facilities. For example, how many stocking points should there be? Should they install a Distribution Requirements Planning system to mimic a pull-system of inventory planning while coordinating manufacturing supply and distribution demand? Should all the slow-moving items be stocked in only one facility, with the fast-moving items assigned to the remaining facilities? Should there be inventory pooling that allows for centralization of some stock-keeping units and then use delivery via couriers? Should they outsource the transportation function or have their own trucks do the distribution? Operations consultants utilize a variety of techniques to model the ideal functioning of a multi-facility system and then advise their clients on using principles of supply chain management and lean operations.

Multiple Facilities/Global Issues

When one adds the global dimension on top of a large number of facilities, the severity of problems increases dramatically (this is a multinational company in Quadrant D). With trade barriers falling and the WTO enhancing the globalization of business, many new international opportunities are facing companies, which each must decide on what types of customers to serve, what suppliers to select, and where their own value-adding facilities should be located.

Consider the case example of a personal computer company, ABC, which uses partners from Asia and the United States to produce standard parts for their notebooks, LCD monitors, and DVD/CD-RW drives. They also rely on suppliers such as Intel and Microsoft for supplying Wintel innards, and Japanese and Korean manufacturers to produce memory chips. ABC does all the final assembly in the United States to customer order. Clearly, ABC cannot increase inventories since product obsolescence will decimate the value of stocks. Time to market is also essential since competition is severe and customers fickle. Worst of all, the challenge of managing new product launches with myriads of suppliers located globally is extremely difficult because a small glitch can account for failure to deliver and a million dollar loss.

Operations consultants are called in to ABC to resolve an internal debate between those who advocate a process focus (i.e., an assembly plant served by central manufacturers and outsourcers) and those who subscribe to a product focus (i.e., all the processes to make the product are self-contained in the plant). For ABC's consultants, the following questions are on their agenda: Should a global production center produce all of a particular component for global demand in order to take advantage of economies of scale? Should there be assembly lines in each marketplace to customize products for that local market? With multiple stocking points in various countries, how does one optimize the level of inventories in the supply chain? What processes/products should the company produce internally and which ones should they outsource? How does one get each of the facilities to be "best-in-class"? How should new product development be coordinated when design, component manufacturing, final assembly, and key customers are spread out across a variety of locations? What kind of software should ABC use, such as collaborative forecasting, product data management, supply chain design and optimization, or enterprise resource planning, in order to connect their far-flung operations and to effectively plan, schedule, and execute efficient operations?

When the OM consultant considers the entire value chain (suppliers, alliance partners, channel) as the total unit of analysis in seeking performance improvements, one can imagine the explosion of consulting work in the global operations management area.

ANALYTICAL TOOLS OF OPERATIONS CONSULTANTS

The operations consultant's tool kit consists of a wide variety of assessment tools, such as gap analysis, plant audits/tours, benchmarking, process analysis, capacity analysis, simulation, and optimization modeling. Gap analysis is commonly used to assess a client's performance relative to the expectations of its customers, or relative to the performance of its competitors along key dimensions. An example is shown in Exhibit 7.3. Portraying data in this graphic form can be useful in gaining the client's attention and understanding of the OM issues involved.

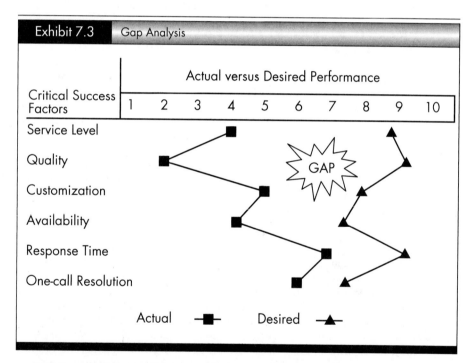

Exhibit 7.3   Gap Analysis

Full manufacturing audits are a major undertaking, entailing measurement of all aspects of the production facility and processes, as well as support activities such as maintenance and inventory stock keeping. Plant tours, on the other hand, are usually much less detailed and can be done in a half day. The purpose of the tour is to get a general understanding of the manufacturing process before focusing on a particular problem area. The rapid plant assessment (RPA) tour,[8] which was created by a professor at Michigan, enables a consulting team to determine the "leanness" of a plant in just thirty minutes. (Sample questions: Are ratings for customer satisfaction and product quality displayed? Is the plant laid out in continuous product line flows rather than shops?) Benchmarking as a process is well understood, and now consulting firms are incorporating write-ups of their benchmarking efforts in white papers to advertise the value of their services to potential clients.

Process analysis and capacity analysis are basic to operations consulting. Process analysis deals with improving each step of a process by changing the way it is done or eliminating it if it doesn't add value to the product or service. It may entail something as minor as eliminating a wasted motion in an assembly operation or something as major as transferring parts directly from the receiving dock to the assembly line rather than placing them temporarily in a stockroom. Capacity analysis deals with matching resource capabilities to production demand requirements over a specific period of time. It might focus on plant-sizing in manufacturing or workforce staffing levels in services. Interestingly, process and capacity analysis are both low tech compared to recent developments in other analytical tools of simulation modeling and optimization modeling. Simple flowcharts and spreadsheet models are about all that are needed for capacity analysis; in contrast, the consulting houses have developed sophisticated software tools for simulation analysis.

PRACTICAL PROBLEMS FACING OM CONSULTANTS

One of the practical problems facing operations consultants is that their work requires quick results and is usually easily measurable. If there isn't an improvement in output, cost, quality, or flexibility as a result of the consultant's suggestions, the engagement is likely to be viewed as a flop. This need for quick results often drives operations consultants to pick low hanging fruit, even if it is better to spend time on tougher problems. To relieve client fears about accomplishing specific results over the long haul, some consulting firms offer service guarantees. For instance, Rath and Strong allow clients to choose from a menu of payouts. For example, if the consultants do not cut lead time by x percent, clients can choose from among such options as refunds and gratis overtime work to get the job done.

A second practical problem is the complexity of data gathering. Production reports, for example, are often highly idiosyncratic and poorly designed, having evolved from a time when the business was young. A case in point is the experience of one of the authors who was working with a major computer manufacturer that sold advanced production control packages while itself relying on homegrown desktop programs to track its own production. Even when various reports within a client's operations are state-of-the-art, the consultant must still figure out how to mesh those that use different time periods or units of measure. Similarly, problems arise when key information systems don't generate across-the-board performance data. Standard ERP systems, for example, provide detailed information on materials flow, forecast accuracy, and schedule performance but don't provide Cost of Quality (COQ) reports. All of this calls for the consultant to possess a bit of the Columbo factor (after the rumpled TV detective of the 1970s)—the ability to ask the right question and the tenacity to follow through to create a coherent picture of a system's strengths and weaknesses.

Sometimes, key clues to solving a production problem may lie in simple documents. For example, every assembly station in a plant has a "parts short list" that identifies the part or component which was unavailable for the production run that day and had to be rush-ordered from upstream operations. An analysis of this list could indicate whether parts were short due to quality problems or scheduling issues.

A third practical problem is that productivity improvements traditionally generate worker resistance. Of course, all consulting leads to changes in some aspect of a client's business, but none has a stronger internal impact than changing the procedures by which work is done. It is no surprise that even a sophisticated workforce will feel threatened by operations consultants. This fear often translates, for instance, into foot dragging by a shop floor supervisor assigned to help the consultants gain access to data or to arrange interviews with appropriate operations personnel.

Finally, there is the challenge of working with other links in the supply chain. If the focus is on a factory, the OM consultant often has to establish a good relationship with suppliers upstream and distributors and retailers downstream because supply chain members can be a valuable source of insight into how a client's processes might be improved.

FUTURE ISSUES FOR OM CONSULTING

We predict several trends will impact the market and skill-set of operations consultants over the next five to ten years.

Service Encounter Design

Although services constitute roughly 80 percent of Gross Domestic Product, and about the same percentage of employment, the most pervasive of all business process—the service encounter between customer and employee—is still approached in a highly unscientific fashion.[9] In fact if we designed cars the way we design most services, they would have five wheels and one axle! Most operations consultants' tool sets contain sophisticated simulations of waiting lines and call centers but are wholly inadequate in even the rudiments of service psychology. Proper service design requires not only an understanding of the basic concepts of service quality (e.g., measurement, recovery planning, critical incident analysis) but also sophisticated psychological concepts flowing from behavioral decision theory. Here close attention needs to be paid to how customers perceive the passage of time and recall the flow of events that make up their service experience.[10] This need for behavioral expertise creates a major opportunity for future consulting in services operations.

What is striking to us is how little attention is paid in the operations consulting community to understanding what is already known about best practices in service encounters that accompany the core services of retailing, health care, education, etc. Consultants would be wise to take a page from the casino Harrah's book in going about achieving service excellence.

Outsourcing and Virtual Integration

The restructuring of companies to focus resources on core competencies often turns to alliances and outsourcing partners to replace low priority activities, and this movement is creating a wealth of opportunities for operations consulting firms. For example, Accenture, while acting as a supplier of logistics services to firms, will contract with suppliers, warehouses, trucking, shipping, etc., and then manage the whole process for clients.

Consulting Insights **On Service**

In 1998, Harrah's was facing a big problem. How could it compete with the architectural splendor of its competitors on the Vegas Strip, given the company's aging, undistinguished Las Vegas hotel and run-of-the-mill casino facilities? Of course, they could invest millions in an effort to create their own Bellagio, Paris, or Caesar's Palace, but at best about all they could do was just catch up. In analyzing the situation, a new management team headed by its current CEO, Gary Loveman, hit upon a novel idea for the gaming industry: How about competing based on *service?* Why service? Analysis showed that what was important to gamblers in the way of service was not having to wait in lines, as well as employee friendliness and helpfulness. Making sure that the customer doesn't have to wait for service to check in to the hotel, to get chips, or to get into the restaurants signals to customers that the company respects the value of their time. Today, if you win a jackpot at Harrah's, you'll have someone there to help within ninety seconds. At other "Strip" hotels, you can easily wait ten minutes or more. To further reduce waiting, Harrah's has invested heavily in self-service technology, such as $125,000 counting machines that allow players to convert their coins into bills without having to wait in line at the cashier's cage. Friendliness and helpfulness create a pleasant overall experience even when losing money. Employees are encouraged to talk to guests and are measured internally by supervisors and externally by mystery shoppers as a part of their "Spotlight on Success" program. Each department supervisor holds five-minute buzz sessions at the start of each shift to communicate knowledge and reinforce elements of Harrah's service culture. Senior management is required to attend at least three departmental buzz sessions per day. To reward good service, Harrah's introduced a bonus program in which every employee receives a bonus of $75 to $200 for each quarter in which the measured level of service goes up by 3 percent or more. After crunching data, taking surveys, and conducting focus groups, Harrah's management discovered that gamblers who were more satisfied with their service experience also increased their gaming expenditures by 10 percent and that those who were extremely satisfied increased their gaming expenditures by 24 percent! The results of these efforts are high levels of customer loyalty and profitability that are the envy of the industry![11]

Another service that operations consulting companies have been trying to provide is the disposal of excess inventories in companies. Rather than sell it to liquidators at a very low price or go through the arduous process of selling through electronic commerce outlets like eBay, consulting companies are offering liquidation services to their preferred clients. Another common phenomenon involves consulting firms using their own personnel to staff such previously untouchable core positions as Purchasing Manager or Logistics Manager. In a similar vein, consultants may actually take on management roles for extended periods to help implement their solutions from an engagement and also help on recruiting and training of their replacements.

Global Supply Chains

As economies become more global and value-adding activities are spread across the world, the need for operations consultants to be capable in dealing with the global supply chain is becoming extremely important. For example, with the shift of so much manufacturing to China, clients now need for their operations consultants to deal with government regulations, state-owned suppliers, and be able to converse in Mandarin.

Consulting firms are now being forced to employ a multicultural workforce that can deal in many aspects of a client's value chain, which may stretch across several countries and continents. For example, Hewlett-Packard employs internal consultants (or procurement specialists) to audit, qualify, and select among potential suppliers from Korea, Taiwan, and China. This means that they, like external consultants, need to understand the work environments, culture, and business practices in these countries, so they can make rational business decisions.

Privatization/Deregulation

The worldwide movement toward market economies has created significant trading opportunities in the East Bloc countries—Russia, China, and India. Indeed, these countries are rushing to marketize their economies and restructure their companies to compete in the world economy. Operations consultants can play a major role in helping to transform large state-owned companies to compete in the private economy. For example, as India privatizes its telecommunication industry, the government needs to know the best ways to structure the ensuing industry, how to set up regulatory structures, how to allow multinationals to enter into the marketplace, and also how to revamp state-owned companies. This also includes work at the firm level where changes will be needed in operations infrastructure, workforce policies, and technology adoption so that these firms can compete in deregulated environments against multinationals.

Real-Time Technology

Information technology has changed the nature and scope of operations in most companies. In the 1970s, 1980s, and even 1990s, multinationals could possibly take from thirty to sixty days to close their accounting books at fiscal year-ending. They needed that much time to figure out where inventories were located around the world. Today, telecommunication and information technologies (e.g., Intranet, client server architecture, global databases, ERP software, CRM software) have made information available and possible anywhere, anytime, and on any appliance (computer, telephone, PDA, etc.). This information revolution offers operations consultants many opportunities to determine how clients can better manage in a real-time environment.

It is quite reasonable to expect that innovative consulting companies will develop war-room versions of operations monitoring and make full use of "real-time" performance measures. For example, Japanese companies are now operating very sophisticated production lines in developing countries, such as China, while using remote monitoring systems and decision controls in Japan.

Mass Customization in Services

The historic approach in services operations has been to: 1) find a successful concept; 2) standardize the service; and 3) scale up by franchising or stamping out the standard format globally. A classic and successful example of this approach is Wal-Mart—so successful that it opened more than 400 new stores in 2003. However, while this cookie-cutter approach has worked in the past, it may be close to running its course as more customers demand having their own way.

There will be an increasing need for consulting firms to design systems for mass customization that apply to both the manufacturing and service sectors. With the advent of real-time information systems and the Internet, data about individual customers are being gathered in large quantities. Data-mining techniques followed by decision support systems can allow services to customize many features that are important to customers and still standardize back-office activities to gain scale economies. An example of this is a McKinsey report on a new method called micro-market modeling, which uses local customer segmentation, operational analysis, and financial evaluation, to customize services offered in different geographic locations.

THE CHALLENGE AND REWARD OF OM CONSULTING

The scene: Arnold's Drive-In in *Happy Days*. Richie is being harassed by a bully, and he scurries over to the booth where Fonzie is sitting. Richie asks Fonzie for advice about what he should do.

> *The Fonze:*   *Don't let him push you around! Act tough and he will back off.*
>
> *Richie:*   (swaggering back to the bully) *I'm warning you, I'm going to take you apart if you give me any more guff!*
>
> *The Bully:*   *Oh yeah. Put up your dukes, wise guy!*

With this, Richie calls "time out" and goes back to Fonzie.

> *Richie:*   *Fonzie, he isn't backing down! Now what?*
>
> *Fonzie:*   *Uh, Richie, one thing I forgot to tell you is that to get a reputation as a tough guy, sometime or other, you had to be seen actually hitting somebody!!! I suggest you run.*

The moral for OM consultants is that to be successful, you actually have to make positive visible changes with a measurable impact on performance. More than any other consultant, you have to make recommendations that result in real improvements in the physical aspects of a manufacturing process or in the subjective experience of customers in services. Even in high-level operations strategy consulting, there is pressure for the rubber to meet the road, whether in strategizing about supply chains, facility location, or technology choice. The visibility of OM consulting contrasts with other types of consulting where results are hard to see and measure. This is the challenge and the reward of operations consulting.

Notes to the Chapter

[1]Treacy, M. and F. Wiersema, *The Discipline of Market Leaders* (Reading, MA: Addison Wesley, 1997).

[2]Taylor, F. W., *The Principles of Scientific Management* (New York: Harper & Bros., 1911).

[3]Peters, T. J., and R. H. Wasserman, *In Search of Excellence* (New York: Warner Books, 1984).

[4]Pugh, S. D., J. Dietz, J. W. Wiley, and S. M. Brooks, "Driving Service Effectiveness Through Employee-Customer Linkages," *The Academy of Management Executive,* 16, no. 4 (2002): 73–85.

[5]For a discussion of the Quality gurus and current TQM practices, see Chase, R. B., N. J. Aquilano, and R. F. Jacobs, *Operations Management for Competitive Advantage,* 9th ed. (Burr Ridge, IL: McGraw-Hill/Irwin, 2000): 258–289.

[6]George, M. L., *Lean Six Sigma: Combining Six Sigma Quality with Lean Speed* (New York: McGraw-Hill, 2002).

[7]The Theory of Constraints was developed by Eliyahu Goldratt and is part of the tool kit of virtually all manufacturing OM consultants. See: Goldratt, E. M., and J. Cox, *The Goal: A Process of Ongoing Improvement* (New York: North River Press, 1986).

[8]Goodson, R. E., "Read a Plant-Fast," *Harvard Business Review* 80, no. 5 (May 2002): 105–113. Also look at: Upton, D., and S. Macadam, "Why (and How) to Take a Plant Tour," *Harvard Business Review* (May–June 1997): 97–106.

[9]A recent call to arms on this issue is presented in: Bowen, D. E., and R. Hallowell, "Suppose We Took Service Seriously? An Introduction to the Special Issue," *The Academy of Management Executive*, 16, no. 4 (2002): 69–72.

[10]Chase, R. B., and S. Dasu, "Want to Perfect Your Company's Service? Use Behavioral Science," *Harvard Business Review* (June 2001): 79–84.

[11]Gary, L., "*Simplify* and *Execute:* Words to Live By in Times of Turbulence: How Harrah's Bet on Loyalty Paid Off," *Harvard Management Update* (January 2003): 12; and personal conversations with Gary Loveman (CEO) and John Bruns (Corporate Director of Customer Satisfaction Assurance) at Harrah's.

sophisticated analytical capabilities to inform the creation and implementation of business strategies.

At the same time, it is essential to identify where IT leaves off in effectiveness and where the qualitative nonprogrammable aspects of human judgment and interpersonal relations become more important.[13] Exhibit 8.1 depicts this relationship between IT, human judgment, and the many HR functions related to the management of human capital in the modern corporation.[14] Some of these areas are more susceptible to the use of IT for automation, such as in the many routine transactions involved in the delivery of Personnel Services, depicted on the right side of Exhibit 8.1. Moving across the diagram to the left and the Strategic Partner role, we see that IT receives much less emphasis. However, it should be noted that there is still a place for IT in each of the major HR roles shown in Exhibit 8.1. Consultants can provide valuable services in each of these areas, including both IT assistance and consulting on the more qualitative and judgmental issues.

Exhibit 8.1	Information Technology and Human Resource Management

Strategic Partner Role	Business Support and Execution Role	Personnel Services Role
Data Analysis, Modeling, and Simulation Capabilities	HR System Administration	
	Employee and Manager Tools, Information, and Advice	Transactional Self-Service Processes
Business Strategy Input	Data and Analysis Tools	
HR Strategy Formulation		
Strategy Implementation	HR System Development, Learning, and Improvement	
Change Management		
Organization Design	Consultation	
	Talent Strategy and Processes	Help-Line Services
Upgrading Analytic Capabilities	Program and System Upgrades	Program and System Upgrades

Shaded = IT/HR Enabled

Routine Personnel Services

As revealed in Exhibit 8.1, the greatest overlap between IT and HR occurs in the routine personnel services role, which involves the transactional parts of HR such as benefits enrollment, claims, payroll, and address changes. Through the automation of these relatively simple transactional processes and by fostering employee self-service, HR can eliminate the multi-step paperwork

CHAPTER 8

Human Resources Consulting

Edward E. Lawler III, University of Southern California and Susan A. Mohrman, University of Southern California

ABOUT THE AUTHORS

Edward E. Lawler III

Edward E. Lawler III is Distinguished Professor of Business and Director of the Center for Effective Organizations in the Marshall School at the University of Southern California. His most recent books include: *Corporate Boards: New Strategies for Adding Value at the Top* (Jossey-Bass, 2001), *Organizing for High Performance* (Jossey-Bass, 2001), *Treat People Right* (Jossey-Bass, 2003), and *Creating a Strategic Human Resources Organization* (Stanford Press, 2003).

Susan A. Mohrman

Susan A. Mohrman is senior research scientist at the Center for Effective Organizations in the Marshall School at the University of Southern California. She researches and writes in the areas of organizational design and effectiveness, knowledge and technology management, and the human resources function. She is the coauthor of three books and several articles and consults to a number of organizations on team-based management.

The future of HR consulting is inseparable from the future of the HR function in organizations. There is little doubt in our minds that the ways in which the HR function is now managed, positioned, and operating in corporations will change dramatically over the next decade and that these changes will significantly alter the future of HR consulting.

Major changes are already occurring for the following reasons: (1) the willingness of companies to outsource numerous functions, including HR, that are not viewed as core to their missions; (2) the prevalence of available electronic Intranet and Web-based services and software; (3) the complexity and variety of new organizational forms such as network organizations and alliances; and (4) the criticality of using human capital as a competitive advantage in the knowledge economy.

Although it is not clear how these changes will settle out, we believe there will still be valuable HR work to be performed but that a significant difference will exist between the work performed by HR functions today and that which will be done by them in the future. As a result of this transformation in HR activities, new and important opportunities for HR consulting will develop.

HR's Current Situation

The HR function in major corporations has a long history of offering administrative services. It is typically positioned in companies as a cost center with a ratio of one HR employee to every 100 employees.[1] The cost of HR administration today is estimated to range from $900 to as much as $4,000 per employee in large corporations. What do organizations receive from this HR cost? The evidence suggests that HR remains a low profile and transaction-oriented function focused mainly on delivering administrative personnel services concerned with compensation administration, benefits, employee counseling, staffing, training and development, and career development assistance.[2]

As for value added, HR is typically not seen as a major contributor to business strategy and organizational performance improvement.[3] Line managers are not inclined to look to HR for consulting assistance on strategy and organization.[4] Moreover, in many companies, HR is not even seen as particularly good at delivering administrative services. Because HR is not viewed as a core priority and competency in many companies, it does not possess the necessary power and expertise to command the resources for providing world-class service. As a result, all too often HR ends up as a high-cost, low-quality bureaucratic provider of administrative services and a no-show in the strategic arena.

HR's Use of Consultants

Corporations have a long history of using consulting firms in the areas of training, compensation administration, benefits, and labor law. HR consulting firms range from small boutiques to major consulting companies, such as Towers Perrin Hewitt; Hay; Watson, Wyatt and Mercer, all of which offer a broad range of HR advice and services. But they are all being challenged by tomorrow's HR needs.

Considerable evidence from recent trends already indicates that HR's use of consulting firms is changing rapidly. First, the use of outsourcing is already appearing in what might be called HR's transactional areas, such as payroll and benefits administration.[5] This trend mirrors changes also occurring in other corporate staff areas (e.g., IT) as companies realize that they cannot build world-class capabilities in all areas, so they turn to outsourcing in hopes of receiving higher quality at lower cost.

A second major trend is currently reflected in the introduction of electronic HR systems (eHR) to provide self-service to managers and employees. Sometimes these systems are developed internally, but in most cases they are designed and sold by consulting firms.[6] In this area, the HR function is following the path of other staff functions as it takes advantage of newly developed IT capabilities to reengineer its processes for greater efficiency and better service.

Another deeper and more profound trend concerns the use of consultants for improving a company's human capital management, which is increasingly seen by senior management as a source of competitive advantage. They realize that the creation of successful business strategies depends heavily on the quality of human input, usually derived from many parties with diverse knowledge and information about a complex and uncertain world. They also know that the effective execution of a promising strategy depends on the quality of leadership from many managers, as well as on the necessity to achieve widespread commitment from the workforce to implement a new strategy.

Given these significant changes and emerging needs for HR, many opportunities are now appearing for consultants to provide new consulting services

in human capital management. To take advantage of this, they must possess leading edge knowledge and implementation skills in two key areas: (1) knowledge about human capital management and (2) information technology for applying this knowledge.

HUMAN CAPITAL AND INFORMATION TECHNOLOGY

Business performance and competitive advantage increasingly depend on the quality of human capital within the firm. Knowledge workers, tools, and tasks are now being integrated to deliver greater value.[7] Information systems and other tools that embody knowledge have become extensions of knowledge workers who are increasingly reliant on advanced analysis, modeling, and communication. Knowledge is not limited simply to data or information. Rather, knowledge is "information combined with experience, context, interpretation, and reflection"[8] that becomes "anchored in the beliefs and commitment of its holder"[9] through collective sense-making and local learning.[10]

While a more extensive discussion of knowledge creation and management is contained in Chapter 17, our focus here is on its implications for HR. A key challenge facing HR consultants is to jointly engage with the HR function and other organizational members so that new frameworks, approaches, and tools from the knowledge economy and information technology can become integrated into the knowledge and systems of the organization and its employees.[11]

Multiple Roles for HR and IT

The IT operational and analytical tools available to HR can empower both themselves and all company employees to add more value. Much HR knowledge can be encoded in algorithmic form, allowing electronically conveyed information to be brought directly to the end user permitting self-service—in essence, this step removes the "knowledgeable" middle person in many transactions.[12] Interestingly, it may also eliminate traditional HR consultants who remain tied to manual paperwork methods for processing HR transactions.

In trying to understand where the knowledge of internal HR professionals should be supplemented by the knowledge of external HR and IT consultants, it is important to realize that their experience bases and formal educations are likely to be very different. Internal HR professionals often possess deep firm-specific knowledge but limited cross-company business experience. External consultants, on the other hand, typically bring strong business education, deeper information technology expertise, and extensive cross-company experience. Where consultants can add value depends on the existing gap between in-house capabilities and the additional knowledge and skills required from the outside to enhance a firm's human capital. Ideally, the external and internal parties should complement each other, rather than seeing the other as a threat.

It is not surprising that, in the current realm of HR consulting, the information technology needs are now big business for consultants. IT is increasingly being intertwined with many HR operations, ranging from embedding knowledge into automated HR transactional processes to the provision of that currently consumes a large percentage of employee time, both in filling out and in processing, which is costly and slow.

To date, this routine transactional area in HR is where IT consultants have been most active in the design, software development, and implementation of new systems. A large consulting business opportunity is maintained in these systems—reprogramming them for changes in the parameters of the system and upgrading their capabilities. Relevant knowledge and skill for performing these activities are not typically found in most traditional HR departments.

However, even with more advanced IT systems for delivering routine services, there remains a need for personally delivered knowledge-based help, often in the form of call centers and help lines to handle complex cases, to answer questions, and to teach employees how to use the automated systems.

Business Support

In the middle column of Exhibit 8.1 is the Business Support role of HR in developing and administering HR systems and services to support the execution of the company's business strategy and its daily operations. These activities include the design and management of systems to secure needed talent, compensate and motivate people, train and develop them, and place people in the right jobs. It also includes HR's internal consultants who work with line managers to help with human resources needs, questions, and issues. These knowledge areas are the ones where HR departments feel most comfortable in terms of their personal capabilities and past performance.[15]

However, many aspects of these traditional HR systems can be codified and automated through IT. Once defined, these activities are usually amenable to self-service through an eHR system. For example, managers can use the system's computer modeling tools, which contain the embedded parameters of the company's compensation system, to perform their own compensation planning—often without assistance from any HR professionals. Another example might be a manager dealing with the potential transfer of an employee who could access the system to find procedures, criteria, and a diagnostic set of questions to help in determining exactly what needs to be done to carry out the transfer.

The development and improvement of HR systems, whether they are automated or not, entails the application of a deep understanding of the principles, regulatory issues, and dynamics of HR systems, especially when crafting systems that support the strategy and the work of the organization. The way employee work is designed has a close relationship to supportive HR systems such as job grades, career tracks, and incentive methods. Therefore, the design of effective HR systems cannot be accomplished without deep expert knowledge, frequently involving consultants.

Although much of this work in the role of Business Support is knowledge-based and judgmental, IT tools remain relevant. Automation of HR systems and transactions makes possible the systematic tracking and evaluation of various systems, such as in determining the relationship between compensation awards and performance evaluation results. Data-based analyses, tracking, and modeling capabilities can provide a future basis for improving HR systems. Many of these data-based capabilities can be Web-based and conducted online, and no doubt these services will become critical to HR's role and effectiveness in the future.

At the bottom of the middle column of Exhibit 8.1, we see the need for a new kind of expertise in designing and upgrading advanced HR systems, both automated and nonautomated for business strategy support and execution. Some of these systems can be automated and turned into self-service, such as talent searches within the corporation. However, others cannot be so easily handled by IT, such as when it comes to developing new organizational designs concerning virtual and network organizations and the redesign of work systems to promote greater employee involvement. Consultants will be able to contribute in all of these areas because many HR departments lack expertise here.

Strategic Partner

The far left column in Exhibit 8.1 shows the Strategic Partner role for HR, which entails providing strategic advice and expertise in advancing the organization's business strategy. Organization design and change management are keys to successful strategy execution. These are areas where organizations have historically sought external consultation, because these activities have been viewed as periodic, one-off occurrences. As a result, HR professionals in corporations are unlikely to possess deep experience-based knowledge concerning them.

The HR function within companies can also play a key role in working closely with top management and outside consultants on strategic issues. Considerable research suggests that strategic planning and complex change efforts that do not consider and involve the human element are doomed to failure. Much of this HR assistance cannot be automated and requires face-to-face interaction. HR can help senior management seek out consultants who are especially skillful at including and involving people in strategic planning, organization design, and change management. And HR can work closely with these consultants during projects to provide internal knowledge.

HR can also play a vital partner role in the use of information technology for strategic purposes. The ability to track and model the company's overall talent pool provides HR with compelling data about whether the human capital within the firm is adequate to enact the business strategy—i.e. asking where the needed talent exists in the company, and how it might be redeployed in order to carry out a changing strategy. IT tools also can be useful for conducting surveys of employee reactions to strategic changes being contemplated or implemented. eHR systems can further enable two-way communication between employees and senior executives, as well as online training for employees to help accelerate learning and the acquisition of new skills required by changes in business strategies.[16]

FUTURE OF TRANSACTIONAL WORK

There is every reason to believe that in the future virtually all HR transactional work will be outsourced. The reason is simple: HR administration is not a core competency of most organizations. Numerous outsourcers and consulting firms now exist that either have or are developing this core competency.

For decades, the transactional work performed by HR has largely been paper-based and labor intensive. This includes many activities involved in advertising and filling a job, the administration of compensation and benefits, preparing personnel policies and distributing them, updating company records, assuring adequate records of performance appraisal, and even purchasing products from vendors. In addition, training in rote skills can be conducted on Web-based systems.

Today, virtually all of the transactional work done by HR can now be accomplished in a self-service mode on eHR computer-based Intranet systems. The traditional, manual way this work has been done is costly and slow, but HR traditionalists often justify it for its personal employee contact. However, it is doubtful that much of this kind of personal contact is even desired by employees, much less worth the added cost involved in delivering it.

Some HR administrative functions have already been outsourced to vendors by many organizations. This is particularly true of benefits administration, for which Hewitt, Fidelity, and other firms have built large outsourcing businesses. They offer substantive knowledge about how to design cost-effective systems and how to deliver administrative services efficiently and accurately. These outsourcers typically operate their own call centers to answer employees' questions and help to migrate employees to Web-based interfaces. They also operate kiosks at company locations to inform and help employees, and they link companies' PC networks into the outsourcer's computer systems.

FOUR TRANSACTION APPROACHES

Basically, organizations can choose from four solutions when it comes to utilizing information technology to handle HR administrative tasks. The four choices are homegrown, best-in-breed, integrated eHR systems, and outsourced HR systems. They all promise to deliver better HR services at lower costs by using Web-based systems, yet they go about it in very different ways. Consulting firms are currently positioning themselves among these choices. Their services range from total eHR outsourcing solutions to single studies evaluating alternatives for clients.

I. Homegrown and Tailor-Made Systems

Technology companies, including Dell, HP, Cisco, Sun Microsystems, and Microsoft, have developed their own Web-based eHR systems. Cisco is perhaps the leader in this field. They use a completely paperless eHR system that runs almost entirely on custom software that it developed in-house. The system includes not only transaction work but offers managers online analytic tools to examine staffing levels, analyze performance results, and perform a host of other services that have traditionally been obtained through face-to-face consultation with the HR department.

This homegrown approach is, and most likely will remain, the least popular of the four alternatives because of its high cost and need for extensive internal expertise. From a company's point of view, the homegrown approach has the advantage of allowing the company to custom-design an eHR system that provides a unique interface with employees. Perhaps the major consulting opportunity here involves the design of the overall HR system and the development of eHR applications. This is often relatively high-level, high value-added consulting that requires deep expertise in HR processes and software applications. In this case, internal HR can combine their in-depth knowledge about the company's needs and capabilities with external expertise.

The overriding question for assessing the value of homegrown approaches is whether they are worth the added cost. Its primary justification rests on serving employees better than they would be by a standardized off-the-shelf system. When it comes to transactional services, it is not clear that individuals necessarily want to have a unique personal interface opportunity; instead, a well-designed, multi-company standardized solution may be all that is needed. For example, the act of changing an address is not something that requires a unique relationship with employees. In other areas, such as embedding unique analytical tools for management decisions about compensation or staffing, the company may in fact derive a competitive advantage through adopting a tailor-made system.

II. Best-in-Breed Systems from Multiple Vendors

An alternative to building a homegrown system from scratch is to buy "best-in-breed" versions of standard software to perform various HR functions. Most companies don't have the expertise or the resources to develop complete eHR applications. An increasing number of vendors can provide software that enables organizations to conduct different kinds of transactional HR services. Some advanced software can perform even more complex advice and knowledge-sharing work that have traditionally been provided in person by the in-house HR staff or by consultants. By choosing software solutions from a variety of vendors, and perhaps building some of their own, organizations can create a complete eHR system.

This approach has a number of potential advantages. It can allow organizations to select the best available system to perform each of its many HR activities. A combination of software systems can be combined and assembled from a variety of vendors to create a total eHR package. It is also possible to combine best-in-breed solutions with homegrown solutions when companies also want a unique set of practices in a particular area of HR administration.

A major disadvantage of best-in-breed approaches is that organizations are required to deal with many different vendors and to be sure that the systems are integrated in the eyes of employees. Software integration problems can be significant, as well as a source of major friction between HR and the company's IT function. Not surprisingly, the IT function typically prefers few vendors and an already-integrated system.

Because of the complexity in creating best-in-breed systems, the opportunities for consulting work are substantial, especially for those firms with skills to integrate software with a deep expertise in compensation administration, staffing, and training. A major issue concerns how to integrate a variety of best-in-breed HR solutions that an organization may want to adopt. This need, if attempted, requires IT expertise that is likely not present inside most organizations or HR departments; indeed, it is probably best done by consulting firms with considerable HR Web systems integration experience across multiple companies.

A best-in-breed approach also can create another consulting opportunity with respect to evaluating how to buy and manage the providers of eHR

CHAPTER 8

Human Resources Consulting

Edward E. Lawler III, University of Southern California and Susan A. Mohrman, University of Southern California

ABOUT THE AUTHORS

Edward E. Lawler III

Edward E. Lawler III is Distinguished Professor of Business and Director of the Center for Effective Organizations in the Marshall School at the University of Southern California. His most recent books include: *Corporate Boards: New Strategies for Adding Value at the Top* (Jossey-Bass, 2001), *Organizing for High Performance* (Jossey-Bass, 2001), *Treat People Right* (Jossey-Bass, 2003), and *Creating a Strategic Human Resources Organization* (Stanford Press, 2003).

Susan A. Mohrman

Susan A. Mohrman is senior research scientist at the Center for Effective Organizations in the Marshall School at the University of Southern California. She researches and writes in the areas of organizational design and effectiveness, knowledge and technology management, and the human resources function. She is the coauthor of three books and several articles and consults to a number of organizations on team-based management.

The future of HR consulting is inseparable from the future of the HR function in organizations. There is little doubt in our minds that the ways in which the HR function is now managed, positioned, and operating in corporations will change dramatically over the next decade and that these changes will significantly alter the future of HR consulting.

Major changes are already occurring for the following reasons: (1) the willingness of companies to outsource numerous functions, including HR, that are not viewed as core to their missions; (2) the prevalence of available electronic Intranet and Web-based services and software; (3) the complexity and variety of new organizational forms such as network organizations and alliances; and (4) the criticality of using human capital as a competitive advantage in the knowledge economy.

Although it is not clear how these changes will settle out, we believe there will still be valuable HR work to be performed but that a significant difference will exist between the work performed by HR functions today and that which will be done by them in the future. As a result of this transformation in HR activities, new and important opportunities for HR consulting will develop.

HR's Current Situation

The HR function in major corporations has a long history of offering administrative services. It is typically positioned in companies as a cost center with a ratio of one HR employee to every 100 employees.[1] The cost of HR administration today is estimated to range from $900 to as much as $4,000 per employee in large corporations. What do organizations receive from this HR cost? The evidence suggests that HR remains a low profile and transaction-oriented function focused mainly on delivering administrative personnel services concerned with compensation administration, benefits, employee counseling, staffing, training and development, and career development assistance.[2]

As for value added, HR is typically not seen as a major contributor to business strategy and organizational performance improvement.[3] Line managers are not inclined to look to HR for consulting assistance on strategy and organization.[4] Moreover, in many companies, HR is not even seen as particularly good at delivering administrative services. Because HR is not viewed as a core priority and competency in many companies, it does not possess the necessary power and expertise to command the resources for providing world-class service. As a result, all too often HR ends up as a high-cost, low-quality bureaucratic provider of administrative services and a no-show in the strategic arena.

HR's Use of Consultants

Corporations have a long history of using consulting firms in the areas of training, compensation administration, benefits, and labor law. HR consulting firms range from small boutiques to major consulting companies, such as Towers Perrin Hewitt; Hay; Watson, Wyatt and Mercer, all of which offer a broad range of HR advice and services. But they are all being challenged by tomorrow's HR needs.

Considerable evidence from recent trends already indicates that HR's use of consulting firms is changing rapidly. First, the use of outsourcing is already appearing in what might be called HR's transactional areas, such as payroll and benefits administration.[5] This trend mirrors changes also occurring in other corporate staff areas (e.g., IT) as companies realize that they cannot build world-class capabilities in all areas, so they turn to outsourcing in hopes of receiving higher quality at lower cost.

A second major trend is currently reflected in the introduction of electronic HR systems (eHR) to provide self-service to managers and employees. Sometimes these systems are developed internally, but in most cases they are designed and sold by consulting firms.[6] In this area, the HR function is following the path of other staff functions as it takes advantage of newly developed IT capabilities to reengineer its processes for greater efficiency and better service.

Another deeper and more profound trend concerns the use of consultants for improving a company's human capital management, which is increasingly seen by senior management as a source of competitive advantage. They realize that the creation of successful business strategies depends heavily on the quality of human input, usually derived from many parties with diverse knowledge and information about a complex and uncertain world. They also know that the effective execution of a promising strategy depends on the quality of leadership from many managers, as well as on the necessity to achieve widespread commitment from the workforce to implement a new strategy.

Given these significant changes and emerging needs for HR, many opportunities are now appearing for consultants to provide new consulting services in human capital management. To take advantage of this, they must possess leading edge knowledge and implementation skills in two key areas: (1) knowledge about human capital management and (2) information technology for applying this knowledge.

HUMAN CAPITAL AND INFORMATION TECHNOLOGY

Business performance and competitive advantage increasingly depend on the quality of human capital within the firm. Knowledge workers, tools, and tasks are now being integrated to deliver greater value.[7] Information systems and other tools that embody knowledge have become extensions of knowledge workers who are increasingly reliant on advanced analysis, modeling, and communication. Knowledge is not limited simply to data or information. Rather, knowledge is "information combined with experience, context, interpretation, and reflection"[8] that becomes "anchored in the beliefs and commitment of its holder"[9] through collective sense-making and local learning.[10]

While a more extensive discussion of knowledge creation and management is contained in Chapter 17, our focus here is on its implications for HR. A key challenge facing HR consultants is to jointly engage with the HR function and other organizational members so that new frameworks, approaches, and tools from the knowledge economy and information technology can become integrated into the knowledge and systems of the organization and its employees.[11]

Multiple Roles for HR and IT

The IT operational and analytical tools available to HR can empower both themselves and all company employees to add more value. Much HR knowledge can be encoded in algorithmic form, allowing electronically conveyed information to be brought directly to the end user permitting self-service—in essence, this step removes the "knowledgeable" middle person in many transactions.[12] Interestingly, it may also eliminate traditional HR consultants who remain tied to manual paperwork methods for processing HR transactions.

In trying to understand where the knowledge of internal HR professionals should be supplemented by the knowledge of external HR and IT consultants, it is important to realize that their experience bases and formal educations are likely to be very different. Internal HR professionals often possess deep firm-specific knowledge but limited cross-company business experience. External consultants, on the other hand, typically bring strong business education, deeper information technology expertise, and extensive cross-company experience. Where consultants can add value depends on the existing gap between in-house capabilities and the additional knowledge and skills required from the outside to enhance a firm's human capital. Ideally, the external and internal parties should complement each other, rather than seeing the other as a threat.

It is not surprising that, in the current realm of HR consulting, the information technology needs are now big business for consultants. IT is increasingly being intertwined with many HR operations, ranging from embedding knowledge into automated HR transactional processes to the provision of sophisticated analytical capabilities to inform the creation and implementation of business strategies.

At the same time, it is essential to identify where IT leaves off in effectiveness and where the qualitative nonprogrammable aspects of human judgment and interpersonal relations become more important.[13] Exhibit 8.1 depicts this relationship between IT, human judgment, and the many HR functions related to the management of human capital in the modern corporation.[14] Some of these areas are more susceptible to the use of IT for automation, such as in the many routine transactions involved in the delivery of Personnel Services, depicted on the right side of Exhibit 8.1. Moving across the diagram to the left and the Strategic Partner role, we see that IT receives much less emphasis. However, it should be noted that there is still a place for IT in each of the major HR roles shown in Exhibit 8.1. Consultants can provide valuable services in each of these areas, including both IT assistance and consulting on the more qualitative and judgmental issues.

Exhibit 8.1	Information Technology and Human Resource Management

Strategic Partner Role	**Business Support and Execution Role**	**Personnel Services Role**
Data Analysis, Modeling, and Simulation Capabilities	HR System Administration / Employee and Manager Tools, Information, and Advice	Transactional Self-Service Processes
Business Strategy Input / HR Strategy Formulation / Strategy Implementation / Change Management / Organization Design	Data and Analysis Tools	
	HR System Development, Learning, and Improvement	
	Consultation	
Upgrading Analytic Capabilities	Talent Strategy and Processes	Help-Line Services
	Program and System Upgrades	Program and System Upgrades

Shaded = IT/HR Enabled

Routine Personnel Services

As revealed in Exhibit 8.1, the greatest overlap between IT and HR occurs in the routine personnel services role, which involves the transactional parts of HR such as benefits enrollment, claims, payroll, and address changes. Through the automation of these relatively simple transactional processes and by fostering employee self-service, HR can eliminate the multi-step paperwork that currently consumes a large percentage of employee time, both in filling out and in processing, which is costly and slow.

To date, this routine transactional area in HR is where IT consultants have been most active in the design, software development, and implementation of new systems. A large consulting business opportunity is maintained in these systems—reprogramming them for changes in the parameters of the system and upgrading their capabilities. Relevant knowledge and skill for performing these activities are not typically found in most traditional HR departments.

However, even with more advanced IT systems for delivering routine services, there remains a need for personally delivered knowledge-based help, often in the form of call centers and help lines to handle complex cases, to answer questions, and to teach employees how to use the automated systems.

Business Support

In the middle column of Exhibit 8.1 is the Business Support role of HR in developing and administering HR systems and services to support the execution of the company's business strategy and its daily operations. These activities include the design and management of systems to secure needed talent, compensate and motivate people, train and develop them, and place people in the right jobs. It also includes HR's internal consultants who work with line managers to help with human resources needs, questions, and issues. These knowledge areas are the ones where HR departments feel most comfortable in terms of their personal capabilities and past performance.[15]

However, many aspects of these traditional HR systems can be codified and automated through IT. Once defined, these activities are usually amenable to self-service through an eHR system. For example, managers can use the system's computer modeling tools, which contain the embedded parameters of the company's compensation system, to perform their own compensation planning—often without assistance from any HR professionals. Another example might be a manager dealing with the potential transfer of an employee who could access the system to find procedures, criteria, and a diagnostic set of questions to help in determining exactly what needs to be done to carry out the transfer.

The development and improvement of HR systems, whether they are automated or not, entails the application of a deep understanding of the principles, regulatory issues, and dynamics of HR systems, especially when crafting systems that support the strategy and the work of the organization. The way employee work is designed has a close relationship to supportive HR systems such as job grades, career tracks, and incentive methods. Therefore, the design of effective HR systems cannot be accomplished without deep expert knowledge, frequently involving consultants.

Although much of this work in the role of Business Support is knowledge-based and judgmental, IT tools remain relevant. Automation of HR systems and transactions makes possible the systematic tracking and evaluation of various systems, such as in determining the relationship between compensation awards and performance evaluation results. Data-based analyses, tracking, and modeling capabilities can provide a future basis for improving HR systems. Many of these data-based capabilities can be Web-based and conducted online, and no doubt these services will become critical to HR's role and effectiveness in the future.

At the bottom of the middle column of Exhibit 8.1, we see the need for a new kind of expertise in designing and upgrading advanced HR systems, both automated and nonautomated for business strategy support and execution. Some of these systems can be automated and turned into self-service, such as talent searches within the corporation. However, others cannot be so easily handled by IT, such as when it comes to developing new organizational designs concerning virtual and network organizations and the redesign of work systems to promote greater employee involvement. Consultants will be able to contribute in all of these areas because many HR departments lack expertise here.

Strategic Partner

The far left column in Exhibit 8.1 shows the Strategic Partner role for HR, which entails providing strategic advice and expertise in advancing the organization's business strategy. Organization design and change management are keys to successful strategy execution. These are areas where organizations have historically sought external consultation, because these activities have been viewed as periodic, one-off occurrences. As a result, HR professionals in corporations are unlikely to possess deep experience-based knowledge concerning them.

The HR function within companies can also play a key role in working closely with top management and outside consultants on strategic issues. Considerable research suggests that strategic planning and complex change efforts that do not consider and involve the human element are doomed to failure. Much of this HR assistance cannot be automated and requires face-to-face interaction. HR can help senior management seek out consultants who are especially skillful at including and involving people in strategic planning, organization design, and change management. And HR can work closely with these consultants during projects to provide internal knowledge.

HR can also play a vital partner role in the use of information technology for strategic purposes. The ability to track and model the company's overall talent pool provides HR with compelling data about whether the human capital within the firm is adequate to enact the business strategy—i.e. asking where the needed talent exists in the company, and how it might be redeployed in order to carry out a changing strategy. IT tools also can be useful for conducting surveys of employee reactions to strategic changes being contemplated or implemented. eHR systems can further enable two-way communication between employees and senior executives, as well as online training for employees to help accelerate learning and the acquisition of new skills required by changes in business strategies.[16]

FUTURE OF TRANSACTIONAL WORK

There is every reason to believe that in the future virtually all HR transactional work will be outsourced. The reason is simple: HR administration is not a core competency of most organizations. Numerous outsourcers and consulting firms now exist that either have or are developing this core competency.

For decades, the transactional work performed by HR has largely been paper-based and labor intensive. This includes many activities involved in advertising and filling a job, the administration of compensation and benefits, preparing personnel policies and distributing them, updating company records, assuring adequate records of performance appraisal, and even purchasing products from vendors. In addition, training in rote skills can be conducted on Web-based systems.

Today, virtually all of the transactional work done by HR can now be accomplished in a self-service mode on eHR computer-based Intranet systems. The traditional, manual way this work has been done is costly and slow, but HR traditionalists often justify it for its personal employee contact. However, it is doubtful that much of this kind of personal contact is even desired by employees, much less worth the added cost involved in delivering it.

Some HR administrative functions have already been outsourced to vendors by many organizations. This is particularly true of benefits administration, for which Hewitt, Fidelity, and other firms have built large outsourcing businesses. They offer substantive knowledge about how to design cost-effective systems and how to deliver administrative services efficiently and accurately. These outsourcers typically operate their own call centers to answer employees' questions and help to migrate employees to Web-based interfaces. They also operate kiosks at company locations to inform and help employees, and they link companies' PC networks into the outsourcer's computer systems.

FOUR TRANSACTION APPROACHES

Basically, organizations can choose from four solutions when it comes to utilizing information technology to handle HR administrative tasks. The four choices are homegrown, best-in-breed, integrated eHR systems, and outsourced HR systems. They all promise to deliver better HR services at lower costs by using Web-based systems, yet they go about it in very different ways. Consulting firms are currently positioning themselves among these choices. Their services range from total eHR outsourcing solutions to single studies evaluating alternatives for clients.

I. Homegrown and Tailor-Made Systems

Technology companies, including Dell, HP, Cisco, Sun Microsystems, and Microsoft, have developed their own Web-based eHR systems. Cisco is perhaps the leader in this field. They use a completely paperless eHR system that runs almost entirely on custom software that it developed in-house. The system includes not only transaction work but offers managers online analytic tools to examine staffing levels, analyze performance results, and perform a host of other services that have traditionally been obtained through face-to-face consultation with the HR department.

This homegrown approach is, and most likely will remain, the least popular of the four alternatives because of its high cost and need for extensive internal expertise. From a company's point of view, the homegrown approach has the advantage of allowing the company to custom-design an eHR system that provides a unique interface with employees. Perhaps the major consulting opportunity here involves the design of the overall HR system and the development of eHR applications. This is often relatively high-level, high value-added consulting that requires deep expertise in HR processes and software applications. In this case, internal HR can combine their in-depth knowledge about the company's needs and capabilities with external expertise.

The overriding question for assessing the value of homegrown approaches is whether they are worth the added cost. Its primary justification rests on serving employees better than they would be by a standardized off-the-shelf system. When it comes to transactional services, it is not clear that individuals necessarily want to have a unique personal interface opportunity; instead, a well-designed, multi-company standardized solution may be all that is needed. For example, the act of changing an address is not something that requires a unique relationship with employees. In other areas, such as embedding unique analytical tools for management decisions about compensation or staffing, the company may in fact derive a competitive advantage through adopting a tailor-made system.

II. Best-in-Breed Systems from Multiple Vendors

An alternative to building a homegrown system from scratch is to buy "best-in-breed" versions of standard software to perform various HR functions. Most companies don't have the expertise or the resources to develop complete eHR applications. An increasing number of vendors can provide software that enables organizations to conduct different kinds of transactional HR services. Some advanced software can perform even more complex advice and knowledge-sharing work that have traditionally been provided in person by the in-house HR staff or by consultants. By choosing software solutions from a variety of vendors, and perhaps building some of their own, organizations can create a complete eHR system.

This approach has a number of potential advantages. It can allow organizations to select the best available system to perform each of its many HR activities. A combination of software systems can be combined and assembled from a variety of vendors to create a total eHR package. It is also possible to combine best-in-breed solutions with homegrown solutions when companies also want a unique set of practices in a particular area of HR administration.

A major disadvantage of best-in-breed approaches is that organizations are required to deal with many different vendors and to be sure that the systems are integrated in the eyes of employees. Software integration problems can be significant, as well as a source of major friction between HR and the company's IT function. Not surprisingly, the IT function typically prefers few vendors and an already-integrated system.

Because of the complexity in creating best-in-breed systems, the opportunities for consulting work are substantial, especially for those firms with skills to integrate software with a deep expertise in compensation administration, staffing, and training. A major issue concerns how to integrate a variety of best-in-breed HR solutions that an organization may want to adopt. This need, if attempted, requires IT expertise that is likely not present inside most organizations or HR departments; indeed, it is probably best done by consulting firms with considerable HR Web systems integration experience across multiple companies.

A best-in-breed approach also can create another consulting opportunity with respect to evaluating how to buy and manage the providers of eHR systems. Few HR functions have the capability to make good decisions concerning which system to buy in each of many areas that need to be Web-enabled. The intertwining of HR system capabilities with software applications poses considerable challenges, such as ensuring that the system has flexibility to deal with changes in a company's strategic direction and anticipating future migration from one generation of software to another.

III. Integrated eHR Systems from Single Vendors

A third approach exists for companies to install a single vendor's wall-to-wall information technology that handles most of its HR administrative transactions through a single sourced integrated software system. Most of these systems are sold today as a subset of ERP (Enterprise Resource Planning) software. PeopleSoft and SAP, along with other providers of ERP systems, offer integrated HR administrative applications. Many of these systems can be linked by ERP software inside the client company with other business information systems, and this can be useful to HR for analyzing data about the human aspects of productivity, quality, customer service, and financial performance.

Integrated single-sourced HR systems assure compatibility, flexibility, and analytical power. However, the installation and management of ERP systems is an extremely complex, challenging, and expensive activity. It requires sophisticated knowledge of software programs, as well as the ability to make good decisions about information management and systems design. Thus, it is not surprising that virtually every existing ERP system is installed and maintained by large firms with outsourcing capability. Some consulting firms, including Accenture and EDS, have grown to enormous size as a result of consulting activities in the ERP space. PeopleSoft and SAP also have their own consulting arms to install and maintain their ERP software. Our research suggests that ERP systems are the most common choice of companies that are seeking Web-enabled HR systems.[17]

However, a number of consulting firms already offer integrated eHR systems that are not part of ERP solutions, although this approach may limit their ability to integrate eHR systems with other business systems in the company. Workscape is a consulting firm that builds Internet solutions to provide a variety of administrative services, with a particular focus on employee benefits administration. They offer both software solutions and ASP hosting, as well as consulting to assess an organization's environment and how services can best be deployed. Other firms are developing a similar model to provide a package of services that allow organizations to purchase whatever eHR services they feel are needed.

Firms purchasing integrated eHR systems face not only a major investment decision but the difficult question of whether to convert all of their existing HR systems to the new system or to pay a large premium to tailor the new system to fit specialized needs. Consultants can help in evaluating these decisions, as well as to aid in the tailor-making process if required.

IV. Outsourced HR Systems

The final alternative is to completely outsource HR administrative tasks. This type of business process outsourcing (BPO) already exists with respect to managing data centers and information technology for companies. It is currently gaining a foothold in HR administration. Several consulting firms now have contracts with major corporations to do Web-based total outsourcing for most HR administration. These consulting outsourcers perform a number of activities, including the design and operation of eHR systems and running call centers.

This total model moves the majority of personnel services, and many business support and execution tasks, to an external firm. In making this decision, it is important for prospective clients to select an outsourcing firm with consulting expertise not only in Web-based applications but with deep experience in HR systems design.

In order for business process outsourcing to be successful, it needs not only to be Web-enabled, but also to utilize highly efficient and effective HR processes. If the processes are not standardized and efficient, then relatively few economies can be realized by moving HR work from paper to computer-based self-service systems. On the other hand, if a BPO firm can bring both process design expertise and Web-enabling technology systems to a company, the opportunities for savings are great. The leading business-process outsourcing firm at this point is Exult, which combines outsourcing transactional support with consulting services that focus on HR process improvement.

BPO firms are potentially in a very good position to learn about the effectiveness of different HR processes. They can gather experience across multiple firms, enabling them to determine which approach to each process is most effective. They can then standardize their systems as a "best practice" and then offer both cost savings and process improvement opportunities. In order to do this, however, they have to be skilled as both an outsourcer and as a consultant to HR.

The size of outsourcing contracts for handling HR business processes frequently run above $100 million and include cost reduction and service guarantees. Because these deals are so large and complex, it raises a key question for potential HR clients: Who is in the best and most effective position to negotiate and monitor these contracts? The internal capabilities of most companies for doing so are quite limited. Executives in the HR function typically know something about what a good process looks like but may not have the applications expertise of the BPO firm. Thus, HR may be poorly positioned to determine whether the process being recommended by the outsourcer is in fact the best one. They almost certainly have neither experience in managing contracts the size of typical BPO contracts nor the ability to evaluate how well the outsourcer is performing.

The BPO model in HR involves a new kind of partnership between the organization and the outsourcer. Both need the other one to be successful. Numerous risks are involved, including low performance by the outsourcer, price increases, and even the outsourcer going out of business. The company using the outsourcer cannot easily change to another outsourcer if it is dissatisfied with the service. Thus, companies need for their outsourcer to be successful, and the outsourcer needs for their clients to be successful; otherwise, both can end up losing badly.

Because of the complexity and newness of this relationship between companies and their BPO provider, numerous consulting opportunities exist to evaluate the outsourcing decision and monitor its progress. Companies need advice concerning how to choose BPO vendors, negotiate contracts, and manage them. Consultants can assess the cost effectiveness of various vendors and compare the choice of outsourcing with internal alternatives. Finally, consulting help is likely needed to facilitate teamwork and collaboration between the outsourcer and the client.

CONSULTING AND HR'S ROLE IN BUSINESS STRATEGY

For the last decade, the Holy Grail for HR functions in large corporations has been to become a Business Partner with senior management in formulating and implementing business strategies. The literature in HR is replete with writings pointing out the advantages to organizations of HR becoming a business partner as well as the advantages to HR itself.[18, 19] The argument is that, because of the major changes that are occurring with respect to the administrative and transactional parts of HR, coupled with the increasing strategic criticality of human capital in the knowledge economy, the HR function needs to dramatically change and elevate its role in order to survive and contribute as an important function.

Business Support Role

Much of the literature contends that the best way for HR to become a partner is to help senior management in aligning their human capital with their existing business strategy. Research points out that strategy execution is often a key problem when an organization tries to change its business strategy.[20] Strategic change frequently fails because of weaknesses in the HR talent of the organization and the inability of the organization to adapt its HR systems to support the new business strategy. These HR activities are depicted in the middle column of Exhibit 8.1, the Business Support role.

If HR is to focus on strategy implementation, it must assure an appropriate reservoir of leadership and technical talent to support the current strategy, and adequate human capital management systems must be in place. Senior executives clearly demand this kind of help; they frequently report that they would indeed like HR to become a partner with them in managing the talent strategy and the employee development agenda of the organization.[21]

Being a Business Support partner requires a broadening of the traditional focus and expertise of HR. In particular, it requires the development of new organizational capabilities that entail expertise in organization design, development, and change management.[22] Rather than HR focusing primarily on an individual employee's capabilities and motivation, HR must address system-wide requirements. In doing so, HR needs to provide assistance in how a company can organize its formal structure and positions in a manner that optimally configure key activities and utilize its talent effectively. It also can help with change management issues to enable the organization to overcome resistance and adopt new behavior patterns.

Many HR functions have installed organization development groups that profess to have expertise in organization design and development. Most of them, however, have been focused more on training and development than on change management and organization design.

Strategic Partner Role

The least developed role for HR is one of acting as a Strategic Partner to help senior management to formulate its business strategy and plan for strategy implementation. Much of the existing literature on HR fails to mention the potentially important role that HR expertise can play and should play in shaping the business agenda of corporations, particularly when human capital is a potential competitive advantage for the firm.

In a company's strategic planning activities, implementation problems can be avoided if a realistic assessment is first made of the organization's ability to carry out any of the alternative strategies being considered. For example, one strategic alternative under consideration may advocate becoming more "marketing driven," but that is not possible without a staff of strong marketing and sales personnel to carry it out. HR can play a key role by identifying the existing performance capabilities of employees and inputting this to the strategic planning process. It also can contribute by identifying other key skills and capabilities not currently recognized or utilized by senior management. If individuals from the HR function do, in fact, understand the business and the capabilities of the organization, and have expertise in diagnosing organizational designs and capabilities, they may be in an unusually good position to help.

We also see a potentially close interplay between the expertise needed to become a Strategic Partner and the use of eHR tools, which can be especially useful in helping strategic change efforts. eHR can provide mechanisms for two-way communication about the HR implications of the business logic underpinning contemplated changes or offer powerful real-time online data about employee reactions to specific change initiatives as they actually happen. New strategic initiatives often require new skills in the workforce; hence, the training of employees via eHR online systems can speed implementation of strategic initiatives. eHR systems can also provide online tools for evaluating HR programs put in place to support a new business strategy.

Despite the potential contributions that HR can make to business strategy formulation and change, little evidence exists that the HR function is as yet acting as a Strategic Partner with senior management in many companies. This raises the key question of why isn't HR changing. Of the possible answers, many have to do with HR's traditional strengths and weaknesses.

On the strength side, HR managers usually possess deep knowledge about their organization's HR systems as well as an understanding of the work of the organization, its culture, and its organizational capabilities. This is valuable information that can make a significant contribution to the formulation of business strategies. However, on the weakness side, the knowledge and worldviews of internal HR staff are often limited by exposure to only one company, making them insufficient to guide strategy formulation and execution. The strategic issues are simply too complex, the knowledge base needed too extensive, and the demands too variable for an internal group to be staffed for adequately meeting these needs.

Therefore, for good reasons, organizations and their senior executives often look outside for consulting help when it comes to strategic planning, organization design, and change management. Many advantages accrue from the broad experience and deep knowledge of consulting firms such as McKinsey and Booz Allen when it comes to providing value-added services. On the negative side, many strategy and general management consulting firms lack specialized knowledge in human resources management or detailed knowledge about a client's HR systems. Even firms that specialize in HR strategy and systems may fall short in understanding a particular client, its culture, and its organizational capabilities. Thus, the collaborative knowledge of both the internal HR function and of external consultants is needed.

Undoubtedly, clients will vary in their preferences for how much strategic HR work is to be done inside and how much is performed by outside consulting firms. At one extreme, there is the company where only a few senior HR people, acting as truly part of the senior management team, devote their attention to consulting firm projects that focus on change management, organization design, and business strategy development. At the other extreme is a firm with an HR group that already has several centers of excellence in organization design, change management, and business strategy analysis; it will only selectively use consulting firms on a limited number of projects and for developing their internal knowledge base.

Either extreme requires fundamental changes in the way that HR operates as well as in its understanding of priorities and criteria for contributing to effective human capital management. Consequently, both approaches described above are likely to need external HR expertise from consultants in order to stimulate the learning of new roles and the development of new systems.

CONSULTING FIRMS AND THEIR FUTURE IN HR

While the HR consulting arena is full of new opportunities for consulting firms, these same firms will need to carefully assess their strategies and competencies as they position themselves for the future market. The two drivers of this market are likely to be: 1) outsourcing services for HR transactions and 2) the human requirements of the knowledge economy, some of which can be automated. Opportunities for outsourcing growth are extraordinary. And the knowledge economy makes human capital a strong leverage point in creating competitive advantage.

We predict that most of the administrative aspects of HR will become self-service and Web-based and that the need for software and systems design will become enormous. In addition, the human capital work involved in developing and implementing business strategies and support systems is potentially a significant growth area for consulting firms. As already noted, consultants possess a number of competitive advantages in this area, especially when compared to most internal HR groups, which are not staffed or experienced for this type of work.

Most likely, the outsourcing of HR transactions will create the greatest disturbance in the structure of the HR consulting market, just as it has already done with the outsourcing of e-business and logistics consulting. The HR outsourcing market is relatively underdeveloped compared to these other types of information outsourcing services.

Recently, a number of IT consulting firms have began to specialize in developing eHR software for performance management, training, compensation administration, career development, and a host of other HR areas. In many respects, these firms are pure software and outsourcing firms rather than HR consulting firms, but in other respects they are consulting firms. Many offer advice to companies on what are the best processes and what are the best systems, but they are neophytes in understanding HR expertise. Nevertheless, they will be serious competitors.

Firm Strategies and the Value Chain

We already see many consulting firms making changes in their domains of expertise and services being offered, as clients assess their value chains and decide what part of HR is to be outsourced, ranging from strategic to transactional work. Will the consulting firms concentrate their services solely on outsourcing, or combine it with some form of systems evaluation consulting? Or will they forsake outsourcing altogether and focus on strategic HR consulting or some other specialized business support area? And might it be possible to put all types of HR consulting services under one roof?

The major business strategy firms, such as McKinsey, Mercer, and Booz Allen, are likely to continue developing their practices in the human capital area but not enter the outsourcing space. Interestingly, some of the traditional HR consulting firms are trying to move upstream into the business strategy arena because of its high value-added and potential growth.

Undoubtedly, a number of successful but small "boutique" firms will continue to specialize in just one HR area, such as change management or organization design or strategic HR. Other firms are likely to move out from their specialties to embrace new areas that are still related to their core competencies. For example, eHR consulting firms may use their knowledge of clients' data systems and processes to move upstream to do strategy consulting, arguing that they are uniquely positioned to combine local knowledge of the organization's existing systems with the kinds of data that are needed to solve strategic issues. However, to make this move, they will need to add considerable skill and knowledge about strategic management, data-mining, and data analysis. The possibility of this happening should not be discounted.

Those large consulting firms that are already active in providing a combination of change management, organization design, and basic HR transactional processes are well positioned to move downstream into outsourcing. They potentially can add outsourcing capability and also enter the eHR space through providing software and ASP services. We think they are likely to do this, as these areas are quite attractive for potential growth. To do so, they will need to develop new core competencies in eHR and information technology. Acquisitions and alliances are a probable route to building these new skills and services.

Many HR consulting firms will want to avoid the outsourcing market altogether, choosing instead to offer only several high value-added strategic HR services. Many client organizations prefer to deal with one vendor in order to get an integrated set of services. One firm that has moved in this direction is the Mercer Consulting Group. They offer strategic consulting, change management consulting, and HR consulting of almost all kinds. The challenge for them and other consulting firms that want to enter this consulting space is to integrate their services. Doing this is not simple, but it has the potential to add considerable value to their offerings.

Finally, a growth opportunity exists for firms to become soup-to-nuts providers of outsourced HR services as well as strategic and organization design services. The ultimate development of this trend might be a super firm that offers "one stop shopping" for everything having to do with HR management. This is definitely easier said than done. It will be very difficult for consulting firms to master all competencies needed to become a full-service provider of HR consulting and outsourcing help. The range of required skills is probably too diverse for one firm to manage. It can try to acquire them, but merging the different cultures with all the different disciplines and values is likely to be an insurmountable challenge.

Strategic positioning will likely require the consulting firm to develop different core competencies and consultant skills from those present today. For those firms choosing to locate themselves mainly in the transactional world, their strengths will come from high volume, low cost, and excellence in execution. On the other hand, if they are in the HR strategy area, then their intellectual and human capital capabilities will be their key success factors; these high-end firms will need to become active in research and development and build close relationships with business schools and gurus who write popular books. To emerge truly as an integrated deliverer of services, these HR consulting firms must avoid the myopic diseases all too common among HR functions within organizations—that is, the "silo-ing" of separate specialties that undermine coordination and integration.

Promising Future

Overall, there is every reason to believe that HR consulting is a growth business that will increasingly produce new types of firms as well as new types of services. There will continue to be issues concerning what HR tasks are best done by internal HR and what are best done by consulting and outsourcing firms. But this will not retard the growth of consulting firms. Indeed, our estimate is that most large organizations will choose to outsource both the design of transactional service systems and also use outside HR consultants for key aspects of formulating and implementing their business strategies. All HR consulting firms are facing major changes within themselves.

Notes to the Chapter

[1]Lawler, E. E., III, & S. A. Mohrman, *Creating a Strategic Human Resources Organization: Trends and New Directions* (Palo Alto: Stanford University Press, 2003).

[2]BNA, *Human Resource Activities, Budgets and Staffs* (Washington, D.C.: BNA, 2001).

[3]Ulrich, D., W. Brockbank, A. Yeung, and D. Lake, "Human Resource Competencies: An Empirical Assessment," *Human Resource Management*, 34 (1995): 473–495.

[4]Ulrich, D., *Human Resources Champions* (Boston: Harvard Business School Press, 1997).

[5]Lawler and Mohrman, *Creating a Strategic Human Resources Organization*.

[6]Lawler and Mohrman, *Creating a Strategic Human Resources Organization*.

[7]Argote, L., and P. Ingram, "Knowledge Transfer: A Basis for Competitive Advantage in Firms," *Organizational Behavior and Human Decisions Processes*, 82, no. 1 (2000): 150–169.

[8]Davenport, T. H., D. W. De Long, and M. C. Beers, "Successful knowledge management projects," *Sloan Management Review*, 39, no. 2 (1998): 43–59.

[9]Nonaka, I., and H. Takeuchi, *The Knowledge-Creating Company* (New York: Oxford Press, 1995).

[10]Orlikowski, W. J., and D. Robey, "Information Technology and the Structuring of Organizations, *Information Systems Research*, 2, no. 2 (1991): 143–169.

[11]Mohrman, S. A., C. B. Gibson, and A. M. Mohrman, Jr., "Doing Research That Is Useful to Practice," *Academy of Management Journal*, 44, no. 2 (2001): 347–375.

[12]Davenport, T. H., *Process Innovation: Reengineering Work Through Information Technology* (Boston: Harvard Business School Press, 1993).

[13]Hammer, M., and J. Champy, *Reengineering the Corporation: A Manifesto for Business Revolution* (New York: HarperCollins, 1993).

[14]Lawler and Mohrman, *Creating a Strategic Human Resources Organization*.

[15]Lawler and Mohrman, *Creating a Strategic Human Resources Organization*.

[16]Tenkasi, R. V., S. A. Mohrman, and A. M. Mohrman, Jr., "Accelerated Learning During Organizational Transition," in S. A. Mohrman, J. R. Galbraith, E. E. Lawler, III, and Associates, eds., *Tomorrow's Organization: Crafting Winning Capabilities in a Dynamic World* (San Francisco: Jossey-Bass, 1998).

[17]Lawler and Mohrman, *Creating a Strategic Human Resources Organization*.

[18]Brockbank, W., "If HR were really strategically proactive: Present and future directions in HR's contribution to competitive advantage," *Human Resource Management*, 38 (1999): 337–352.

[19]Ulrich, D., M. R. Losey, and G. Lake, eds., *Tomorrow's HR Management* (New York: Wiley, 1997).

[20]Michaels, E., H. Handfield-Jones, and B. Axelrod, *The War for Talent* (Boston: Harvard Business School Press, 2001).

[21]Mohrman, A. M., J. R. Galbraith, E. E. Lawler, III, and Associates, *Tomorrow's Organization: Crafting Winning Capabilities in a Dynamic World* (San Francisco: Jossey-Bass, 1998).

[22]Bossidy, L. and R. Charan, *Execution: The Discipline of Getting Things Done* (New York: Crown Business, 2002).

Part 3

Consulting in Different Contexts

INTRODUCTION

Management consulting is "contextually bound"—or in plainer words, "one size doesn't fit all." The challenge facing every consultant is to strike a balance between relying on the generalizations inherent to many consulting concepts and models, while also ensuring relevance and adaptation of unique solutions to specific client situations. In many ways, every client is special and different, yet the astute consultant cannot start over each time. Rather, an intermediate ground advocates that the consultant be aware of certain broad classifications of contexts, such as financial services versus high-tech manufacturing, where certain patterns of client behavior and consulting issues can be anticipated.

This section highlights three important contexts among the many that exist in management consulting—the CEO and boardroom consulting, global consulting, and public sector consulting. We selected these three major areas because they are likely to become more important and perhaps even dominant in the future. Not covered here, but still very important, is the uniqueness of certain industries, such as pharmaceuticals, communications, high technology, retailing, and so forth. Also not recognized here is the varying size of firms where some clients may be small entrepreneurial ventures while others are mega-holding companies. We have drawn the line rather arbitrarily around our chosen three practice areas, which are less known or experienced by many consultants. We hope their coverage will alert the reader to be broadly sensitive to all contexts and to be more alert to the kinds of issues—economic, organizational, or technological—that will likely be encountered.

Chapter 9 on "Consulting to CEOs and Boards" provides us with an inside look at many of the issues facing these two parties as each struggles to be effective. The chapter points out the powerful advantages of having a CEO as a client yet warns us that this client requires a form of consulting unlike most other kinds of consulting. Most consultants are not prepared for consulting at this level. Many pressures face CEOs today that were not present five years ago, from having to deal with strident stakeholders to winning over an entire workforce in its commitment to major changes in strategy and organization. There are also stages to a CEO's tenure, with each stage presenting unique problems and solutions. The chapter concludes by closely examining Boards and the need for them to become a team, not a loosely connected group. It also considers the complex relationship between the CEO and the Board and how the consultant can sometimes assist both parties but runs the risk of becoming trapped in the middle of a complex political context.

Another important context for consulting is clearly the global arena, which is covered in Chapter 10 on "Globalization Consulting." Most companies today, including even small ones, find themselves doing business on an international basis, and frequently they need assistance in dealing with complex issues arising from different cultures, economies, and political systems. This chapter presents a model of *Nine Steps to Globalization* to describe the evolution of a complete globalization consulting project for a client. Each of the nine steps can represent a separate consulting project. The nine steps also fall into one of three major practice areas common to international firms: strategy consulting, operations consulting, and leadership consulting. Each of these three practice areas raise issues and suggest solutions that are often different from what is practiced in one's home country, ranging across cultural practices to security concerns to channel distribution to public infrastructure problems. The author concludes with advice about the skills required by global consultants in order to develop a "global mindset" for working more effectively across nations in helping clients.

Chapter 11, on "Public Sector Consultation," explores a third unique context—local and federal government—a rapidly growing sector but one where private sector trained consultants often stub their toes. The public sector has recently become a significant market for consulting firms, especially in IT consulting, which contributes upwards of 25 percent of today's consulting market. The authors make clear that consulting in the public sector requires a special understanding and sensitivity on the part of consultants to the multi-purposes of government and the cumbersome bureaucracy that affects decision making. A major reality is that many stakeholders often have to be included in reaching a decision, which is unlike the private sector where a single client may alone have the authority to decide. Much of this chapter is devoted to the types of consulting projects that are likely to arise under the need for "reinventing government." These include projects involving information technology for making government more reachable to the public, and designing new metrics and rewards to establish accountability in a system where profits are obviously not the bottom line. The chapter concludes by arguing that private sector consultants have much to offer to the public sector, yet certain private sector methods and mindsets have to be left at home.

CHAPTER 9

Consulting to CEOs and Boards

David A. Nadler, Mercer Delta Consulting

ABOUT THE AUTHOR

David A. Nadler

David A. Nadler is Chairman of Mercer Delta Consulting, a management consulting firm. Dr. Nadler consults at the CEO level, specializing in large-scale organization change, executive leadership, and corporate governance. He has written numerous articles and book chapters and has authored and/or edited fourteen books. He is a member of the Academy of Management and was elected a Fellow of the American Psychological Association.

For decades, CEOs and Boards of Directors have availed themselves of a wide array of consultative services. However, the nature of these services, the role of the consultants, and the relationships between consultants and senior-level clients have undergone important changes over the years. Two particular years in recent history have each anchored radical changes in these roles and relationships—1993 and 2002.

The year 1993 was truly a watershed year in the history of corporate governance in the United States. That year, the CEOs of more than two dozen major corporations were dismissed or forced to resign by their Boards. It was a wholesale corporate housecleaning unlike anything experienced before by U.S. business, extending to the pinnacle of the corporate establishment and enveloping such corporate icons as General Motors, IBM, Westinghouse, and American Express.

The second watershed year was 2002. Major changes occurred in the wake of the Enron and Arthur Andersen disasters and the subsequent problems at Tyco, Global Crossing, Worldcom, Qwest Communications, and elsewhere. In the face of broad-based outrage by the public concerning management and Board malfeasance, various constituencies began to act. Actions taken by the SEC, new guidelines from the New York Stock Exchange[1] and the NASDAQ,[2] and legislation from Congress[3] have all contributed to changing the fundamental landscape of corporate governance. The result has been a dramatic shift in the balance of power between Boards and CEOs. And for those of us whose business is to consult with corporate leaders, the implications are just as profound.

Our intent in this chapter is to provide a perspective on the special nature of consulting to CEOs and Boards. We begin with why there is a need for consulting at this level, then we turn specifically to consulting to CEOs, next to

Boards, and then we end with the relationship between the two parties and some of their potential conflicts.

Although our focus is on issues and consulting work in the context of the United States, much of what we have to say is likely to apply to corporations based abroad as well. While the United States is in the vanguard of consulting to CEOs and Boards, similar trends in the problems of corporate governance and concern for CEO performance have developed in Canada, the U.K., and much of Western Europe.

Need for Consulting Assistance

During the late 1980s, CEOs recognized that their jobs were becoming significantly more challenging, complex, and difficult than in the past. Faced with a job that presented a daunting array of personal and professional demands on a daily basis, more and more CEOs began seeking assistance from lawyers and investment bankers outside the corporate chain of command.

At the same time, the economic downturn of the early 1990s, coupled with the emergence of the shareholder activist movement and increased pressure from Boards, served to reshape the dynamics and measures of CEO success. No longer was the CEO's job a lifetime sinecure, insulated from the ups and downs of corporate performance and the vagaries of Wall Street. This new fear of failure, coupled with the increasing complexity of the CEO's job in a highly competitive global economy, fueled recognition by CEOs that outside help wasn't just nice to have—in many cases, it was essential.

We have simultaneously witnessed a major shift in the role of Boards and in directors' perceptions of their responsibilities. Prior to the 1990s, corporate Boards in the United States had largely served as cosmetic appendages to the corporate governance structure. They met infrequently in highly ritualistic settings. In general, their role was to fulfill a bare minimum of responsibilities required by law without interfering in the real business of managing the enterprise.

As the 1990s progressed, more and more Boards began to perceive their role in more activist terms. They began to see themselves as important and unique components of corporate governance, as bodies with real work to do and with real accountability for the quality of their work and decisions. After 2002, due to top management corruption and SEC action, Boards must now become more proactive, more productive, and more performance oriented.

They are also beginning to understand that they need to replicate the dynamics of effective executive teams, with more explicit roles, efficient structures, and thoughtful processes designed to accomplish value-added work on an ongoing basis. That involves much more than perfunctory meetings of the Audit and Compensation committees; it requires a fundamental rethinking of how the Board works together and with the CEO. And that kind of change, as many Boards have realized, usually requires help from outside professionals.

The changing nature of Boards must, by definition, result in a different relationship between the CEO and the Board—and again, the need for outside help in designing and developing those relationships is increasingly evident. Accordingly, we've seen the rapid emergence of a specialized field of consulting to both CEOs and Boards.

In comparison with other forms of management consulting, much of the work with CEOs and Boards retains an aura of mystery. Few out of many thousands of management consultants have had direct, personal experience with what actually happens behind the closed doors of the CEO's office or in the inner sanctum of the Boardroom. The consultation that takes place in these obscure venues, by its very nature, is sensitive and confidential, leading to a variety of fantasies and misconceptions about the nature of the work and relationships between consultants and senior executives.

Nevertheless, the need for consultative services to CEOs has been prompted over the past decade by a growing body of experience and occasional research on CEOs and their shortcomings. Also, we've seen a similar but more limited expansion of our understanding about what's involved in consulting to Boards of Directors.

CONSULTING TO CEOS

The key to consulting to CEOs—particularly to CEOs of large, complex public companies—is to understand the world in which they operate. It is a world like no other. The popular stereotype of the CEO is that of an all-powerful figure—of a ship's captain setting a course and issuing orders to a crew that responds without question or pause. Nothing could be further from the truth.

In reality, the CEO sits at the center of a universe of stakeholders, both internal and external, who constantly attempt to impose difficult and often conflicting demands on the CEO and the organization (see Exhibit 9.1). Each set of stakeholders has its own expectations, its own interests, and its own standards for assessing the CEO's performance. The resulting challenge for the CEO is to constantly weigh the importance of these stakeholders and balance their demands against the CEO's own vision, strategy, and expectations.

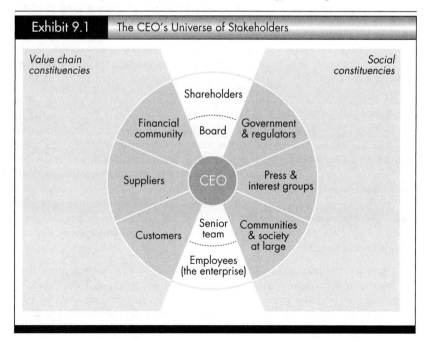

Exhibit 9.1   The CEO's Universe of Stakeholders

The exact nature and relative importance of different stakeholder groups will vary with any given company, but some of these constituencies are always present. At the most basic level, they can be identified as either internal or external stakeholders. The external stakeholders include what we refer to as the *value chain constituencies*—customers, suppliers, strategic partners, and the financial community. There are also external *social* constituencies—which often exert demands that conflict with those of the value chain constituencies—including government agencies, regulators, the press, interest groups, local communities, and society at large. Internally, the CEO deals with several stakeholder *employee* groups who, again, can impose conflicting demands— from the Board to senior management, to the union, and more generally from disgruntled workforce groups. The final stakeholder group, which encompasses both internal and external constituencies, is the *shareholder investor,* ranging from huge institutional investors to day traders, employees, and retirees.

The one aspect of the CEO's job that makes it so unique is that he or she is the only individual in the organization who is in direct contact with—and directly held accountable by—the full universe of stakeholders. No one else in the organization has a job that comes close in terms of scope of responsibility and complexity of major decisions.

Today's CEO is also required to fill a wide array of roles—ambassador and chief spokesman to the outside world, chief strategist, leading deal-maker, articulator of the corporate vision and role model for the company values, cultivator of top talent, immediate supervisor of the top executives, leader of the senior team, and, in most U.S. companies, Chairman of the Board.

On a daily basis, the CEO, more than anyone else, is dealing with the demands, concerns, and expectations of multiple constituencies. In every interaction of every day, CEOs are confronted with issues that represent either a personal or institutional agenda. People seeking access, attention, and approval surround them. As David Kearns, CEO of Xerox through the early 1990s, said shortly after his retirement, "The burden of the job is enormous and you don't realize it fully until you leave it." CEOs are now acutely aware that more than ever before, any misstep can dramatically increase the chances of failure.

One other factor defines the world of the CEO: the old but true cliché that "it's lonely at the top." Anyone who has worked closely with CEOs can attest to the isolation experienced by these powerful executives. They have no peers within their organization. Rarely can they even temporarily step out from behind the desk and share their fears and concerns with anyone in the company. Recently, a new CEO said to me, "The thing that is the greatest surprise to me in this job is the intense and profound loneliness." They are convinced— and rightly so—that every person who comes to see them is there for a reason and with a personal agenda that will color the tone and substance of their interactions. They can never allow themselves the luxury of accepting advice or suggestions at face value.

That's a very difficult way to live and work. Many CEOs harden themselves to that reality and come to the conclusion that the only way to do the job is to keep their own counsel and trust their own instincts. But a growing number have come to realize that they do need unbiased advice, feedback, coaching, new ideas, and fresh perspectives. So they look to professionals who can provide any or all of that. The most prominent among these advisors are lawyers, investment bankers, and, of course, management consultants.

CEOs Are Attractive Clients

Let's be honest; many consultants seek CEO clients for the status this level of work confers. If you are consulting to the top of the organization, it must mean you are at the top of your profession. The nature of the issues involved is challenging and intellectually stimulating. A vicarious thrill comes from being personally involved—even from the sidelines—in decisions that shape a company's future. And if we're truthful with ourselves, we'll admit to the personal satisfaction that comes from having these important, powerful, and sometimes magnetic personalities turn to us for guidance and advice. It would be both silly and dishonest to discount the personal gratification that often comes from consulting at this level.

But more importantly, consulting directly to CEOs offers the greatest opportunity for providing real value to client organizations. The CEO is the key driver of strategic and organizational change. My own consulting experience clearly indicates that profound, sustainable, enterprise-wide change is most often led from the top. As frustrating as the CEO's job might be, only he or she has access to all the levers for implementing major changes—the ability to shape the strategy, the organization structure, the culture, and the talent. The CEO enjoys more degrees of freedom for taking broad action than any other leader in the organization. In the vast majority of situations, he or she is the final decision maker and the ultimate arbiter of all appeals. Consulting directly to the CEO acknowledges that leaders farther down in the organization, no matter how capable, lack the leverage to chart strategy and sustain large-scale change.

By virtue of his or her unique position, the CEO, as we discussed earlier, is in greater need of outside advice. He or she has no peers to turn to in the organization, no internal aide whose advice isn't colored by some agenda. The CEO needs the advice and counsel of an experienced professional whose only agenda should be one of enhancing the CEO's effectiveness and likelihood of success.

Quite often, the kinds of consulting assistance that the CEO needs will depend on certain stages that operate in parallel with the CEO's tenure in office. To be sure, these scenarios vary with changing business conditions, but in general, we find four critical time periods in a CEO's tenure where the consulting needs to be performed differently.

Perplexed New CEO. Many CEOs spend much of their careers working and hoping to land the top job. But once they find out they're actually going to get it, their first reaction is frequently, "Now what do I do? How do I get started, and what should I do first?" Depending upon the circumstances— whether they've been promoted from within or recruited from the outside, whether they're assuming control of a company that's doing well or one that's in deep trouble, whether they've landed the job through an orderly succession plan or been appointed to replace a predecessor who's been suddenly removed, whether they're an industry veteran or newcomer, whether they're inheriting an intact senior team or need to create one overnight—the new

CEO will require help on any number of fronts, ranging from organizational studies to turnaround advice or strategic planning.

Frustrated Sophomore CEO. In this case, a new CEO takes office with a clear strategy and plan of action yet finds after the first year in office that none of the expected changes are actually happening. A few years ago, the second-year CEO of a large pharmaceutical company came to visit me, complaining that he felt like he was on the bridge of a large ship, pulling at the controls and finding that they weren't attached to anything. This individual was confronted by a syndrome that frustrates many sophomore CEOs; they're doing all the things they thought were necessary to set a new course to improve performance, but none of their tactics seem to have much impact. They turn to the outside for help in identifying the barriers and in locating the real levers for implementing successful organizational change.

Worried Mid-term CEO. Given the nature of today's business environment, it is inevitable that every CEO will experience at least one—and probably more than one—episode of major crisis that will require radical, large-scale change in the organization, including its structure, systems, and culture. It might result from new forms of competition, disruptive technologies, and shifts in public policy. But whatever the cause, the organization has to find fundamentally new ways of doing business. Few organizations have the internal capacity to design, lead, manage, and sustain that kind of transformational change without outside help.

Reflecting Late-term CEO. As they approach the natural end of their tenures, many CEOs become concerned with managing the selection and development of their successor and with shaping their own legacy. On numerous occasions, I've been approached by CEOs with very few years to go, realizing that they had significant succession problems, yet no one to talk to about the candidates and the evaluation criteria—except perhaps an uninformed and passive Board. These CEOs require confidential advice and candid soul-searching that only outside experts can provide.

Understanding the Spectrum of Consulting Roles

The ability of senior consultants to provide value beyond their particular areas of expertise underscores the paramount importance of the relationship between the consultant and the client and highlights the critical relationship between the content of the consulting issue at hand and the behavioral approach that is employed to engage the client with the content. In other words, every outside advisor is interacting with the CEO along two key dimensions, represented as the vertical and horizontal axes in Exhibit 9.2.

- **Ideas versus Actions:** Does the advisor bring fresh perspectives, information on best practices, or a new "Big Idea," or is he assisting the CEO to identify specific actions to take in order to address a specific issue?

- **Prescriptive versus Facilitative:** Does the advisor recommend a specific decision, or does he see his role as helping the client to identify a range of alternatives and providing a process through which the client can make the most appropriate choice?

Exhibit 9.2	Roles for Consulting to CEOs

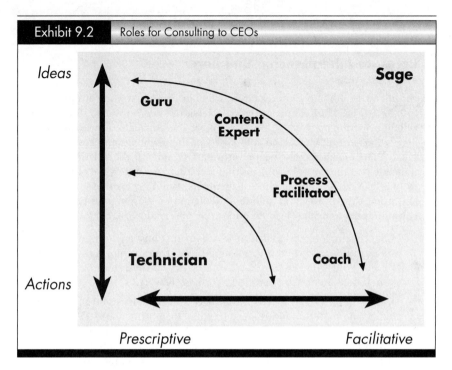

The work of every consultant, specialist, and advisor to CEOs combines some mix of these two dimensions. Their interplay suggests that most CEO-level consulting falls into one or more of six roles, which we define as follows:

- **Technician:** Highly prescriptive about specific actions the CEO should take (e.g., crisis communications, legal strategies for handling specific litigation).

- **Guru:** Also highly prescriptive, but with focuses on concepts or ideas at an abstract level, rather than specific actions.

- **Content Expert:** Somewhat prescriptive, offering strategic advice and opinions on areas of specialization to the individual consultant, such as leadership, strategy, or organization change.

- **Process Facilitator:** Brings participative skills and approach to help clients identify for themselves the problems facing them and to create their own solutions.

- **Coach:** A pure facilitation role to individuals, focusing on the client's personal development rather than on broader organizational issues.

- **Sage:** A rare and unique role where the CEO has a relationship with an advisor who brings new ideas but interacts in a facilitative manner to help the CEO think through significant issues. This role is usually enacted in combination with one or more of the other roles.

Of course, these role designations are somewhat narrow and arbitrary; consulting relationships, particularly those that extend over a period of years, become quite complex, and the dividing lines between categories grow fuzzy. And that's our point; consulting relationships, like any other relationships, are dynamic and evolving. If they're successful, they change, deepen, and grow with the passage of time and the CEO's time in the position.

Roles and Relationship Building

As we reflect on these different approaches and roles, we assume that the consultant is ultimately interested in two objectives. First, the consultant seeks to have *impact*. The real measure of professional and personal effectiveness is whether anything is different as a result of the engagement with the client. Second, at the CEO level, the complexity of the problems and context usually mean that impact cannot occur without *continuity* in the relationship over time. Most of the critical problems that the CEO encounters are not amenable to one-shot single interaction engagements. Building on these assumptions and using this approach as a general depiction of the range of possible CEO consulting relationships, I would offer these observations:

- Successful, long-term advisors can start in almost any of the roles but almost invariably end up combining two or more roles. Less effective consultants tend to get stuck where they started, both in terms of their content domain and single form of delivery.

- In addition to specific roles, the successful consultant must always fill the role of "trusted advisor." In their insightful book, *The Trusted Advisor*,[4] Maister, Green, and Galford suggest that trustworthiness results from the interplay of four key components: credibility, reliability, intimacy, and, the one to be wary of, self-orientation. It's an interesting way of defining a complex relationship; as the term "trusted advisor" continues to gain currency, there will undoubtedly be others. But the underlying idea is right: Technical expertise, in the absence of a trusting relationship, will result in seriously diminished opportunities for impact.

Again, the consultant's technical expertise or superior knowledge is usually the natural starting point for a consulting engagement but only the first step toward becoming a long-term, trusted advisor to the CEO. So it is important to understand how these rare relationships are developed and sustained over time.

Developing the CEO Relationship

The role of "trusted advisor" to a CEO is the goal, not the starting point, of a consultative relationship. Almost always, the relationship begins with a specific assignment and a particular piece of work. If the relationship progresses well, the focus moves from narrow, segmented work to a broader role that can involve helping the CEO to develop and implement a much wider range of decisions. The important point is that the relationship has to evolve naturally; consultants who walk into the room for the first time and immediately attempt to create an artificial "trusted advisor" relationship are doomed to failure.

My own experience suggests that several elements are critical to building this relationship—a list not too dissimilar from that suggested by *The Trusted Advisor*.[5] First and foremost, the relationship must be built on a foundation of substantive, *high-quality work*, and beneficial advice. It doesn't matter how terrific the personal chemistry may be between the consultant and the CEO if the substantive work doesn't add value and the advice doesn't make sense; here, the relationship isn't going anywhere.

The second critical element goes to the tone of the engagement process; the consultant should be *respectful* of the client yet willing to confront him or her on critical issues. It's a delicate balance, to be sure but the point must be made early on that the consultant is not just another member of the CEO's staff and is prepared to push back—and push back aggressively—if the CEO seems to avoid an issue or discount important data.

Trust is the third critical element. Over time, the consultant must demonstrate a commitment to total confidentiality and the ability to consistently deliver information accurately, completely, and dispassionately, without distortion, exaggeration, or "spin." The CEO must become completely confident that the consultant isn't taking advantage of their special relationship. The trusted consultant cannot send inappropriate messages to others in the organization or, conversely, to act as a conduit for underlings who want to pursue personal agendas by conveying information through the consultant.

The final element is *positive personal engagement.* In essence, this is the corollary of the first element. Without substantive, value-added work and advice, the relationship goes nowhere; yet, as one of my clients once observed, "If I don't enjoy the personal relationship, it doesn't matter how smart you are—I won't keep working with you." Personal chemistry is critical to the trusted advisor relationship.

Process Determines Content

The process of consulting to CEOs has certain similarities to consultation with other clients, but there are also important differences. For one thing, asking questions can often be far more effective than providing answers to CEOs. By nature, most CEOs tend not to be highly introspective; they are oriented toward action. In that role, it's essential to be able to make decisions and then quickly move on, not spending much time on reflection or second-guessing. Given their range of responsibilities, they have to be able to do that. The consultant can play an important and unique role by providing the CEO with a safe space in which to step back and reflect privately and confidentially on concerns, doubts, and sources of anxiety about impending business decisions. The simple question, "What's keeping you awake in the middle of the night?" may sound a bit trite, but it's amazing the revealing responses it often elicits.

The process of consulting to CEOs emphasizes discussion over explanation and authoritative conclusions. The real value of this consultation comes from informal give and take, not formal presentations. Certainly, there are situations—generally, in group settings—where the CEO will want to see data presented in a formal way. Nor does the idea of discussion diminish the importance of careful preparation for each private meeting with the CEO. But these meetings have to be tailored to the CEO's schedule, energy, and priorities, and the consultant must have the flexibility to use whatever time is available in the most beneficial way.

A good deal of value that the consultant may provide comes from structuring information so as to give a fresh viewpoint. It is not that the consultant brings brand new information (although he or she might), but that the consultant provides a cognitive "frame" to structure significant bits of information in ways that are informative, insightful, and meaningful to the client. One can think of the consultant as not only gathering data but transforming these data into new knowledge about the situation and, ultimately, this knowledge into action. The value, therefore, comes from helping the client to look at an existing situation in a new way.

Sometimes the most important service the consultant provides to the CEO is to simply listen. As mentioned previously, the CEO experiences a tremendous sense of loneliness and isolation; his or her typical day is frequently filled with issues and problems that can't be discussed candidly with anyone in the organization. Like any of us, a CEO sometimes needs an outlet to just vent anger, frustration, or anxiety. The consultant should understand that at times the best way to help is to listen, because the CEO isn't really looking for advice—just a safe audience.

Dilemmas in Consulting to CEOs

Consulting to CEOs not only requires some unique processes, it also presents the very real possibility of encountering some difficult dilemmas that arise in the relationship. These are among the most challenging issues:

- **Insulation:** Over the course of their tenures, CEOs tend to become more isolated.[6] In their early years in office, they reach out to the organization and develop multiple contacts and sources of information. As time passes, and they become more comfortable in their jobs, they tend to rely on a relatively limited number of trusted subordinates for their information. Consultants must be wary of duplicating that same pattern. All too often, in the latter stages of the relationship, consultants restrict their interactions to the CEO and perhaps one or two other senior executives, which severely limits the value they can bring to the CEO in terms of objective information and different perspectives. Consultants to CEOs must seek information from many sources, not just ones recommended or arranged by the CEO.

- **Clientship:** Sooner or later, many CEO consultants face an incredibly difficult question: Who is the real client—the individual or the organization? The simplistic answer is that there's no conflict; by helping the CEO perform effectively, the consultant is providing value to the entire enterprise. But in some situations, it becomes evident that the CEO is simply incapable of providing the kind of leadership that the organization needs in order to address severe challenges, and no amount of coaching or advice will help. Consequently, is there some point at which the consultant should conclude that the organization would be better off with a different CEO? There is no easy answer; it's important to recognize that it's a perplexing dilemma that comes with the territory. One approach I have taken is to consciously and deliberately discuss with the CEO whether he or she is capable and willing to undertake the tough decisions required by the situation. If not, then I have, at times, terminated my relationship with the CEO and the organization rather than collude with the CEO to sustain the perception that the festering issues are being solved. I refer to this as "calling the question"—the point at which a consultant needs to question whether the CEO client has the capacity to do the job.

- **Influence Balance:** CEO consultants run the constant risk of being perceived in the organization as having either too much or too little influence. The role requires an endless balancing act. If you're perceived as having insufficient influence, it becomes difficult to get on people's calendars, to get invited to the right meetings, and to be privy to necessary information. On the other hand, consultants can sometimes be perceived as a kind of Svengali, the mysterious figure behind the curtain who is really pulling all the strings—a role people come to resent and one that severely limits the consultant's effectiveness. It is important for the consultant to display an aura of independence while displaying openness without violating anyone's confidence.

- **Backstairs Channel:** As mentioned previously, people who perceive a close relationship between the consultant and the CEO will seek ways to use the consultant as a conduit to the executive office. The consultant must be careful to maintain relationships with others in the organization without being used as a tool for advancing other people's agendas. And if from above the CEO asks, "Who said that?" you reply in words that are slightly more polite than "It's none of your business."

- **Over-Identification:** It's inevitable, over time, that a close association with the CEO will color the consultant's view of people and issues in the organization. That's a natural consequence of being privy to information that others don't have; you begin to tell yourself, "If they knew what the CEO knows (and what I know), they'd understand this decision." It's essential not to become so close to the CEO that your perspective becomes indistinguishable. At that point, the consultant loses the ability to broaden the CEO's thinking.

- **Inflated Ego:** Some CEO consultants tend to forget that they are consultants, not CEOs. They get carried away with their own sense of influence, power, and access. They become insufferably arrogant; they forget that they're in the room to give advice, not to make decisions. Another variant of this is frequent dropping of the CEO's name, which can easily become perceived as transparent self-enhancement. The ego-inflated consultant becomes intoxicated as a result of closeness to "the throne."

- **Assessing People:** In the course of the relationship, as the CEO gains trust in the consultant's judgment, it's inevitable for the CEO to seek the consultant's assessment of certain individuals in the organization. That is a dangerous path to go down; it's risky, even irresponsible for the consultant to offer an assessment based on limited interactions with those being assessed. And if word gets out that the CEO is obtaining these assessments, the nature of the consultant's dealings with other executives becomes tainted by fear and suspicion. The consultant's independent role needs to be made clear, and if executives are to be assessed, the consultant can help assure a fair process and assessment of the job to be filled, without personally entering into the selection of the individual. But the fact remains that the CEO will want to know what the consultant thinks, and will continue to ask, so be ready with a response.

Clearly, the relationship between the trusted advisor and the CEO is fraught with danger. To be successful, and to provide real value to the client, the consultant must bring to the table a rare combination of content knowledge and process skills. He or she must understand that consulting to CEOs requires the same abilities needed to succeed with clients at lower levels, and then a whole set of unique capabilities beyond that. It is a role that requires maturity, confidence, keen intellect, and emotional insight. Not too many consultants can play successfully at this level, but those who do earn the satisfaction of influencing the direction and performance of entire organizations.

CONSULTING TO THE BOARD

The pressure on Boards to accept greater accountability for their companies' performance has grown dramatically through the 1990s and into the twenty-first century. Spurred on by shareholder demands for consistently high stock performance, by outside pressures from "good governance" groups such as the CALPERS pension fund, and by greatly intensified scrutiny by the business press, Boards have begun paying much closer attention to "scorecard" issues such as Board composition, compensation, and meeting frequency. The Enron collapse accelerated attention to Board oversight issues (e.g., revised NYSE and NASDAQ corporate governance rules and the Sarbanes-Oxley Act), causing directors to quickly become concerned about their legal exposure related to their handling of Board oversight responsibilities.

As was already the case with CEOs, Boards are now looking to outsiders for guidance and expert help. However, the content and process of Board consultation offers some marked contrasts with CEO consulting.

Content of Board Consulting

To date, the legal responsibilities of Corporate Boards in the United States are actually fairly minimal. According to the respected legal handbook, *Liability of Corporate Officers and Directors,*[7] the Board's role generally encompasses six basic responsibilities:

- Approving major corporate actions (e.g., acquisitions, divestitures, stock splits, etc.)
- Providing counsel to senior management
- Overseeing management's performance, setting executive compensation, hiring and dismissing the CEO
- Ensuring effective audit procedures
- Ensuring that nonmanagement perspectives are heard and considered when major decisions are made
- Regularly monitoring the company's investments for legal compliance

A Board can limit its activities to these five areas and comply with its statutory obligations. However, growing public concern for improved Board performance suggests that this level of compliance is likely not enough. In their recent book, *Corporate Boards: Strategies for Adding Value at the Top,*[8] Conger, Lawler, and Finegold argue that Boards should go beyond their legal mandates to focus on five additional areas that will assure better governance:

- **Strategic direction and advice:** a largely advisory role to the CEO and executive team, but one that capitalizes on the variety of business skills and backgrounds assembled around the Board table.

- **Oversight of strategy implementation and performance:** Approving major financial and capital investments, setting benchmarks for organizational performance, and holding the CEO and executive team responsible for meeting strategic goals.

- **Developing human capital:** Overseeing succession planning and compensation strategies for senior management and evaluating CEO performance, exercising ultimate authority on hiring and dismissal of the CEO.

- **Crisis management and prevention:** Planning for the Board's role in various crisis situations, brainstorming crisis scenarios, and instigating processes that will raise "red flags" that might signal potential crises.

- **Procuring resources:** Assisting management, particularly in smaller or newer companies, in obtaining the necessary financing, talent, technology, and strategic relationships.

Board's Unique Process Issues

Both of these frameworks that we've just discussed—the chartered legal obligations and additional areas of responsibility—focus on the substantive content of the Board's work. These set the Board's working agenda, and an effective Board will address it with serious intent. It is a large agenda, going beyond what most Boards in the past saw as their limited responsibility.

In addition, one of the most interesting developments in the evolution of corporate governance over the past decade has been the growing realization that the Board's working processes—the ways in which its members engage each other and senior management—constitute a critical component of Board performance and effectiveness, and for two key reasons.

The first is that in legal proceedings—a cause of increasing concern to Boards—the courts have established the so-called "business judgment rule" as a legal defense that can be invoked by directors in liability cases. Recognizing that judges and courts are not necessarily qualified to second-guess the correctness of complex business decisions, the courts have chosen instead to focus on a Boards' decision-making processes. In other words, rather than trying to evaluate the precise content of Board decisions, the courts are weighing the processes and procedures used in reaching decisions. Special attention is being given to whether the Board acted with the corporation's best interests in mind, was well informed, acted within the bounds of the law, and avoided conflicts of interest.[9, 10]

A second factor that has elevated interest in Board processes is the growing emphasis on the need for Boards to do "real work," as opposed to performing mainly ceremonial duties. In the past, Boards were merely disparate groups of individuals who gathered four times a year to rubber stamp management's recommendations and then adjourn for cocktails. It didn't really matter whether the Board's work processes were designed to achieve high performance; it was simply irrelevant. Now, as Boards feel growing pressure to demonstrate their active involvement and sharp oversight over important corporate issues, the Board's ability to collectively perform substantive work, and to perform it well, is a serious issue. In fact, new regulations and guidelines create clear responsibilities for the Board and specifically for certain committees, such as the audit committee and the nominating/corporate governance committee.

Levels of Board Engagement

One way of thinking about Board performance is to consider the level of engagement of the Board in the affairs of the company. As illustrated in Exhibit 9.3, engagement can be thought of as a continuum of nonaction to being highly active. At one end is the Passive Board, essentially disengaged from the running of the company. This model, while prevalent historically, is no longer viable. At the other end is the Operating Board, which is actually attempting to manage the company on a day-to-day basis. While this latter model may be used during a crisis period (such as following the removal of a CEO), it is clearly not a long-term solution and violates the basic principal of the Board's legal role to ensure effective management but not to usurp management in making daily decisions.

The Board's challenge, therefore, is to attempt a balancing act in the middle of the engagement spectrum where active policy guidance and oversight are given for the business, for the stakeholders, and for the individuals involved—while at the same time avoiding acts of micro-management. Given current public scrutiny on Boards, they need to resist the temptation to tilt toward operational management (see Exhibit 9.3).

This balancing act leads to two implications: First, CEOs and Boards need to determine the appropriate level and scope of engagement for a particular Board in a specific company context. Second, CEOs must develop what I call "constructive engagement strategies," or carefully planned approaches to engagement through making changes in a range of levers that affect direction of the company, including structure, process, composition, and leadership. This is where consultants can be of considerable help.

Implications for Consulting to Boards

Traditionally, Boards have sought assistance from outside specialists whose technical expertise is limited to activities encompassed by the Boards' legal obligations. These advisors generally included lawyers, auditors, investment bankers, compensation experts, and executive recruiters. Over time, the "good governance" ground-swell has led gradually to more Boards seeking out a small group of consultants—primarily academics and single practitioners—to advise them on such issues as Board composition, committee roles and structures, meeting frequency, and appropriate agenda.

Today, the growing emphasis on Board processes and new corporate governance requirements is creating a demand for a new form of consulting—new, at least, in the realm of corporate governance. In particular, Boards are beginning to ask for expert help concerning the Board's own internal processes—how the directors engage with each other to fulfill their legal obligations and pursue their other governance activities in ways that truly add value. A second and related area involves the Board's interactions with the CEO and the Chairman—who might or might not be the same individual.

Taken together, these new developments lead me to suggest four major implications for consulting to Boards:

1. While Boards will continue to need and to seek out technical expertise in a variety of legal and financial areas directly related to their statutory obligations, there will be a dramatic expansion of Board interest in improving the process and dynamics of governance itself.

| Exhibit 9.3 | Levels of Board Engagement |

The Passive Board	The Certifying Board	The Engaged Board	The Intervening Board	The Operating Board
• Functions at discretion of CEO • Limited activity and participation of Board • Limited accountability • Ratifying management preferences	• "Certifies" to Shareholders that CEO is doing what Board expects; Management is capable of taking corrective action when needed • Emphasizes outside/ independent directors; meets independently without the CEO • Stays informed of current performance; designates external Board members to evaluate CEO • Establishes an orderly succession process • Is willing and able to change management to be credible to shareholders	• "Partners" with CEO to provide insight, advice, and support to CEO and management team on key decisions and implementation • Also recognizes ultimate responsibility to oversee CEO and company performance; dual role of guiding/ supporting as well as judging the CEO • Board meetings characterized by useful two-way discussions of key issues/ decisions facing the company • Board members need sufficient industry and financial expertise to add value to decisions • Time and emphasis spent on defining role and behaviors required of Board members; boundaries of CEO/Board responsibility	• Typical mode during a "crisis" situation • Board becomes intensely involved in discussions of key decisions facing the organization and in decision making • Frequent and intense Board meetings, often called on short notice	• Board makes key decisions; management implements • Not uncommon in early "start-ups" where Board members selected to "fill gaps" in management experience

2. The key to process improvement involves dynamics rather than mechanics. If the Board is willing, the mechanics of its work processes—composition, committee structures, meeting agendas—can be fixed fairly easily with help from consultants operating in the content expert role. But the essence of Board performance lies in the group's dynamics, not the mechanics. You can fix the mechanics but still fail to achieve high performance if the dynamics are wrong.

3. Consequently, the consulting work with the biggest payoff to Boards will take what we already know about high-performing executive teams and adapt relevant concepts to the unique dynamics of the Board. This approach implies a fundamentally new view that an effective Board should operate as a real team, not as a collection of individual stars with big resumes. They should work collectively and cohesively to accomplish outcomes that they couldn't achieve individually. It assumes that Board members will interact and actively engage to perform real work, a marked difference from the traditional pattern of one or two Board members acting in concert with senior management to lay the groundwork for periodic meetings that consisted of nothing more than perfunctory votes and well-rehearsed presentations.

4. Corporate governance will be enhanced when the Board functions as an effective team, using appropriate levels of engagement and building a collaborative relationship with the CEO. My prescription for a collaborative relationship between CEOs and Boards differs dramatically from what has been the norm in many companies. Some CEOs view their Boards as a necessary evil at best or as an interfering nuisance at worst. Others view their Boards as a valuable sounding board but little more. Conversely, from the board members' perspective, those directors who believe they've been anointed with an honorary position requiring nothing more than filling a seat at occasional meetings and the radical idea of partnering with other directors and the CEO to do real work will require a major attitudinal shift.

Transforming the Board into a Team

Without question, Boards differ in significant ways from other teams: The Board's work tends to be episodic in nature, occurs in a unique legal context, involves varying patterns of inclusion because of its committee structure, and generally takes place when the team is all together rather than communicating during the intervening periods between meetings. But there are also major similarities to teams, in general, involving the dynamics of leadership, the importance of communication, and the diffuse distribution of power.[11] As stated earlier, the key for effective consultants will be to understand both the differences and similarities and to adapt what we already know from executive team building to the Board's unique requirements.

My consulting experience with Boards suggests that, despite the characteristics that differentiate Boards from other teams, a team-building approach that we have used successfully with CEO-led executive teams over the years also applies, in large part, to transforming Boards into high-performance teams.

This approach spells out two key dimensions of team performance. The first is *production of results* —the team's ability to fulfill its obligations and to provide valuable leadership. The second dimension is what I describe as *maintenance of effectiveness*—the team's ability not only to work together effectively but also to continue doing that over time in the face of new situations or challenges. The two are closely linked; the team's effectiveness must be maintained to ensure consistently high results.

What is it, then, that influences these two dimensions of performance? Three core processes are critical:

- **Work Management:** How the team organizes and manages itself to perform work, set agendas, make decisions, and coordinate the activities of its sub-teams (i.e. committees)

- **Relationship Management:** How the team manages personal interactions on issues such as conflict resolution and decision making in ways that engender trust, openness, and cohesiveness

- **External Boundary Management:** How the Board defines its relationships with the rest of the organization and with important individuals and major constituencies outside the organization (e.g., the investment community, the press, government regulators, etc.)

The effectiveness of these three key processes is heavily influenced by the Board's composition and structure. The "good governance" movement has focused on composition in several areas—the balance of internal versus external directors, the individual's age and CEO experience, potential conflicts of interest, and the use of "professional directors" who serve on so many Boards that they can't possibly give sufficient attention to each Board. These issues are important, although it is by no means clear that even when Boards meet the "good governance" composition criteria they are more effective than Boards that do not.[12] Instead, my experience suggests that the more important dimensions are the willingness of directors to engage in hard work and their ability to work collaboratively with the CEO in a positive team environment. Today, we are seeing strong support for a team approach amidst the current trend away from Boards dominated by only a few active and influential committee chairmen.

As more and more Boards begin working with consultants on their internal processes, much of this effort should focus on the real work of team building (see Exhibit 9.4), which addresses five leverage points for shaping effective processes:

- **Goals:** Exactly what is the value-added work the Board can and should be doing collectively—in other words, what is the most beneficial way for these time-constrained people, who meet fairly infrequently, to spend their time together?

- **Roles:** What requirements should each Board member be expected to meet, and what specialized roles are necessary?

- **Procedures:** How will the team design and manage its agendas, structure its meetings, and share its information?

- **Interactions:** What "rules of the road" will guide the behavior and personal interactions among directors?

- **Quality Assurance:** What processes should the Board use periodically to monitor their own effectiveness as a team? This has now become a requirement, since the NYSE is expecting regular assessment of both the Board as a whole and its individual committees.

It is in the above areas that Boards will benefit most from expert consulting assistance. The successful consultant should possess both strong content knowledge and facilitation skills regarding executive team building. It will also likely require the consultant to sit in on Board meetings to observe the interaction and to help the Board critique itself.

Exhibit 9.4	Team-Building Framework

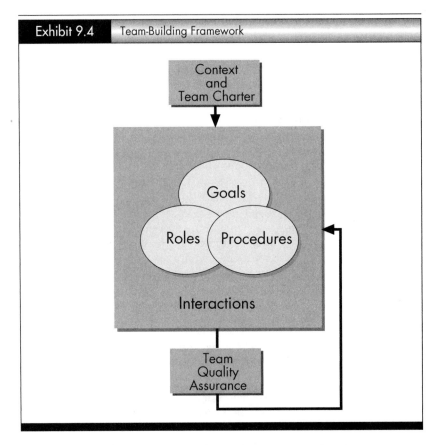

RELATIONSHIP BETWEEN BOARDS AND CEOS

Throughout this chapter, I've largely dealt with consulting to CEOs and Boards as separate issues, but they are obviously related. The CEO is directly accountable to the Board for the organization's performance. Collectively, the Board is the "boss" with ultimate authority for the CEO's compensation, terms of employment, and selection of a successor. As the representative of the shareholders, the Board constitutes one of the CEO's most important stakeholder groups. So it is impossible for a consultant to work closely with a CEO on matters affecting strategic and financial issues, the CEO's performance, and succession planning without also helping the CEO to think through and work on his or her relationship with the Board.

For those consulting either to Boards or to CEOs or to both, it is important to recognize that the CEO is the single most important individual in terms of the Board's ability to exert influence over the company's management, direction, and performance. And in the majority of companies, the CEO also chairs the Board, which makes him or her a critical player in any serious work intended to address the Board's work processes and dynamics.

Thus, the intricate relationship between these two clients—the CEO and the Board—raises some difficult and challenging questions for the consultant. These dilemmas do not yet have standard solutions, and so I haven't provided any. It's doubtful if there will ever be any obvious and uniform solutions because each situation is unique.

Who is the client? For a consultant working with both the CEO and Board of a company, who is the real client? For instance, more and more Boards are reconsidering the sufficiency of their processes for assessing the CEO's performance. In theory, both the CEO and the Board—not to mention the enterprise as a whole—should benefit from an explicit, transparent, and collaborative process that provides regular oversight while avoiding any rude surprises to any of the parties involved. In reality, not all CEOs favor a more formal process. When push comes to shove, whose interests are the consultant there to serve? The fact of the matter is that there might well be an inherent conflict in consulting to both the CEO and the Board.

Where there are potential conflicts, three alternative approaches are available in defining the client relationship. The first approach is where only the CEO retains a consultant to help him or her deal with the Board and its relationship with the CEO. The second approach is where the Board retains a consultant on its own. A third approach is where both the Board and the CEO agree to collaborate to obtain help. Obviously, when one party wants a consultant and the other objects (either to hiring a consultant or to the specific choice of advisor), then a very problematic condition is created where it is difficult to provide services in a constructive manner. In all of these situations, it is important to define explicitly for all parties involved who will receive what forms of information and advice, and when.

How are the trusted advisor and advocacy roles balanced? As consultants become more involved in corporate governance, they are likely to develop points of view about what constitutes good governance. At the same time, many sitting CEOs have been reluctant to institute major changes in governance processes. As the consultant becomes more committed to change and the client becomes more resistant, the consultant may find him or herself pushed into the role of advocate rather than advisor, thereby complicating the relationship.

How do you work when the roles of CEO and chairman are separate? How does this type of consulting play out when the CEO is also the chairman versus when the CEO may sit on the Board but another individual is the chairman? This separation of the CEO and chairman roles is relatively rare in the United States—only about 25 percent of companies employ this and mostly for purposes of transition. Outside the United States, and especially in the U.K. and Western Europe, this structure of separation is more prevalent.

How do you maintain continuity? By their very nature, Boards are episodic. They meet together, but only periodically. Virtually every nonexecutive director has other demands and obligations that consume more attention (most of the time) than any one Board on which he or she serves. When consulting to this type of client, the question is how to maintain continuity so that the work during one period builds on the work done previously to have an impact on the Board.

How do decisions get made? The efficacy of a consulting relationship ultimately depends upon the ability of the client to make and implement decisions—to take action. By definition, Boards are usually reactive—they respond to situations, questions, and decisions placed before them by the Chairman/CEO. When a Board may have to make a decision "by itself" (including the decision to retain a consultant), it may run into problems. The frequent lack of clear decision-making processes and rules combined with the episodic nature of the Board make it difficult for them to make decisions when on their own. This is an example of the old consulting dilemma that I call "the problem is the problem." The problem the Board is trying to solve concerns its group processes, but these very same problems get in the way of making a decision to seek help.

Reflecting on these dilemmas, I follow some simple general guidelines when I encounter any of them:

- Avoid, to the extent possible, getting involved in political conflicts between the Board and the CEO.

- Be open and honest with all parties, yet protect confidential communication.

- Work to facilitate solutions that are helpful to both the Board and the CEO through well-informed discussion and mutual agreement.

The consultant must be aware that conflicts and dilemmas are always present and needs to be ready to deal with them. Specific "tailor-made" answers have to be developed for each situation. Although there's a considerable body of knowledge and experience regarding consulting to CEOs, we are just now witnessing the first stages of an entirely new discipline of process consulting to Boards. The broad outlines are taking shape, but the details and nuances will become much clearer through more practical experience.

KNOW THYSELF AND THY CLIENT

Consulting to the senior-level figures in corporate governance offers enormous opportunities, both for consultants and their clients, yet this unique role presents serious questions and significant risks. It is no place for amateurs or rookies; only the most talented and experienced consultants are likely to succeed, while drawing upon a wealth of personal experience and a deep reservoir of confidence, courage, empathy, and integrity. Beyond that, consultants who try to swim in these deep waters must possess an unusual degree of self-awareness and self-confidence, meaning they must understand their personal strengths and weaknesses and be exceptionally clear about the kinds of technical expertise, content knowledge, and intervention steps that will work best, both for themselves and for their demanding clients.

Notes to the Chapter

[1]"Report of the NYSE Corporate Accountability and Listing Standards Committee," June 6, 2002.

[2]"Nasdaq Approves Rule Changes to Modify Key Corporate Governance Standard," Nasdaq Press Release, May 24, 2002.

[3]"Corporate and Criminal Fraud Accountability Act of 2002 (Sarbanes-Oxley Act)," Pub. L., No. 107–204, 116 Stat. 745, July 30, 2002.

[4]David H. Maister, Charles H. Green, and Robert M. Gailford, The Trusted Advisor (New York: The Free Press, 2000).

[5]Maister *et.al.*

[6]Sydney Finkelstein and Donald C. Hambrick, *Strategic Leadership: Top Executives and their Effects on Organizations* (Mason, Ohio: South-Western College Publishing, 1996).

[7]William E. Kepper and Dan A. Bailey, *Liability of Corporate Officers and Directors* (Charlottesville, Virginia: The Michie Co., 1998).

[8]Jay Alden Conger, Edward E. Lawler, III, and David L. Finegold, *Corporate Boards: Strategies for Adding Value at the Top* (San Francisco: Jossey-Bass, Inc., 2001).

[9]Jay W. Lorsch and Elizabeth MacIver, *Pawns or Potentates: The Realities of America's Corporate Boards* (Boston: Harvard Business School Publishing, 1989).

[10]Conger *et al.*

[11]David and Spencer.

[12]Conger *et al.*

Additional Bibliography

Carucci, Ron A., and William A. Pasmore. *Relationships That Enable Enterprise Change: Leveraging the Client-Consultant Connection.* New York: John Wiley & Sons, 2002.

Charan, R., and C. Crocker. *Boards at Work.* San Francisco: Jossey-Bass, Inc., 1997.

Chautard, C. Personal Communication. 2002.

Conger, J. A., Edward E. Lawler, III, and David, L. Finegold. *Corporate Boards: Strategies for Adding Value at the Top.* San Francisco: Jossey-Bass, Inc., 2001.

Finkelstein, Sydney, and Donald C. Hambrick. *Strategic Leadership: Top Exec and Effect.* Mason, Ohio: South Western College Publishing, 1996.

Knepper, William E., and Dan A. Bailey, *Liability of Corporate Officers and Directors,* 2 vols. Charlottesville, VA: The Michie Co., 1998.

Lorsch, Jay W. and Elizabeth MacIver. *Pawns or Potentates: The Reality of America's Corporate Boards.* Boston: Harvard Business School Publishing, 1989.

Maister, David H., Charles H. Green, and Robert M. Galford. *The Trusted Advisor.* New York: The Free Press, 2000.

Nadler, David A. (1998). "From ritual to real work: The board as a team." *Directors and Boards,* Summer Issue, 28–31.

Nadler, David A., and Janet L. Spencer. *Executive Teams.* San Francisco: Jossey-Bass, Inc., 1998.

Nasdaq Press Release, May 24 (2002). Nasdaq Approves Rule Changes to Modify Key Cororate Governance Standard (May 24, 2002). Available at: http://www.nasdaqnews.com/news/pr2002/ne_section02_113.html; http://www.nasdaqnews.com.

Report of the NYSE Corporate Accountability and Listing Standards Committee, June 6 (2002). Available at: http://nyse.com/press/NT00565884.html

Sarbanes-Oxley Act. Corporate and Criminal Fraud Accountability Act of 2002. Pub. L., No. 107–204, 116 Stat. 745, July 30, 2002.

Tushman, Michael L., David A. Nadler, and Donald C. Hambrick, eds. *Navigating Change: How CEOs, Top Teams and Boards Steer Transformation.* Boston: Harvard Business School Publishing, 1997.

CHAPTER 10

Globalization Consulting
Stephen H. Rhinesmith, CDR International

ABOUT THE AUTHOR

Stephen H. Rhinesmith

Stephen H. Rhinesmith is a partner in CDR International and focuses on global business strategy implementation and human resource development. Dr. Rhinesmith has served as a consultant to many Fortune 100 corporations on the development of global competencies and corporate cultures. His recent book, *A Manager's Guide to Globalization,* is used in management and leadership development programs throughout the world.

The word "globalization" today evokes diverse and often negative images in the public media. In Seattle, Prague, and Washington, D.C., young people hold banners denouncing what they see as the abuses of "globalization." In Frankfurt, London, and Hong Kong, anxious traders wait to see the impact of volatile markets in the United States. And in Tehran, Singapore, and Jakarta, people complain about the impact of Western values and technology on the religious and cultural traditions that have given meaning to their lives and the lives of their forefathers.

While these political portraits of globalization dominate headlines throughout the world, many business people experience globalization in a very different way. They are challenged by market entry into China, the adaptation of products for newly emerging Russia, competitive forces from Korea, and the new demands of global customers everywhere. For these executives, globalization presents numerous challenges for new leadership and management practices, such as: what kind of global strategy and structure to adopt for their organizations; how supply chains can be designed and managed most efficiently; and which managers will be successful in leading new initiatives in foreign lands?

Imagine you are the managing director of a European firm in 2005, establishing a beachhead for new operations in Russia. You do not know entry conditions for your business or the potential risks of doing business there. Your first reaction is to examine your experience in other Eastern European or newly emerging countries to determine what lessons can be learned. You may conduct an inventory of your managers to see who has foreign experience that could allow them to be redeployed. Or, if you lack internal resources and experience, you may turn to McKinsey, Monitor Company, Booz Allen, or the Boston Consulting Group to conduct a study on the feasibility of developing a competitive business for you in Russia.

Growth of Globalization Consulting

In response to these needs, a new field of "globalization consulting" is clearly an attractive opportunity. Over the last forty years, a wide range of professionals from countless disciplines have developed theories, methods, and practices to meet the challenges of operating globally. To date, however, "globalization consulting" has not been formally analyzed as a professional practice. A quick search of Amazon.com books reveals zero matches under "Globalization Consulting" or "Global Consulting."

The only general management consulting firms explicitly offering services defined as "Globalization" are McKinsey through its Global Strategy Practice and the McKinsey Global Institute, and the Boston Consulting Group through its "Globalization Practice" that "helps companies navigate the opportunities and risks of the new global business environment."[1] In addition, many IT-oriented consulting firms have multiple offices covering the world, including Accenture and IBM Global Services, and there are numerous smaller national, regional, and local consulting firms offering assistance to clients with interests in particular geographies.

In this chapter, I will identify several key issues facing clients attempting to globalize; look at the main emerging practice areas; examine future opportunities in globalization consulting; and explore qualities and characteristics of consultants and firms working in the global arena.

Globalization Defined

What does "globalization" mean for a business, and what is globalization consulting? Globalization is more than simply exporting or "going international." A company may conduct business in 100 countries around the world, and still not be global. Globalization is not *where* you do business, but *how* you do business. It involves the transfer of knowledge and resources from one country to another to achieve competitiveness and profitability through new product development, economic efficiency, or customer responsiveness (see Consulting Insights on Colgate-Palmolive Vision).

FRAMEWORK FOR GLOBALIZATION CONSULTING

Nine Step Model

The first major challenge in globalization is convincing senior executives to develop a multi-year, integrated, and multi-step strategy for global development. Based on my consulting experience, I have developed a roadmap, Nine Steps to Globalization (see Exhibit 10.1), which outlines the key steps and the overall processes that an organization must go through to become more truly global. These nine steps enable executives to understand the key components of a total globalization process. Without some form of template indicating what is ahead, it is difficult for senior executives (and consultants, I might add) to understand and manage the overall globalization process. Throughout this chapter, I will build on these nine steps.

Consulting Insights | **Colgate-Palmolive Vision to Become Truly Global**

"This means we bring together the world's best people, creative ideas, technology, and processes to meet the needs of our customers wherever they live. We create and sustain superior business performance through global teamwork."[2]

Companies like ABB, Sony, GE, Nokia, and Ford have worked for many years to achieve strategic global advantage by locating various aspects of their supply chain in areas around the world. Their aim is to deliver products and services to the most profitable markets in the world by sourcing money, raw materials, technology, and labor from lowest cost markets and transferring these assets to markets where they can be sold for the greatest profit. In the process, they have had to develop organizations that are diverse and resilient in their corporate cultures and staff them with people who possess the global mindsets and skills needed for a broader perspective.

Integrating the Nine Steps

Each of these nine steps represents a unique practice area in globalization consulting; some consulting firms specialize in each of them. However, we must realize that simply following the nine steps is not enough. They need to be considered within an integrated end-to-end globalization process where everyone benefits from thinking in more systematic and integrated ways about globalization, its businesses, organizations, and people challenges.[3]

As a result, in order to move toward a more integrated approach, I have also divided and combined the nine steps into three broad areas of specialized consulting practice that I will discuss in more detail in this chapter. The three major areas and their related steps are: *I. Global Strategy Consulting* (Steps 1 through 3); *II. Global Operations Consulting* (Steps 4 through 6); and *III. Global Leadership Consulting* (Steps 7 through 9). Exhibit 10.2 reflects my integrated view of how these three broad areas of consulting intersect within a dynamic global environment composed of constantly changing market, political, and economic events.

While global clients are increasingly interested in an integrated approach to globalization, it is not easy for them or consultants to achieve in practice. The ideal view is one of building a global business that is competitive, supported by an integrated strategy, structure, and corporate culture, and led by people with mindsets and skills to work globally. This end goal is obviously not possible for consultants to achieve in one engagement or even several; in fact, most clients encounter different global problems at different times, resulting in the use of different consulting firms for specialized projects. Perhaps only in a small company might large strides toward integration be possible, especially with an enlightened founder/CEO who can see the whole system at once.

Still, even if one is consulting in a specialized area, it is essential to keep an integrated approach in mind. Otherwise, the company becomes a patchwork of quick fix solutions that don't reinforce each other.

The Three Practice Areas

Large consulting firms, such as McKinsey, BCG, and Booz Allen, tend to focus on *global strategy* consulting. Their objective is to assist clients with issues of global growth and competitiveness. In contrast, firms like Accenture and

Exhibit 10.1	Nine Steps to Globalization™

GLOBALIZATION DRIVERS
1. Global Environment
Socio-economic-political Risks and Opportunities

2. Global Business Case
Specific Benefits of Becoming More Integrated

3. Global Strategy
Cost, Customer, Innovation, and
Competitive Performance Indicators

4. Global Structure
Product/Business, Function, Geography
Integrated, Coordinated, Differentiated Activities

GLOBALIZATION CAPACITY
5. Global Paradox Management
Global-Local Paradoxes Identified to Achieve Balance

6. Global Metrics
Responsibility, Accountability, Authority
Decision Matrices, Decision and Baseline Metrics

7. Global Cultural Supports
Values, Processes, Systems

8. Global People Capability
Mindsets, Skills, Behavior

9. Global Performance Metrics
Market Share, Risk Management, Shareholder Value,
Competitive Positioning, Short-term/Long-term Strategy

CGE&Y emphasize *global operations* consulting solutions focusing on supply chain management. Their objective is to improve a client's operating efficiency and effectiveness from supplier to the customer. Independent con-

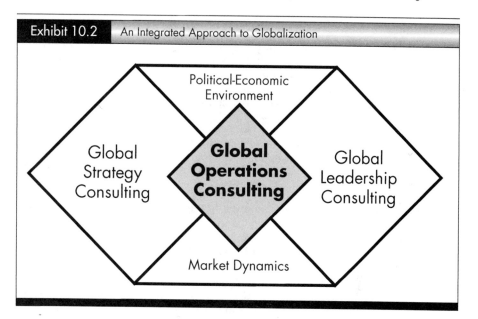

Exhibit 10.2   An Integrated Approach to Globalization

sultants, small boutique firms, and university business schools mainly populate the *global leadership* consulting area. Their objective is to build leaders who can adapt locally while managing with a global perspective.

In general, firms have had difficulty embracing all three major practice areas—economies of scale and limits in consultant capabilities are not easily transferable from one specialized practice to another or from one consultant to another. Large global consulting firms need a fairly replicable process that can be sold on a leveraged basis through younger, less expensive, and less experienced consultants. A practice focused solely on leadership and team development, for example, is less leveragable and, therefore, tends to be provided by smaller firms.

GLOBAL STRATEGY CONSULTING

In 1990, Harvard Business School professor Michael Porter wrote *The Competitive Advantage of Nations,*[4] and an era of global strategy consulting was launched. McKinsey & Company quickly followed with its Global Consulting Practice, spearheaded by its Japanese managing partner Kenichi Ohmae, writing *The Borderless World.*[5]

Global strategy consulting continues to be the mainstay of most globalization consulting. Corporations throughout the world face complex challenges in planning for new market entry and well-coordinated global organization structures. As a result, many companies turn to large consulting firms to assist them in the analysis of their strategies and organization structures.

Six typical types of consulting studies underlie global strategy consulting: 1) global social-cultural and economic trend analysis; 2) global security risk monitoring; 3) emerging markets studies; 4) competitive positioning studies; 5) complex organization design; and 6) managing the big-small paradox.

Global Social-Cultural and Economic Trends Analysis

Henry Kissinger once said that people would look back at the Cold War as one of the most stable periods of the twentieth century. This seems odd to many of us who grew up under the "nuclear overhang" and the fear that the world would be blown up through a nuclear power confrontation between the United States and the Soviet Union, but in fact, the world has become more unstable and threatening since the fall of the Berlin Wall in October 1989.

With the fall of the Berlin Wall and the end of the Soviet Union, the world has grown more interdependent in economics, markets, and communication. At the same time, social and cultural conflicts in various countries have emerged as critical forces affecting global businesses worldwide.

In a little known but prophetic publication in 1995, Samuel Huntington, a Harvard professor, raised the ominous picture of a twenty-first century dominated not by the competition of economic and political philosophies, but by a clash of civilizations.[6] Huntington maintained that differences in worldview, philosophy, religions, and culture would create friction on a global scale. He specifically studied the potential conflict between Islamic nations and Judeo-Christian countries as well as between the Chinese, Japanese, and Slavic worlds. He concluded that there would need to be new theories and institutions to deal with these issues in the twenty-first century.

Corporations operating internationally today need much greater awareness of the diverse cultural and religious forces shaping the world and their potential for opportunity and disruption of global operations. Corporations continue to require economic trend analysis for them to understand complex market forces and the implications for locating their businesses around the world. This involves the study of market opportunities, labor supply, cost efficiencies, treasury operations, and other factors affecting business profitability in various countries.

Both public and private institutions offer this kind of advice. In the public sector, the U.S. State Department Commercial Service produces a wide variety of publications advising companies about the business environment in various countries, as do foreign governments and international organizations such as the IMF, Import-Export Bank, and United Nations. In the private sector, most major banks and investment firms track global trends.[7] McKinsey's Global Institute and Monitor's Global Business Network work closely with companies to examine the impact of social, cultural, and political trends on international business opportunities.

This area will no doubt receive increasing attention in years to come; professional consulting services will grow substantially, requiring country, regional, and global specialists who understand mega trends that affect everything from consumer preferences to labor and government relations.

Global Security Risk Monitoring

Tensions and clashes between nation states, as well as religions, have captured the attention of the world and raised serious concerns about global corporate security. The rise of security consulting is evident everywhere; corporations are hiring security firms to protect their employees, to provide guidance with regard to travel policies, and to protect their manufacturing, research, and IT sites and systems throughout the world. A sample of consultants includes Kroll International and Control Risks, Ltd., which provide city briefs for 300 cities and offers crisis management and kidnap negotiating teams.[8]

IBM, Compaq, and many other computer companies provide global security and privacy assessments and protection for the architecture, design, and management of IT services. SOS International, the world's largest international medical assistance company, operates crisis centers that monitor international emergencies and assist corporate executives in arranging evacuation to the nearest safe haven. Founded in 1850, Pinkerton, a member of Securitas Group listed on the Swedish stock exchange, covers more than 80 percent of the U.S. Fortune 1,000 as its clients.

Emerging Markets Studies

Many new emerging markets are located where numerous corporations have never been, which creates a need for consultation regarding how to operate in places where just a few years ago business was done in a very different way. All the former socialist countries have little experience working with the developed world, and many companies in the developed world have little experience working in emerging markets.

As countries like Kazakhstan, Kirghizia, and Poland opened their markets to foreign trade and investment, Western companies began to seek advice from global consulting firms regarding government regulations, market opportunities, and cultural differences. The big consulting firms like McKinsey and BCG offer advice on government regulations and market opportunities, while smaller firms and universities like Brigham Young and Thunderbird offer training and insights into cultural differences affecting business practices.

Competitive Positioning Studies

Simultaneously, the rise of new markets has rearranged global competition. European investment in the United States is growing rapidly, while U.S. investment is making China one of the fastest growth areas in the world. Cross-border mergers and acquisitions are changing the landscape of telecommunications, financial services, and pharmaceuticals on a monthly basis. Business intelligence units, many of which are located in consulting firms, now scan the globe for the emergence of promising opportunities and the entrance of new competitors.

Complex Organization Design

As businesses turn to new markets, they face the inevitable question of how to best design their organization structures for global operations. For example, should they be set up on a geographic basis (e.g., Asia, Europe, North America) or should they be set up by product (e.g., Global Consumer products, Global Pharmaceutical products, Global Animal Care products), or should it be some combination of both geography and product?

Inevitably, when organizations try to coordinate their responsiveness to local customers, their global needs for economic efficiency, and their global and regional need for knowledge transfer, a matrix organization structure is usually the result. However, the complexities of managing in a matrix organization are among the most difficult issues in globalization. Sometimes it is better to use a simpler formal structure, product or functional, and rely on good informal relationships across the organization to make decisions and coordinate activities.

In all these choices, there is a trade-off between how close the firm should get to its local markets versus how similar and coordinated its services worldwide should be. Bruce Pasternack and Albert Viscio, founding partners of Booz Allen's Leadership Practice, have laid out the company's philosophy of global organization structure in *The Centerless Corporation*,[9] in which they advocate the division of responsibilities between the "global core" and subsidiaries in a way that only assigns functions to the center that add value to the total company.

BCG's Globalization Practice suggests four guidelines for managing the global-local paradox:

1. Begin with the fundamentals of the business: competitive economics, customer value and segmentation, and process capability. Examine opportunities for value creation by leveraging global scale and scope.

2. Identify the biggest opportunities for active cross-border process interaction. Keep the number of processes small, and determine where decision-making authority should be placed.

3. Suppress discussion of organization structure until there is a high-level definition around the fundamentals developed in 1 and 2 above.

4. Follow through relentlessly on supporting mechanisms and infrastructure that will enable the new strategy to work.[10]

Whether one follows BCG's advice or the advice of other consulting firms in this area, the global-local paradox will need to be managed on a continuous basis. Firms specializing in global-local organizational consulting will discover a steady source of business for the foreseeable future.

Managing the Big-Small Paradox

Closely related to the global-local paradox is the big-small one. A good case description of the big-small paradox is revealed in an interview with Percy Barnevik, former Chairman and CEO of ABB, in the *Harvard Business Review*.[11] Barnevik describes how he structured ABB to be simultaneously "big and small" by dividing 220,000 employees into 1,300 companies and 5,000 profit centers. In this way, while ABB's employees worked for a big company, they also felt considerable personal responsibility and ownership of their jobs in smaller companies and profit centers.

Barnevik called his organization structure a "multi-domestic" model. He became an overnight sensation, and throughout the 1990s, consultants and companies worked on various schemes to ensure that "glocalization," as the Japanese termed it, would ensure that global needs for efficiency were combined with local needs for responsiveness. This was achieved by becoming global in upstream parts of the business and local in the downstream parts. ABB also found it very difficult to manage its complex matrix, causing managers frequently to focus more on the inside at problems of conflict resolution than on the outside toward customer needs.

The six challenges described above are symptomatic of a myriad of opportunities/issues facing consultants dealing with global strategy. Some of these, like the global-local and big-small paradoxes, have enough experience behind them to suggest some possible best practices for dealing with them, although every situation is different. Others, like global security issues, are still emerging and require further development of new solutions and techniques.

GLOBAL OPERATIONS CONSULTING

Spearheaded in the 1990s by "cycle time reduction" introduced by the Boston Consulting Group, and "reengineering" by Hammer and Champy at CSC, operations consulting came of age on a global scale with technology and systems consulting. Most global operations consulting is oriented toward increasing a company's production and labor efficiency. A wide range of operations consultants provide assistance to various functions along the value chain—from R&D to engineering, manufacturing, finance, marketing, sales, human resources, and information technology. Each function has its own challenges and requires specialists with the technical knowledge and expertise to address these complex issues in an international context.

Typical types of operations studies include:

- R&D consulting services designed to determine the configuration of research and development centers on a global basis.

- Supply chain studies to deliver savings in purchasing on a regional or global basis.

- Logistics consulting to decrease transportation costs over a standard intercontinental route through a range of computerized options that provide more flexible, faster, and efficient delivery.

- Engineering searches for the most advanced technologies to be included in local or regional production.

- Manufacturing optimization through the location of manufacturing facilities after considering such issues as customer proximity versus transportation costs.

- Information technology studies to develop common global platforms for cost efficiencies, better global coordination of information, global planning, knowledge management and transfer, and competitive positioning.

Consultants who work on global operations often find themselves dealing with two fundamental and underlying issues that need to be addressed, regardless of their specialized practice area. These include: 1) developing a global technology infrastructure; and 2) locating responsibility for decision making.

Technology Infrastructure

The drive for functional efficiency is one of the major reasons companies choose to go global. During the 1960s, many companies in textiles, telecommunications, and toys moved their manufacturing operations to Taiwan, Korea, and Hong Kong in order to achieve greater efficiencies from cheap labor. Later, software development, pharmaceuticals, and financial services began to move operations offshore to take advantage of highly skilled but less expensive IT and R&D professionals.

Today, labor-based industries are gaining less advantage from going offshore because of the increased use of technology at home to reduce labor content in products. The development of global platforms for everything from finance to engineering, manufacturing, logistics, and human resources is a driving force for organizations to make their "upstream" activities as cost efficient as possible.

Most human resource executives who are globalizing their operations immediately confront the need to identify and develop a global employee database. Many companies have little ability to find, access, measure, track, or develop qualified managers; unfortunately, detailed employee records are unavailable because company information systems have been decentralized to local units, or if a database exists, the necessary information for determining global qualifications is not recorded.

Therefore, the first step in designing a truly global human resource system is the installation of a global IT platform and the integration of all the disparate HR information systems throughout the world.[12] Accenture, PeopleSoft, and others have shown that they can add great value to global HR information processes. The same can be said for almost every function in a company involving transactions or facts that can be stored for easy access and analysis. This will be an area of continued opportunity for IT consultants for years to come.

Location of Responsibility for Decision Making

The drive for efficiencies through the consolidation, centralization, and integration of various functional activities always produces a counterforce that emphasizes the need for decentralized, customized products and services to respond to the preferences of local markets. Managing the global efficiency versus local responsiveness dilemma is a major challenge faced by value-chain consultants.

Large general management consulting firms and the IT-based firms provide services to determine how management responsibilities for these decision processes should be defined and handled. Typically, decision matrices are designed to determine specific responsibilities concerning who makes final decisions, who needs to be consulted, and who needs to be informed for a wide range of basic decisions. These matrices allocate authority and accountability by global, regional, and local managers.

GLOBAL LEADERSHIP CONSULTING

In the end, decisions regarding efficiency and responsiveness require a manager to have a keen political sense for not only the local culture but the one's own organization culture as well. Many companies have found that the ability to manage both internal and external conflicts is an important aspect of managerial success. Personal skills at negotiation, conflict resolution, and change management are essential for today's global executive.

Currently, many large global companies have some form of global leadership training and, in most cases, have developed a talent management process that ensures that top performers from subsidiaries around the world have an opportunity to move up through the executive ranks. Companies like IBM, Citigroup, Motorola, GE, Nestlé, Nokia, Sony, and Samsung are representative of major companies that have aggressively worked to develop leaders capable of operating on a global basis (see Consulting Insights on Samsung's approach to developing global mindsets).

Overall, a manager's ability to execute plans and solutions has become the mantra of all aspects of global operations. Years ago, a McKinsey study showed that 80 percent of the failure in global strategy was in execution, not analysis. Larry Bossidy and Ram Charan have written a thoughtful book entitled *Execution*,[13] in which they argue that the key to execution is having leaders who know the details of the business and are relentless in pursuing "how" things will get done. The formula for executing global strategy, as the book's authors note, depends very much on the interplay between strategy, operations, and people. The authors claim that the most crucial ingredient is people and their ability to identify opportunities, execute decisions, and solve problems.

Consulting Insights	**Samsung Develops Global Mindsets**

For over a decade Samsung has been a leader in developing executives to operate internationally. Realizing that the number of Korean executives who could run foreign operations would limit expansion, Samsung has established a Global Leadership Institute where it trains large cadres of middle and senior manages to operate globally. In 1989, Samsung began a long-term program designed to develop regional or national experts who "think and act as local residents." Under this program, 400 high-potential managers were gradually sent to one of forty foreign countries for a year to master the local language, experience the local culture, and prepare a report on "Threats and Opportunities" for Samsung in their assigned country. When they returned, they entered the Samsung Global Leadership Institute for a three-month debrief of what they had learned from their experiences. The participants were then assigned to new jobs at Samsung and subsidiary headquarters where they could use their global training in enhancing Samsung operations throughout the world. Samsung continued this practice for several years until they had developed enough managers to run Samsung's operations successfully on a global scale. They believed this leadership development investment was critical to their capacity to grow internationally.[14]

Most authors and consultants agree that, in the end, the success of an effective global organization depends on the quality of its people and especially its leadership. Unfortunately, few corporate leaders today have extensive experience working in even a fraction of the hundred or so countries in which many companies operate. Theoretically, it would take an aspiring global leader a lifetime to understand all the countries in the company's portfolio, and even then the leader would fall short.

Is there any kind of shortcut? This gap in global experience has led to three important opportunities in global leadership consulting: 1) preparing people to operate in multiple cultures; 2) building global teams; and 3) developing global leaders.

Preparation for Multicultural Experiences

Much of the early activity in cross-cultural training has focused on how to prepare an executive and his or her family for experience in other cultures as expatriates. By the 1980s, however, executives were engaged in global team-work and travel to multiple countries around the world. Increasingly, their ability to work with people from many cultures and across many different societies has become more essential.

Consultants have quickly realized that it is not possible to conduct briefings on all countries that a busy executive might visit during two or three weeks abroad. From this dilemma has emerged the idea of focusing on "cultural self-awareness;" that is, developing an executive's knowledge about one's own culture and the cultural values and predispositions he or she carries around that might be different from patterns held by people in other countries where they might be working or visiting.

Fons Trompenaars and Charles Hampden-Turner in their excellent book, *Riding the Waves of Culture*,[14] popularized cross-cultural thinking for business executives. Their most recent work, *Building Cross-Cultural Competence*,[15] is a comprehensive sourcebook for dealing with some of the fundamental cultural paradoxes that executives confront in global situations.

In many countries, there are cross-cultural training services provided by small firms and independent consultants. Consulting opportunities abound, and so do the suppliers. But the number of consultants with both a broad range of business as well as cultural knowledge is limited. Competitive positioning for consultants in this area depends not only on personal knowledge, but on the development of country profiles, cultural tests, and other instruments that executives can use to improve their knowledge of multiple cultures. Training Management Corporation in Princeton, New Jersey has teamed up with E&Y to develop an excellent source for information and testing on a global basis. One of the oldest companies providing this service is Tucker International in Boulder, Colorado.[16]

Multicultural Team Building

Global corporations are increasingly using multicultural teams to coordinate far-flung activities around the world. These teams, separated by time, distance, and culture, are challenged to develop rapidly an understanding of the team's purpose and individual roles, and responsibilities, while also being alert to cultural differences.

The need for building effective multicultural teams is particularly relevant to strategic alliances and joint ventures. In cross-border mergers and acquisitions, corporations may buy a company that does business in a particular country with which they are not deeply familiar. The local company, on the other hand, often has little international experience. In these situations, some form of multicultural team building is needed.

Independent consultants who are trained and experienced in group dynamics, team development, and cross-cultural relations provide most multicultural team-building services. Over the last ten years, a substantial body of literature has developed about best practices in leading, managing, and building global teams. GlobalWork by Mary O'Hara-Deveraux and Robert Johansen[17] is a landmark study that outlines four basic skills that leaders need for effective global team management: 1) knowledge of cultural differences; 2) ability to use technology for team meetings and operations; 3) skill in facilitating teamwork across time and distance; and 4) ability to successfully direct a team to accomplish its tasks efficiently.

Most multicultural team-building services use a combination of cross-cultural exercises, clarification of team roles and goals, and the setting of operating norms to guide team interaction. Companies providing these services include Hewlett Associates, Tucker International, and TMA International in London.[18]

Global Leadership Development

Last, but hardly least, is the need for global leadership development. Globalization creates the need for a new kind of corporate leader, one who can deal with complex intellectual and technical issues on the one hand, while also being sensitive to cultural differences and local needs on the other.

The main form of global leadership development offered over the years has occurred in select business schools. In the United States, the Thunderbird School of International Management is one of the first to have specialized in preparing executives to work in other cultures. By the 1990s, however, several business schools like Harvard, Stanford, and Chicago were adding global elements to their curriculum. In Europe, the London Business School, INSEAD, and IMD are today in the vanguard of preparing leaders to operate globally.

In addition to business schools, some professors and independent consultants have developed programs utilizing behaviorally oriented methods to help executives learn how to work in the midst of global uncertainty and ambiguity. Companies such as CDR International, and independent consultants such as Noel Tichy, Henry Mintzberg, and Yury Boshyk, began global leadership programs that involve four to six weeks of training in different parts of the world. In many cases, these programs also use "action learning" in which real business issues are studied by small teams from a global perspective.

In Europe, the leader in the use of action learning for global leadership development is MiL, which was founded in Sweden in 1977 by Lennart Rohlin. This organization has worked to pioneer the use of action learning for facilitating the global development of Scandinavian organizations and their managers. MiL's learnings have been summarized in two excellent books, *Strategic Leadership in the Learning Society*[19] and *Earning While Learning in Global Leadership: The Volvo-MiL Partnership*.[20] This same type of action learning process was followed by CEO Jack Welch and Chief Learning Officer Steve Kerr at GE when managers were brought to its Crotonville campus. One such team went off to South America to study and recommend how GE should organize its Latin-American operations, and a member of the team was placed in charge of the new organization for Latin America.

MINDSET AND SKILLS FOR GLOBAL CONSULTANTS

If the qualities and characteristics of global leadership need nurturing and development, it is also true that the qualities and characteristics of globalization consultants need development. Lewis Pinault, a former consultant with BCG, Gemini, ADL, and Coopers, writes in his book, *Consulting Demons*,[21] that, while there is no ideal consultant, the following profile suggests many of the desired qualities:

The consultant would have the best possible education for both business and analytic problem solving; say, a Cambridge undergraduate education in math or physics and a Harvard MBA, and be equipped to make any intellectual challenge in business seem dead easy, given the requisite fluency in analytic technique. . . . skilled at finding tolerable pleasures in the chaos of travel and long hours, the consultant would nonetheless savor opportunities apart from consulting to reaffirm his own identity and recreate the inner self from which the consultant's energies are drawn. Low of ego, multilingual and at ease becoming immersed in the struggles of others, the consultant is at home in almost any environment where there is a business need. Amazingly, this composite, or something very close to it, occasionally surfaces as a real person.[22]

Having spent twenty years as a global executive and another twenty coaching and developing global executives, I have developed a formulation of the mindsets and skills needed for global effectiveness. An overview is included in Exhibit 10.3.

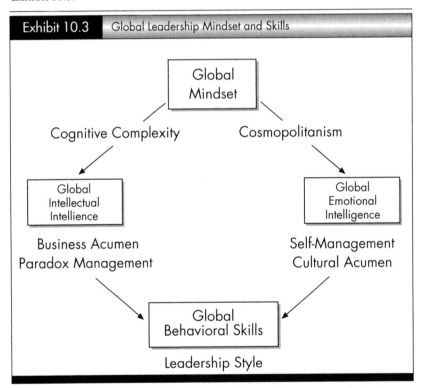

Exhibit 10.3   Global Leadership Mindset and Skills

To be successful as a global consultant one must develop a global mindset. This, in turn, requires "global intellectual intelligence" and "global emotional intelligence." Global intellectual intelligence—comprised of business acumen and the ability to analyze and recommend solutions to the complexity of global organizational paradoxes—is a necessary but insufficient condition for global success. The landscape of global operations is littered with the bodies of brilliant technical experts who lacked adequate interpersonal skills across cultures.

Global interpersonal skills for consultants are represented by what I call global emotional intelligence. This involves elements of Goleman's emotional intelligence—self-awareness, self-regulation, empathy, and social skills—but also augmented by cross-cultural acumen and sensitivity. The result is a consultant who possesses cultural self-awareness, the ability to adjust to new cultures, and the capacity to show empathy for people with other value systems.

NO TURNING BACK

In this chapter, I have tried to define the main components and issues of the new field that I call "globalization consulting," which, as I suggest, signals major new opportunities accompanied by difficult challenges ahead.

As we proceed, many new concepts and methods will no doubt emerge to aid the global consultant. Every global consulting firm will need to update its consultants frequently as well as to debrief them on their experiences. Many business schools have been slow to take up the global challenge, but they too will soon begin turning out better educated future global consultants.

Globalization is clearly not a phenomenon that will fade away. The world is not going to revert to a nation-state focus. Economic regions, such as the EU and Asia, are growing in economic and political power. For better or worse, the world is now interdependent, not only technologically and economically but socially, politically, and culturally. It will need all the help consultants and their firms can give to assist their clients in building their capabilities to succeed in an interdependent and fast moving global community.

Notes to the Chapter

[1] Boston Consulting Group Web site http://www.bcg.com/home.jsp.

[2] Michael Marquardt and Angus Reynolds, *Global Learning Organization* (Burr Ridge, Ill: Richard Irwin, 1994): 66.

[3] George Yip, a Professor at the London Business School, has also written a guidebook for developing a global organization. In *Total Global Strategy II,* he focuses on such basics as diagnosing industry globalization potential, designing global products and services, locating global activities, and building a global organization (Upper Saddle River, NJ: Prentice Hall, 2003).

[4] Michael E. Porter, *The Competitive Advantage of Nations* (London: Macmillan, 1990).

[5] Kenichi Ohmae, *The Borderless World* (New York: Harper Business Press, 1990).

[6] Samuel Huntington, *The Clash of Civilizations and the Remaking of World Order* (New York: Simon & Schuster, 1995).

[7] For further reference, see Thomas L. Friedman, *Lexus and the Olive Tree* (New York: Farrar, Strauss, Giroux, 1999).

[8] For further reference, see Bill Phillips, *Corporate Security Handbook* (New York: McGraw Hill Textbook Press, 2002); Jerry Rogers, ed., *Global Risk Assessments: Issues, Concepts and Applications in Business Environment Risk Assessment, Country, Investment and Trade Risk Analysis* (New York: Global Risk Assessments, 1997).

[9] Two of the best works on complex organization design are Jay R. Galbraith, *Designing the Global Corporation* (San Francisco: Jossey-Bass, Inc., 2000); Bruce A. Pasternak and Albert J. Viscio, *The Centerless Corporation* (New York: Simon & Schuster, 1998).

[10]BCG Web site http://www.bcg.com/home.jsp.

[11]William Taylor, "The Logic of Global Business: An Interview with Percy Barnevik," *Harvard Business Review,* 6, no. 2 (March–April 1991): 91–105.

[12]For a useful and comprehensive discussion of human resource challenges in globalization, see Paul Evans, Vladimir Pucik, and Jean-Louis Barsoux, *The Global Challenge: Framework for International Human Resource Management* (New York: McGraw-Hill, 2002).

[13]Larry Bossidy and Ram Charan, *Execution* (New York: Crown Business, 2002).

[14]Fons Trompenaars and Charles Hampden-Turner, *Riding the Waves of Culture: Understanding Diversity in Global Business,* 2d ed. (New York: McGraw-Hill, 1998).

[15]Charles Hampden-Turner and Fons Trompenaars, *Building Cross-Cultural Competence: How to Create Wealth from Conflicting Values* (New Haven: Yale University Press, 2000).

[16]See Elizabeth Marx, *Breaking through Culture Shock* (London: Nicholas Brealy Publishing, 1999); Robert Rosen, Patricia Digh, Marshall Singer, and Carl Phillips, *Global Literacies: Lessons on Business Leadership and National Cultures* (New York: Simon & Schuster, 2000).

[17]Mary O'Hara-Devereaux and Robert Johansen, *GlobalWork: Bridging Distance, Culture and Time* (San Francisco: Jossey-Bass, Inc., 1994).

[18]For further information on global teams, see Lynda C. McDermott, Nolan Brawley, and William W. Waite, *World Class Teams* (New York: John Wiley & Sons, Inc., 1998).

[19]Lennart Rohlin, Per-Hugo Skarvad, and Sven Ake Nilsson, *Strategic Leadership in the Learning Society* (Vasbyholm, Sweden: MiL Publishers AB, 1998).

[20]Lennart Rohlin, et. al., *Earning While Learning in Global Leadership: The Volvo MiL Partnership* (Vasbyholm, Sweden: MiL Publishers AB, 2002).

[21]Lewis Pinault, *Consulting Demons: Inside the Unscrupulous World of Global Corporate Consulting* (New York: HarperCollins, 2001): 198.

[22]Personal observation in visit to speak at the Samsung Global Management Institute.

CHAPTER 11

Public Sector Consultation

Alan M. Glassman, California State University and Morley A. Winograd, University of Southern California

ABOUT THE AUTHORS

Alan M. Glassman

Alan M. Glassman is Professor of Management and Director of the Center for Management and Organization Development, California State University, Northridge. He has served as Chair of the Managerial Consultation Division of the Academy of Management and as editor of *Consultation: An International Journal.* He consults actively with municipal governments, the criminal justice system, and social services.

Morley A. Winograd

Morley A. Winograd is a Managing Principal of Governmentum Partners, L.L.C. and Executive Director of the Center for Telecommunications Management and Associate Professor of Clinical at the Marshall School of Business at the University of Southern California. He served as Senior Policy Advisor to Vice President Gore and Director of the National Partnership for Reinventing Government. He is the coauthor, with Dudley Buffa, of *Taking Control: Politics in the Information Age.*

In the historical record of management consulting, the public sector has frequently gone unmentioned or undifferentiated from the private sector. Or when addressed, private sector consultants are frequently advised to avoid the public sector because of its rules, regulations, and low fees. In our opinion, these two seemingly contradictory views both reflect two very misleading assumptions that fail to understand the public sector consulting space; namely, that: 1) public sector consultation is identical to private sector consulting; and 2) successful public sector consultation is severely limited by an impenetrable and unrewarding bureaucracy. If a consulting firm adheres to this false mindset, it can cost the firm millions of dollars in overlooked opportunities, lost proposals, and failed projects.

Indeed, the government market today offers significant opportunities for both consulting and individual consultants, provided they can master the public sector's unique features and become an "industry expert" at this type of consulting. Many consulting firms today are deriving a substantial amount of revenue from the public sector.

In this chapter, we examine several important questions related to the context and practice of public sector consultation, and we discuss how it will likely evolve into the future. For example, what is the market for public sector consulting? How do the public sector and private sector settings differ? What are the current and future opportunities? How do the federal, state, and municipal settings differ? What has been the impact of the information revolution on public agencies and the role of consultants? What key institutional variables are likely to impinge on public sector consulting engagements? In answering these questions, we offer some keys to successful public sector consulting.

THE PUBLIC SECTOR MARKETPLACE

While the origins and growth of management consulting reside historically in the private sector, recent years have seen the public sector emerge as a significant source of consulting activity and revenues. For example, during 2002, Accenture reported a 31 percent increase in revenues for its Government Operating Group, far exceeding the combined revenue growth rate of its other four groups. Indeed, Accenture's Financial Services' Group, a traditionally strong contributor, actually suffered a 9 percent revenue loss.[1] And BearingPoint's public services practice, mainly in IT work, is now their largest, generating $966M or 40 percent of their revenues in 2002. While the actual size of the U.S. public sector marketplace is difficult to determine, we estimate that the combined federal, state, and municipal spending on consulting constitutes approximately $30 billion of the approximately $120 billion worldwide consultation industry. The earliest consulting entrants to the public sector, such as Booz Allen and McKinsey, have focused mainly on the federal level market; meanwhile other consulting firms moving away from their accounting heritage, such as KMPG (now BearingPoint), Accenture, and PWC (now IBM), have all greatly increased their overall share of the U.S. public sector market, especially at the state and local levels. And, as highlighted in the sidebar on the United Kingdom, the overseas public sector marketplace offers many additional opportunities.[2]

Consulting Insights | **The United Kingdom Marketplace**

A recent report entitled *Delivering World-Class Consultancy Services to the Public Sector—A Statement of Best Practice* by the British government, in conjunction with the National Audit Office, the Management Consultancies Association, and the Institute of Management Consultancy, provides guidance on how public sector buyers and private sector suppliers of consulting services can ensure the delivery of more effective services to government. The impetus for the report was the recognition that the central government had increased consultation spending to over £.6 billion and that nearly every major consulting firm was focused on fortifying their relationships with government agencies and public officials.

Both the domestic and global markets for public sector consulting are likely to expand during the next decade. For example, within the United States, many state governments and local municipalities have entered an era of reduced revenue streams due to a slowing economy and the unwillingness of legislators to raise taxes. Consequently, many public entities are now seeking advice on how they can deliver public services, such as education, health care, transportation, and social programs, in a more efficient manner.

Similarly, many national governments worldwide are engaged in administrative reform of their core functions; numerous countries have sought to cut the size of their public bureaucracies while simultaneously making government more efficient, more modern, and more responsive to citizens' needs.

Among the more notable experiments have been: 1) the United Kingdom's *Prior Options Review,* which mandates that the government's leadership determine every five years whether a service should be provided by the government or by the private sector; 2) Italy's *Bassini Laws,* which provide for the delegation of centralized national services to regional governments; and 3) New Zealand's movement toward outsourcing the management of government agencies, while leaving Ministers in oversight positions to represent taxpayers' ownership interests and set policy. Taken collectively, all of these domestic and international initiatives provide a significant opportunity for management consulting firms to seek contracts from both national governments and local municipalities.

The key to winning these contracts is to recognize the distinctive features of government when marketing one's own expertise and offering counsel. Attempts to simply transpose private sector solutions to this market are likely to be rejected out of hand by public sector prospects. They want insights unique to their decision-making environment that can be implemented within the same spirit of public service that likely animates their own careers. For example, in government, improved efficiency for its own sake is rarely a compelling argument for hiring a consultant; rather, the promised outcome has to be linked to a larger public goal (social good) that finds acceptance from several stakeholders, such as better service to citizens.

Two types of consultant companies have demonstrated their ability to make this transition in their marketing approach. On one side are well-known, major consulting firms emphasizing their full-service capabilities; these firms are largely concentrating on the federal market, especially in their attempts to win large IT projects involving systems integration (CRP and ERP). The federal acquisition reform movement of the 1990s has greatly stimulated this type of business through promoting two types of contracts: 1) performance-based contracts with specified outcomes; and 2) "share-in-savings" contracts where the contractor receives an agreed upon percentage of the money saved. This growing IT consulting focus represents enormous dollars in revenues and profits, especially when compared to fees paid to consultants in the past. Much of Accenture's recent growth is due to their aggressive pursuit of these new types of consulting contracts, with a heavy emphasis on the integration of IT systems.

On the other side, the public sector market has increasingly favored small *boutique* firms that maintain expert knowledge in one or two areas of consultation while specializing in government practice. These *boutique* firms, frequently founded by ex-government employees, bring a unique level of understanding to the contemporary challenges confronting government in such areas as human resource management, strategic planning, e-government, and performance measurement. Their "tailor-made" approaches can often prove superior, in the client's eyes, to the more generalized knowledge and standardized approaches of the major firms, and usually less expensive. Indeed, the more local the government entity (e.g., small city, town), the more attractive are these boutiques. We are also witnessing the emergence of university-based boutiques that combine research and consultation for government, such as the Public Sector Group at UCLA and the Center for Management and Organization Development at California State University, Northridge—both located within colleges of business.

PUBLIC SECTOR REALITIES

To gain a share of the public marketplace, consultants need to understand how this sector differs from the private sector. Overall, it is commonly accepted that the dual purposes of government throughout history have been primarily to serve its citizens through: 1) providing physical protection; and 2) enhancing their economic and social well-being. These twin purposes are fundamentally different from the well-understood purpose of private sector organizations, which is mainly to achieve superior economic returns for its owners.

This major difference in purposes between the two sectors creates an entirely different context for public sector consultation. The criteria through which proposals and projects are judged is decidedly different—the private sector assesses consultants for their probable impact on economic results, while the public sector places high value on delivering a broad array of services that cannot be easily measured for their financial return (nor should they be!). As a result, public sector consultants face a unique and demanding challenge in selling their proposals.

This context requires that consultants, when importing methods and approaches from private sector, do so with care in their adaptation so as to meet both the political and complex organizational needs of the public sector client. In essence, public sector consultants must propose solutions that not only deliver results, but votes as well.

It is also important for consultants to understand that governments have complex and well-established multi-level structures at the federal, state, and municipal levels. These are created to respond to different levels of constituency interests. For example, in the United States under its system of federalism, the focus of the national government remains on the larger purposes of defense and economic prosperity; however, the relationship between constituents and their governments are closer at state and local levels where policies and programs make a more direct impact on daily lives (e.g., sales taxes, maintenance of roads, school funding, social service policies, criminal offenses). Local municipalities, at the county, city, and school district levels, offer a number of services that provide the best opportunity for citizen participation (e.g., town meetings, access to lawmakers and elected officials).

Taken together—the unique purposes of government and the complex architecture of multi-level government organizations leads to three overriding challenges facing the public sector consultant. Let us examine each of these challenges in some depth, because unaware and ill-prepared consultants will fail in dealing with them.

Public Omnipresence

Consultants must accept that the public is an active party to all decision making, and therefore consultants must consider this "unspoken agenda" when framing recommendations. First, there is the client audience—many public sector employees choose government careers (e.g., health and mental health services, public safety, social services) as a means for improving the well-being of the general population. While it may seem idealistic to private sector consultants, this personal commitment of public sector employees to helping others often becomes their overriding criterion when assessing consultant proposals and recommendations.

Second, politically active groups, such as advisory committees, industry lobbyists, community action organizations, and "grass roots" organizations, frequently use the opportunity to comment on and influence the acceptance of consultants' proposals and recommendations. These groups have access at many points (to elected officials, to department and program administrators, and to media) that permit them to exert pressure on the outcomes of decision making. Thus, their relative strength and even active involvement must be considered when making recommendations to public sector clients. Discussions and decisions about major recommendations usually occur in public forums under public scrutiny. As told to us by an elected official, "I wonder how any corporate CEO would feel if every major decision on a new program or expenditure was conducted in front of the shareholders?" Moreover, even if the consultants' advice is given privately, the consultants must assume that their counsel, whether verbal or written, will someday find its way into the public domain, and they must be prepared to defend it in that venue.

Complexity, Complexity, Complexity

Once government is recognized as a unique industry, consultants must think beyond the unit or agency for which they provide advice and consider a multitude of factors that may impact their recommendations. A short list of such factors includes private sector firms that seek contracts to replace government agencies, community and citizen demands, internal resource allocations, and the complex "web of rules" that sometimes lead to conflicts between different levels (e.g., federal versus state rules on social service requirements, municipal dependence on the distribution of state tax revenues).

Consultants must look upon the public sector as an "industry" made up of many highly differentiated market services (e.g., health, education, defense), all conducted by various units at several levels with an intricate set of interdependencies and vested interests. Like any industry, there are competing forces and continuous change.

As a result, it is often difficult to get agencies at any level to work together to provide seamless service. Freedom of action is limited due to others' regulations and/or the agency's willingness to cooperate. Flexibility is further limited by the industry's structure. For instance, states and municipalities cannot 1) refuse to implement federal laws and regulations, even when they are passed without accompanying funds or 2) withhold a service from those who qualify even when this service requires disproportionate expenditures. So, unlike the private sector, the activities of government units are highly proscribed; these units cannot simply drop a service or choose a preferred "market niche." Nevertheless, working within these constraints offers numerous opportunities for consulting input.

It's All Politics . . . And That's the Way It Should Be!

A frequently cited comment by disgruntled public sector consultants is, "It was all political." In uttering this phrase, these consultants indicate a lack of understanding that "politics" is the dominant frame for decision making in government! In this context, the traditional private sector Four Ps of marketing—price, product, position, and promotion—morph into a different set of public sector Ps—politics, public relations, policy, and performance. And with rare exceptions, they occur in that order.

This political view accepts the reality that politicians must get reelected and that many public constituencies, including customers and suppliers, all can make reasonable and unreasonable demands on government agencies. Thus, there exists among them constant dialogue and negotiations to ensure that the final decision has a positive political outcome. For the consultant, this produces a challenging dilemma: "How can I recommend transformational change possibilities when politicians tend to be risk adverse and department heads and agency executives must be responsible to elected officials?" Yet, this constant "give and take" between politician and public constituencies (often invisible to the public) is an essential component of the democratic process. It is the public sector equivalent to the dominance of the market in determining the viability of private sector decisions. Any public sector consultant who fails to heed this fundamental truth about the primacy of political considerations will inevitably fail.

Consultant sensitivity to these three dimensions—public presence, architectural complexity, and political considerations—is a prerequisite for consulting success. That does not mean that learning and methods from the private sector are irrelevant. To the contrary, there is a great deal of transferability, but it requires a different mindset and a willingness to adapt. Indeed, with increasing frequency, numerous private sector consultants understand this different mindset and are experiencing considerable success.

REINVENTING GOVERNMENT: CREATING A CONTEXT FOR CONSULTING

Many opportunities for consulting are now occurring under the rubric of *Reinventing Government*—which is generally referred to as a movement designed to 1) meet increased service demands from the public, 2) through the application of information-age technologies, and thereby 3) enable major changes in public sector organizations, their cultures, and workplace processes that serve the public. We will discuss in this section four major consulting opportunities that are currently attracting high priority under the umbrella of reinvention: 1) strategic planning; 2) e-business and customer service; 3) strategic human resources; and 4) performance management.

Exhibit 11.1 broadly depicts the intersection of the complexity of variables that come together under government reinvention, which as a total context must be considered by consultants, both in their diagnoses and recommendations.

As part of this movement, government agencies are adopting many of the techniques, systems, and philosophies that the private sector uses to operate more efficiently while delivering better service to customers. Many agencies are now: 1) relying on markets and competition to determine winners and losers; 2) focusing on the targeted customers of government services (rather than on voters or citizens) to measure the success of programs; and 3) establishing more flexible workplaces with a greater degree of employee involvement in decision making. Government employees are increasingly being encouraged to become risk-takers, entrepreneurial, and active participants in cross-functional teams so as to promote the widespread sharing of information and services across unit boundaries.[3]

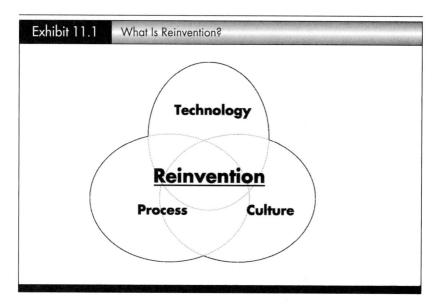

Exhibit 11.1   What Is Reinvention?

While many people in government recognize the challenge of reinvention, the path from an industrial-era method for doing business to a new information-age approach is not plainly marked. Clearly the new institutions and practices of government will have to reflect the underlying dynamics of the information age. Continuously, we find that government leaders are looking for guidance from consultants on: 1) what types of new structures can be put in place to better serve stakeholders and fulfill the fundamental purposes of government; and 2) what leadership and change strategies can be used to transform units into adaptive agencies able to cope with an increasingly tumultuous public environment. Indeed, it is not unusual to find government leaders reading the same leadership and transformational change books that are popular in the private sector. Some of the more notable government successes with reinvention from around the world are highlighted in the sidebar, *A String of Successes.*

The reinvention challenge, however, is frequently made difficult by the sheer size of government entities. Few private sector companies compare in budget size or number of employees to any federal level cabinet department (e.g., Defense, Agriculture, Homeland Security, Commerce) or even regulatory agencies (e.g., Federal Trade Commission, Federal Communication Commission). Similarly, the municipal level covers a large scope of operations. Los Angeles County consists of thirty-seven departments employing over 90,000 people and has a yearly combined budget of $16.5 billion, which is larger than the budgets of forty-one states, all reporting to an elected five-member Board of Supervisors with both legislative and executive power.

Strategic Planning

It is not surprising, then, that government agencies have increasingly turned to strategic planning as a process and mechanism for launching reinvention efforts. This activity helps the senior managements of agencies to: 1) rigorously assess the environments in which their agencies will be operating in the future; 2) debate and determine the agency's mission, values, and goals; and 3) develop appropriate yet flexible initiatives for achieving goals in a rapidly changing environment.

Consulting
Insights   **A String of Successes**

In 1998, the U.S. government surveyed its 1.8 million frontline employees to determine what impact the *Reinventing Government* initiative had made in their work lives. Nearly 33 percent of those interviewed indicated that the reforms had changed their daily routine and that they felt an increased sense of empowerment. While critics noted that this was scant progress after six years, other observers asserted that, in absolute numbers (approximately 600,000 people), this was the most significant change in a large organization ever achieved in such a relatively short amount of time in either the public or the private sectors. Below, we list some specific, albeit more modest, government successes.

- Indianapolis' Competition for Public Services: Mayor Goldsmith bid out $500 million, saving 20 percent; public employees won a majority of the competitions.
- New York City's CompStats: Provides for biweekly borough reviews of current crime statistics, identification of trends, and the immediate shift in resources to meet identified needs.
- Baltimore's CitiStats: Provides for biweekly departmental reviews of service performance judged against specific outcome measures; seeks understanding of reasons for underperformance; and as necessary, the development of action plans to address service delivery shortcomings by area of the City.
- Minnesota Board of Government Innovation: Power to grant agencies waivers from regulations to better meet customer (i.e., citizen) needs.
- Veteran's Health Administration's VISION: Reorganization from a hospital-based assessment system to geographical teams measured on the improved health of the population; required cross-functional teams and new information sharing systems.

However, only minimal success has been reported from many of these planning efforts, and government officials often express "pain" when discussing their experiences with strategic planning. Based on our own experience and conversations with consulting colleagues, we conclude that many government agencies have faltered in their planning efforts because they have defined changes in their external environment as *one-time* events rather than understanding that strategic planning must be a continuous process where strategies are being constantly reinvented.

Many public agencies have also been too quick to adopt planning models from the private sector, several of which have been introduced by consultants. But there is a real difference! In the private sector, the planning emphasis is on accelerating strategic decision making as a means for attaining competitive advantage. In government, however, agencies must spend significant time seeking agreement from a wide range of stakeholders before a decision is implemented (see Exhibit 11.2). From our observations, private sector consultants often fail to grasp the differences between the readily identifiable triad of customers, employees, and shareholders in the private sector and the innumerable potential stakeholders in the public sector who expect to "have input."

A closer look at the public sector stakeholder environment reveals the complexity of stakeholders that strategic planners and consultants must consider

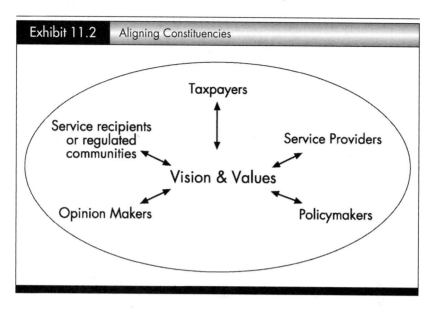

Exhibit 11.2   Aligning Constituencies

and balance off against each other. For example, millions of taxpayers supply the revenue for operations and interact with government as service recipients, yet decisions about priorities are usually made by legislators and executives selected by only a subset of this population. In addition, the most powerful constituents often decide the budgets and rules for judging performance—and these decisions can easily be in conflict with the desires of the agency's leaders. Then there are the media and NGOs (nongovernment organizations) that tend to reflect very narrow interests, but they are highly visible and can create a distorted picture of an agency's performance.

A consensus is emerging that strategic planning execution often fails to meet expectations due to the inability of agency leaders to recognize the practical problems of implementation that cause them to omit the needed organizational changes and the accompanying integration steps. Organizational barriers and turf protecting behavior also get in the way of implementation. Over and over, we hear government clients express the need for cross-functional teams to work on strategies, openly share information, and reallocate resources. Fortunately, consultants can reach across agency and department boundaries more easily than agency leaders to form teams with other consultants, often learning from each other. In one instance, we saw two consultants from competing firms "team up" and then seek out other independent consultants to guide a major strategic planning effort in a large state correctional agency. They used their willingness to cooperate as a link for getting the health care staff and correctional staff to set joint strategies for improving inmate care.

We suggest, therefore, that strategic planning in the public arena needs to become more inclusive and more disciplined than the private sector. One approach that accomplishes this goal is the *Five Star Framework* developed by Governmentum Partners, LLC.[4] It is organized around the five "As"—key questions that determine the degree to which any government entity, or agency within it, can make changes as fast as the environment that surrounds it.

- **Analysis**—Given the *purpose* of the organization, what are its key external *relationships* and internal *readiness* to meet its *challenges*, and what *objective information* supports the analysis?

- **Alignment**—Does the *leadership* have a *vision, set of values, mission* and *strategies for innovation* and promoting *learning and growth*?

- **Action**—Are *program structures* and internal *action plans* designed to fully incorporate enhanced *human capital*, revised *work processes*, and the creative use of *technology*?

- **Accountability**—Has *integrity* been recognized, and have *outcomes* been clearly established in terms of *overall objectives* and *specific goals* tied to *budgetary and other resources*?

- **Acceptance**—Do *customers, employees*, and the *public* value the *outcomes achieved* and agree with the *methods* inherent in creating and communicating the *policies* that are being implemented?

In the Five Star model, when the answers to the five questions are reviewed within the context of key governmental processes (identified by italics above), a governance system can be developed that provides feedback loops and organizational learning in strategic planning.[5]

Customer Service and E-Government

The basic goal in introducing Web-based technologies is to create a government that is online twenty-four hours a day, seven days a week—total availability to meet the performance expectations of the citizen customer. In advocating a move to e-government, a joint study by the United Nations and the American Society of Personnel Administration argues, "It is a permanent commitment by government to improving the relationship between the private citizen and the public sector through enhanced cost-effective and efficient delivery of services and information. This effort can be the practical realization of the best government has to offer."[6] Turning that vision into reality provides a fast-growing opportunity for consultants to apply both technical and organizational guidance for improving public sector entities.

E-government is a key strategy for improving customer service. It was introduced under the Clinton administration and is now continuing under President Bush. For example, in the United States, individuals seeking a place to vacation can go to a single Web site, http://www.recreation.gov, and make reservations for a campsite or other places to stay at any one of our national parks or forests. Interestingly, due to historical protocols and statutory requirements, three different agencies are responsible for recreational services. But in the e-government world, these stovepipes become transparent. The three agencies have now jointly funded the Web site and acted to make the processes identical. In other areas, the Web is being used to accept employment applications, obtain required forms and documents, register patents, transfer funds, submit taxes, and answer general questions.

The Bush administration is currently attempting to save millions of dollars by providing a single Web-based platform that will host a set of common government processes such as processing grants, paying employees, and determining eligibility for government benefits. All federal agencies will be asked to use this platform in conducting their business. Whichever consulting firms become the vendors for this project will gain a significant and almost permanent advantage in providing future advice to improve Web-connected processes throughout all federal agencies.

Other countries have also adopted a variety of models for e-government that can be used by consultants to help shape state and local portal designs. Some countries organize their e-government services by patterns in a citizen's life. Thus, one Web site might provide the information necessary to record the birth of a child and accompanying information (e.g., ranging from physical characteristics to family genealogy); a different Web site can track a child's school progression; another can focus on adult life (e.g., work experience, marriage, home sites); and another exists for senior citizens living on pensions. The key design parameters are determined by organizing the site around the needs of each "customer type." The next step is to make available all the services government offers customers on one Web site. These new Web sites for kids or workers or seniors or vacationers become the virtual agencies of a new information-age government.

At the state and municipal levels, most governments now provide informational Web sites, but few of them offer the functionality that allows citizens to do business with specific government units. One reason for this failure is that there has often been little integration of strategic planning with e-government processes, a conclusion also reached in a recent study by the International City/County Management Association and Public Technology, Inc.[7] Indeed, this study suggests that the lack of technological expertise and adequate financial resources remain major barriers. It is clear to us, however, that, as the private sector continues to advance the use of information technology to meet public needs, pressure will mount on state governments and local municipalities to accelerate their adoption of similar approaches. This will provide many opportunities for consultants to integrate information technology with public purpose.

It is important to recognize that efforts at e-government can become truly transformational by going beyond simply making the existing structure of government operate more efficiently or even effectively. It must respond to specific citizen needs rather than seeking to control those who interact with government. Thus, the act of advising government clients requires a framework and process that delivers an entirely new experience for the citizen customer. A one-size-fits-all approach needs to be avoided; rather, customized services for various citizen segments should be established.

To lead this shift toward the increased use of technology, it is essential that consultants define their roles broadly and accept that citizens are the customers to be served. This permits them to raise the right, fundamental questions from the beginning regarding the use of information technology. Still, the introduction of information technology into government suggests the need for a phased approach so that existing agencies can evolve into their roles without disrupting service. By adopting an evolutionary approach to transformation, governments can gradually begin to address demands from citizens for online services and at the same time provide technical training to government workers who are new to the information environment. The key is to ensure a customer focus at every stage of the process.

Consultants can help agencies begin by adapting their existing methods to the existing online environments in each agency and then systematically make progress toward the creation of a fully interactive, participatory government—a desired end-state where the government's relationship with citizens is transformed. We want to emphasize that there is nothing in this shift to e-government to suggest that the process requires the immediate redesign of public bureaucracies (e.g., elimination or addition of departments) or new laws to move forward. While the ultimate impact of e-government will eventually cause many agency activities, especially in service delivery, to wither or disappear, the gradual introduction of e-government can be done with a minimum of disruption.

Strategic Human Resource Management

Traditionally, the function of human resources management (HRM) in government has been viewed through a negative lens. Included among the many harsh criticisms of public sector HR are its: 1) narrow recruitment of security-oriented employees; 2) obsessive focus on record-keeping and manual operations; and 3) defense of the status quo and its burdensome civil service rules. The primary focus of HRM has often been on monitoring legal compliance in employment practices and avoiding "people" problems. A myriad of stories exists within all government agencies regarding the inability of HR to discipline employees, its creation of massive volumes of paperwork necessary to authorize new positions or reclassify employees, and its advocacy of reward systems that place seniority before merit.

In this era of unprecedented change, however, public sector human resources management is now a constant target for performance improvement. The goal is to professionalize the human resources function. In a recent study, Hays and Kearney concluded, "HRM is presently experiencing a near revolution in its operating practices. Cherished techniques are reportedly being abandoned, and a profusion of new approaches to the HRM function is taking hold within the personnel profession. Pervasive control techniques are yielding to a consultative role for the personnel office."[8]

This revolution in HRM is creating many untapped opportunities for public sector consultants to provide needed advice. At the federal level, for instance, the reinvention movement has sought greater flexibility for line managers, including the scrapping of the 10,000 page personnel manual, decentralization of recruitment and hiring processes, revision of classification and pay systems to reflect market conditions, and bonuses for exceptional performance. Labor-management partnerships have also been formed for problem solving and process reengineering, and training programs with measurable performance outcomes established.

We also note that these dramatic changes in HRM have some vocal critics. First, those changes that focus only on single departments inevitably create a lack of consistency in HR policies across agencies and between different units in the same agency. Second, there are ever-increasing reports of grievances due to perceived arbitrary and discriminatory managerial behavior. Some HR critics argue that the behavioral axiom of "any good carried to an extreme will become a negative" has taken hold. The most severe critics of human resources reinvention, many of them in Congress, argue that it has resulted in lost accountability, political shenanigans, and even higher costs. Regardless, agreement remains that change must continue and that a dynamic human resource function is required to keep up with today's information age environment. Helping government find the right balance between flexibility and fairness is a challenging assignment for public sector consultants.

State and municipal level governments have also undertaken reform of their human resources functions. Some have significantly altered civil service rules by changing their approach to classification (e.g., broad banding), developing performance outcome training and evaluation processes, and giving less weight to seniority and written examinations in promotional decisions. Most radical, however, is the recent action by the State of Florida, which outsourced all human resources functions to a private firm at a cost of $280 million over seven years; the state expects to save $173 million. The award was given to Convergys Corporation, a private sector firm specializing in integrated billing, employee care, and customer services. Convergys promised not only increased efficiencies, but the use of the Web to enable state employees to exercise greater control over their career planning through access to training courses, job opening information, and a resume databank. Additionally, the firm will be involved in the development of marketing tools for employee recruitment.

The goal of all these efforts is to allow states and local entities to focus on their primary mission of providing better and more varied service to citizens. There is clearly room for innovation, and some interesting examples are being set.[9]

Perhaps, the most difficult human resources challenge facing state and local municipalities is to find ways to cope with the replacement of an aging workforce. Compared to the private sector, the public sector has a significantly higher and accelerating retirement rate. Moreover, due to budget freezes and cutbacks during the 1990s, many agencies are today understaffed. Yet, at the state level of government, unlike the federal government, there is little evidence of making a strategic issue out of workforce planning. A notable exception is the Los Angeles County Training Academy, which has adopted a corporate university model and a commitment to prepare the county's 90,000-employee workforce for future leadership and technical competency.

Given the centrality of human resources issues in any transformational change effort, the next logical step requires that government HR leaders become strategic partners with senior management in their strategic planning and change programs. Similar to the private sector, the opportunity exists for HR professionals to: 1) improve the efficiency of transactional processes through the use of information technology; 2) plan the recruitment of a more skilled workforce based on strategic decisions and ensure that the right people are ready at the right time; 3) use training and development programs to support strategic directions, including the development of teams, the alignment of organizational goals, and the need for transformational change and lifelong learning; and 4) become the repository of organization development skills to help more technically oriented managers learn to implement changes effectively.

By becoming a strategic partner, HR professionals can highlight the human issues involved in transformational change and draw attention to the steps needed to increase human capital (see Chapter 8 for more discussion on this issue). At this point, due primarily to its past negative image, we do not see many HR leaders being included at the strategy level. We recommend that whenever consultants are involved in significant change programs (regardless of functional area), they should recognize and include the HR implications in their recommendations.

Performance Measurement

Nearly everyone agrees with the adage, "What gets measured, gets done." Yet, for most of this century, academics and practitioners have lamented the unwillingness of public sector agencies to measure the outcomes of their programs. While we know that the better performing private sector companies rigorously set objectives and use systematic measures to evaluate progress, lagging behind are public sector agencies that have historically remained steadfast in their use of limited performance measures (e.g., size of budget, headcount, number of arrests, number of clients served). Scant attention has been given to measures of resource utilization efficiency or program effectiveness (i.e., outcome benefits to the public).

Most public sector performance reports tell us how much work has been done, but we cannot determine from them how well it was done. Public sector agencies have often justified this approach by citing the complexity and high cost (rarely funded by fiscal bodies) involved in developing meaningful performance measurement systems. Others note that the lack of competition and bottom-line accountability removes any incentive for them to gather better performance data.

Today, with the current public sector focus on customer service, performance measurement has finally emerged on the front burner for public agencies. Performance measures can now be found in most reinvention proposals and strategic plans. However, from our perspective, developing and using performance measures has not been an easy task. First, it requires an exceptional educational effort because public employees have little experience in this arena. Also, the problem of choice of terminology and actual measures has lead to many debilitating debates over what constitutes an appropriate indicator for a given outcome. Next, the necessary data needed to determine "success" has often gone uncollected. Consequently, all of these require the allocation of new resources and the design of new systems at a time of resource scarcity. Given the choice between focusing on the long-term benefits of performance measurement and the need to allocate resources to other immediate problems, the latter usually wins. Thus, there is a constant need to balance the workload demands involved in designing a viable performance measurement program with the day-to-day workload requirements in delivering services to the public. From our observations, for progress to be made in improving performance measurement, a major commitment in money, time, and people must be made. In addition, the involved agencies must be prepared for much learning through trial and error, as well as the need to maintain constant vigilance to prevent slippage back to traditional input measures.

As performance measurement has advanced as a "cause" throughout the public sector, numerous federal, state, and local municipalities have begun to design innovative systems and even share information. Thus, Oregon is known for its quality of life measures and New York City for its use of CompStats to reallocate resources in order to reduce crime, while the City of Baltimore has progressed to the point where many of its agencies now have a set of performance outcome measures that can be monitored regularly, thereby providing for the identification of problems, development of new strategies, and better reallocation of resources. Indeed, Baltimore's CitiStats has created a new level of public sector accountability that others will surely emulate.

Also, the growth of performance measurement has enabled agencies to benchmark themselves against others. When used properly, these benchmarks can help agencies and their constituents determine the best performance measures for their programs and spur agencies to improve their services. Our experience suggests that by providing objective performance data to the public, government agencies can build greater credibility and "rally" resources when performance is not meeting expectations. Better and more transparent outcome data can help to focus many constituencies on fixing the problem, rather than on assigning blame.

As citizens demand higher quality services and as more government agencies adopt a customer orientation, public sector consultants can play an influential role. Currently, few consultants offer performance measures with their proposals and recommendations (and they are often not required to do so in RFPs (Requests for Proposal). We suggest that public sector consultants take the opportunity to advance the quality of service delivery by adding performance measures to their proposals and reports. Such actions will: 1) increase awareness of the importance of measurement; and 2) encourage "deeper" discussion of the intent of the recommendations and how an agency evaluates its success.

STAKEHOLDER AND CHANGE ISSUES

At this point, a cautionary note is appropriate. Because of the presence of the public voice, large-scale change in government takes longer to implement. Consultants who have aided other organizations on transformational change projects need to remember that the "clock speed" for government is considerably slower; but, given the foundations of democracy, this slower pace is necessary.

As summarized in Exhibit 11.2, every government leader must deal with a wider range of stakeholders than does the CEO of a major corporation. This multiplicity of forces that can impede progress is one reason for the relatively slow pace of change. First, the leader is often distracted from the job of communicating a new vision and gaining support for it by the demands of the media or legislative entities for answers to today's newsworthy crisis. Unlike their private sector corollary, public sector leaders cannot duck these requests with a simple "no comment" or turn the task over to their public relations spokesperson. Consultants need to be sensitive to the continuous public scrutiny faced by clients.

Further, public employee unions perceive many reforms to be simply an attempt to reduce their membership enrollment and power, and therefore, this concern requires additional time from government leaders to gain their support. In the Clinton/Gore administration, this task was raised to the level of an Executive Order of the President that required each agency to establish labor/management partnership councils to discuss proposed changes. Similar partnership council was even formed at the Cabinet level to underline the importance of employee involvement in the reinventing government process. Any advice that implies job loss or even reconfiguring the responsibilities of the workforce must, therefore, include suggestions for how to gain support from employees and particularly the unionized groups.

Finally, the voice of the taxpayer is always monitored by elected officials, especially in biannual and quadrennial election cycles. Consequently, those working for elected officials often judge the introduction of a change proposal and/or the pace of implementation based on their assessment of the political implications (i.e., election fallout). This is antithetical to the textbook admonition that fundamental changes require sustained and focused efforts that are not interrupted by other concerns.

In addition to the problem of gaining support from a wide variety of stakeholders, agency leaders, when introducing major changes, face the challenge of communicating with and educating large numbers of public servants about proposed changes. As summarized by a CIO for one large state agency, "One of the real differences in managing the introduction of new information-based processes in public organizations is the tremendous educational process that must occur." Taking the employee population from awareness to understanding of the required changes uses up precious time and resources and is often therefore given short shrift in the budget process. Yet failure to ensure this transfer of knowledge can easily lead to the failure of the overall effort. For instance, when the State of California adopted its procurement reform efforts, they failed to provide the necessary education and training in new procedural processes to be used by newly empowered frontline workers. The result was a steady deterioration in the procurement process.

One creative solution to the challenge of communication has occurred through the use of the "hammer awards" by the National Partnership for Reinventing Government. These symbolic awards were given in public settings to teams of federal employees who implemented the recommended reinvention reforms. The process served to spread the word on what changes were desired; even the process of submitting nominations to the reinventing taskforce provided a steady stream of best practices that could be further shared with the workforce on the Web and through newsletters. Still, no amount of creativity and effort can fully overcome the fundamental challenge of size and time in bringing change to government organizations.

WATCH OUT FOR THE POTHOLES

Throughout this chapter, we have emphasized the need for consultants to focus on certain needs of the public sector and to demonstrate sensitivity to the political environment while working with multiple constituencies. We close now with four consultant pitfalls that seem to occur all too frequently in the public arena.

Overlooking Behavioral Expectations

With increased frequency, both consultants and government agencies have recognized during the negotiation process that they need to agree upon defined outcomes in the consulting contract. This outcome focus has ameliorated many past disputes where consultants have completed the required work (e.g., designed a new software program, conducted the required focus groups), but the client was later dissatisfied (e.g., cost factors made full implementation impossible).

However, from our perspective, a new issue has emerged that must also be addressed during the contracting process—the client's behavioral expectations. In the public sector, in particular, clients often expect consultants to be available for unanticipated meetings (often of short duration), constant telephone conferrals, and even additional presentations to various constituency groups—many of which were not anticipated in the original contract. As one IT consultant told us, "They want me to adopt their same public service commitment, but when I can't meet their time demands, they start to see me as an adversary." Some consultants have tried to negotiate both an outcome and an hourly rate for these additional services, but finding the proper balance remains elusive. Our advice is to be ready to spend extra time on these requests, some of which can be planned for and budgeted, but others can't be. In the long run, being available to clients, even when it may seem like donating pro bono time, will go a long way toward cementing the client relationship, usually leading to more work for the consultant.

Playing "God"

It is well established in the consulting literature that clients can become highly dependent on the advice of their expert consultants. While some degree of dependency is understandable, the attentive consultant needs to move clients toward greater self-sufficiency. In IT projects, for instance, government clients, anxious to provide better services to citizens but lacking in-depth knowledge of advanced platforms and applications, have been particularly susceptible to complete reliance on outside expertise. However, as shown in the sidebar, this has lead to some very expensive IT debacles in California.[10]

Consulting Insights **California's Rocky IT Road**

As with other states, California experienced a decade of IT project failures: 1) 1992: $52 million state lottery application; 2) 1994: $51 million Department of Motor Vehicle database plan; 3) 1997: $111 million Automated Child Support System. As a result, the legislature created the Department of Information Technology (DOIT) in 1995 to set overall IT policy, the position of Chief Information Officer in 1999 to advise the Governor on IT policy, and the Office of E-government in 2000 to move procurement into the information age. The Department of General Services established a series of educational programs for those involved in procurement as well.

These efforts unraveled in 2002 when DOIT was a willing partner in the award of a $95 million enterprise licensing agreement with Oracle, allowing 270,000 state employees to use Oracle database software, only to discover during legislative hearings that there was limited competitive bidding and that the contract contemplated more licenses than the state had employees. The subsequent well-publicized rash of high-level resignations by the CIO, director of the Department of General Services, and the head of the Office of E-government, plus the refusal of the legislature to extend the sunset clause on DOIT, highlighted the dangers of allowing consultants to overreach.

Unfortunately, some public sector consultants become power intoxicated as they take advantage of their influence over elected officials and agency executives. While a loss of perspective by consultants may be due to a real desire to affect public policy, the unintended effects can be harmful; we have seen consultants 1) attempt to establish "cults" of client advocates in an attempt to spread and sell a specific approach or technique further in the public sector or 2) venture into areas that exceed their contract obligations and expert knowledge.

Isolating Potential Allies

At the opposite end of the spectrum are public sector consultants who try to maintain exclusivity with their clients. These consultants eschew collaboration with others, repeatedly offering reasons why the involvement of others will create more discord than benefit. It reminds us of the private sector competitive model where the goal is to capture the ground and then protect it against outsiders. Recently, we have observed two instances where consulting firms lost future business because of their unwillingness to negotiate contracts that included working with other consulting firms.

This go-it-alone approach clashes with the public sector movement toward cross-functional team approaches and the desire to build integrated services. As noted earlier, many public agencies and consultants are forming new alliances in their efforts to provide better customer service. Thus, while consultants may indicate that they prefer to operate independently, their isolationist style and approach may undermine the client's ability to form new alliances.

Overlooking Educational Needs

A common characteristic of public sector employment is that nearly all new employees enter government on a technical track and can only transition onto a managerial track after many years of employment. As a result, even at the managerial level, the leadership's focus is often technical and short term. Furthermore, most employees remain within a single agency and, therefore, express a rather narrow perspective on the world of management. Thus, when consultants introduce recommendations for "doing business" differently, it can require significant relearning by the client organization to gain acceptance. Even simple ideas from the private sector may be seen as too complex for implementation and likely to meet with strong resistance. Unfortunately, we see few attempts by public sector consultants to link their proposals to supportive and complementary educational programs. This leads to both a greater percentage of rejections and a less positive view of consultants than is necessary.

BRIDGING THE DEVELOPMENT GAP

Throughout this chapter, we have emphasized both the unique aspects of public sector consultation and the growing opportunities for expanded consulting services. Yet, many consultants lack experience in the public sector, with even fewer specializing in this domain. This raises the developmental question of how can management consultants increase their learning and savvy about the public sector?

As we survey the educational landscape, we find the educational playing field relatively barren when compared to the private sector. For instance, the Management Consulting Division of the Academy of Management focuses almost exclusively on the private sector, while the Public Sector Division of the Academy offers few applied sessions and virtually nothing on consulting. Similarly, many Colleges of Business offer courses in managerial consulting that emphasize only the private sector, and relatively few comparable courses can be found in Colleges of Public Administration. Simply stated, if we are going to improve the quality of public sector consultation, we must establish programs to educate those who wish to consult in this arena.

We believe that public sector consulting is an exciting field that will only grow in the future. Its complexity and bureaucratic barriers no doubt appear, at first glance, to be an overwhelming challenge and perhaps even a deterrent to eager private sector consultants. However, this very complexity and set of hurdles can lead to interesting and rewarding consulting projects. The public sector environment of problems and opportunities is both intellectually stimulating and highly demanding from an implementation perspective, providing conditions that will surely make for stronger consultants. Today it is also financially rewarding. The public sector wants and needs consulting assistance, and those who are well prepared and accept the challenge will benefit immensely.

Notes to the Chapter

[1]Top-consultant.com, dtd 12/12/02.

[2]Ibid.

[3]D. Osborne and T. Gabler, *Reinventing Government: How the Entrepreneurial Spirit Is Transforming the Public Sector* (Reading, MA: Addison-Wesley, 1992).

[4]Governmentum Partners, L.L.C. is an example of a government-oriented *boutique.* The firm focuses on transformational change with a special niche in the use of technology to improve performance and establish new levels of customer service. At http://www.governmentum.com.

[5]DeSeve, Ed., Managing Principal, Governmentum Partners, L.L.C.

[6]United Nations and American Society for Personnel Administration, Global survey of e-government (2001). Available at http://www.unpan.org/egovernment2.asp.

[7]Reported by J. Moon, "The Evolution of E-government Among Municipalities: Rhetoric or Reality?" *Public Administration Review,* 62 no. 4 (2002): 424–433.

[8]S. Hays, and R. Kearney, "Human Resource Practices in State Government: Findings from a National Survey," *Public Administration Review,* 61 no. 5 (2001): 508–607.

[9]For information on Florida system, access: http://www.myflorida.com/dms, dtd 9/5/02.

[10]A. Glassman and M. Winograd, Using multiple frames to understand and rebuild California's Procurement Process, Grant proposal for PWC Foundation (2002).

Part 4

Implementation
and Change

INTRODUCTION

From the client's perspective, the acid test of a consultant's value resides in achieving real improvement in performance. Otherwise, it is difficult for clients to justify their added investment in consulting. The inability of consulting firms to produce results can easily damage their reputation and cause prospective clients to shy away.

Unfortunately, too many clients have experienced projects that either fail or fall short of expectations. Not many years ago, and even in some cases today, this failure in implementation was blamed by consultants on the client because the consultants adhered to their expert role of only making recommendations while leaving implementation to the client.

However, the tide has clearly shifted over the past decade to place much more responsibility on consultants for producing results. Many consulting firms now employ intervention approaches that are designed to ensure ownership and commitment to change by the client's workforce, and they often stay longer into the implementation period. But these changes do not occur easily or naturally. Most clients prefer stability while adhering to past practices, and there are always senior executives who resist changes that threaten their power base.

Chapter 12, "Intervention Strategies in Management Consulting," argues that consultants often apply the wrong intervention approach to client situations. As a result, resistance arises and the change effort fails. The chapter goes on to describe four major intervention strategies, from expert-based to process-based, each of which works only under certain conditions in the client situation. The challenge for the consultant is to understand the client's situation in-depth and to choose the appropriate intervention strategy. Unfortunately, it is not easily accomplished because consulting firms often have a "preferred" intervention approach (their own set of best practices) that they apply in most situations. The author makes a plea for greater flexibility in the consultant's choice of intervention strategies as they relate to certain conditions in the client firm.

Mergers and acquisitions, the subject of Chapter 13, "Consulting to Integrate Mergers and Acquisitions," covers another important change situation fraught with frequent failure. Two-thirds of all merger deals fall short of expectations, with half of those becoming outright failures. The chapter points out that most advisory work on current M&A transactions takes place before the deal is consummated, usually conducted by lawyers and bankers. However, a real need for consulting assistance exists, not only in the due diligence period but with the difficult problems of post merger integration. The initial technical advisors often underestimate the subsequent post-merger implementation issues, which are the focus of this chapter. Highlighted are the barriers to integration, such as lack of preparation, divergent cultures, and disagreement among top managers about the goals of the merger. The author suggests various consulting strategies to deal with these issues, including listening deeply to the various parties and clarifying their intentions. Despite their high failure rate, mergers will no doubt continue, and consultants will need to provide post-merger integration services.

Assisting a client through organizational change is one of the most demanding consulting tasks, since it requires a high level of persuasion skills but also deep personal insight into the consultant's own strengths and weaknesses. Chapter 14, "On Becoming a Transformational Change Agent," argues that the consultant must serve as a behavioral role model for the client and become "one" with the change effort if he or she is to be successful. More typically, as the chapter points out, the consultant is reluctant to recommend changes of great significance because the client ultimately doesn't believe in enduring disruptions that upset the status quo, thereby ending the consulting relationship. This hidden collusion between consultant and client endures despite words and recommendations about change.

The two authors of Chapter 14 take the reader on a career journey, presented in letters back and forth between themselves, father and son, concerning the developmental challenge in becoming a successful change agent. The letters focus on the required journey of a consultant in acquiring the skills of a masterful change agent. The developing consultant must learn to enhance his or her skills through experiencing four growth stages ranging from novice to expert and then to master. A framework for "advanced change theory" comprising strategies for changing human systems is presented as a guide for learning by the masterful change agent. The chapter provides a valuable mirror for the reader's personal reflection on his or her attitudes toward clients and the change process.

CHAPTER 12

Intervention Strategies in Management Consulting

Thomas G. Cummings, University of Southern California

ABOUT THE AUTHOR

Thomas G. Cummings

Thomas G. Cummings is Professor and Chair of the Department of Management and Organization at the Marshall School of Business, University of Southern California. He has authored and coauthored nineteen books and is currently Vice President and Program Chair of the Academy of Management. His major research and consulting interests include designing high-performing organizations and strategic change management.

Consulting firms typically describe their services in marketing brochures in terms of their specialized practice areas, such as strategic planning or the financial services industry. Although these features help to explain what services the firm provides to what kinds of clients, they reveal relatively little about how the firm actually intervenes with clients to deliver these services. This is the unspoken iceberg that lies beneath the surface of marketing pizzazz, and yet it is what I believe determines success in consulting outcomes.

Like all practical professions, management consulting faces persistent questions from researchers and critics of the profession about the efficacy of its applications. This is especially true when it comes to implementing proposed changes in organizations. Management consultants frequently discover that their recommendations, no matter how valid or relevant, make little if any impact on how their client organizations function. As a result, their advice fails to translate into real organization change. Explanations and excuses for this unfortunate execution gap existing between recommendations and implementation can come from consultants (e.g., no top management support to implement) and from the client (e.g., recommendations were impractical).[1]

The explanation for this gap lies in the way consultants choose to intervene in organizations. They frequently use the wrong intervention approach for the problem at hand. Or the client resists a recommended approach that indeed might work but which the client doesn't understand and therefore objects. Consulting firms are often wedded to their unique intervention approaches, the "XYZ firm way," regardless of the situation. And clients are often naive about what questions to ask regarding what types of interventions may or may not work in their organizations. As a result, they buy the wrong intervention only to learn too late about their mistake.

---

*Consulting
Insights*   **Case of Implementation Failure**

Alpha Inc., a large multi-service consulting firm, is renowned for its advanced models and techniques for assessing and determining corporate strategy. Employing the brightest MBAs from mostly top-ten business schools, Alpha has built a solid reputation for delivering the "goods" when it comes to assessing clients and their markets and recommending appropriate strategies. Moreover, Alpha responds rapidly to client needs. As one amazed customer remarked: "Alpha is like the Army in Desert Storm. A dozen or more of them descended on us almost overnight, collecting data, crunching numbers, and making proposals." Unfortunately, Alpha's approach to management consulting is increasingly coming under attack from critics who suggest that "good analyses and proposals" are not enough to achieve success. Rather, "execution" of corporate strategy is what matters. Indeed, the CEO of one of Alpha's clients was recently cited in a popular business magazine as saying: "Alpha did a good job for us. The market analysis was insightful and the recommended business strategy made sense. Where we ran into trouble was getting middle managers to buy into it. They just didn't seem to understand where we needed to go and what needed to be done to get there. Perhaps this isn't Alpha's fault, but they could have warned us. We wasted a large investment."

Greater knowledge about interventions is essential to consultants and clients alike for improving consulting practice and enhancing implementation success.[2] Consultants can benefit by knowing more clearly what kinds of interventions may or may not work under certain conditions. And perceptive clients can become more aware of the right questions to ask of potential consultants about their intervention approaches before deciding to accept a specific proposal.

This chapter addresses both sides of the consulting relationship and shows how the nature of consulting interventions can affect outcomes, negatively or positively, in different situations. It presents a framework based on two key dimensions underlying most interventions: delivery mode and content focus. Delivery mode refers to how consulting is conducted (e.g., types of involvement) with the client, and content focus refers to the substance (e.g., theories and issues) being considered by the consultants. Then it describes how these two dimensions intersect in practice to give rise to four possible intervention strategies: expertise-based, organization-based, teaching-based, and process-based. Each strategy will be discussed for its strengths and weaknesses under specific conditions in a client's organization. The chapter concludes with broader implications for the future development of consultants, clients, and the consulting profession.

KEY DIMENSIONS IN CONSULTING INTERVENTIONS

As shown in Exhibit 12.1, the two dimensions of delivery mode and content focus lay behind the four basic intervention strategies in management consulting. The two dimensions in themselves provide useful insights into the assumptions and dynamics that underpin the intervention strategies.

Delivery Mode Dimension

The delivery mode in consulting represents a continuum with two different modes of delivery at each end, from study and recommend to facilitate and learn (see horizontal dimension in Exhibit 12.1). As these terms imply, the

Exhibit 12.1	Intervention Model

Delivery Modes

		Study and Recommend	Facilitate and Learn
	Technical Systems	Expertise-Based Strategy	Teaching-Based Strategy
Content Focus			
	Social Systems	Organization-Based Strategy	Process-Based Strategy

former mode involves analyzing the client's situation and proposing solutions; the latter mode emphasizes helping clients learn for themselves about how to improve their organizations. Similar distinctions made elsewhere in this book include describing consultants as "experts" versus "advisors" (Maister, Chapter 2); "prescriptive" versus "facilitative" consulting roles (Nadler, Chapter 8); and in other literature, such as "consultant-centered" versus "client-centered" change.[3]

Exhibit 12.2 presents these two opposing *delivery modes* in terms of their history, basic assumptions, and other aspects that highlight their major differences.

Study and Recommend. This is the oldest and most prevalent *delivery mode* in management consulting. Consultants analyze clients' organizations and propose solutions to their problems. Its historical roots go back over seventy-five years to the rapid emergence of management consulting as a profession following World War I. At the time, engineering was the most developed of the applied sciences with specific applications for business firms. Thus, its rational problem-solving approach heavily influenced how consulting services were delivered to management. Indeed, the profession's first society was called the Association of Consulting Management Engineers (ACME), which later changed its name to the Association of Management Consulting Firms (AMCF) as companies came to dominate the industry and other applied disciplines, such as accounting and economics, entered the field.

From its engineering origins, it is not surprising that the *study and recommend* mode treats organizational change as an empirical-rational process. It assumes that managers are guided by reason and evidence and will use rational criteria to make decisions about changing the organization. Because the chief threat to rationality is ignorance or superstition, managers need scientifically based empirical information to make good decisions. It is assumed that such so-called "facts" will persuade them to change.

Exhibit 12.2	Alternative Delivery Modes	
	Study and Recommend	Facilitate and Learn
History	Engineering; ACME	Humanistic psychology
Assumptions about organization change	Empirical-rational process; Change via persuasion	Normative-reeducativeprocess; change via involvement
Underlying values	Effectiveness, efficiency	Collaboration, openness, trust
Major objectives	Getting it right	Increasing capacity of client to solve own problems
Consultant expertise	Discipline based	Clinical based
Role of consultant	Solution giver	Facilitator
Role of client	Solution implementer	Co-learner
Intensity and length of engagement	Arms length; periodic	High; continuous

Based on these assumptions, the study and recommend mode emphasizes hard data and bottom-line results. It promotes organizational effectiveness and efficiency, with the goal of finding the right solution to a clearly defined management problem with profit-and-loss consequences.

This *study and recommend* mode tends to view management as a "science" where change is implemented via rational persuasion. Consultants study the client's situation to provide objective evidence about the causes of problems and give expert advice on what to do about them. To be successful, *study and recommend* consultants need to be seen by clients as objective experts. Thus, they work hard to differentiate themselves from clients. They act as detached solution givers and not involved implementers; they engage with clients in arms-length relationships where they meet only periodically.

To enhance their perceived expertise, these consultants draw heavily on theory and knowledge from the academic business disciplines (e.g., economics), which provides them with analytical models and prescriptive solutions, such as Porter's Five Forces model or the BCG matrix. All this helps to assure, and reinforce the belief, that consultants are unbiased and professionally proficient. Such views are fundamental to the *study and recommend* delivery mode.

Facilitate and Learn. At the other end of the *delivery mode* continuum, the *facilitate and learn* mode focuses on helping clients learn how to improve their own organizations. It dates to the 1950s with the emergence of humanistic psychology and applications of nondirective therapy to management consulting. Many training programs eventually evolved out of this movement, such as the Managerial Grid and Six Sigma. The *facilitate and learn* mode emphasizes the developmental nature of people and organizations. This approach assumes that the more developed an organization, the better able it is to solve its own problems and to improve itself. Thus, management consulting under this mode is concerned with transferring skills and knowledge to organizations so they can self-improve their capacity to solve future problems.

The *facilitate and learn* mode considers organization change as a normative reeducative process. It does not deny human rationality but assumes that in social contexts, people's behavior is heavily influenced by social norms and their commitment to them. For change to occur, people must modify norms and values and develop commitment to new ones. This cannot be simply accomplished by changes in the amount of information available and intellectual logic alone. It requires the active involvement of people in changing the attitudes, values, skills, and relationships underlying their behavior. Thus, people must participate in their own reeducation and, thereby, change themselves if they are to change at all.

Given these assumptions, the *facilitate and learn* mode emphasizes learning and commitment to change. It values consulting relationships that promote collaboration, openness, and trust among participants, which in turn facilitate helping clients learn how to change and improve themselves. *Facilitate and learn* consultants instruct clients on how to change their organizations through active participation of employees in the change process itself. Therefore, consulting engagements tend to be highly intense and continuous. If clients are to grow and develop, they must transcend their natural dependency on consultants. This places a heavy demand on a consultant's clinical expertise and social acumen. The consultant must act more like a facilitator and trainer than an expert as clients develop their own competencies for implementing change and improvement.

Content Focus Dimension

The second key dimension that underlies most interventions concerns the *content focus* of a consulting engagement. This involves the substantive aspects of the "problem" that consultants must address for the client, such as value chain analysis, reward systems, information systems, organization design, and team decision making. It also includes the content of knowledge and methods brought to bear by the consultants, such as psychological theories, marketing models, or operations techniques.

Content focus differs enormously in management consulting and often serves as the basis for a firm to advertise its specialized knowledge and services in a particular practice area, such as human resources or marketing or operations. Content focus falls along a continuum from *"technical systems"* to *"social systems"* (see vertical dimension in Exhibit 12.1). The former has to do with the functional business disciplines, tools, and methods through which client organizations make and deliver products and services; while the latter involves the human relationships that occur among employees as they organize, coordinate, and control their efforts to make decisions and communicate with each other.[4] These two aspects of content focus are described further in Exhibit 12.3.

Technical Systems. Like the *study and recommend* delivery mode, the *technical systems* focus is the oldest and most pervasive content focus in management consulting. It dates back to Frederick Taylor's pioneering work in scientific management in the early 1900s, which emphasized efficiency at work

Exhibit 12.3	Content Focus	
	Technical Systems	Social Systems
History	Scientific management	Organization development
Primary emphasis	Solving problems correctly	Making things run smoother
Assumptions about the nature of organizations	Objective; independently measured	Subjective; socially constructed
Assumptions about knowledge utilization	General knowledge applies to specific situations	Local knowledge necessary
Action levers for change	Strategy, task structure, and business functions	Individuals, groups, and their relationships
Pertinent data	Manifest Industry and competitors; client company; business functions	Latent Leadership; decision making, communication, and problem solving processes; interpersonal relations, group process
Consultant selection criteria	Technical expertise and industry knowledge	Interpersonal competence
Consultant retention criteria	Demonstrable work and financial results	Trust

through the analysis and redesign of jobs and work methods. Because organizations tended to be highly inefficient, the initial success of scientific management fueled widespread demand for this consulting expertise. Thus, early management consulting concentrated on the technical side of organizations, primarily on the shop floor. Over time, this focus extended to marketing, finance, information and control systems, and more recently, corporate strategy.

Underlying a technical focus are certain assumptions about how to understand issues of concern to clients. It is assumed that a specific body of knowledge exists that can be drawn on by educated consultants from different disciplines. Such knowledge is viewed as applicable across situations. Thus, consultants intervene to apply general expertise and others' experiences to different clients facing similar problems. Moreover, client organizations are treated as objective entities with their own properties and features. Therefore, consultants believe they can independently measure and analyze these features.

Based on these assumptions, the technical systems content focus addresses the more manifest or observable aspects of a client's problems. It emphasizes technical variables as action levers for improvement, including the client's marketing strategy, task structure, or information systems.

Technically oriented consultants generally collect and analyze information about the organization's industry and competitors, its design elements, and how it achieves on various performance criteria. Based on that information, they apply technical knowledge and expertise to develop specific innovations for improving the organization. Thus, clients select management consultants for their strong technical expertise and knowledge of the client's industry. They often retain them again for demonstrating measurable improvements in client functioning and performance.

Social Systems. This content focus involves the human side of organizations, and it is rooted in the emergence of the knowledge fields of organization design and organization development in the 1950s and later in leadership theory and change methods in the 1990s. As organizations grew larger and more bureaucratic, they experienced a host of unintended social problems; members found it increasingly difficult to communicate both laterally and vertically, to resolve problems within and across groups, and to respond energetically to managerial directives. Also, consultants experienced growing resistance to technical solutions.

The fields of organization design and organization development, drawing heavily on the disciplines of psychology and sociology, responded to these problems with a variety of interventions for improving social processes and overcoming resistance to change, such as innovative organization structures, team building, process consultation, and conflict management. In focusing on social content, management consultants placed heavy emphasis on resolving social ills and making things run smoother. They addressed social processes as the key to implementing organization change.

This content focus, supplemented by research on leadership and change, treats organizations from a subjective perspective, both in their design and in their evolution. Organizations are viewed as socially constructed out of employee intents, values, and perceptions. They involve members taking action and making sense out of their behavior, thereby creating shared meaning for organized activities. Thus, to understand organizations, it is necessary to see them as the members of the organization see them.

Subjective experiences play a key role in applying knowledge to organizations. Because members' sense-making is unique to each organization, generalized knowledge must be adapted to fit specific organization contexts. So called "local knowledge" is essential to this adaptation process.

Given these views, the social systems content focus treats individuals and groups as the key action levers for improving organizations, primarily through social processes having to do with structure, leadership, decision making, communication, and problem solving. Consultants typically spend considerable time with organization members to understand how they perceive those processes. Then, they apply their expertise to help make these social processes run smoother and more effectively. Clients tend to select management consultants with strong interpersonal competence and a belief that solutions lie within the members of the organization. They retain consultants they can trust and be open with during their contacts.

FOUR ALTERNATIVE INTERVENTION STRATEGIES

The two underlying dimensions of interventions—delivery mode and content focus—interact in the real world to produce four basic intervention strategies for consultants (depicted earlier in Exhibit 12.1). I have labeled these four strategies as: *expertise-based, organization-based, teaching-based,* and *process-based.* In this section, I describe each strategy in some depth, exploring its strengths and weaknesses, and suggest situations where each is likely to be more or less effective. Later in this chapter, I will consider how the four intervention strategies can be used in combination during certain types of consulting engagements and at different stages in a project.

Expertise-based Strategy

This intervention strategy combines the study and recommend, delivery mode with a content focus on technical systems. From its roots in engineering and scientific management, the *expertise-based* strategy has come to dominate management consulting. Today, it is used by most large consulting firms to intervene with clients.

The *expertise-based* strategy is relatively straightforward.[5] Consultants collect and analyze data about technical aspects of the client organization, such as its products, markets, operations, and economic conditions. They then recommend specific solutions to client problems, such as formulating a new global strategy, product structure, or implementing a JIT inventory control system.

To be unbiased observers and advisors, *expertise-based* consultants clearly divide the consultant and client roles; the former is concerned with recommending while the latter with implementing. As experts, consultants work hard to show how their general technical knowledge applies to specific client situations.

A typical example of the *expertise-based* strategy involves a large management consulting firm hired to advise a company's top management team on possible changes in its business strategy. Led by a seasoned project manager with experience in the client's industry, several junior consultants are assigned full time to the consulting engagement, which lasts from three to six months. They gather data on the client and its competitive environment, usually drawing on market research and industry dynamics. Based on this information and analysis, the consultants recommend specific changes to the client's business strategy. This is accomplished in a multi-media presentation to the top management team and backed by a written report containing supporting data.

The *expertise-based* intervention strategy has a number of distinct strengths. It offers clients an objective and independent assessment of their situation, which can uncover problems and opportunities that clients may not have addressed or considered. *Expertise-based* consultants bring new perspectives to clients; their knowledge of client industries and competitors will suggest benchmarks and best practices that clients can implement.

In recent years, *expertise-based* consultants have increasingly applied their capabilities to perform tasks or provide services that clients normally do themselves, particularly support functions such as accounting, human resource management, and information processing. This external capability provides clients with viable options to outsource tasks that are not part of their core competence and that consultants can do better and cheaper.

Perhaps the greatest strength of the *expertise-based* intervention strategy is that clients can easily understand it and defend its use to relevant stakeholders.

Using experts to solve problems is generally considered normal and highly rational. In case of failure, clients can reliably blame consultants rather than themselves.

The *expertise-based* strategy also contains certain downsides, however. It is unlikely to lead to high levels of employee commitment to change, thus resulting in implementation problems. While expert consultants will brief the client occasionally on their progress, they typically do not involve the client in data gathering, analysis, and formulating recommendations. As a result, the client's employees may not support the proposed changes and may resist or even sabotage them.

The *expertise-based* strategy involves a division of labor where consultants design improvements and clients implement them. This division can lead to differences in design criteria and change orientation between consultants and clients. *Expertise-based* consultants are likely to favor change programs with explicit schedules, goals, and change activities, while underplaying the ability of the client to implement the recommended change program. Moreover, consultants seek solutions with proven records of success and, consequently, rely on change programs that have worked well in other settings and that can be readily packaged and adopted by clients. These features are intended to assure that the consultants' expertise will be recognized and valued by clients and that the integrity of their recommendations will persist.

Clients, on the other hand, often prefer change programs that afford maximum freedom to modify and adjust the changes to fit their specific situation, including its culture, politics, and capabilities. They seek flexibility and local control over changes. These fundamental differences can lead to consulting reports that simply gather the proverbial dust on the CEO's bookcase or that result in overt conflicts between consultants and clients.

Probably the most troublesome limitation of the *expertise-based* strategy is that it does little to improve the client's ability to improve itself. *Expertise-based* consulting is aimed primarily at solving client problems in a single engagement, not at providing managers and employees with the skills and knowledge necessary to analyze and solve future problems. Because the expertise to assess organizations and propose improvements resides with the consultants, clients tend to become dependent on them and see little need to gain such skills themselves.

Despite these inherent problems, the *expertise-based* intervention strategy is well suited to particular situations. It is especially relevant when client's problems are clearly defined, limited in scope, and require minimal amounts of organization change. In these settings, clients are likely to be clear about the "problem" but believe they do not have the knowledge or resources to understand and resolve it. Thus, they are likely to choose experts who meet their needs. The consultants can then apply their technical expertise without needing high levels of client involvement. Whether the client will then implement the recommendations remains highly problematic.

Organization-based Strategy

This intervention strategy blends the *study and recommend* delivery mode with the content dimension focused on social systems. In dealing with the social side of organizations, *organization-based* consultants address client issues related to leadership, decision making, communication, power and politics, and interpersonal and group dynamics.[6]

Like the previous strategy, it is expert driven; consultants analyze and advise while clients implement change. Consultant expertise is generally rooted in the organizational behavior disciplines involving social relations, group process, and the like. *Organization-based* consultants seek to provide clients with the right solutions to their organizational problems, especially ones that make things run smoother and more effectively.

Consultants applying the *organization-based* strategy typically look at organizations from a subjective viewpoint. They seek to understand client organizations as members see them and thus employ diagnostic methods, such as interviews and surveys, that tap into employee perceptions.

Like expert consultants, *organization-based* consultants tend to regard organization change as a rational persuasion process supported by theory and evidence. To convince clients to change, they provide expert insights about members' subjective experience; they then draw on those interpretations to make skilled recommendations (e.g., new organization structure) for how clients can improve themselves. This application of external expertise to internal subjective data can change how clients view their situation; it can reveal new possibilities and show them how their local knowledge can inform change.

To make this work, *organization-based* consultants display a good deal of independence from the client's situation. They remain unbiased toward clients yet establish a close enough relationship with them to elicit relevant social data. Clearly, this is no easy task for even the best organization consultants.

An example of the *organization-based* strategy involves a consulting firm that is hired to help a company understand and solve its stated "morale" problem. A small team of experienced consultants is assigned to the project, and they negotiate a six-month project to study the problem and make recommendations. The consultants collect and analyze data using an organization-wide survey that includes measures of several organizational features that might affect employee morale, such as communication, leadership, pay, and working conditions. Based on the survey results and their diagnosis, the consultants discover that the morale problem is merely a symptom of deeper problems with the client's reward system and bureaucratic practices. They then recommend to the client in a lengthy report and oral presentation several specific changes, including a performance-driven reward system and greater decentralization in the organization structure.

The *organization-based* intervention strategy has many of the same strengths and weaknesses as the expert strategy. On the plus side, it provides an independent view of client organizations and can reveal problems and possibilities that clients may not have considered. This is especially important when dealing with social issues, where clients are likely to be emotionally involved and may need an outside expert to help them sort things out.

On the negative side, the *organization-based* strategy can have problems with commitment to change and client dependency. Because clients are not generally involved in analyzing the organization or making proposals for change, they might not develop sufficient support to implement the consultants' recommendations. Moreover, organizational change can be difficult and stressful, and clients may find it less painful to defend the status quo than to change it. *Organization-based* strategies, like *expertise-based* strategies, are particularly vulnerable to clients becoming excessively dependent on consultants to solve their social problems. Because social expertise can be difficult to acquire, clients can overly rely on external experts to provide that skill and knowledge.

The application of *organization-based* intervention strategies are particularly appropriate in situations where clients recognize they have social problems and do not have the expertise or resources to solve these problems themselves. It is also relevant when clients want to get an objective assessment of the social and human side of their organizations. Social audits are increasingly being used to supplement more common financial assessments. Finally, the *organization-based* strategy works well in situations where clients want experts to direct them in learning specific social skills. Executive coaching, for example, is a rapidly growing practice in management consulting.

Teaching-based Strategy

The *teaching-based* intervention strategy is relatively new in management consulting. It is a combination of the *facilitate and learn* delivery mode with a content focus on technical systems.[7] *Teaching-based* approaches are responsive to the increasing need of organizations to adapt to environments that are changing rapidly and unpredictably. In these situations, organizations must continuously transform themselves; this requires building the capacity to change and improve into the organization itself so it becomes a core competence.

To help organizations accomplish this, *teaching-based* consultants impart skills that get clients directly involved in analyzing and improving their organizations, particularly the technical features such as management structure, work design, and information systems. Consulting engagements tend to be long and continuous; some consultants work as trainers while others work alongside clients as facilitators helping them learn skills and knowledge while they are changing their organization. Thus, clients become co-learners with consultants; they learn how to change their organization by doing it.

Teaching-based consultants typically have technical expertise in the content of their discipline, and some have facilitation skills as well. Some act more as teachers, while others act as internal on-the-job consultants. They apply clinical skills to facilitate client involvement and to help create the collaboration, openness, and trust that are essential to member learning.

What is unique about this approach to management consulting is that the consultants focus on the social dynamics related to the technical side of the organization. In essence, social process is used to engage technical content, such as proposing a new work design based on high involvement teams in manufacturing.

Teaching-based consultants generally view organizations objectively, and they seek to impart knowledge, theories, and methods to client employees. They treat corporate strategy, structure, and business functions as subjects to learn about and also as key action levers for change. They help clients to analyze technical features and redesign them accordingly. General knowledge is applied to client organizations primarily through members learning how to tailor it to their setting. Clients typically select *teaching-based* consultants based on their technical expertise and clinical skills; they retain them based on how well they can facilitate learning and how well the change process produces measurable results.

An example of the *teaching-based* strategy involves a pair of consultants with skills in corporate strategy and group dynamics who work with a senior executive team to develop and implement a new strategic direction for its firm. The consultants negotiate an initial eight-month project that includes a series of off-site retreats where the top team learns how to create strategy by doing it. Members learn how to conduct a SWOT analysis of their situation, determine a competitive logic for the business, set appropriate financial goals, determine guidelines for designing and managing the firm, and develop specific initiatives and action plans to implement the strategy. The consultants design the format and periodically present educational inputs to teach the team how to perform these strategy-setting tasks. The consultants also facilitate the process through which team members jointly carry out these tasks. Based on the success of this initial project, the consultants agree to work with the client team for several more months to help it implement the strategy. They teach the client's employees how to redesign the company and manage change. They help employees apply that knowledge to changing the company and learn from those efforts how to improve it continuously. As the client gains skills and experience, the consultants play a less active role, returning periodically to help members assess overall progress of both the strategic changes and the learning process itself.

The *teaching-based* strategy has a number of strengths. Because clients are directly involved in diagnosing, redesigning, and changing their organization, they are likely to become more highly committed to implementing the changes. Such commitment is essential for transformational changes that involve most levels of the organization. Client involvement also increases the chances that consultants' content wisdom will be appropriate to the setting. Indeed, much of the learning is directed at helping clients translate general knowledge into situation-relevant structures, practices, and behaviors. This external vantage can also be helpful in coaching executives to develop leadership skills. Clients are likely to be less defensive about receiving feedback and direction about their leadership behaviors from outside experts than from colleagues or bosses. *Teaching-based* consultants can provide executives with the psychological support that is needed for trying out new behaviors and learning from mistakes.

Probably the greatest strength of the *teaching-based* strategy is that clients learn how to change the organization, thus gaining the internal capability to change and improve it continuously. Paradoxically, successful *teaching-based* consultants work themselves out of a job.

A major downside of *teaching-based* interventions is the long time it generally takes to complete them. Clients must first gain rudimentary knowledge and skills to diagnose and redesign their organizations. They must then spend time doing those activities and implementing the results, which can take one to two years or more. Clients may not have the time or persistence needed for *teaching-based* consulting; they may find it too long to meet their immediate needs.

Another problem stems from the fact that the *teaching-based* strategy is inherently more chaotic and uncertain than more common consulting interventions such as the *expertise-based* strategy. A *teaching-based* intervention typically involves multiple stakeholders who can have conflicting interests; because clients are involved in all stages of the intervention, it is difficult to predict how quickly they will learn and what direction they will take. These attributes of *teaching-based* consulting can be disturbing to clients, especially when they are used to dealing with more clearly defined, expert-driven consulting interventions.

Teaching-based interventions are ideally suited to organizations facing environments that are changing rapidly and unpredictably. To adapt to these conditions, organizations must continuously change and transform themselves, and *teaching-based* consulting can help them develop that capability. It can help clients gain the core competence to continually change and improve themselves; because such expertise is not easily imitated or acquired, it can provide a strong competitive advantage in turbulent environments.

The *teaching-based* strategy is especially applicable to organizations that must radically transform themselves from efficient bureaucracies into leaner, more flexible structures. To succeed, such large-scale change requires a great deal of member reeducation, commitment, and willingness to change. The client involvement intrinsic to *teaching-based* interventions can enable that to occur.

Process-based Strategy

This last intervention strategy combines the facilitate and learn delivery mode with a content focus on social systems. From its origins in humanistic psychology and organization development, the *process-based* strategy has been used extensively in management consulting to help clients address social issues and acquire social skills.[8] Expertise in *process-based* consulting is rooted in the clinical disciplines having to do with individual, group, and inter-group behavior. Consultants strongly value openness, trust, and collaboration among people and believe those values underlie healthy organizations that can perform well and satisfy members' needs.

This strategy views organizations as socially constructed and employs a normative-reeducative approach to change them. Organizational problems are addressed through the eyes of those who create them, and clients are directly involved in diagnosing and solving them. *Process-based* consulting tends to be highly intense and continuous. Social issues are often emotionally charged, and acquiring skills to understand and improve them can take considerable time.

Process-based consultants play a facilitative role. They work closely with clients to help them understand how their perceptions and behaviors contribute to social problems, such as inter-group conflicts, poor team problem solving, and miscommunication across managerial levels. Clients are taught how to apply their local knowledge to develop and implement appropriate solutions. They act as co-learners, making changes in their own behaviors while acquiring the skills and knowledge to make social processes work smoother and more effectively in the organization. *Process-based* consultants, for example, can help to resolve or mediate conflicts between members or work teams; they bring a neutral stance to such disagreements and can help the involved parties to de-escalate the conflict and discover a joint solution.

An example of *process-based* consulting would be a consultant who is hired to help a work team make faster, more effective decisions. The engagement starts with the consultant describing to the client what this strategy is all about, particularly the need for members to take ownership over their poor decision-making behaviors and be directly involved in learning how to improve them. Then, the consultant attends several team meetings where actual decisions are being made. He or she helps members periodically assess their decision-making behavior, which involves short assessment periods at the midpoint and end of each team meeting. Members are encouraged to lead these assessments and, based on them, to suggest and implement necessary changes. Over time, team members learn how to become better decision makers; they also learn how to assess and improve decision making in teams.

Process-based consulting is particularly strong at getting clients to own their social problems and do something constructive about them. Like the *teaching-based* strategy, clients are directly involved in all phases of the consulting engagement and thus increase their commitment to solutions. Moreover, because those solutions derive from clients' local knowledge, they are clearly relevant to the situation.

Process-based consulting not only helps clients to solve social problems, it also provides them with the skills and knowledge to improve the social side of their organizations continuously. Such social expertise provides a strong competitive advantage, especially in today's customer-driven organizations with lean, flexible structures.

The *process-based* strategy has certain downsides, however. It generally takes considerable time and effort, and clients are often not willing to commit sufficient resources to what they consider to be "soft" problems not directly related to bottom-line results. Because social problems are inherently emotional, clients may naturally feel uncomfortable with a consulting intervention that encourages them to confront and resolve such issues. They may find it easier and less stressful to turn to more expert-driven consulting, such as the *organization-based* strategy, for help. *Process-based* consulting focuses on social content and may ignore technical features of the organization that contribute to social problems, such as the organization structure, reward systems, and work designs. Unless these features are addressed, social problems may recur continually even with effective *process-based* consulting.

The *process-based* strategy is highly relevant to situations where clients have social problems and where those directly involved are willing to confront and resolve these problems. Such member commitment is essential for taking ownership over problems and developing relevant solutions. *Process-based* consulting also applies to settings where members want to gain the skills needed to address and improve social processes. Such expertise generally requires practice to acquire. *Process-based* consulting enables clients to learn by doing; they gain skills while learning to apply them to their own situation.

IMPLICATIONS FOR CONSULTANTS, CLIENTS, AND PROFESSION

This typology of four intervention strategies provides a broad overview of the major approaches used in management consulting today. It offers insights into how management consulting is applied to organizations and the likely results in different situations. The typology also suggests a number of implications for consultants, clients, and the consulting profession itself.

For Consultants

Management consultants generally specialize in a particular intervention strategy. They acquire expertise and experience in applying a strategy and, if successful, tend to repeat it with future clients. Specialization is a normal outgrowth of the evolution of the consulting profession and has certain advantages. As the problems facing organizations have become more complex, consultants tend to focus on particular issues, clients, industries, and of course, interventions. In all but a few large consulting firms, consultants do not have the broad expertise and experience to address the full range of client needs; specialization enables them to concentrate on a particular consulting niche and excel at it.

A major problem of specialization, however, is that it easily leads to "intervention myopia." Consultants overlook important client features and dynamics that contribute to organization success, thus causing consulting failures despite consultants' best intent and effort. Consultants applying an *expertise-based* strategy, for example, are likely to ignore the social dynamics underlying technical problems; they are unlikely to see value in involving clients in the intervention process. Such neglect can result in excellent technical recommendations not being implemented. Conversely, consultants using a process-based strategy will probably ignore key technical issues underlying social problems; thus, the same social problems may recur regardless of effective process consultation.

These intervention failures could be lessened if management consultants had greater appreciation for intervention strategies other than ones they typically use. However, gaining this broader perspective is not an easy task. Consultants tend to be heavily invested in specific intervention strategies and are unlikely to consider alternatives without compelling reasons to do so. Moreover, intervention strategies are generally reinforced with use and become habitual; consultants rarely question the assumptions and biases underlying them and instead take their strategies for granted.

To overcome these problems, consultants might start with an explicit re-evaluation of their favored intervention strategy, surfacing underlying assumptions about when it has worked and run into trouble. Then, these consultants could use their assessment as a baseline against which to compare other intervention strategies and to learn more about them. This effort at self-reflection can heighten awareness of critical blind spots in favored strategies and might reveal entirely new steps that would improve future interventions. For example, consultants might further choose to broaden their own expertise or consider teaming with other consultants who have complementary skills and knowledge.

The typology of four strategies outlined in this chapter can help to guide this reevaluation by giving consultants more informed choices about alternate intervention strategies. It can also direct speculation about how consultants might combine the four strategies to complement each other and thereby achieve more powerful results, like in a multiplier effect.

Probably the easiest way is to blend two strategies that share a common dimension, such as broadening one's content focus from technical systems to include social systems while adhering to the same study and recommend delivery mode. In doing so, consultants would benefit from a different yet related content perspective under the same mode of delivery. Because both types of content share a study and recommend delivery mode, this shift does not involve such an enormous change in capabilities. An *expertise-based* consulting firm moving in this direction might then decide to hire *organization-based* consultants with advanced content knowledge about social systems.

A more difficult yet powerful way to combine strategies is where neither strategy shares a common dimension. Here, consultants would have to acquire an entirely different approach to consulting involving both a new content focus and a new delivery mode. For example, consultants using a study and recommend approach relying on technical systems content might attempt to broaden their approach to include both social systems content focus and the *facilitate and learn* delivery mode. This leap would require a drastic change in consultant skills and knowledge; so rather than learning the expertise themselves, consultants could form an alliance with a firm whose consultants subscribe to the other strategy.

While blending intervention strategies can take advantage of complementary perspectives, just how these combinations can be applied to specific client situations is still highly speculative. One plausible scenario, for example, might start with consultants using the *expertise-based* strategy to diagnose a client's technical systems content and make recommendations for change. Next, the consultants would apply the *organization-based* strategy to propose particular social systems processes needed to implement the technical changes. This could be followed with a *process-based* strategy where the consultants work directly with client members helping them to surface concerns about the change and reduce resistance. Finally, as employees gain social skills and become more involved in the change process, the consultants could apply a *teaching-based* strategy where new skills are taught to employees so they can cope better with the changes.

For Clients

Prospective clients can use the proposed typology of intervention strategies to make informed choices about management consultants. They need to first familiarize themselves with the strategies and the conditions under which they are more appropriate. Then, based on their consulting needs, executives can determine which of the strategies (or combination of them) best fits their situation. That information can then be used to choose a suitable consultant. For example, executives might interview consultants and ask pertinent questions about how they intervene with clients: What are their assumptions about organizations and change? What organization features and processes do they diagnose? What action levers do they employ? How do they measure success? What is their primary expertise? What role will they play, and what role do they expect clients to play?

Answers to these questions will provide added insight into a consultants' preferred intervention strategies. Such information can be then used to assess how well prospective consultants fit with the client's needs; it can also reveal limitations inherent to proposed strategies. Executives might, for example, select different kinds of consulting firms for different consulting needs; they might also employ them simultaneously or in a certain temporal order depending on how the situation evolves. Knowledge about different intervention strategies can help executives make these difficult choices.

For the Consulting Profession

The typology presented in this chapter raises important implications for the consulting profession, especially with regard to how consultants acquire competence at making interventions, and how the profession considers the value of different intervention strategies.

Management consultants generally gain skills and knowledge in only one of the strategies. The vast majority are trained in business schools, which strongly emphasize the study and recommend delivery mode with a content focus on technical systems and occasionally on social content. Very little, if any, training is given in the *teaching-based* or *process-based* strategies.

This concentration of business schools on learning an *expertise-based* strategy of intervention is not surprising. It is what business schools do well, and it is the primary intervention strategy for the large consulting firms that do much of the hiring. A smaller yet significant number of management consultants receive training in the helping professions, such as clinical psychology and social work, or in organization development. This education centers heavily on the *facilitate and learn* delivery mode with a focus on social systems; it prepares consultants for the *process-based* strategy on intervention.

Current training in the consulting profession contributes to a natural division in the field between hard-nosed, *expertise-based* consultants and softer, *process-based* consultants. Rather than perpetuate this schism, the typology proposed in this chapter strongly suggests that consultants will likely be more effective if they receive broader training that encompasses more than one intervention strategy. They do not necessarily need to become specialists in other strategies, but they should gain rudimentary skills and knowledge so they know how the strategies work under certain conditions. Such multi-strategy education should go a long way to overcoming the intervention myopia described previously. Management consultants might then begin to appreciate and may even practice the other strategies.

Like consulting education, the profession itself is split into different camps roughly along the lines of the intervention strategies described here. The dominant approach to management consulting is by far the *expertise-based* strategy. As shown in this chapter, these divisions are a natural outgrowth of the varied assumptions and practices that underlie the different strategies. Because the *expertise-based* strategy is so dominate in the consulting profession, it is far more valued than the other strategies and, thus, is afforded a great deal more legitimacy. This not only perpetuates the intervention myopia and narrow training that still permeate the profession, but worse, it makes it far more difficult for other strategies to attract talented recruits and clients.

If anything, I hope this chapter demonstrates the value and relevance of all four intervention strategies. It shows that none alone can succeed in all situations and that all are often needed to satisfy a client's changing and varied needs, especially in today's world of global competition, complex organizations, real-time communication, and workforce diversity.

Notes to the Chapter

[1] M. Beer, R. Eisenstat, and B. Spector, "Why Change Programs Don't Produce Change," *Harvard Business Review* (November–December 1990): 158–166.

[2] C. Argyris, *Intervention Theory and Method: A Behavioral Science View* (Reading, MA: Addison-Wesley, 1970).

[3] T. Cummings and C. Worely, *Organization Develop and Change,* 7th ed. (Cincinnati: South-Western College Publishing, 2001).

[4] E. Trist, G. Higgin, H. Murray, and A. Pollock, *Organizational Choice* (London: Tavistock Publications, 1963).

[5] See, for example, "Part 4: Prescriptive Interventions" in R. Blake and J. Mouton, *Consultation* (Reading, MA: Addison-Wesley, 1976).

[6] See, for example, "Part Three: Data-Based Strategies of Social Intervention" in H. Hornstein, B. Bunker, W. Burke, M. Gindes, and R. Lewicki, eds., *Social Intervention* (New York: The Free Press, 1971).

[7] C. Argyris, R. Putnam, and D. Smith, *Action Science: Concepts, Methods, and Skills for Research and Intervention* (San Francisco: Jossey-Bass, 1985); S. Mohrman and T. Cummings, *Self-Designing Organizations: Learning How to Create High Performance* (Reading, MA: Addison-Wesley, 1989).

[8] E. Schein, *Process Consultation Revisited* (Reading, MA: Addison-Wesley, 1998).

CHAPTER 13

Consulting to Integrate Mergers and Acquisitions
Anthony F. Buono, Bentley College

ABOUT THE AUTHOR

Anthony F. Buono

Anthony F. Buono is a Professor of Management and Sociology at Bentley College. He has written and edited seven books and is editor of the *Research in Management Consulting* book series. Dr. Buono is past Chair of the Academy of Management's Management Consulting Division. His research and consulting interests include the management consulting industry, organizational change, and mergers and acquisitions.

Over the past decade, a quick perusal of the business section in most newspapers suggests that, while merger and acquisition (M&A) activity may have been at a high point, many M&A deals were experiencing severe digestion pains.

- "ABC Corporation announced yesterday that quarterly earnings would miss Wall Street estimates because of weakness in its brokerage operations. ABC, which has posted erratic earnings during its struggles to integrate its operations after several acquisitions, reported another drop in earnings. . . ."

- "At its annual meeting last week, XYZ Company announced that it is jettisoning some of the most distinctive pieces that Target Company brought to the merger in an attempt to reduce its exposure and regain its focus in the industry. . . ."

And on it goes.

The poor performance of combined firms continues to raise questions about the efficacy of mergers and acquisitions as a value creation strategy. While the criteria to evaluate the success of M&As vary considerably (e.g., share value, post-merger profitability, market share growth, or R&D innovation and new products), it appears that roughly one-third of all M&As fail outright and another third fall short of their operational, financial, and strategic objectives.[1]

Echoing a cover story "Do Mergers Really Work?" from 1985, seventeen years later a *Business Week* analysis concluded that both the merging and acquiring companies continue to make the same mistakes, destroying shareholder value in the process.[2] As a result, while recent years have witnessed one of the biggest M&A booms in history, it has also been one of the largest waves of divestments and spin-offs.[3]

DYNAMICS OF M&A CONSULTING

The highly complex nature of the M&A process, however, leads client firms to seek out a broad range of consulting services that go well beyond those typically delivered by general management consulting firms. Typically, merger deals are dominated by lawyers, investment bankers, and accountants, and the need for management consultants is too often left out until major problems arise.

Transaction Advising Versus Merger Integration Consulting

It is useful to distinguish between management consultants and transaction advisors.[4] Occasionally, the initial transaction advisors are actually management consultants hired by the firm to plan its acquisition strategy and then locate an acquisition target that fits with the proposed M&A strategy. More often, the transaction advisors involve financial and legal specialists who offer technical assistance leading up to the deal itself—a process typically characterized as "from contact through contract." Clearly, the complexities associated with pre-deal decision making (scouting for deals, due diligence assessments, forecasting value) and combination-related negotiations (which lead to general agreements on the value and details of the deal) are important determinants of M&A success.[5] For example, if an acquirer pays too much, it may never earn its money back. Clients rely on specialists who recommend how to proceed or turn back based on their expert advice. In large companies, they often run their own acquisition efforts and then hire transaction advisors to consummate the deal.

However, these transaction experts (and the managements themselves) frequently overlook, ignore, or underestimate the problems of post-merger integration. This omission is understandable since the guiding assumption underlying much of their pre-deal work suggests that, "if a deal is done well, the deal is done." Most transaction advisors are paid on a contingency fee basis tied to the value of the deal. So, while these advisors may strive to be objective and careful, it will come as no surprise that they often are fairly optimistic about the synergy prospects from the combined parties. Finally, most transaction advisors are hired to focus on narrow but complex technical issues rather than on broader strategic, cultural, and political dynamics associated with the integration of two companies. Thus, they lack perspective for anticipating what may turn out to be a major issue after the merger.

From a post-combination and integration perspective, this is where the real management and leadership challenges begin, and where management consultants can be highly valuable. Unlike the transaction advisor role where the advisor's judgment serves as the basis for a decision, merger consultants are called upon to help but not decide in planning and supporting the integration process. M&A integration decisions are best made by the affected executives because they are the ones whose destinies are linked to the long-term success of the combined entity.

Merger integration consultants tend to embed their expertise in a process consultation mode. My experience suggests that the consultant's most effective interventions, rather than playing guru and "being right," evolve around what Maister and his associates refer to as the "trusted advisor."[6] This approach seeks to support and facilitate management in making their own decisions about integration.

An underlying dilemma, however, is that it takes time to become a "trusted advisor" in the eyes of a client. Given the frenetic pace that typically accompanies an M&A, consultants do not have much time or latitude to gain credibility. Instead, it is usually their past reputation that carries the most weight going in, and then the consultant must be quickly adept at bringing forth issues and helping management to plan specific steps in the integration process. The initial skill and speed with which this is done often determines the consultant's fate and opportunities for a continuing relationship.

Throughout this process, it can be difficult to maintain the level of objectivity that we strive for as consultants. As much as we might not like to admit, there is a certain element of excitement and gratification that comes from being part of the inner circle of advisors deciding on the fate of an organization.[7] Following months of preparatory work on building competency in acquisition integration, for example, I recall being part of a pre-acquisition working session with the senior-level integration team as the target of an impending acquisition was announced. As a buzz of excitement quickly spread through the room, I found myself getting caught up with the fervor—thinking "so that's who *we* are acquiring"—as the meeting turned to specific strategic and operational planning issues.

Thus, while much M&A consulting involves pre-merger financial and strategic analysis, along with deal support, this chapter will focuses on post-merger issues of integration that are so often neglected. Our discussion addresses the specific challenges that merger integration consultants will face, and we will consider ways of dealing with these issues.

Integration Defined

Compared to the financial orientation of many past mergers and acquisitions, where being over-leveraged was the main risk, the recent M&A boom reflects deals that are more strategically driven. Today's deals are influenced by technological advances and R&D investment needs, the increased importance of accelerating speed to market, attempts to broaden geographical presence, and the need to react to industry overcapacity and related global pressures for cost cutting. The 1960s era of conglomerate acquisition of any type of promising business has given way to a basic philosophical shift for acquirers who now pursue targets more closely related to their core businesses. The main risks associated with these latter-day M&As, therefore, have much more to do with concerns around assimilation and integration,[8] pressures that have created a vital need for highly focused, post-combination strategies and plans.

At the same time, we need to be clear about what the word "integration" means and implies. It does not mean that all acquired companies should be completely absorbed into the acquiring company and thereby cease to exist. Rather, there are degrees of integration. Some acquisitions, like those made by Johnson & Johnson, are left more as freestanding entities retaining their former company names. However, they are brought onboard in terms of strategic planning, operations budgeting, compensation, and the cultural values specified in J&J's Credo. On the other hand, if the acquisition is small and its purpose is to fold its product line into the acquirer's existing product line, then the absorption is likely to be more complete. Either case presents integration issues that, while different, can spell the difference between success and failure.

Lack of Preparation

Many factors account for the disappointing track record in M&A performance—from paying too much for a target company, to choosing the wrong partner, to misperceiving the potential synergies. However, the combination of misunderstood cultural differences and poorly conceived integration strategies is typically a potent factor contributing to failure.[9]

All too often, the reality is that the acquiring company's management is ill prepared to face the complex implementation dynamics once the deal is signed.[10] Studies indicate that even those firms that do develop systematic processes for selecting and dealing with acquisition targets, few actually operationalize and follow these plans.[11] A KPMG survey of 750 of the largest deals during the latter 1990s concluded that, while acquirers typically had a fundamentally good strategy, there was an overreliance on the financial model that drove the deal. As a result, poor integration planning and execution of the combination itself undermined the companies' ability to enhance shareholder value.[12] Similarly, a global survey of 115 M&A transactions by A. T. Kearney revealed that 53 percent of the respondents saw post-merger integration as the greatest failure risk.[13]

No Single Best Strategy

Integrating two previously autonomous companies is an exceedingly complex and idiosyncratic process. Based on over twenty years of experience in studying and working with companies going through the M&A process, it has become very clear to me that such combinations are riddled with uncertainties, paradoxes, and dilemmas. Merger integration consultants do encounter some fairly common consulting challenges, regardless of the M&A assignment. At the same time, several challenges are created by the characteristics of the specific M&A deal in question, and still other issues can easily emerge during the consulting assignment itself.

Yet, despite the reality that there are different types of mergers and acquisitions, we often group all M&As together.[14] The underlying hope, it seems, is that there is a core set of "best practice" strategies and tactics that will facilitate their success. But that hope is too general and idealistic! The strategy underlying a specific merger or acquisition dictates the unique aspects of the level of integration (financial, strategic, operational) necessary, the speed through which the integration should be achieved, and the ways in which the integration should be planned and implemented. Complete operational integration raises the most challenges and is clearly the more difficult to accomplish.

M&A Stages and Consulting Roles

As depicted in Exhibit 13.1, consulting roles during mergers and acquisitions evolve around three different but overlapping phases: 1) pre-combination preliminary planning, 2) early integration implementation during combination, and 3) the post-combination aftermath.[15]

| Exhibit 13.1 | Illustrative Merger and Acquisition Integration-Related Consulting Interventions |

Preliminary Planning (Pre-Combination)

- Strategy and selection
  - Vision casting and strategy setting
  - Inter-firm fit: Partner/target evaluation
  - Broadened due diligence foci (e.g., culture, HR practices, marketing, operating systems, IT)
  - Synergy and revenue enhancement analyses
- Announcement
  - Stakeholder analysis
  - Communication strategy: Internal and external
  - Level of integration analysis
- Creation of integration plans
  - Assessment of business and cultural impediments to integration success
  - Initial organization structure planning
  - Initial transition plans, selection of integration manager, and formation of integration teams
  - Key talent retention program(s)
- Focus on immediate feelings and concerns of organizational members
  - Stress reduction and merger sensitization workshops
  - Focus groups

Early Integration Implementation (First 1–6 Months)

- Enhance inter-firm cooperation
  - Orientation meetings and realistic M&A previews
  - Two-way communication (meetings, hotlines, newsletters)
  - Intergroup mirroring and team building
  - Transition teams and steering committee
  - Refine and implement integration plans
- Focus on transition and integration
  - Focused reward systems (material and symbolic)
  - Focused use of organizational rituals
- Work through merger syndrome-related problems and concerns
  - Focus groups and survey feedback
  - Coach senior and middle managment to model desired attitudes and behaviors

Post-combination Aftermath (Next 6–18 Months)

- Track the combination and support integration initiatives
  - Integration audits
  - Build capabilities
  - Exit interviews
  - Continued integration activities and transition-related rituals
- Assess and attempt to correct dysfunctional behaviors
  - Confrontation meetings and team building initiatives
  - Focus groups and survey feedback

During pre-combination, the consultant's interventions need to focus on ensuring that senior managers have a deeper understanding of and are clearly aligned with the strategic rationale for doing the deal. Emphasis should be placed on broadening the client's perspective and awareness for the need to include nonfinancial factors in their analysis (e.g., cultural factors, human resource capabilities, IT systems) and then to assist the client in assessing the implications for post-integration needs and outcomes. In essence, the focus should be on drawing out what it will take to make the merger or acquisition a success.

In the next stage of combination, early integration implementation efforts concentrate on the transition itself, drawing out ways to enhance inter-firm cooperation, bringing the two organizations together, and working through merger syndrome-related problems and concerns, such as who will have which jobs and what the new organization structure will be.

Finally, during the post-combination aftermath period, the focus shifts toward tracking the combination, supporting ongoing integration initiatives, and assessing and attempting to correct dysfunctional reactions and behaviors.

Although there are different foci within each of these three stages, the emphasis of consultants should be continuously placed on enhancing the capability of both organizations to: 1) clarify and understand the intent of the combination and the requirements for integrating the two companies; 2) deal with the anxieties and uncertainties that accompany the M&A process; and 3) refocus their energies on combination-related goals and objectives (see Consulting Insights).

Consulting Insights   **The Focus of M&A Integration Consulting**

An increasing number of consulting firms—from virtually all of the large consultancies to a broad array of smaller, boutique firms—have begun to offer merger and acquisition integration support. While the specific proprietary tools and approaches may vary, the essence of their offerings is essentially the same—to provide early planning and intervention to facilitate the combination of the two client organizations. As examples, Accenture emphasizes "strategic due diligence," focusing on identifying and testing "future value levers" of a deal and analyzing what will need to be accomplished during post-M&A integration to make the transaction a success. McKinsey & Co. stresses sources of future revenue growth, supported by strategic assessment and the need to identify and retain key talent that will enable the organization to meet those growth goals. Bain & Company highlights the need for a "strategic implementation plan," focusing on establishing the post-merger organizational structure, resolving back-office technology issues, and maintaining "seamless customer interfaces" throughout the process. Towers Perrin emphasizes the alignment of human resource capabilities with merger-related goals and objectives, change management and communication strategies, and determining an appropriate timeline and set of integration processes for the merger. Mercer stresses a strategic perspective on integration processes, suggesting that "how you combine should be driven by why you combine." While the pace of mergers and acquisitions may ebb and flow over the years to come, as research by senior consultants from A. T. Kearney forecasts, the continued consolidation of firms and industries is "unstoppable, . . . continuous, and inevitable."

Ideally, the consultant's interventions should span all three stages. However, much M&A consulting is far more piecemeal and reactive, as different consultants are brought in to help resolve a particular problem that emerges in the overall M&A process. In the pre-combination stage of preliminary planning, transaction advisors typically drive the process without the involvement of merger integration consultants. Unfortunately, merger integration consultants are often not brought in until problems arise late in the post-combination, aftermath stage, long after the merger or acquisition has been consummated. At this point, clients often have unrealistic expectations about what can be accomplished from their consultants.

Temporal Constraints

Three time-related factors shape the challenges facing consultants when intervening in a merger or acquisition. The first set of issues is shaped by *when* the consultant is brought into the process. Consultants are faced with different challenges depending on the stage of their intervention. Working with a client during the pre-combination, preliminary planning phase (e.g., facilitating an initial integration planning assessment) is extremely different from intervening during the early integration implementation period (e.g., getting leaders to clarify strategic intent after the fact). Too often merger consultants are only called in during the post-combination aftermath stage with the intent of "fixing" a problem (e.g., the exodus of key personnel).

The second time-related factor is whether the consulting assignment is a long-term engagement or an isolated, "hit-and-run" project. When working with two organizations over an extended period of time, it can be difficult to maintain an unbiased perspective vis-à-vis the two companies. I have found that it is all too easy—even at an unconscious level—to develop an allegiance to certain managers and one of the organizations, especially toward the acquirer who likely hired you. This can readily influence what you "see" and how you interpret different situations. On the other hand, in a short-term engagement, the consultant's problem becomes one of obtaining sufficient information about the details of the merger or acquisition. Everyone is busy on many different sub-aspects of the merger, and it is difficult to track down a lot of data and opinions in a short time.

A third underlying problem facing consultants is that they are not around all the time, which makes it difficult to penetrate the aura of game-playing and veil of secrecy often surrounding the M&A process. As third parties, consultants may not be as intimately involved as may initially appear—even in long-term assignments. For example, in one of my engagements, I underscored that I should be kept involved in the decision process on an ongoing basis. But as the acquisition unfolded, however, I found that I was not privy to a host of key decisions that had taken place when I was absent—financial and operational—that created a different context for what the organization was attempting to accomplish. It is difficult to carry out an accurate diagnosis and offer meaningful advice when operating from a partial understanding of what is happening.

COMMON INTEGRATION ISSUES

In some mergers and acquisitions, holding on to key people, especially technical talent, is one of the keys to success. In another, the people in the target firm might be less important to retain, and the emphasis, for example, should be placed on integrating the information systems of both companies. In still another, if a company acquires a firm in the same industry due to excess capacity, key challenges include which operations to shut down, which employees to lay off, and how to effectively resize the organization. Considering the different goals and outcomes associated with these disparate strategies, each of these combinations places different pressures and requirements on the integration process—and on consultants.

What Comprehensive Due Diligence Really Means

As part of the strategy and partner selection process, a key factor in successful pre-M&A integration is comprehensive due diligence. Clearly, financial, legal, and regulatory analyses—in essence, risk assessment—dominate most due diligence efforts. Although financial projections typically accompany such assessments, the basic focus is usually placed on the history of the target firm more than its future potential.[16] Comprehensive due diligence, however, incorporates a broader array of concerns, including sales and marketing strengths and weaknesses, human resource capabilities, supplier networks and commitments, and so forth. The key is that due diligence assessments should emerge from the future strategy and vision for the merger.

The greatest challenge for management consultants in this area is related to the technical complexities involved in each dimension of due diligence assessment. Transaction advisors drive the process. For example, accountants focus on the valuation of assets and liabilities, the tax consequences of the combination, and fulfilling regulatory reporting requirements. Lawyers concentrate on jurisdiction and incorporation issues, securities law ramifications of structuring the deal, anti-trust concerns, and so forth. The underlying assumption that consultants must challenge is that favorable judgments about financial, legal, and regulatory aspects means automatically that the strategic benefits of the merger will necessarily fall in line with the numbers. The reality of a merger or acquisition is often quite different from the M&A deal that exists in numbers and on paper.

The idea of comprehensive due diligence can be overwhelming because time pressures, legal restrictions, and limited resources prevent organizations from fully following idealistic "best practices" recommendations. Consultants can, however, emphasize the importance of *strategic* due diligence by getting the acquirer to closely examine and clarify the strategic intent of the acquisition and then to spell out all of the likely factors that have to fall into place to make the strategy happen in practice. Usually, a checklist is required to prompt the acquirer to think of nonobvious criteria, such as the target company's talent pool, technical capabilities, its organization structure, cultural values, and prevailing management philosophy toward decision making.

Capturing Merger-Related Synergies

As suggested by John Bogush, managing director of KPMG (now BearingPoint), complexity in M&A integration revolves around the key strategic drivers rather than the size of the combination per se.[17] The strategic intent of the acquisition might be to reduce manufacturing and distribution costs, gain access to new customers or new markets, or obtain technical talent or gain access to new technologies. Given the underlying objectives sought after, the strategic due diligence review should focus on the probability of attaining these desired synergies.

Recent studies by Towers Perrin and PricewaterhouseCoopers found, however, that acquiring firms tend to fall short in achieving desired synergies in such areas as growing market share, enhancing brand strength and reputation, and accessing talent capabilities and "know-how" in the target company.[18] Depending on the extent to which "softer," more intangible synergies are a driving factor (see Exhibit 13.2), the marketing and human sides of the integration process become increasingly critical.[19] While companies may have a relatively clear understanding of why they selected a particular acquisition target, there usually remains significant uncertainty as to *how* exactly to capitalize on the intended synergies through integration.[20]

From a consulting perspective, it may seem to be relatively straightforward work to assess the extent to which tangible assets might be transferred from

Exhibit 13.2	Illustrative Merger and Acquisition Strategies

"Hard" Synergies/ Relatively Easy to Attain

Financial Engineering
- Managing the cost of capital (e.g., refinancing target's debt, pooling working capital requirements)
- Managing tax benefits

Cost Reduction
- Consolidation
- Elimination of duplication (jobs, facilities)
- Economies of Scale

Revenue Enhancement
- Bundling product lines
- Enhancing brand strength and reputation
- Combining customer segments (cross-selling)
- Cross-utilizing distribution channels
- Growing market share

"Soft" Synergies/ Relatively Difficult To Attain

Process Improvement
- Transferring/combining core competencies and/or best practices
- Integrating human capital
- Creating next generation products
- Enhancing product development processes

one firm to another. Yet political dynamics, cultural overtones, and general "win-lose" mentalities among M&A partners can readily complicate what might appear to be relatively clear-cut.

USAir's acquisition of Piedmont Airlines provides a good illustration of these tendencies. Prior to the acquisition, USAir's reservation system and customer service were so poor that customers deemed the airline "Useless Air."[21] Yet, rather than engaging in an analysis of the relative disadvantages and costs associated with maintaining USAir's system compared to building on Piedmont's capabilities, which were noted to be much better, USAir's power politics prevented the combined airline from taking full advantage of potential operational synergies. Acquiring companies tend to impose their own systems on target firms rather than engage in a true joint diagnosis and analysis of the situation, a tendency that external consultants need to counteract.

Synergy-related challenges are particularly acute in those industries where intellectual capital is one of the determinants of organizational success. Ultimate M&A success in high technology companies, for example, can take years and successive generations of new products. In several of my consulting experiences, I have found that the lingering effects of previous mergers or acquisitions further exacerbate current combination integration efforts. Hewlett-Packard's acquisition of Compaq, for example, is complicated by Compaq's hangover from its acquisition of Digital Equipment Corporation. Within Compaq, organizational members still differentiate themselves as "Digital Classic" and "Compaq Classic" employees. Such stereotyping suggests that Compaq's acquisition of Digital is still not complete, which adds a layer of complexity to H-P's acquisition of Compaq.

Technology firms often believe that they can take the best of each other's businesses and, thereby, generate end-to-end packages that will be attractive to a wider range of consumers. However, simply repackaging existing products and product lines is rarely sufficient. Rather it is the second- and third-generation products—through the innovation and creativity that a merged group of R&D experts can create—that ultimately translates into long-term success. Thus, rather than simply acquiring patents, products, or facilities, an underlying key to success lies in getting the talent in each organization to adopt a cooperative attitude and a willingness to collaborate on new products and processes. An early exodus of key personnel—"brains with legs" and "frogs in a wheelbarrow" (they can jump out at any time) as they are often referred to[22]—can quickly create problems for the combined organization. The turnover and departure of key personnel following America Online's acquisition of Netscape, for example, delayed the scheduled release of Netscape's browser for two years.[23]

Retaining Talent

Depending on the nature of the merger or acquisition and its underlying strategy, different levels of attention must be focused on the human element of the combination. Yet, even in those acquisitions where the strategic intent is to keep the target's core talent, it is crucial that these plans are made clear and explicit and announced as soon as possible. The uncertainty and anxiety that go along with being acquired can be debilitating and literally drain value from an acquisition.

As part of its diversification strategy, for example, SteelCo acquired a petrochemical company (Petro) and focused its initial energies on capturing short-term, financial gains.[24] Based on initial diversification planning, the positions of the technical experts, engineers, and scientists at Petro were not threatened. In fact, SteelCo had mainly acquired the firm to secure the expertise of its technical employees. During the early integration implementation period, however, SteelCo's senior management focused on attaining immediate costs savings (the "hard" synergies depicted in Exhibit 13.2), consolidating basic functional areas and support groups—such as human resources, finance, and legal. They never explicitly communicated their intended strategy to the organization or reached out to the target's technical core. Petro's technical staff interpreted the changes and terminations in other sections of the company as "a sign of things to come" and began bailing out of the company. Even the scientists who were willing to "give SteelCo's management a chance" found themselves under significant pressure from colleagues and coworkers to exit the firm. By the time SteelCo realized what was happening, it found itself in control of the petrochemical company but without the core of technical professionals that made Petro a desirable acquisition target.

Consultants are often brought in at this point to help the organization "stop the hemorrhaging," but such efforts are frequently too little, too late.

Who Is the Client?

Inter-firm dynamics can also raise questions about who the "client" really is, as multiple parties jockey for position and attempt to exert their influence. While many of us might like to think that the "system" is our ultimate client, we are often faced with divided loyalties when parts of the system clash with each other. Our contact clients (i.e., the individual(s) who bring us into the organization) may be different from our primary clients (those who ultimately "own" the problem or issue). Similarly, our primary clients may also be different from our "intermediate" clients (the individuals or groups that we interview and interact with as part of the intervention).[25] Since the needs and expectations of each of these "clients" may be quite different, what we think we know about a client is, at best, a hypothesis that needs to be tested constantly.

INTERVENTION STRATEGIES AND TECHNIQUES

The nature of possible consulting interventions in M&As varies widely, influenced by the specific task at hand, the intent of the merger or acquisition, and the timing of when the consultant enters the process. Given the heightened anxieties, insecurity, mistrust, and power dynamics that accompany the M&A process, intervening in one raises many unique challenges. It is hard to decipher real motives and deal with the inevitable conflicts that arise (e.g., creating collaboration versus undermining internal opposition or ensuring objective analysis versus protecting vested interests).

Most useful prescriptions about the consulting process emphasize the need to develop rapport and a collaborative relationship with one's client. As in any large-scale change intervention, one of the basic challenges is to motivate employees to refocus from their own self-interest to the collective interests of the combined entity. Earning the trust and confidence of organizational members in a merger environment is quite challenging, as is generating valid data for understanding people's reactions about what is happening both to and around them.

In Exhibit 13.3, we see that goodwill and a cooperative spirit often characterize public exchanges at the deal announcement ceremony, with both parties emphasizing the promise of the merger or acquisition. But just under the surface, people are experiencing quite different feelings. Referred to by some observers as the *merger syndrome*,[26] these reactions reflect high levels of anxiety and stressful reactions. Heightened self-interest and preoccupation with job positions in the combination, culture clashes, and restricted communication are all too commonplace. The result is a host of problems emerging at the individual and organizational level. Most client resistance stems from feelings of vulnerability and losing control.

| Exhibit 13.3 | Typical Human Reactions in Mergers and Acquisitions |

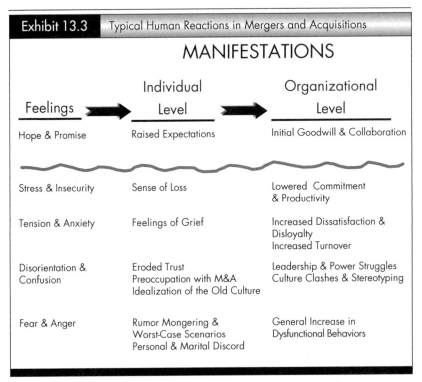

MANIFESTATIONS

Feelings ➡	Individual Level ➡	Organizational Level
Hope & Promise	Raised Expectations	Initial Goodwill & Collaboration
Stress & Insecurity	Sense of Loss	Lowered Commitment & Productivity
Tension & Anxiety	Feelings of Grief	Increased Dissatisfaction & Disloyalty Increased Turnover
Disorientation & Confusion	Eroded Trust Preoccupation with M&A Idealization of the Old Culture	Leadership & Power Struggles Culture Clashes & Stereotyping
Fear & Anger	Rumor Mongering & Worst-Case Scenarios Personal & Marital Discord	General Increase in Dysfunctional Behaviors

As an M&A consultant, it is important to realize that organizational members tend to be overly sensitive to literally everything around them, including the terminology used to describe the combination. The idea of a "merger," for example, is frequently stated and interpreted publicly as a merger of "equals." Yet, in most instances, one of the merger partners is "far more equal" than the other. The reality is that most mergers are actually acquisitions. In acquisition after acquisition, for example, it is not uncommon for the majority of one of the partner's management teams to be terminated. If the intent is to assimilate one company into another, companies should resist the temptation to characterize the combination as a merger of "equals." Perpetrating the ideal of equals only breeds confusion, contempt, and mistrust on the part of those being acquired when expectations are not fulfilled—and M&A consultants can quickly be drawn into this turmoil.

Given these heightened emotions and reactions, people going through a merger or acquisition tend to be guarded and are often less than forthcoming. They withhold or distort critical information when interacting with their M&A counterparts and related stakeholders—including consultants. Even attempts to model authentic behavior on the part of the consultant—that is, putting into words what you are experiencing as you work with a client, trying to build a base of trust and commitment—can be met with skepticism and even cynicism. A unique dilemma faced by consultants in this environment is that efforts to gain trust and commitment from one member of the two organizations can quickly create doubts and suspicions on the part of the other member. In essence, organizational members grapple with such concerns as whose "side" is the consultant really on and whether the real client is that "other" organization.

Listening Deeply

As a way of dealing with this dilemma, a guiding approach that I have used throughout many types of interventions over the years is one of "listening deeply" to all parties affected by whatever the intervention. This includes many discussions and interviews where I use my experience with M&A dynamics to get individuals in carefully arranged meetings to reflect on integration and implementation challenges. In doing so, I try to assess and compare reactions and perceptions across organizational members and then attempt to get individuals to listen to each other with greater attentiveness, compassion, and understanding—especially on issues where there are strong differences of opinion.[27]

As objective third parties, consultants often meet with top executives and managers from different divisions or sides of the companies to discuss and assess their reactions—positive and negative—concerning the merger or acquisition and its future business prospects. As part of this interaction, I attempt to learn about the organization's cultural system, emotionally encompassing as much as possible in order to help describe and interpret it to its members. An underlying goal is to facilitate their understanding and knowledge about the breadth and depth of their own culture and its ramifications for the combination they are envisioning.

Within this listening and clarifying context, I often serve in a coaching capacity, helping the management team to understand the likely outcomes and reactions to various decisions and events. A key here is the extent to which the consultant can help the client to learn from his or her experiences and feelings and then to build on these insights in adapting to the merger. An underlying challenge—especially when working with senior-level managers—is to get people who are far more action-oriented than introspective to engage in this reflective level of analysis.

Given the anxieties and political dynamics that are an inherent part of the M&A process, drawing these feelings out can be a challenge. Thus, in many instances, identifying what needs to happen may be relatively straightforward; working with the emotions of two organizations to actually make it happen is not.

Clarifying Strategic Intent

It is a given that the strategic rationale underlying the merger or acquisition in question should be fully understood by the acquirer's senior management team. As such, consultants typically advise their clients that it is critical to fully think through their M&A strategy, understanding the risks as well as the potential benefits. Given the aura that permeates deal making, however, there are times when actually accomplishing this task is very difficult.

In a recent consulting engagement, for example, the CEO of an acquiring company and I decided that I should play a devil's advocate role during an acquisition-planning session with the firm's senior management team. I had previously undertaken a series of one-on-one interviews with each member of the team. Drawing on this information, the intent was to ensure that everyone fully understood the rationale underlying the acquisition and its potential difficulties. A key goal was to reach consensus on whether the firm should move forward with its acquisition plans.

During the planning session, I continually raised a series of questions and concerns, pushing each member of the team to clarify his or her thinking about the combination and what the company was trying to accomplish. The team ultimately reached consensus on the strategy and decided to move forward with their acquisition plans. In our debriefing discussion after the meeting, however, the CEO was furious, feeling that I was being overly negative and that I was attempting to lead the team to reject the acquisition. All of our pre-meeting talks about the irrational exuberance that often accompanies M&A game playing and the need to step back for a critical look at the proposed acquisition were lost amid the CEO's emotional fervor to see the deal through.

Facilitating Integration Decisions

Integration issues encompass a broad array of change-related challenges, including: meshing operating systems; determining new roles and responsibilities; combining corporate functions and processes; setting priorities; enhancing cross-organization teamwork and collaboration; and forging a new organizational identity. All of this needs to be accomplished while maintaining sufficient flexibility to maneuver around inevitable roadblocks and barriers.[28] A general rule of thumb I have found is that the integration process typically takes more time and costs more money than initially anticipated—a message that clients rarely want to hear.

Part of my consulting role in M&As is that of problem finder, bringing to the surface potential problems that can derail integration plans. This very activity, however, can create resistance as already stressed-out organizational members are reluctant to take on what they see as yet another challenge. A related difficulty is that while integration planning is typically conducted at the highest corporate levels, its implementation is invariably a line responsibility. This essentially requires organizational members at all hierarchical levels to "think big" while "acting small" by focusing on the details and implementation intricacies associated with successful combination.[29] Thus, one of the consultant's goals is to facilitate the problem-solving process and decision-making process within by providing a broader perspective on how different decisions relate to each other and to the overall integration challenge.

As a way of creating supportive conditions for M&A integration, I recommend that, as early as possible, organizational members should be provided with the basic knowledge they need to reduce change-related anxieties. This information should help people take care of personal and professional needs, identify with the merger or acquisition partner, and accomplish job-related tasks. Thus, organizational members require information on roles and positions, compensation, reporting relationships, organizational policies, and initial transition assessments and planning efforts.

Some common techniques that I use include: 1) holding orientation sessions and disseminating information packets; 2) get-acquainted "town meetings" with cross-organization and cross-function mixes of employees that allow people from the two organizations to meet and interact with each other; and 3) executive and top management visits to selected key sites to answer questions and "walk around." Such visits and appearances, however, must be carried out with sensitivity and caution. As one of the partners in a merger I worked on a few years ago lamented, "I felt little more than a used car, with the other management team kicking my tires."

Working with Integration Managers

One finding that has clearly emerged from studies of M&A activities is the importance of establishing a dedicated senior integration manager as early as possible. These individuals oversee merger integration teams and task forces, helping to create guidelines, metrics, and accountability measures. They attempt to provide sufficient coordination so task forces do not go "off track" and specific needs and details do not "slip through the cracks."

Integration managers should serve as internal consultants, helping to guide the M&A process on a daily basis and acting as a conduit between the organization and its upper management.[30] Usually, this same person is a member of the acquirer team, and that can constrain how they approach different situations and limit the willingness of organizational members to cooperate. Thus, in many instances, I have worked with these individuals as an external consultant, acting as a resource and sounding board for their decisions.

While working with an integration manager, I try to fill an "onstage" role — operating more in public, in open forums—which is distinctly different from more typical consultant "backstage," confidential roles.[31] As part of my "onstage" role, for example, I often facilitate focus groups, conduct merger-syndrome workshops, and work with integration planning teams to discuss and analyze integration-related plans and activities. My role with integration managers, however, tends to reflect more of a "backstage" role, involving private conversations and exchanges. In these situations, I often engage in attachment-oriented behaviors—communicating empathy, respect, and regard—the goal being to help the integration manager cope with the surrounding uncertainty by giving encouragement and comfort as well as practical assistance and technical guidance.

Over time, these interactions create the conditions for the consultant to become a "trusted advisor." An underlying dilemma, however, concerns how others perceive the consultant's role and relationship with the integration manager. Since much of the information involved in "backstage" discussions can be highly sensitive, people are often wary about being too open with the consultant, concerned about how far confidentiality might really extend. Thus, merger consultants must walk a fine line when working with integration managers. It is important to develop trust and close ties with them, while also attempting to maintain one's position of objectivity and openness to others in the organization.

Serving as Morale Auditor

Consultants can also serve as a "morale auditor," providing a basis for an organizational "health check" and focusing on helping employees better understand and manage merger-related stress. Of course, the idea that the human side of mergers and acquisitions must be attended to is not a novel idea. Yet, one of the frustrating realities of M&A consulting is that, in far too many instances, "people issues" continue to be placed relatively low on the list of success measures, despite their eventual importance in driving the new business forward.

Most managers understand these dynamics on a cognitive level. A problem I've often faced, however, is that they are not prepared to deal with the emotional realities of the situation. Moreover, the romance of deal making, coupled with impatience to get the deal done, often make it difficult for M&A consultants to be fully heard over the recommendations of transaction advisors. Thus, even when pre-combination, transition-planning teams are created, they continue to be disbanded too early. Communication plans about merger integration, which are often well intentioned and thoughtfully planned at first, quickly begin to deteriorate. Many of the insights that are generated through systematic assessments of acquisition targets or merger partners fall into a literal interorganizational void due to time pressures and internal politics. It is far too easy for managers to get overwhelmed by the day-to-day pressures in a merger, with limited ability to step back and carefully think through next steps and action plans. Moreover, since a merger or acquisition is often seen as a one-time event, most managers try to get them over with rather than attempting to understand how to do them better.[32]

Within this context, I find merger-syndrome workshops and focus groups to be useful because they: 1) acknowledge the reality of peoples' fears, anxieties and uncertainties, 2) provide them with direction for M&A-related changes, and 3) prepare them for the stresses and tensions that accompany such transitions. It is important to ensure that the voice of the merger partner or acquisition target is clearly heard, allowing people to vent their feelings, concerns, and frustrations. It is even more important, however, to use these activities as a bridge for people to let go and move on.

A key challenge in planning these workshops is the need to establish discussion of priority "business" initiatives that reflect immediate, short-term results. Organizational members typically become inwardly focused, especially on "me issues," instead of on business-related activities, meeting the needs of customers and staying attuned to changes in the marketplace. Thus, as a way of building momentum for the merger or acquisition, it is useful for the participants to identify specific projects that can produce business results in 100 days or less. Focusing on these projects, cultural and psychological impediments can be identified, along with specific strategies for dealing with them. Successfully accomplishing these projects not only enhances operations but also begins to contribute to a new mindset as to how people view the combination.

Dealing with Culture

No other area of M&A is more frustrating for consultants than culture change. But not every merger or acquisition necessarily requires the same cultural integration strategy. In some instances, and probably too often, the acquiring company will seek to totally integrate the target into its operations, including an attempt to assimilate the culture into its own. In others, firms may follow a cultural pluralism strategy, attempting to build on cultural differences in the target company. Ed Liddy, Chairman and CEO of Allstate, has noted that although his company has made a number of acquisitions they do not try to "Allstate-ize" all of them.[33] In some instances, Allstate completely integrates the target firm. In others, the strategy is to keep the acquired firm operationally separate, leaving it to rely on the unique characteristics—whether product, channels, or key people—that made the company attractive in the first place.

Rather than trying to change an organization's culture—which can take years to accomplish—a key to successful integration is to focus on discussing and understanding the typical behaviors and practices in each organization. While organizational cultures often clash during a merger or acquisition, the cultures themselves do not have to be the problem. Rather it is better addressed in terms of the relatively low level of understanding of how one's culture—and the culture of the merger partner or acquisition target—has served to shape its management practices over the years. The well-known example of Hewlett-Packard's "Stepford Wives" and Apollo Computer's "Hell's Angels" provides a good illustration.[34] When H-P initially acquired Apollo, its managers experienced difficulties integrating Apollo into its operations. It was easy to point to the distinctly different cultures of the two organizations as an intractable problem. An intergroup mirroring exercise during a consulting engagement, however, drew out the Stepford Wives-Hell's Angels analogy. Discussion centered on how members of the two organizations approached typical business challenges. Instead of attempting to change the cultures, the intervention focused on increasing mutual understanding about how the cultures of each organization had shaped their behavior. Once this became clear, greater mutual respect was realized, and the focus turned to creating appropriate behaviors for how they could work together in the future, rather than trying to change their underlying values.

Hired by the Acquired Organizations

Despite the growing appreciation for the type of interventions discussed above, numerous instances still occur where consultants are contacted by the acquired firm rather than the acquiring company. The acquiree is often in a difficult situation because of how it is being treated by the acquirer. For example, a survey by Pittiglio Rabin Todd & McGrath, a global consulting firm to technology-based businesses, found a number of common problems among unsuccessful acquirers. The mistakes centered around the failure to communicate less than one-quarter of the ongoing integration activities to target company members and key stakeholders, the absence of a dedicated transition team, and the lack of a clearly understood and supported business strategy for the new entity.[35]

In these situations, consultants are faced with several unique challenges. I typically try to initiate an explicit strategy to increase open interaction between the firms (e.g., data-sharing strategies, joint action-planning, and offsite team-building meetings). But I have found that target firm executives are understandably uneasy about initiating such efforts because of their secondary role in the merger. It is, therefore, important to inform the acquirer that the acquiree would like to hire a consultant to help its employees adjust to the new situation.

While the prevailing view among many consultants is that long-lasting change will only occur when intervention begins at the top, some things can be done at lower organizational levels through workshops and other means of communication.[36] One of the most effective ways to assist organizational members in this process is by guiding them through a series of questions that assist them in coming to terms with their situation and their spheres of control. The essence of these questions is to prompt employees to identify 1) the exact nature of their situation; 2) what it will take to resolve any problems and/or concerns; and 3) whether they currently have or might be able to generate sufficient resources to deal with these issues. The objective is to enable individuals to distinguish between those aspects of their work environment that they can and cannot control, as well as alerting them to issues that they can manage through direct action, behavioral change, or even a change in attitude.[37]

As employees are shown how to concentrate on those areas where they are able to exert some influence, they can be encouraged to work constructively on possible solutions. When one set of issues is resolved, the next solvable problem often becomes more visible, encouraging people to become more proactive in dealing with it. In complex organizations, such "small wins" do not necessarily connect in a logical sequential form, but they can develop momentum toward inter-firm cooperation and more positive attitudes.[38]

Clearly, there are limitations to this approach. One decision by the acquiring organization can quickly undermine what the target company and its members have attempted to do. Thus, in these instances, "helping" is limited to enhancing the ability of the client in the target firm to better handle their feelings of frustration and helplessness.

THE FUTURE OF M&A CONSULTING

The overarching reason why firms enter into a merger or decide to acquire another company is the belief, albeit frequently naive, that the combination will allow the new entity to attain its strategic goals more quickly and less expensively than if the firm attempted to do so on its own. Yet far too many M&A deals are dominated by the content of financial analysis, a focus on historical data rather than future sources of revenues, and power plays that turn strategy into gamesmanship. Many companies still seem to meander through the post-combination integration process, literally paralyzed by the myriad dysfunctions that surround them.

Despite the poor performance and track record associated with merging and acquiring firms, future projections suggest that M&A activity will become more far-reaching and more complex than anything we have experienced thus far.[39] Many will take place across national boundaries and cultures.

These deals will continue to be strategically driven, requiring a level of integration that makes key challenges as much cultural and psychological as they are financial and operational. A likely change is that merger integration consultants will share the table more frequently with transaction advisors earlier in the process of due diligence. Consulting engagements will become longer term, going beyond isolated interventions to focus more on the entire process of merger planning and integration. Thus, from a consulting perspective, post-M&A integration will continue to become an increasingly important service.

Notes to the Chapter

[1]See, for example, R. W. Coff, "Human capital, shared expertise and the likelihood of impasse in corporate acquisitions," *Journal of Management*, 28, no. 1 (2002): 115–137; P. M. Elsass and J. F. Veiga, "Acculturation in Acquired Organizations: A Force-Field Perspective," *Human Relations*, 47, no. 4 (1994): 431–453; and M. Lubatkin, "Mergers and the performance of the acquiring firm," *Academy of Management Review*, 8, no. 2 (1983): 218–225.

[2]Compare the two *Business Week* cover stories: "Do Mergers Really Work?" June 3, 1985 and "The Merger Hangover: How Most Big Acquisitions Have Destroyed Shareholder Value," October 14, 2002.

[3]See "Establishing Strategic Guideposts for Corporate Buyers in the 21st Century," *Mergers and Acquisitions,* 36, no. 5 (2001): 18–27.

[4]See, for example, A. R. Lajoux, *The Art of M&A Integration* (New York: McGraw-Hill, 1998), 49–53.

[5]See, for example, R. G. Eccles, K. L. Lanes, and T. C. Wilson, "Are You Paying Too Much For That Acquisition?" *Harvard Business Review,* 77, no. 4 (1999): 136–146; and M. N. Clemente and D. S. Greenspan, *Winning at Mergers and Acquisitions* (New York: Wiley, 1998).

[6]See D. H. Maister, C. H. Green, and R. M. Galford, *The Trusted Advisor* (New York: Simon & Schuster, 2000).

[7]David Nadler talks about a similar dynamic when consulting with CEOs and Boards of Directors in Chapter 9 in this volume.

[8]A. F. Buono, "Technology Transfer Through Acquisition," *Management Decision,* 35, 3 (1997): 194–204; D. Carey, "Lessons from master acquirers: A CEO roundtable on making mergers succeed," *Harvard Business Review,* 78, no. 3 (2000): 145–154; and P. Pritchett and R. D. Gilbreath, *Mergers: Growth in the Fast Lane* (Dallas: Pritchett & Associates, 1996).

[9]A. F. Buono and J. L. Bowditch, *The Human Side of Mergers and Acquisitions: Managing Collisions between People, Cultures, and Organizations* (San Francisco: Jossey-Bass, 1989); and D. Kidd, "Who Goes, Who Stays? Many Mergers Do Not Create the Shareholder Value Expected of Them," *Harvard Business Review,* 79, no. 1 (2001): 9.

[10]A. F. Buono, J. W. Weiss and J. L. Bowditch, "Paradoxes in Acquisition and Merger Consulting: Thoughts and Recommendations," *Consultation: An International Journal,*8, no. 3 (1989): 145–159.

[11]See A. L. Velocci, "Merger "Experiences Yield Valuable Lessons," *Aviation Week & Space Technology,* 154, no. 19 (2001): 80–81; and P. Haspeslagh and D. B. Jemison, *Managing Acquisitions: Creating Value through Corporate Renewal* (New York: Free Press, 1991).

[12]Reported in *Mergers and Acquisitions,* "Establishing strategic guideposts."

[13]M. M. Habeck, F. Kroger, and M. R. Tram, *After the Merger* (London: Financial Times/Prentice-Hall, 2000), 3–5.

[14]For a thoughtful discussion of M&A strategies and their ramifications, see J. L. Bower, "Not all M&As are alike—and that matters," *Harvard Business Review,* 79, no. 2 (2001): 93–101.

[15]Exhibit 13.1 has been influenced by a number of sources, including M. L. Marks, "How to Treat the Merger Syndrome," *Journal of Management Consulting,* 4, no. 3 (1988): 42–52; M. L. Marks and J. Cutcliffe, "Making Mergers Work," *Training and Development Journal,* 42, no. 4 (1988): 30–36; and Buono and Bowditch, *The Human Side of Mergers and Acquisitions.*

[16]For a fuller discussion of the shortcomings of traditional due diligence efforts, see Clemente and Greenspan, *Winning at Mergers and Acquisitions,*Chapter 1.

[17]Reported in Mergers & Acquisitions, "Establishing Strategic Guideposts for Corporate Buyers."

[18]See J. A. Schmidt, "The Correct Spelling of M&A Begins with HR," *HR Magazine,* (June 2001): 102–108; and M. L. Feldman and M. F. Spratt, *Five Frogs on a Log: A CEO's Field Guide to Accelerating the Transition in Mergers, Acquisitions, and Gut Wrenching Change* (New York: HarperBusiness, 1999).

[19]Exhibit 13.2 draws from R. G. Eccles, K. L. Lanes, and T. C. Wilson, "Are You Paying Too Much for That Acquisition?" *Harvard Business Review,* 77, no. 4 (1999): 136–146; and R. Coff, "Human Capital, Shared Expertise, and the

Likelihood of Impasse in Corporate Acquisitions," *Journal of Management,* 28, no. 1 (2002): 115–137.

[20]A good illustration of this can be found in P. H. Mirvis and M. L. Marks, "The Human Side of Merger Planning: Assessing and Analyzing Fit," *Human Resource Planning,* 15, no. 3 (1992): 69–92.

[21]Reported in Marks, "Making Mergers and Acquisitions Work."

[22]Reported in M. P. Ennen, "The War for Talent: Physicians in Management Consulting," *Journal of the American Medical Association,* 285, no. 17 (2001): 2252.

[23]See Coff, "Human Capital, Shared Expertise, and the Likelihood of Impasse in Corporate Acquisitions."

[24]This case is drawn from Buono and Bowditch, *The Human Side,* Chapter 8.

[25]E. Schein, "Managerial Consulting: Who Is Our Client? Who Should Be Our Client?" Distinguished speaker presentation, Management Consulting Division, Academy if Management, Cincinnati, Ohio, August 1996; see also E. Schein, "The Concept of 'Client' from a Process Consultation Perspective: A Guide for Change Agents," *Journal of Organizational Change Management,* 10, no. 3 (1997): 202–216.

[26]See P. H. Mirvis and M. L. Marks, *Managing the Merger: Making it Work* (Englewood Cliffs, NJ: Prentice-Hall, 1992).

[27]The discussion of listening deeply is based on A. F. Buono and A. J. Nurick, "Intervening in the Middle: Coping Strategies in Mergers and Acquisitions," *Human Resource Planning,* 15, no. 2 (1992): 19–33; and H. F. Stein, *Listening Deeply* (Boulder, CO: Westview Press, 1994).

[28]For an in-depth discussion of these integration challenges see Buono and Bowditch, *The Human Side;* Clemente and Greenspan, *Winning at Mergers and Acquisitions;* and Haspeslagh and Jemison, *Managing Acquisitions.*

[29]See Clemente and Greenspan, *Winning at Mergers and Acquisitions;*and Habeck, et al, *After the Merger* for a fuller discussion of these dynamics.

[30]A good illustration can be found in R. N. Ashkenas and S. C. Francis, "Integration Managers: Special Leaders for Special Times," *Harvard Business Review,* 78, no. 6 (2000): 108–116.

[31]The distinction between onstage and backstage roles is drawn from P. Mirvis, "Midlife as a consultant," in P. J. Frost and M. S. Taylor, eds., *Rhythms of Academic Life* (Thousand Oaks, CA: Sage), 361–369.

[32]R. N. Ashkenas, L. J. DeMarco, and S. C. Francis, "Making the Deal Real: How GE Capital Integrates Acquisitions," *Harvard Business Review,* 76, no. 1 (1998): 5–15.

[33]Reported in D. Carey, "Lessons from Master Acquirers," 152.

[34]A fuller discussion of the H-P/Apollo culture clash can be found in A. F. Buono and A. J. Nurick, "Intervening in the Middle: Coping Strategies in Mergers and Acquisitions," *Human Resource Planning,* 15, no. 2 (1992): 19–33; Mirvis and Marks, *Managing the Merger;* and T. L. Legare, "The Human Side of Mergers and Acquisitions: Understanding and Managing Human Resource Integration Issues," *Human Resource Planning,* 21, no. 1 (1998): 32–41.

[35]Reported in Velocci, "Merger Experiences Yield Valuable Lessons."

[36]See Buono and Nurick, "Intervening in the Middle."

[37]A good illustration of this dynamic can be found in M. L. Marks, *From Turmoil to Triumph: New Life after Mergers, Acquisitions, and Downsizing* (New York: Lexington Books, 1994), 162–165.

[38]This approach is an application of K. Weick, "Small Wins: Redefining the Scale of Social Problems," *American Psychologist,* 39, no. 1 (1984): 40–49.

[39]For an intriguing assessment of the future of M&A activity, see "Merger Outlook: You Haven't Seen Anything yet" in Habeck, et al, *After the Merger,* 1135–1140.

CHAPTER 14

On Becoming a Transformational Change Agent

Robert E. Quinn, University of Michigan, and Shawn E. Quinn, Creativity-at-Work

ABOUT THE AUTHORS

Robert E. Quinn

Robert E. Quinn holds the Margaret Elliot Tracy Collegiate Professorship at the University of Michigan. Dr. Quinn's research and teaching interests focus on organization effectiveness and leadership. Quinn has written several articles and books, including *Letters to Garrett* (Jossey-Bass, 2002), *A Company of Leaders* (Jossey-Bass, 2001), and *Change the World* (Jossey-Bass, 2000). He has consulted with nearly 100 of the Fortune 500 companies.

Shawn E. Quinn

Shawn E. Quinn is a full-time consultant and project manager at Creativity-at-Work. He specializes in designing and facilitating organizational change processes, with particular emphasis on aligning vision, strategy, technology, and human systems. He holds a master's degree in Organizational Psychology from Columbia University.

Fifty percent of all major organizational change efforts fail.[1] They fail for many reasons, but a main one is the lack of personal authenticity in the person attempting to lead the change. While many CEOs and other executives espouse their support for a given change and invest considerable time and money in it, they are usually not, in fact, fully committed to the change they indeed espouse. In the end, they are unwilling to make changes in themselves that are necessary for the organization to be transformed. Most experienced consultants, when they reflect back on failed engagements, will recognize and agree about this weakness in self-change among senior executives.

The same problem extends beyond executives to consultants. Consultants are also agents of change, and many organizational changes fail because consultants lack the integrity to fully play out their role and their recommendations to create transformational changes when they are needed.

All human beings, including the authors of this chapter, spend much of their time being externally driven and self-focused. In planning an organizational change, consultants seek to persuade others by demonstrating expertise and wielding authority. We try to introduce change through the transfer of knowledge. We expect to diagnose the situation and tell people how and why they have to change. When people are not responsive, we default to a backup strategy in which we look for ways to force change through the use of authority, power, and external influence. While this strategy may obtain compliance in the short term, it frequently occurs at a high cost in the commitment of the people involved, causing a downturn in long-term results.

This "telling and forcing" model of change permeates all of administrative theory, executive leadership, and most consulting practices. It permeates every business school. It permeates our entire culture. While the model is seemingly functional in its theoretical appearance and logic, it is also deeply flawed by its one-sided arrogance in its negative attitude toward the contribution of people—a flaw that lies within the psyche of the change agent. Instead of focusing on instrumental methods to bring about change, as we usually do, we might be wise to focus more deeply on ourselves and how we think, feel, and act during the change process.

In this chapter, we ask the reader to rethink his or her approach to change, and in so doing, to perhaps consider becoming a transformational change agent. A consultant who becomes a transformational change agent is a consultant who becomes more masterful in elevating the level of value creation within the consulting relationship and for the client. What does this mean? A comparison to management may be helpful.

Management and Leadership

Most executives tend to be managers who seek to preserve value. They tend not to be leaders who create value. Managers preserve value by maintaining equilibrium: "Thank you for this new job, and I can assure you that for the next three years there will be no problems here." This mindset is fundamentally reactive and transactional; the manager's job, in this mindset, is to survive by dampening disruption and conflict. The manager's job is to recognize the political self-interests of people and to transact business in such a way that they all do what is necessary to keep things running smoothly. The job, so defined, is to preserve value.

Leaders create value by destroying the existing equilibrium and establishing a new equilibrium: "Thank you for the new job, and in three years you will not recognize this place." This mindset seeks a higher order. Such a leader is a transformational leader, one who alters the status quo by lifting everyone from transactional self-interest to a state in which everyone makes personal sacrifices for the collective good. In this transformed state, there is synchrony. The personal self-interest and the collective self-interest become one. A transformational leader brings fundamental change by enticing people to a higher level of relationship between themselves and the organization and community. It is then that the system accelerates its evolution, developing new collective competencies as it changes. It is through this evolutionary process that new levels of value emerge.

Consultants

Many consultants are like managers. They seek to preserve a relationship in which they can be paid for contributing their expertise. As the assumptions of transaction dominate the executive world, the assumptions of transaction also dominate the world of consulting. A subtle but deadly problem follows. These consultants often believe that their first priority is to bring about change in the client's organization. However, this belief is more likely to be a self-deception. If consultants are honest with themselves, their first priority is usually to maintain a working relationship with those in authority, which includes both the client and the consultant's boss. They seek to avoid negation and rejection. They seek to survive by making money for the consulting firm and themselves.

The client authority figure, like the consultant, also sincerely believes that he or she is committed to change. Yet organizations are systems. If the organization has a problem, the authority figure is usually part of the problem. For the organization to change, the authority figure must change. The notion of having to make personal change is seldom appealing to the authority figure. So the authority figure typically defines the problem to be somewhere other than where it really is. This distortion makes it difficult for anyone to deal with reality.

To survive in a transactional system, the consultant must serve and please the client. The consultant must knowingly or unknowingly begin to collude, applying his or her expertise to various issues in the name of change. But, in many instances, they only seek to preserve the equilibrium that currently exists while introducing superficial "fine-tuning" changes. The result is that both the manager and the consultant sincerely claim that they are committed to change, while engaged in an unconscious conspiracy to prevent change. Two examples may be helpful.

This book emerged from a conference attended by the authors and many consultants. Some of the presentations and discussions had an instrumental and financial bias. A few less than elevating practices were defended as necessary for financial survival of the consultant. At one point, the CEO of a large consulting firm told of a principle by which he and his firm operated, saying that each project is regularly "called to question." "Is this project contributing true value to the client?" If the answer is no, the project is cancelled. He then told of a case in which he cancelled a contract for millions of dollars that accounted for one-fourth of his firm's revenue. Some attendees found this notion incomprehensible.

A week later, one of authors of this chapter had lunch with a former doctoral student who had been working for a well-known consulting firm. He was leaving. His decision to leave was tied to a single incident. His team was working on a large technology project. The client was unable to organize in such a way as to move forward. The consulting team could see that they were just wasting the money of the client and came to a consensus that the project should be ended. When they took their decision to their senior partner, he became furious, read them the riot act, and required them to continue with the project. They were intimidated and frustrated. The former student said he could no longer work under those conditions.

Think about that situation. The remaining consultants were adding little value. The responsible executives in the company were maintaining the expensive contract for political reasons. They did not want to signal that there were problems. Everyone, the executives and the consultants, were colluding to maintain the equilibrium of the present organization and engagement.

Over time, some consultants come to an awareness of this pattern and feel guilty about the collusion trap. To manage their shame, they, like the manager, define the problem to be elsewhere. As they increase these rationalizations, they become increasingly disconnected from their own emotional reality. They lose vitality and effectiveness, yet they see no way to change the situation. They continue to feel trapped.

The above description is challenging and uncomfortable. We believe it also applies beyond the world of executives and consultants. It applies to virtually everyone, including the authors and the reader. We all have long periods when we live by our fears, react rather than create, and collude in the preservation of the status quo regardless of its dysfunctionality.[2]

Unusual Nature of This Chapter

This chapter is about finding a way out of the collusion trap. It is about the process of becoming a transformational change agent. Our belief is that organizations can be transformed when meaning, dialog, and behavior are transformed. To accomplish this process, transformational leaders must behave outside the box. Among other things, they must model behaviors that are out-of-pattern, engage in risk taking, display vulnerability, and model what we call "moral power." One has moral power when other people are enticed and inspired to engage reality by speaking both the cognitive and emotional truth.

In this chapter, we try to move toward that level, knowing our thoughts will be imperfect. First, we will go outside of the pattern of collusion. The tone of this chapter will be different from the other chapters in this book. It will be a dialog. The dialog will be risky because it is intimate. The dialog is a model. It models what the reader must do to become more transformational, examine one's self, find courage, engage reality, experiment with new patterns, develop new competencies, and experience the empowering process of increasing value.

The dialog is an exchange between the two authors, Robert Quinn and Shawn Quinn. Robert is in the later stages of an academic career focused on change research and consulting. His son Shawn is in the process of becoming a change agent. Shawn entered the master's program in Organizational Psychology at Columbia University in September of 2001. As he did so, it was agreed that he would keep a journal. Robert would read journal entries and provide responses. During his first two semesters, Shawn wrote nearly thirty lengthy entries. Many of the issues embedded in those entries were discussed by email and by phone. Then came the invitation to write this chapter. It seemed like an excellent opportunity to examine the question at the core of those journal entries: How do I become a transformational change agent? What follows is a summary of our many emails and phone conversations, which we have combined into two letters back and forth. We invite you to listen in.

MASTERY AND THE NATURE OF THE JOURNEY

Dear Shawn,

I have recently reread your journal entries. I am grateful for your discipline and for your insights. You have come a long way. I think back to the first week of September 2001 and driving with you and Lisa to New York City. A memorable moment occurred when we were in New Jersey, ten minutes from the George Washington Bridge. Suddenly Lisa tensed up and was filled with anxiety. The thought of living in New York City and starting an entirely new life phase seemed overwhelming. Then, we reached the bridge. You looked at the view of Manhattan. As we crossed the bridge your anxiety turned to wonder and then excitement. You said, "Look at this, look at this, a year ago, we would not have dreamed that we would be here doing this!"

Now, you are nearly finished and ready to start what seems like a new journey. Yet it is not a new journey. The Hudson River was just a punctuation mark. When you crossed the George Washington Bridge, you were moving into a new phase of the same journey you have always been on. When you graduate and move to a new job, it too will become a new phase in that continuous journey. It is important to be clear about the nature of the journey.

Becoming More Masterful

It seems to me that life is about the process of becoming, of continually learning, of moving to a higher and higher level of consciousness and capacity. When we are not growing in this fashion, we choose slow death.[3] Each of us is full of potential. When that potential is expanding, we are filled with positive emotions. When we get stuck and stop growing, we begin to stagnate and die. Human beings are always choosing to grow or die. When our potential is expanding, we tend to be in a creative, life-giving state.[4] We become empowered and empowering. When our potential is blocked, we behave in a more reactive, disempowered state.

Life continually calls us to change. Our challenge is to keep accepting that call. If we do, we become increasingly more Masterful. Let's consider the process of becoming more Masterful. In taking on the role of a change agent, you can perform at different levels. You begin as a novice and then work your way to higher levels of Mastery. A novice is a beginner, a trainee, or apprentice. There are academic models that describe the process of developing Mastery. One is a five-stage journey described by Dreyfus, Dreyfus, and Athanasion.[5] Here is a summary.

1. In the *novice* stage, people learn facts and rules. The rules are learned as absolutes that are never to be violated. For example, in playing chess, we learn the names of the pieces, how they are moved, and their value; in parenting, we take classes and read books; in management, we are exposed to the manuals and books of procedures.

2. In the *advanced beginner* stage, experience becomes critical. Performance improves as real situations are encountered. Understanding begins to exceed the stated facts and rules. Observation of certain basic patterns leads to the recognition of factors that were not set forth in the rules. A chess player, for example, begins to recognize certain basic board positions that should be pursued. The parent notices that the baby responds to a certain kind of soothing. The manager notices that people seem to regularly struggle with certain problems.

3. The third stage is *competence*. Here we begin to appreciate the complexity of the task, and now we recognize a much larger set of cues. We develop the ability to select and concentrate on the most important cues. With this ability, our competence grows. Here our reliance on absolute rules fades. We take calculated risks and engage in complex trade-offs. A chess player may, for example, weaken board position in order to attack the opposing king. This plan may or may not follow any rules that the person was ever taught. The parent begins to ignore certain kinds of cries. The manager begins to anticipate

misunderstandings and prevents them.

4. The fourth stage is the *proficiency* stage. In this stage, calculation and rational analysis seem to disappear, and unconscious, fluid, and effortless performance begins to emerge. Here we hold no single plan sacred. We unconsciously "read" the evolving situation. We notice and respond to cues that a casual observer wouldn't notice. Our attention shifts to new cues as our response to old ones becomes automatic. New plans are triggered in our minds as emerging patterns call forth plans that worked previously. Here there is a holistic and intuitive grasp of the situation. We are talking, for example, about the top one percent of all chess players, the people with the ability to intuitively recognize and respond to change in board positions. Here are the parents who maintain an extraordinary implicit communication with their children. Here is the manager who regularly obtains extraordinary performance. Such people are rare, of course, and there is much to learn from them.

5. The final stage is the *expertise* stage. Those in this fifth stage do what comes naturally to the expert. They do not apply rules but use holistic recognition in a way that allows them to deeply understand the situation. They have maps of the territory programmed into their heads that the rest of us are not aware of. They see and know things intuitively that the rest of us do not know or see. They frame and reframe strategies as they read changing cues.

A *novice* tends to focus on learning the facts and the rules. You read about many of these facts in your textbooks. The *novice* tends to see rules as absolutes. These become less absolute in the next stage. In the advanced beginner stage, experience comes into play. You go out and you take on your first consulting experience. This is when you really begin to stretch, and you start to learn. Your journal entries about your first intervention verify this. Since you have always struggled with reading, I am moved by the following observation from you:

> One thing I have found as I prepare for my first intervention is that my desire to read has increased. I have read a ton over Christmas break and continue to look for times to read books beyond my required readings. Knowing I am going to be consulting soon and that I know so little has motivated me. I want to gain more knowledge. Having a real experience like this consulting project makes school so much more interesting. Since the company is a financial company, for the first time I am excited about my finance class. I have already read two books from my change class.

For me, engaging reality gives a reason to acquire knowledge. Much of the educational enterprise is devoid of reality and devoid of meaningful learning. As you begin to gain experience in the advanced beginner stage, your understanding starts to exceed the stated facts and rules. Careful observation leads to the recognition of factors that were not set forth in the rules. For example, in setting up your first intervention, you discovered all kinds of lessons about how to arrange a contract and set up expectations with the client. As you have more and more such experiences, you will find yourself moving up to competency, proficiency, and finally into the expert stage.

The description of the final stage sounds almost mystical. Here calculation and rational analysis seem to disappear, and unconscious, fluid, and effortless performance begins to emerge. Here we hold no single plan sacred. We unconsciously "read" the evolving situation. We notice and respond to cues that a casual observer wouldn't notice. Our attention shifts to new cues as our response to old ones becomes automatic. New plans are triggered in our minds as emerging patterns call forth plans that worked previously. *Masters* (and this also includes *Masters* in consulting) tend to do what comes naturally. They do not apply rules but use holistic recognition in a way that allows them to deeply understand the situation. They have maps of the territory programmed into their heads that the rest of us are not aware of. They see and know things intuitively that the rest of us do not know or see. They frame and reframe strategies as they read changing cues.

As I said, this description sounds almost mysterious. Yet it can be accomplished in any activity.[6] Consider the following statement from Robert Pirsig from *Zen and the Art of Motorcycle Maintenance* about flowing with performance.[7]

> Sometime look at a novice workman or a bad workman and compare his expression with that of a craftsman whose work you know is excellent and you'll see the difference. The craftsman isn't ever following a single line of instruction. He's making decisions as he goes along. For that reason he'll be absorbed and attentive to what he is doing even though he doesn't deliberately contrive this. His motions and the machine are in a kind of harmony. He isn't following any set of written instructions because the nature of the material at hand determines his thoughts and motions, which simultaneously change the nature of the material at hand. The material and his thoughts are changing together in a progression of changes until his mind is at rest at the same time the material is right.

At the level of Mastery, the change agent and the consulting relationship are changing together in a creative interaction. The Master and the Master's reality are cocreating each other. This is not as mysterious as it may seem. In fact, you understand it very well from other experiences. Think back to your time as a point guard in basketball. A Masterful point guard does not just follow a set of rules; he or she flows with the situation, continually making choices. His or her behavior creates the situation and the situation creates the behavior. Great teachers, great leaders, and great change agents learn to do the same thing. They engage in the flowing process of cocreation.

The Process Model

In organizations, a premium is typically placed on information and knowledge. Expertise tends to be equated with the possession of information and knowledge, which, however, is a distortion of expertise in the five-stage journey. The information-based expert is not a Master expert engaged in cocreation; rather, the former is a possessor of knowledge who transfers the knowledge by informing less-informed people. The information-based model of expertise is so pervasive that many people can conceive of no other model. It is dominant in management consulting. Yet, you are aware of an alternative. Because of your athletic and missionary experiences and because of your many workshops at the National Training Labs, you are comfortable with and strive to employ the *process* model. The process model suggests that a change agent can play the role of a facilitator who becomes a catalyst in the process of human learning and discovery. The facilitator does not tell a person, group, or organization what to do. A facilitator helps the system embrace reality, exercise courage, resolve conflict, and move to where it needs to go.

One of the major themes in your journal entries is the frustration you have experienced trying to help others to understand and embrace the process model. In your class projects, you indicate that some of your peers cannot comprehend what you are talking about. In making a presentation, you have been rejected out-of-hand by the grader for not using the information-based expert model. Apparently, she does not even know what you are talking about when you confronted her with the notion of the process model. Then you talked to a professional consultant. He shrugs off your interest in the process model and tells you that there are only a few consulting firms that specialize in team building; otherwise, there are no jobs for such people. He smiles down upon you from the loftiness of his information-based perch.

Here is an interesting thing. At the heart of all value creation is the process model. Just as above, I said, a "facilitator helps the system embrace reality, exercise courage, resolve conflict, and move where it needs to go." The word *move* is critical. The facilitator is creating a new kind of dialog giving rise to hope, courage, trust, and action. When these virtues increase in their authenticity and intensity, the group moves forward to face uncertainty. As the group moves, it develops new competency. The development of new competency, not the possession of information and knowledge, is the source of value creation. Most information-based experts cannot produce hope, courage, trust, and action. They transfer information but it usually creates fear and stops action. Little of value is created.

Unfortunately, most managers, faculty members, and consultants see limited value in the process model. They consign it to what they see as a "weak" and limited area of activity known as team building, and they carry images of facilitators as low-level process people who lead group discussions. I consider their position valid. A novice facilitator often is very weak and adds little value. A Master of facilitation, however, is a Master of change and carries power that cannot be understood from the framework of the information-based expert. Consider why the gap exists.

One answer is that most people in authority are embedded in the journey of intense achievement. They have high needs for control. They are very results-oriented, and they see the choice between the information-based model and the process model as an either/or proposition. In one of your journal entries, you provide a wonderful example.

However, you say that one of your professors seems to greatly value the process or learning model, and she seems to teach it well. She makes it clear that the model requires the change agent to give up the illusion of control that comes with the information-based, expert role, to stand naked of external validation, to engage reality, and to cocreate the new future. The class has difficulty with this. You describe a classic response. "A man in my group raised his hand and talked about how it seems unprofessional to admit that you have no idea what you are doing, or that you don't have an answer in situations where you really don't have one." The assumption is that the very definition of being a professional is to be an information-based expert, to always know the answer. People see no other alternative.

The information-based expert is always fearful. Their authority is always in danger. They can only be confident as long as they are in their comfort zone. Since changing reality is always calling on us to cocreate a new future, changing reality is highly threatening to the information-based expert.

Remember that the practice of the process model should embrace and be driven by a genuine commitment to results. Most of us, when in the reactive state, espouse a desire for results, but our commitment is not real. If results require us to leave our comfort zone and endure change, our commitment wanes because we do not want our vulnerabilities to be exposed. We want to be in control. The important point is that the issue of results versus process are not an either/or issue. We see them as one. You will be continually tempted to reject the information-based expert model in defense of the process model. Do not fall into this trap!

Again, it is not knowledge that is bad but the lack of authenticity and the unwillingness to engage changing reality. The Master does not reject existing knowledge but neither is the Master trapped by it. The Master embraces and releases existing knowledge while continually creating and embracing new knowledge.

Advanced Change Theory

The work of the consultant and change agent is always concerned with the issue of change. Without it, their work is not done. The change agent must therefore become one with change. Gandhi understood this when he said, "Be the change you want to see in the world." To a graduate student, this may sound like strange stuff. So I would like to share a framework that may help. Then I would like to ask you a question that may help even more.

The framework comes from my book, *Change the World*.[8] In that book, I introduce what I call Advanced Change Theory or ACT. I believe ACT deals with the most advanced issues in management consulting. There I examine the principles of change practiced by Martin Luther King, Jr., Gandhi, and Jesus Christ. It is not a religious book. It is a book about practicing change in modern organizations. When people read the book, they never say that ACT is wrong. Instead, they argue that it is impractical. "No ordinary person can do what you are asking." Actually, they are partially right.

Everyone is ordinary or average in some way. It is when we practice ACT that we become extraordinary. So it is not that ordinary people cannot practice ACT; it is that most ordinary people do not practice ACT. When ordinary people do practice ACT, they become extraordinary, and ordinary people feel the power of their authenticity. In the ordinary state, everyone "knows" ACT is nonsense. Now let's take a look at the ACT framework, shown in Exhibit 14.1, as it applies to change agents.

The first three strategies are telling, forcing, and participating. These labels are adapted from a classic article on organizational development written by Chin and Benne.[9] The authors identified three general strategies available to change agents for changing human systems. You can understand each strategy by examining the questions in Exhibit 14.1 that the wise change agent might

---

| Exhibit 14.1 | Four Strategies for Changing Human Systems |

Level 1. The Telling Strategy

Method: Telling others to change

Objective: Align the change target with established facts

- Am I within my expertise?
- Have I gathered all of the facts?
- Have I done a rigorous analysis?
- Will my conclusions withstand criticism?
- Are my arguments logical?
- Do I have a forum for instruction?
- Do the people understand my argument?

Level 2. The Forcing Strategy

Method: Leveraging others to change

Objective: Align the change target with established authority

- Is my authority firmly established?
- Is the legitimacy of my directives clear?
- Am I capable and willing to impose sanctions?
- Is there a clear performance-reward linkage?
- Am I controlling the information flow?
- Am I controlling the design of the context?
- Are the people complying?

Level 3. The Participative Strategy

Method: Engaging others in conceptualizing change

Objective: Alignment of the actors in a "win-win" dialog

- Is there a focus on human process?
- Is everyone included in an open dialog?
- Do I model supportive communication?
- Is everyone's position being clarified?
- Are the decisions being made participatively?
- Is there a commitment to a "win-win" stratgy?
- Are the people cohesive?

Level 4. The Transformational Strategy (ACT)

Method: Modeling change by others

Objective: Alignment with changing reality

- Am I aware of the realities of the emergent system?
- What are my patterns of self-deception?
- Are my values and behaviors aligned?
- Am I freed from external sanctions?
- Do I have a vision of the common good?
- Do I operate at the edge of chaos?
- Do I maintain reverence for others?
- Do I inspire others to enact their best self?
- Am I engaging in unconventional or paradoxical ways?
- Have I changed myself as a model for the system to change?

Source: Adapted from Quinn (2000).

---

ask him or herself. I believe that the second strategy is more complex than the first, and the third is more complex than the second.

The fourth strategy is the essence of ACT. It is the most difficult of all because it does not begin on the outside. It begins on the inside and is based on my study of the three change agents identified above—Gandhi, King, and Christ. It suggests that we transform human systems by modeling change for others and that our objective is always to be aligned with the changing reality around us. Instead of simply reacting to reality as we encounter it, we need to think of ourselves as cocreating this reality in which we are engaged. When we are living in the creative state rather than the reactive state, we are living out the essence of ACT.

Clearly, ACT is not ordinary. It requires that we live and work at a very high level of accountability. As change agents, it asks that we do the hard things that we ask of those people, groups, and organizations we seek to help. As I indicated above, most ordinary people run from ACT by arguing it is impractical. They much prefer to live in the safety of the information-based model. Hence, many change agents and consultants are transactional and not transformational. They collude with executives in the avoidance of the real work that will bring change.

Now, given the difficulty of accessing ACT, what possible use can it be to a novice or information-based expert? As a graduate student, how could you ever be expected to understand or use ACT? I think there is a very clear answer; it is that you already have begun to embrace it in your early life experiences. At the outset of this letter, I said graduate school is not a new journey. "The Hudson River was just a punctuation mark. When you crossed the George Washington Bridge, you were moving into a new phase of the same journey you have always been on. When you graduate and move to a new job, it too will simply be a new phase in a journey you have always been on."

I have a request of you. If you fulfill it, I think you will render a great service to the reader of this chapter. So far I have played the role of the information-based expert. To help the reader, one of us has to be transformational. I ask you to play that role.

How could you be transformational? I ask you to shape your future and the future of the reader by examining your past. You carry a treasure trove. I would like you to utilize it. As an athlete, you experienced personal and collective transformation. As a missionary, you experienced personal transformation and facilitated the transformation of others. As a college student, you again experienced transformation. As a manager, you facilitated the transformation of the systems and groups in your company. Here I would like you to go back and identify the most meaningful transformations in your life. I would then like for you to identify the lessons they hold in helping you to move forward on the path of becoming an extraordinary change agent.

Such an effort in increasing your consciousness may model for the reader the change you and I would like to see in all of us. That is, you may help us to discover how to find the transformational power that already exists in our lives.

MOVING TOWARD PROCESS-ORIENTED EXPERT

Dear Dad,

The challenge you issue is a difficult one. You alluded to my struggles with reading. I also have struggles with writing. While I have grown in my writing skills, I still find this task intimidating. You may expect too much, like most fathers.

I am not sure if I feel intimidated because it means I will have to work hard, or that I will have to open myself up to the public, or if it is that I am worried that I have not yet reached a transformational level in my experience—which I surely haven't. Also, to think back and discover that I have not learned as much as you think I have could prove painful.

My temptation is to say that I worry about disappointing you or being embarrassed in public. While both these fears are present, they are not my most potent fears. In the face of this challenge, I hear you suggesting that there may be greatness in me. I want to believe that. Yet a voice whispers that if

I really look inside myself, I will find only weakness and inadequacy. My most central fear is that, if I look, really look, I may find that I have little value.

Thankfully, I have had enough experience with such fears to know that when I feel this way, the thing to do is move forward. I will do the following. I will share three stories from my earlier life and then examine each story in terms of the concepts in your letter. Then I will try to extend the implied principles to my immediate future of trying to become a professional change agent.

Basketball

The first change agent experience that comes to me has to do with my high school basketball team. In my senior year, we had a team with great potential. We started the season 11 and 1. Despite the success, we had serious morale problems. One of our players quit. Others complained a lot. Things finally began to fall apart. We went 2 and 6 over the rest of the season. In that period, I was also unhappy because I was seeing limited playing time.

Meanwhile, I was having a problem with an authority figure in the school. On an important issue, the person treated me in a way that I felt was a huge injustice. That night I lay in bed sobbing. At midnight, mom came into my room. We talked for a while. She cried with me and encouraged me to pray. Afterwards I did pray, and a clear thought came into my head. It was a verse of scripture about loving your enemy. I had always thought that the enemy meant the people we fight in wars. For the first time, I understood the real meaning of the verse. I realized that I had come to hate the person in question, and that hate was a disease that was killing me. I needed to change.

So I decided to try to appreciate the person, to see the good in him. I started to go out of my way to compliment him. After a lot of effort, I noticed that the hatred was gone. I also noticed that I felt much better about myself. I felt more centered and grounded. This seemed to influence other decisions. At basketball practice, for example, I stopped worrying about what my coach thought. I started playing for myself, for the joy of the game. I worked very hard, but I was no longer trying to impress anyone. For the first time in my high school career, the work was fun.

As the regular season ended, one of the assistant coaches called a "players only" meeting, just before the district tournament began. He asked us to express our feelings. The room grew quiet. To the surprise of everyone, including me, I stood up. I talked about the potential I saw in the team and what we could do in the tournament. I also talked about how hard I had worked and how little playing time I got. I said I could live with it if the people with more playing time also worked hard. I told them I struggled with those who were being lazy. I encouraged them to play for the team. I was surprised by what I said. Yet my comments seemed to move people. A few others made comments, and then everyone expressed together their commitment to work harder. What followed was one of the biggest turnarounds I have ever witnessed.

In the first district tournament game, we blew out the other team. During the next district game, things remained close into the second quarter. I went in, and in three and a half minutes I had five steals, four points, and a few assists. We took a big lead into halftime and never looked back. In the district final, the other team did not score until our lead was 22 to 0. We won both the district and regional championships. The average victory margin over five tournament games was twenty-nine points a game. Our next opponent was ranked thirteenth in the nation. We lost in a close game.

Lessons. This was my first experience at trying to change the process of relationships, which in itself involved changes in my behavior. Previously, I tended to be idealistic, dedicated to the service of others, reflective, open, and intuitive. I was also externally directed. I was unsure of myself and lived to please others. When I changed, I became more internally directed. For the first time in my life, I chose my own emotional state. I focused on how I felt about the team, not whether I was playing or not. I think that is why they accepted what I said. They knew I was concerned more about the team than me. I was asking them to put the team first, to get involved with their hearts, to again become a winning team. I was offering an alternative vision—to become winners, and calling them to it. It was a plausible vision, and it raised enthusiasm, optimism, and inspiration. Perhaps, in standing up, I was modeling the risk-taking behavior that they would also have to engage in to change. In short, I was changing myself and had the power to call others to change. I believe that I was beginning to practice what you call Advanced Change Theory.

Missionary Work

One of the greatest challenges that I ever took on was becoming a missionary. It meant working twelve hours a day, six and a half days a week. It meant finding people who were interested in changing their lives. It meant being continually rejected by the many people who were not interested. It meant I had to become a teacher. I had to learn to inform others as most teachers do, but I also had to learn to transform others as few teachers do. For me it was a huge challenge.

As a new missionary, my most central challenge was to memorize and teach the provided material. It consisted of six, one-hour lessons. During the early weeks, I read from notes that I had scribbled on the back of the materials I was presenting. My only focus was on the knowing and on communicating the content.

Finally, I memorized the material and did not need the notes. During that period, I was focused on presenting my material. I wanted to get the information out. I was not very anxious to have them ask questions or disrupt what I was doing.

As I started to pay attention, I could see that they were often bored. Other times they had a concern or question, but they knew that I did not want them to ask a question or express their concerns. I was pouring information on them, but much of it was unheard or had had little impact.

With discomfort, I began to focus on their needs rather than mine. First, I became more sensitized to the physical environment. I got into the habit of rearranging rooms, opening or closing windows, doing whatever was needed so we could better communicate. Then I started to pay attention to what they were feeling. If they looked like they had a concern, I would pause and give them a chance to ask a question. If they did not, then I asked them if they had a concern. Soon I learned that listening was more important than informing.

Sometimes I would listen to their concerns for a very long time, not even going back to the lesson material.

Then I noticed something about their responses. They were influenced most if I first listened and then spoke with greater authenticity. So I started to more deeply analyze the principles that I was presenting. Then I discovered that I was not fully practicing them. I was being a hypocrite. My sudden shame drove me to work harder at applying the principles. The effort changed me. I began to increase my integrity. The more I did, the more internally directed and other focused I became. It was then that I made my biggest breakthrough. I let go of my ego.

At that point, when I talked about a principle, I did so with greater conviction. When they had questions, I could answer them by telling a personal experience. I began to let go of the memorized materials. I began to learn how to pursue an objective, surface their concerns, and teach to those concerns. I did so in my own words and using my own examples. I tried to express genuine feelings of respect and even love, always looking to help them as much as possible.

Lessons. In the beginning of my missionary training, I was a novice seeking to become an information-based expert. I focused on learning content. This was a good and necessary step. Yet, once I reached that stage, I began to focus on process. I learned to listen better to concerns. I began to study more diligently the topics I was teaching so that I could understand and apply them at a deeper level. I started feeling good about myself as a teacher. Then I learned the importance of service and matching my actions to what I was teaching.

I know it sounds idealistic, but I felt like I began to flow in the moment, becoming more genuine in my interactions while also challenging others to consider a higher purpose. It is probably claiming too much, but I honestly felt like I was able to lead them to a state of self-discovery. I was no longer interested in being an instructor. I realized that the instruction part was just an excuse to be in a relationship. Once there was a relationship, they could behave in ways that would increase the possibility of transformation for all of us.

First Management Job

My first job out of college was working for one of the country's fastest growing trucking companies. I was the assistant to the president of the Western Division, and I had frequent opportunities to work with the CEO. After a short period, the CEO and I developed a trusting relationship. I think that relationship was a function of what I learned in the previously mentioned two cases.

At one point, he decided to invest in a company offering a new information technology. They had an innovative information system that would allow for tracking and managing our trucks and trailers. We believed that implementing the system would greatly improve our bottom line. Yet the implementation process did not go well. There were many problems and much resistance. The utilization rate was 5 percent. At that point, I was asked to take charge of the project.

After a couple of weeks of analysis, I decided to do two things. First, each time a driver was sent to me with questions about the system, I sent the driver back to get his manager. I would then teach the manager how to use the system. When these managers came in, they were often resistant but as they gained a sense of control, they got excited about what they could do. They went back and coached their other drivers. Second, I spent a lot of time talking to people at higher levels. I continually pushed for them to include competency with the system as part of the job evaluation procedure. Gradually, this happened, and it helped a great deal.

Despite measurable progress, there were still a number of drivers and driver managers who were not using the new technology. At first, I was tempted to blame them, but instead I decided to own the problem. If they were not using the system, I had to bear some responsibility. So this realization forced me to develop new strategies. I tried to talk to everyone, at every level, about the bigger picture. I explained that if we could make the technology work, it would help the technology company to go public and, since we owned part of the company, it would help our bottom line. I did this relentlessly. I continually shared data showing the improvements in time utilization. I did interviews and distributed questionnaires seeking to learn about every problem they were encountering. I made sure we took action to remedy each one. I identified the nonusers and started spending my time with them. I did whatever was necessary to free them up to learn and teach the system.

Utilization rates started to climb. In four months, we went from 5 percent to 60 percent utilization. As this happened, we discovered some of the real problems with the technology. Here my integrity failed. I worried a lot about pleasing the CEO. He wanted the new technology company to be successful. So I had a tendency to soften my accounts of the problems with the new technology. I also failed to confront people in the technology company. I should have challenged them to be more honest with themselves, to deal with real problems. They did not want to face the pain of reality, and I did not have the courage to impose the pain. In the long run, they had to drop a part of their product line. They suffered, and we suffered.

Lessons. Looking back at my managerial experience in the trucking company, I think about the four strategies in your ACT diagram (Exhibit 14.1). I think they were all present in my behavior. In the first phase, I did a lot of rational explanation, telling people why they should change. I also used political leverage by getting management to evaluate people. I used a number of participative techniques, involving people in the learning process. Yet, even after all that effort, we were still only partially successful. At that point, I very much wanted to blame others. Instead, I tried to change myself, trying to take more accountability for results and increasing my integrity. That led to greater commitment, effort, and change from myself and from others. It brought a lot of success.

Yet, in perhaps the most key area, I had a failure of integrity. I was more concerned with impressing the CEO than I was with the good of the enterprise. Notice how many times I say "I" in this letter—part of it is the nature of the letter, but it shows too much concern for myself. As I tried to move forward at the edge of chaos, my fears triumphed. I now see things in that episode that I could not see. I see things I was denying. Being transformational is a function of our ability to constantly engage that which we least want to engage, our own hypocrisy. I think it will help me to approach such situations differently in the future. I am sure I will often fail, yet I am also sure that I will more frequently and consciously be able to apply the principals of your ACT model.

Moving Forward

In trying to become a professional change agent, I have had the experience of negotiating and designing some interventions for clients. In these initial interventions, I felt very much like a novice. I found myself saying and doing things that a novice would do. I have been too worried about what authority figures think. I have tried to say what I think they want to hear. Other times I have tried to do what I thought was right, but then I made statements that only led to discomfort. I was challenging but not supportive. I need to learn how to model tough love. I need to stop describing and trying to sell the process model. Instead, I need to live it, to behave its power.

When I consider the insights derived here, I see myself behaving differently in the future. I know that by being more internally driven and other focused, I will begin to make decisions that can benefit more people than myself. I will try to look past my deceptions and the deceptions of others. I will constantly need to ask myself, what can I change to improve a relationship or situation? I will seek to free myself of rules and scripts so that I can grow toward a state of co-creation. I know these things are far easier to say than to accomplish. However, recognizing that I have taken these steps in a few cases in the past should help me move forward.

Last week I watched a movie about a woman living a superficial life and denying the pain associated with such a life. She finds out that she is going to die and begins to clarify what really matters to her. She begins to make choices at work that most people are afraid to make. She immediately becomes more authentic. She takes risks and creates new relationships while achieving greater success.

My challenge is to do what she did, without death to motivate me. I need to live authentically because I choose to do so. I hope to move closer to becoming a transformational change agent, because, if I am growing, it may help others to grow.

Shawn

CONCLUDING CHALLENGE

In closing, we pose a challenge for the reader. You can read this chapter, like most people normally read, intellectually considering the concepts and the issues. On the other hand, you might consider reflecting on your past, like Shawn has done. This second strategy, we believe, can yield more value. Take these thoughts and dare to look inside. Discovery will empower you and make you more empowering. Discovery will hasten your journey toward becoming a transformational change agent, a person who is Masterful in elevating the level of value and richness in any relationship. That is when transformation takes place.

On the other hand, transformation is not an easy business. It requires a great personal price. It is always met with resistance. Many people have designed their lives so they never have to leave their comfort zones; they become hostile when threatened by the presence of a person who is truly committed to change. In addition, not all situations call for transformation. Some changes only need to be incremental and the expert model is fine. It is also possible to corrupt the transformational model. Many people can get themselves into a self-absorbed and purely internally driven state, while thinking they are serving others. They then become very dangerous. That is the cult of James Jones, the fanatic who led so many people to their death in Guyana. The challenge is to become both internally driven and other focused without imposing one's beliefs on others. At that point, we put the good of the community first, and then the system has a better chance of moving where it needs to go. At such times, we experience transformation and increased understanding of how to become transformational. That, in the end, is the purpose of this chapter.

Notes to the Chapter

[1] K. S. Cameron and R. E. Quinn, *Diagnosing and Changing Organizational Culture: Based on the Competing Values Framework* (Reading, MA: Addison-Wesley, 1999).

[2] R. E. Quinn, *Deep Change: Discovering the Leader Within* (San Francisco: Jossey-Bass, 1996).

[3] *Ibid.*

[4] R. Fritz, *The Path of Least Resistance: Learning to Become the Creative Force in Your Own Life* (New York: Fawcett Columbine, 1989).

[5] H. L. Dreyfus, S. E. Dreyfus, and T. Athanasion, *Mind Over Machine: The Power of Human Intuition and Expertise in the Era of the Computer* (New York: Free Press, 1986).

[6] M. Csikszentmihalyi, *Finding Flow: The Psychology of Engagement with Everyday Life* (New York: Basic Books, 1997).

[7] R. M. Pirsig, *Zen and the Art of Motorcycle Maintenance* (New York: Morrow, 1974): 148.

[8] R. E. Quinn, *Change the World: How Ordinary People Accomplish Extraordinary Results* (San Francisco: Jossey-Bass Publishers, 2000) 27.

[9] R. Chin and K. D. Benne, "General Strategies for Effecting Changes in Human Systems" in W. G. Bennis, K. D. Benne, and R. Chin, eds., *The Planning of Change: Readings in Applied Behavioral Sciences* (New York: Holt, 1969).

Part 5

Managing and Growing the Consulting Firm

INTRODUCTION

Consultants are attracted to consulting careers because the work itself is interesting, and it often provides a career gateway and shortcut to securing a senior executive position upon leaving the consulting firm. Rarely are consultants interested in long-term careers in consulting or advancing to its senior executive ranks. Instead, they prefer to be out with clients, not staying in the office to hold meetings and manage expense reports. Moreover, they are quite aware that consultants are themselves quite difficult to manage because they typically have big egos and prefer autonomy over supervision. As a result, many consulting firms suffer from poor leadership, lack of coordination, and inability to change when confronted with competitive threats or strategic opportunities.

Ironically, today's highly competitive consulting environment requires that consulting firms be successfully led by capable senior management. Competition is fierce, clients are more demanding, and the structure of the industry is changing rapidly. The successful consulting firm leader will not only have to manage the firm's resources efficiently day to day but also inspire and motivate the staff to improve the firm's ability to compete. Without exceptional leadership, the firm is likely to falter and even fail.

This section examines the consulting firm from three different angles of effectiveness— Chapter 15 on managing growth stages of the firm, Chapter 16 on the characteristics of high performance firms, and Chapter 17 on creating and sharing knowledge within the firm—all three areas of concern are highly significant for mobilizing the intellectual capital of the firm and achieving greater competitive advantage in the marketplace.

Chapter 15, "Managing Growth Stages in Consulting Firms," focuses on how these firms cope with growth and why they either fail or succeed over their life cycle. The chapter presents four stages of growth, with each stage culminating in a major crisis that needs to be resolved by the firm's leadership before growth can be resumed. Each stage is different and requires a different management approach. Unfortunately, most consulting firms do not make it through all four stages of growth; instead, they bog down with disagreement among the senior partners, some of whom want to grow and others who do not. The chapter concludes with advice to senior partners about how they need to let go of past practices, even their own power, in order to facilitate growth of the firm.

Chapter 16, "High-Performance Consulting Firms," describes the "best practices" employed by highly successful consulting firms. The author builds on results from his research to offer evidence of common practices across high performing firms. These practices range from a shared strategic identity throughout the firm to the attraction and retention of consultant "stars." Also, the senior leadership challenge requires wearing three hats at once and equally well: those of producer, leader, and owner. In the end, if the firm is to be successful, strong alignment is required by the consulting firm across its strategy, goals, people, culture, governance, and leadership.

Chapter 17, "Knowledge Management in Consulting," contends that consulting firms are more likely to attract clients through establishing both the perception and reality that they are indeed on the leading edge of management knowledge. This requires the consulting firm to attract, develop, and retain highly qualified consultants. To do so, the firm must not only share its accumulated experience with its consultants but also engage in knowledge creation. The first part of the chapter explores how knowledge is created in consulting firms, including the types of research involved and how it can be used for competitive advantage. Examples from three large consulting firms: Accenture, IBM, and McKinsey are used as illustrations for how they create knowledge. The second part highlights how knowledge is managed, shared, and used in the same three firms. A key challenge here is how to get consultants to share their knowledge with each other when they are often deterred from this task by an opposing reward and reporting system designed to keep consultants out in the field working on projects.

CHAPTER 15

Managing Growth Stages in Consulting Firms

Larry E. Greiner, USC, and James K. Malernee, Cornerstone Research

ABOUT THE AUTHORS

Larry E. Greiner

Larry E. Greiner is Professor of Management and Organization in the Marshall School at the University of Southern California. Dr. Greiner has served as Chairperson of Managerial Consultation Division of the Academy of Management. He is the author of numerous books and articles on organization growth, management consulting, and strategic change, including *Consulting to Management*, with Robert Metzger.

James K. Malernee

James K. Malernee, cofounded Cornerstone Research, a litigation research and consulting firm, in 1989. Dr. Malernee is CEO of the firm and heads its New York City office. Prior to that, Dr. Malernee was a senior vice president of The MAC Group, a general management consulting firm. He has taught finance at the University of Texas at Austin and business strategy at the Stanford Graduate School of Business.

From 1960 to 2000, the consulting industry experienced phenomenal growth, prompting many industry leaders and pundits to predict continued high rates of growth long into the future. The economic signs all seemed favorable; consulting firms were selling larger and larger contracts to clients; MBA recruits were receiving astronomical salaries and signing bonuses; and more and more firms were lining up to do IPOs with fast run-ups in market value.

Yet, as we all know with hindsight, this golden era of growth came to a rude and resounding slowdown, if not a complete halt for many firms, shortly after the start of the new millennium. Even as late as 2004, numerous firms in a stagnant economy were still struggling, trying to grow again but realizing that it may be more up to their management know-how and ingenuity than simply relying on the industry's coattails.

The purpose of this chapter is to take a close look at how individual consulting firms cope with growth and either fail or succeed. While we all recognize that the industry's growth rate depends heavily on the general state of the economy, we are much less aware of how this growth takes place within individual consulting firms. It is common to think of a firm's growth as merely a performance outcome that is measured by revenues, profits, project size, and number of employees. Instead, as we shall point out in this chapter, growth is much more than a simple "outcome"; it is a deeper complex process that is continuously and privately at work inside each consulting firm. Furthermore, growth has to be managed and planned for on a daily basis; otherwise, regardless of the economy, a single firm can easily fall on hard times and become a tombstone in the already large graveyard of defunct consulting firms.

The consulting industry landscape is littered with the victims of bad growth management. While numerous reasons account for the success and failure of consulting firms, growth management issues have to be near the top of the list. Looking back just twenty years ago, who would have thought that Andersen Consulting, which was smaller than Arthur D. Little at the time, would today be one of the largest consulting firms in the world and renamed Accenture? Or that Arthur D. Little would enter bankruptcy? Or that in 2003, IBM's consulting arm, IBM Global Services, would be larger than its hardware business?

Consulting
Insights   **Case of Failed Growth**

A notable case of failure occurred in 1997 for the once-promising strategy consulting firm Mitchell Madison Group (MMG), which in five years had expanded to fourteen offices around the world and 800 employees. Moreover, ex-McKinsey partners who presumably knew something about good management led it. The story of MMG's demise is extensively reported in the March 2001 issue of *Consulting*, but below is a telling quote from an ex-MMG partner about the numerous problems created by the firm's leadership and its obsession with growth:

> Growth quickly became a divisive issue for the firm's board of directors, as well as for those partners who routinely asked the question: "Why not grow at a rate we can actually afford?" By early 1998, the push for growth had begun to take its toll on the firm in other ways. Distrust of the firm's compensation scheme had spread as more new partners were hurried into the firm using new perks and special arrangements. Moreover, as more partners were added to the payroll, a number of MMG's founding partners and directors sensed the board's powers decaying as well as it efficacy as a vehicle of governance.[1]

Growth Study

Given the difficulties experienced by so many firms in managing their growth, we decided a few years ago to begin a study to determine if professional services firms (PSFs) pass through discernable stages of growth. Our study examined a range of PSFs, including consulting, accounting, legal, advertising, and investment banking firms. Our interest in making this study grew out of Professor Greiner's earlier *Harvard Business Review* classic, "Evolution and Revolution as Organizations Grow,"[2] and Dr. Malernee's managerial background as cofounder and CEO of Cornerstone Research, a rapidly growing economic research consulting firm. Professor Greiner's earlier work had focused primarily on industrial firms, not professional services firms, which were only in their ascendancy at the time.

We will report here our findings on growth stages in consulting firms for the first time. During the course of our research, we performed an extensive examination of documents and articles written about many PSFs, including several consulting firms. We also conducted over 200 interviews with partners and staff from current firms and ones that had failed or been acquired. All of the current firms are well-established ones that have grown through their own wholly owned resources, full-time staff, and management; in other words, they were not franchises or networks of independent consultants, neither of which have grown to any substantial size. Our interviews covered each firm's history, the types of organization structure employed, major strategic decisions made, financial and marketing problems encountered, management systems and controls introduced, and changes in key leadership.[3]

Interestingly, our research results across all the PSFs appear strikingly similar, revealing clear discernable stages of growth. Of course, in this type of qualitative research with a relatively small sample, we caution that more research is needed. Readers of this chapter who work in consulting firms should match their own experience against our findings.

Growth Issues

Most consultants do not start or join a firm because they want to climb the firm's hierarchy to become CEO. Rather, their primary motivation is to practice consulting and perhaps eventually to become a partner, though usually they move on to executive positions. They often view participation in the consulting firm's management as a "necessary evil" that, in most instances, should be delegated to lesser-paid, "nonprofessional" administrators.

Unfortunately, these consulting professionals, when they eventually assume leadership positions in consulting firms, often fail in their attempts at managing the growth process. Only a few out of the thousands of start-up consulting firms actually become large, thriving organizations. The great majority of firms either fail or remain small "mom and pop" operations of five to fifteen employees. Even the few firms that grow very large frequently experience serious setbacks; for example, consider what happened to Arthur Andersen after the Enron scandal. Even the prestigious strategy consulting firm Bain and Co., in the early 1990s, faced the departure of top partners, followed by a business downturn. At the time, *Business Week* reported:

> Today Bain is the one that seems to need a consultant. The firm's workforce, about 1000 professionals and support staff is down 30 percent, thinned by two rounds of layoffs and by the defections of key executives. "We were very good consultants, but not very good managers," says one executive.[4]

So why do leaders of consulting firms choose to grow their firms in the face of such difficulties? Clearly, one reason is to take advantage of the rising tide of a growing and expanding industry. Since 1983, the industry has grown from $3.5 billion to approximately $120 billion in revenues. Other reasons, all quite rational, include the need to broaden services in order to serve growing clients and to attract larger clients; to be able to take advantage of the leverage effect on profits by hiring junior professionals and billing them out at higher rates than their salary cost; and to reach a size where the firm can go public and secure growth capital, as well as shares to reward partners.

GROWTH STAGES AND CRISES

Despite the advantages of growth, those consulting firms that launch themselves on a growth path are hardly assured of success. For the firm, growth creates significant strategic, marketing, and organizational challenges that have to be managed. Our research suggests that most surviving firms grow through a life cycle of four distinct stages, with each stage requiring a different strategic

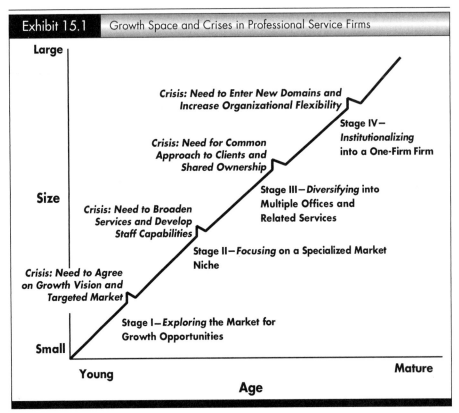

Exhibit 15.1   Growth Space and Crises in Professional Service Firms

approach to its marketplace and a unique set of management practices.[5] In addition, each stage is followed by a crisis that needs to be resolved for the firm to advance into the next stage of growth. Below are the four stages and crises identified in our study, which are also depicted graphically in Exhibit 15.1.

- *Stage I: Exploring* the Market for Growth Opportunities

  Crisis: Need to Agree on Growth Vision and Targeted Market Segment

- *Stage II: Focusing* on a Specialized Market Niche

  Crisis: Need to Broaden Services and Develop Staff Capabilities

- *Stage III: Diversifying* into Multiple Offices and Related Services

  Crisis: Need for Common Approach to Clients and Sharing of Ownership

- *Stage IV: Institutionalizing* into a One-Firm Firm

  Crisis: Need to Enter New Domains and Increase Organizational Flexibility

Role of Crises

A consulting firm's passage through the four stages is not automatic; instead, toward the end of each stage, it encounters a major crisis that must be resolved for the firm to move forward. Few firms survive all the way through the four stages; instead, most do not grow beyond the first stage; others manage to grow through Stage II but then are sold or split-up when they fall victim to conflict among the partners.

The impetus for a crisis can be internal when one of the partners advocates a new growth path and the others disagree or external when there are signs of falling behind major competition. Crises can be short if a solution is found quickly or prolonged by continuous partner disagreement, thereby stopping growth and perhaps causing the sale of the firm.

The onslaught of a crisis, however, appears necessary to provoke the partners into action and change. Crises seem inevitable because resistance often arises when partners and employees are confronted with the necessity to introduce new practices required to move to the next stage. Reluctant partners and employees frequently oppose change because they are attached to past practices that they see as the source of success. So it is difficult for them to understand why these once successful practices cannot continue. They hang on to old habits and refuse to let go. Sometimes the crisis is mild if the partners have agreed upon and prepared a solution much earlier, or it can be severe if the partners continue to be in strong disagreement.

Management Practices

Exhibit 15.2 summarizes the different management practices that are characteristic of each stage in the growth life cycle. These practices are described in detail in the remainder of this chapter. They provide a "roadmap" for leaders of consulting firms and also for those who are currently working for or may aspire to work for a consulting firm, so they can understand better what lies ahead.

While the stages presented here are shown with distinct boundaries so as to illustrate more clearly their sequence and effects, in actual practice each stage and crisis is likely to overlap as new management practices are introduced and old ones are abandoned. The average length of a growth stage for firms in our study was approximately seven years, ranging between four and ten years, with the later stages lasting longer than the earlier stages. The crises lasted from a few months to one year, although the longer crises usually ended in the sale of a firm or its continued decline.

STAGE I: EXPLORING THE MARKET FOR GROWTH OPPORTUNITIES

The origin of a new consulting firm typically begins when an experienced professional "hangs out his or her shingle," often after leaving the security of a larger firm. This entrepreneurial step is frequently taken in collaboration with one or two other partners who are colleagues from their former firm. They agree to share ownership, pool their efforts, and hope that revenues will cover modest draws and limited office expenses. (Throughout the remainder of this chapter, we will use the term "partner" to refer to the leading owners of a firm, even though the legal form of ownership may be either a partnership or a corporation.)

The founding partners typically go through an initial period of testing both the market and each other. Each partner attempts to attract clients who are receptive to his or her particular expertise. For example, one partner may pursue clients interested in compensation plans, while another may seek clients

Exhibit 15.2	Life-Cycle Model and Management Practices	
	Stage I—Exploring	Stage II—Focusing
Strategy	Each partner sells his/her individual expertise to a diverse range of clients. Search for clients and market feedback.	Focus on single market niche, selling specialization to a targeted group of clients or industry.
Organization Structure	Centered around founders, their personalities, values, and practices.	Project team formed for each client. Partners act as project leaders, sharing junior professionals among them.
Systems and Rewards	Training is on the job; no policies. Founders split profits evenly. Firm is staffed with principals only and a few clerical employees. Minimal systems needed. Little development of people.	Office/Administrative Manager installed. Minimal training. Founders split profits and pay bonuses to select juniors—even one or two might be made junior partners.
Management Style	Authoritative but informal. Deference to founders' decisions.	Founders divide roles. One founder specializes in internal management, while others develop business.
Decision Process	Consensus among partners, but sometimes dominated by one founder with most clients.	Reliance on consensus among partners, after perhaps checking for input from top juniors.
Culture	Informal, family-like atmosphere, individualistic, and entrepreneurial.	Task oriented. Adherence to founders' values and their methodologies.
Sources of Conflict	Founders can easily have different visions of the firm. Will this venture work? Do we want to grow the firm or stay small? Should we focus on a particular market or take a more individualistic approach?	Should we expand services to meet client needs or continue to focus on our core competency? Some senior partners advocate expansion, while others resist diversification.

with production problems. It is unclear to the partners as to which specific service will succeed in the market, what types of clients will be attracted, or which partners may be more adept at selling. Here is how one partner described his firm's "shotgun" approach to the market during its start-up stage:

Exhibit 15.2 continued		
	Stage III—Diversifying	Stage IV—Institutionalizing
Strategy	Expansion into new offices and closely related practice areas, sometimes through acquisition. Begin international expansion.	Marketing the firm's image and cross-selling the firm's reputation in various areas of its expertise. More uniform services to clients. Major acquisitons. Strong overseas presence.
Organization Structure	Decentralized profit centers led by younger managers. Executive committee of senior partners—in addition, perhaps larger advisory council of office and practice managers.	Matrix structure with partners appointed to lead practice areas and regions/ offices. Full-time Managing Director, often elected, manages the administrative side of the business.
Systems and Rewards	More complex information systems for reporting on each office and service. Policies codified and written. Business plans begin to appear. Bonuses for unit performance, especially to head of each sub-unit.	Training programs formalized to teach the "firm approach." Strategic plans are routinely drafted. Career tracks and performance evaluation become more standardized. Accounting, HR, and MIS formalized as staff functions. Rewards for both sub-unit and corporate performance. Broader ownership.
Management Style	Founders delegate increase responsibility for daily operations to leaders of offices and practice areas.	Collaborative management style in teams and committees.
Decision Process	Operating decisions made at sub-unit level. Promotion and policy decisions continue to be made by founding partners.	Founders step aside. New leaders take over. Strategy and capital decisions made at corporate headquarters.
Culture	Diverse units with each of the practices centering on values of their respective leaders.	Firm's values extol its history and reputation. Employees hired to fit a common profile that complements the culture. The culture becomes cohesive and monolithic.
Sources of Conflict	Rivalry between satellite offices and the head office. How do we prevent fragmentation? What should be the equity stake of key business developers in relation to the founders? Should we build this organization into an institution?	Are we becoming too depersonalized? Are we becoming bureaucratic? Is the firm becoming insulated from the market? How do we create innovation and more growth?

Potential clients would ask us, "What do you do?" and we would say "What do you want?" We did all kinds of projects. We did business brokering . . . we did sales training . . . you name it.

Also confronting the partners is the difficult management challenge of learning to work together in making decisions. They gradually discover whether they share the same ideas on how the firm should be run, if their commitment to the venture is similarly high, and if their work styles are complementary. With little formal organization structure, the partners meet informally to decide various issues by consensus, whether it be the design of a brochure or the purchase of a computer.

In the firm's quest for economic survival, the partners set their billing rates lower than rates charged by their larger competitors. Overhead expenses are restricted to spartan offices and contracted services. The partners' wages are based on a minimal but livable salary, which usually remains fixed for the first year unless there are negative interim results. At the end of the year, profits are divided among the partners or reinvested in the firm. Growth will require more money going to reinvestment, and this will provide a test of partner commitment to further growth.

Most start-up firms never grow beyond this entrepreneurial stage. Instead, their partners choose to remain small, with their partners using the firm as an efficient overhead shelter while they go about their individual marketing efforts. They each manage to sell enough business to support themselves and make a contribution to overhead. Occasionally, one partner will obtain a project large enough to include another partner or assistant. They respond to workload problems by hiring a secretary and employing occasional subcontractors.

Those few firms that grow successfully beyond this start-up stage do so only after discovering a promising market niche for a particular service and only after all the partners agree to focus their energies on pursuing this specialized niche.

First Major Crisis: Need to Agree on Growth Vision and Targeted Market Segment

When a promising and profitable niche becomes evident, the founders must make a strategic choice. Do they continue as before with each partner pursuing his/her separate specialization and personal set of clients, or do they collectively focus their energies and resources on the more promising specialization that one or two of them have found while exploring the market?

At this point, open communication among the partners is essential to examining what each one wants the firm to become and in determining what each is prepared to contribute. They need to ask themselves: Is the promising specialized market niche large enough to support our further growth if we all agree to focus on it? Do all of us want the firm to grow larger? If so, how willing are we to let go of what we have been doing to focus on one major service (e.g., human resources consulting to financial services industry)? How should we work together? What roles should each of us play? Who will look out for administration? Who will sell business? Who will run projects? How many junior people should we hire, and what should be their skills?

As the partners address these difficult questions, underlying differences often emerge among them. They are often surprised to learn that they are not all in full agreement on whether to grow further or on what to specialize, as evident in this example from a small consulting firm:

> *We didn't realize that there were problems because we all thought we were talking about the same thing. And then, a year later, it was very clear to me that our motives and goals were very different. One partner wanted to be the single person in-charge, while the other two wanted to run it by committee.*

Consequently, many firms flounder and break up at this point, including the small consulting firm just mentioned, as its demise is recalled by one of its ex-partners:

> *Robert began to feel like he was putting a lot more effort and revenues into the firm than the others. He knew there was a good market for his specialty, but he began to question our ability to support him, so he left. We then folded.*

Those few firms whose partners do finally reach agreement and choose to grow larger will typically implement a highly focused strategy, which includes a new and very different set of management practices from the first stage.

STAGE II: FOCUSING ON A SPECIALIZED MARKET NICHE

Stage II begins when the partners decide to join together in selling one unique service to a focal set of clients. They no longer go their separate ways to sell only their individual talents to a diverse list of clients. Thus, for example, a consulting firm in Stage II might decide to sell only training programs in information systems to the middle market in the retail industry, because this market opportunity was discovered to be most promising during Stage I. The CEO of a now large management consulting firm reflects back on how he and his partners made this strategic choice:

> *We began by doing an array of projects, anything the client would buy. And then we came to a point where we had to decide if we were going to go anywhere, we needed to define some things. So the first big decision was: Who are we, what is our competence, and what should we become? We decided we would be the productivity people, and we honed in on the real estate industry. We attacked it through making speeches, writing articles, and joining trade associations. One of our partners left, and we had to recruit new people who knew more about real estate.*

Having chosen to specialize, the firm also faces a challenge in developing a core competency in its area of expertise. The firm's staff and internal practices must be reoriented toward improving its capability to deliver the chosen specialization. To do so, the partners decide to hire and train several junior associates. This step allows the firm to take on larger projects with lower priced staff, thereby enhancing the economic leverage of the firm and freeing partners from the vicious "do-sell" cycle. Previously, partners felt compelled either to work on projects at the expense of developing new clients or to take time off to sell new business and thereby cause delays in project completion. Now they act more efficiently by assigning less expensive, junior employees to work on existing projects while they devote more time to developing new business.[6]

In moving ahead, it is necessary to introduce a new project-type organizational structure and more formal procedures to handle the growing client load and expanded workforce. Each partner now acts as a project leader while sharing junior professionals across projects. The partners also divide their roles; one partner handles administration, while the others concentrate on selling. Basic accounting and computer systems are installed for processing invoices, project costs, and payroll. An increased administrative load eventually prompts the partners to hire a full-time office manager. Additional clerical staff are added under the office manager for preparing proposals, typing reports, and maintaining the firm's information system.

Decision making continues to reside with the founding partners who rely on achieving consensus among them before acting. They occasionally check with younger associates for their input on major decisions, but they still retain sole responsibility for hiring, assigning, evaluating, and compensating all employees. At the end of the year, the partners allocate bonuses among themselves and to a few high performers in the staff.

Success in Stage II gradually sows the seeds for the firm's second major crisis involving the need to serve increased client demands and to reach out to new markets as a further stimulus to growth. Simply remaining a one-product company in one location is insufficient to fuel continued growth.

Second Major Crisis: **Need to Broaden Services and Develop Staff Capabilities**

This crisis often begins when the firm's larger clients ask to be served in new ways, either with additional services or in new locations. They may even threaten to take their business elsewhere if the firm does not respond. Some clients request services not currently being performed by the consulting firm, such as a client asking for training programs once the consulting firm has installed a new information system. Still others may want the same service delivered to their operations in other locales. This crisis often becomes severe because the firm does not possess the necessary range of services in-house for expansion, nor does it have a trained staff able to deliver new services or possessing the willingness to move to a new office.

In order to grow, the partners need to decide if they want to open a new office or if they want to add a new service or both. To do so, they must assess their internal capabilities, since, during Stage II, the large majority of staff has specialized on delivering a single type of service out of one location. This decision by the partners includes not only assessing the skills of the staff to provide a new service but determining if any partners are willing to move and open a new office.

The client mix of the firm has likely changed during Stage II as some of the firm's clients have grown larger and become more sophisticated in their demands. As a result, the firm's staff requires more advanced skills to perform larger and more complex projects. Frequently in short supply are competent managers and technically qualified staff.

So the central issue becomes one of not only how to broaden the services offerings but also to build capable staff . The partners' awareness for this need is usually late in coming. It typically happens when they find that they can't do everything themselves, which has included long hours of selling, managing, and performing projects. They have been so busy and task focused that they have neglected the developmental needs of their staff.

As a result, the partners find themselves in a difficult situation—to live with and retrain the current staff or go outside for new talent and run the risk of alienating the original staff. The original staff is likely not up to standard in handling newer, more complex types of clients. They were hired earlier for their willingness to assist the partners with minor assignments and to be technically focused. Rarely, has any training been given to them; they have learned on the job. Unfortunately, not many of the staff know how to sell or manage projects, nor are they willing to relocate to a new office.

The partners must choose among three strategic alternatives: 1) remain the same and probably stop growth in their current location; or 2) continue to grow by diversifying the line of services while continuing to operate out of the same office; or 3) grow through opening new offices and delivering the same existing service. They worry that services diversification, even in the same locale, may dilute the firm's specialized focus and undermine its established efficiencies and competencies. On the other hand, the choice of opening new offices raises the troubling issue of staffing, especially in deciding which partner will have to uproot and move.

Some firms respond to this crisis by choosing the first alternative of remaining at their current size level in the same place, hoping that the future market for their existing specialized service is large enough to replace the loss of clients requiring broader services or the same service in other locales. Still other firms experience severe conflict, as their partners are unable to reconcile their differences about growth versus nongrowth, or to open new offices or to add new services, prompting some partners to depart or even forcing the sale of the firm. The partners become the critical stumbling block because none of them want to move, nor do they want to stop performing their current specialty and launch into a new one.

For those few remaining firms that choose to grow larger and take on the risk of diversifying into new practice areas or opening new offices, the next step requires another major shift in the firm's strategy and organization structure.

STAGE III: DIVERSIFYING INTO MULTIPLE OFFICES AND RELATED SERVICES

Most Stage III firms typically choose first to open additional offices for their existing service instead of diversifying into new product lines. Stage III firms tend to pursue the new office route and stick with their current specialty service because it is their core competence. The partners feel more comfortable and confident in being able to pull off this type of expansion. To begin an entirely new service area threatens the skills of the current staff and the existing culture. It is also easier for them to staff the new offices with current personnel than add a new service. But even this decision proves difficult because one of the partners will most likely have to move since they don't trust an unknown to run another office.

Only a very few consulting firms try to open both new offices and add services at the same time, because they risk diluting resources and overextending their staff. This step often fails as it creates significant management problems for senior partners who try to coordinate multiple services across multiple offices, to say nothing for finding qualified staff for both offices and practices.

It is a challenge that most founding partners are not up to at this point. A better and more workable strategy is to proceed sequentially—opening an office or two and then gradually expanding services one at a time. This is the process we found in the more successful growth firms.

The partners are likely to decide to broaden the firm's line of services only after opening a few offices delivering their original service as a starting point. However, these firms cannot effectively provide all services that every client may desire, so most firms will select only services that are closer to their core competency. For example, we observed an information systems consulting firm that decided to add hardware selection and training programs to its existing systems design service, while avoiding something as diverse as strategic planning. Similarly, the location of new offices is usually determined by where the firm's major clients are located and where senior managers are willing to live. One mid-size IT consulting firm, Clarkston Consulting, has four established offices but allows its consultants to live in other cities while focusing on clients in three industries—life sciences, manufacturing, and high technology.

As the firm grows and becomes financially stronger, it may also begin to make acquisitions of smaller firms as a way of adding related services and additional offices. Later in Stage III, a few of these firms will begin to expand globally, usually through acquisitions. Right Management Consultants, a rapidly expanding human resources and outplacement consulting firm, has actively pursued this policy around the world, adding more than five international acquisitions a year in recent years. However, acquisitions present a further challenge to acquirers who must integrate new partners and diverse cultures. The preferred merger integration process in successful firms is to absorb the acquiree completely into the acquirer's systems and practices and to buy out any partners who do not seem to fit.

All senior employees at the management level in Stage III firms are expected to specialize, either by office or practice area. Younger members remain specialized but are usually shared across offices on larger projects. Training programs are introduced to develop junior staff members faster than might occur on the job. In addition, it often proves necessary to recruit experienced "lateral hires" from competitor firms, although this poses a risk because "outsiders" may not share the firm's values and goals. These hires are carefully screened for compatibility.

To support diversification, a decentralized organization structure is introduced to manage the greatly broadened scope of offices and services, as well as to open up career opportunities. The new offices become relatively self-contained sub-units managed by younger, high-potential employees desiring more responsibility. They act as profit center managers, accountable for obtaining new clients, managing their sub-units efficiently, and developing their unit's employees.[7]

In the firm's new decentralized structure, formal management systems are implemented to control and reward performance in each profit center. The various offices and service areas are each expected to develop a budget and profit plan, and the firm's information system is redesigned to record each unit's performance results. The reward system is changed to provide substantial incentive bonuses for the heads of each practice area and office. Eligibility for bonuses is gradually extended to the entire professional group. A senior committee is established at the firm's headquarters to evaluate performance and make compensation recommendations.

The managing partner of a large international consulting firm describes below how, during Stage III, he introduced a new budgeting system to fit with his firm's recently decentralized structure and new practice areas:

> We had formalized the practice areas but we still had a top-down planning and control system. I transformed revenue setting to a bottom-up method. Practice leaders would then have to think about how much business they are going to generate from existing and new clients. The process forced people to quantify what had previously been implicit in top-down annual goals.

However, in most Stage III firms, the partners only allow the younger leaders to make operating decisions at their sub-unit levels, excluding them from key firm-wide decisions about promotion, compensation, and expansion. Therein lays the next major crisis. The firm's diversification and decentralization efforts in Stage III eventually pose a major challenge for reuniting and coordinating the firm as "one firm" in its next growth stage.

Third Major Crisis: Need for Common Approach to Clients and Sharing of Ownership

Signs of this crisis begin to appear in competitive rivalries and parochialism among the decentralized sub-units spawned during Stage III. Local offices have been conditioned by the firm's reward and control system to behave separately as profit centers—to look out more for themselves than the firm as a whole. As a result, lack of cooperation between offices and practice areas eventually makes it difficult to cross-sell different services and to interchange personnel for staffing large projects. Increasingly, the various sub-units begin to ignore and resist directives from headquarters. The firm starts to fragment into a loosely disjointed organization of fiefdoms.

Large clients also begin to complain about the firm's uncoordinated practices across offices. They want assurance that the same level of service will be delivered consistently across all the client's operations domestically and worldwide. Unfortunately, this is difficult to achieve since each office and practice area have developed different cultures guided by leadership personalities who want to remain in control of their units. Some units were acquired and not fully absorbed and, therefore, retain their pre-acquisition practices.

A closely related challenge also involves the firm's junior leaders, who now expect to share in a "piece of the action" with the founding partners. These young leaders are the new "rainmakers" for the firm, having successfully managed new offices and practice areas, secured additional clients, and contributed significantly to profit growth. Yet they feel under-rewarded and excluded by the senior partners from making firm-wide strategic and personnel decisions. They become less willing to cooperate despite pleas for commonality from the "in-group" of senior partners. They want to be better rewarded with ownership and greater power for decisions affecting the firm as a whole. In their frustration with senior management, some junior partners decide to leave, accepting attractive offers from competitors and clients; still others split off to form their own firms. Our interviews revealed one such rebellion among junior partners, as recounted to us by one of its co-conspirators:

A colleague of mine wanted a greater amount of equity, compensation, and recognition for his business development efforts. We agreed with him, so he tried to orchestrate the notion of a name change for the firm, and then a change in the system where he would get rewarded by a higher annual bonus and more point allocations. This was met by enormous resentment from the older partners. So we tried to arrange a spin-off of a select group of consulting colleagues . . . and that caused the old partners to give-in.

This Stage III crisis poses a major dilemma for the founding partners—either they opt for growth through taking on more coordination responsibility to build a common approach toward clients, as well as sharing ownership and power with new leaders, or they choose to stop growth and retain exclusive control for themselves. These twin issues of coordination and ownership are closely related because the firm's senior leadership, without support from the younger leaders, lacks sufficient power to reunite the firm and coordinate its resources. Those firms that fail to come up with a solution are often sold to an acquiring firm as the original partners decide to cash in their equity. Still other firms may begin to decline as their partners stubbornly resist change, even as junior leaders depart with established clients.

The remaining firms, whose founders retain a vision of growth, choose to make the difficult transition to Stage IV. This effort to share and reunite the firm is not an easy decision for the founding partners to make. In deciding to share senior leadership and ownership, the founding partners must dilute their equity without substantial, monetary incentive to do so. They also realize that their retirement will likely occur before earning back sufficient income to offset their lost equity and that they will need to give up power and step back into the shadows as new senior leadership takes over.

STAGE IV: INSTITUTIONALIZING INTO A ONE-FIRM FIRM

To bring the firm together, the senior partners frequently turn to one of the younger, more respected leaders now running a practice area or an office, and they ask him or her to become the firm's new managing partner. This move, which we observed in several firms, helps to win over the younger leaders, who then join as a team in unifying the firm. The new senior "owner" managers of the firm move rapidly to orchestrate a transition from Stage III's loose confederation of offices and practices to a strong, highly coordinated entity with a worldwide reputation. They become the firm's senior management as the founders gradually step aside and retire. The dominant working styles of the new leaders are ones of collaboration and teamwork as they promote unity throughout the firm. Together, they subscribe to a "professional" and corporate form of management.

In Stage IV, the primary challenge is to pull the firm back together through uniting decentralized units and establishing a strong institutional image in the marketplace. These changes are demonstrated not just through external advertising but also by establishing consistent internal practices to create a "one-firm firm" with delivery of uniform services around the globe. The marketing emphasis shifts to promote the name and reputation of the firm itself, not the names and capabilities of individual partners or offices, as was the case in Stage III. The firm becomes a "brand name" recognizable worldwide; McKinsey is an outstanding example.

While some firms in prior stages may have launched marketing and advertising campaigns to promote themselves, Stage IV firms emphasize a deeper process of institutionalization to establish a strong "firm identity," including a core set of values and practices that unify employees under a common culture and delivery approach to clients. This new identity becomes pervasive throughout the firm, ranging from the types of people recruited, to training programs, and to consistent approaches toward clients. Here we see the emergence of the "Andersen Way" or the "Bainies."

Strategically, these large firms usually move to differentiate themselves from other firms by staking out a clear domain among one of five broad types of management consulting: IT, strategy and organization, marketing, operations, or human resources, which are then supplied to wide variety of industries. Rarely do they become known as superior in more than one domain, though they may offer services in these other domains. Under its chosen domain, the firm also builds a range of closely related sub-services and delivers them in a uniform way wherever a client's operations may be located. Thus, a firm in the IT domain delivers systems design, hardware and software selection, training, and outsourcing services.

At this point in their evolution, most Stage IV firms have established themselves globally with offices in many countries. They assure large international clients that they can deliver the same service with the same quality worldwide. More acquisitions are made, including even mega-mergers, such as occurred between Cap Gemini and Ernst & Young. These mergers help to provide global scale, acquire a larger client base, weed out underperforming partners, and close redundant offices.

The organization is reshaped from its Stage III decentralized profit centers into a highly coordinated global matrix based on geography (e.g., North America, Europe, and Asia) and practice/industry areas (e.g., change management and financial services). Numerous offices are grouped under regional managers whose responsibility is to coordinate projects and personnel across local offices to assure a more uniform level of service. They are also likely to appoint regional and global practice leaders, especially for industries, who coordinate and develop resources for their special focus.

Sophisticated management systems are introduced to manage this complex matrix as well as to ensure consistent treatment of clients. Extensive employee training becomes essential for educating all consultants in the firm's preferred "approach" to serving clients, including Web-based virtual training and centralized face-to-face training. One such example is Accenture's central training facility in St. Charles, Illinois, which was described as follows to us by one Accenture partner:

> We have a centralized training facility—a university type campus for many more than 1,000 participants—and we use it to teach everyone our methods and approaches to clients. The partners do much of the teaching, and they communicate our values along with technical skills. Everyone is expected to practice the same approach worldwide.

Increased emphasis is given by the firm's senior management to strategic planning so as to allocate firm-wide resources toward the best opportunities and priorities. To coordinate and review strategic plans, an executive council of senior partners from offices and lines of service is appointed or elected. Various communication forums, such as annual partners' meetings and newsletters, are established to keep employees well informed. At headquarters, new staff groups are created in Human Resources, Information Technology, Marketing, and Accounting to serve the line operating units and promote uniform practices.

The human resources system is redesigned to encourage rapid career advancement for those individuals who not only perform at a high level but also subscribe to the firm's values and standardized approach toward clients. Clear and uniform policies are established for employee selection, promotion, performance evaluation, and ethical conduct. The recruitment of consultants is conducted worldwide. Year-end rewards are based on a combination of total firm, sub-unit, and individual performances. The array of awards includes cash bonuses and shares, along with promotion to partner and officer status. Planned turnover is used to weed out low performers and those who deviate from the firm's prescribed norms and standards.

In Stage IV, the sheer size of the firm and the magnitude of its overhead expenses cause it to pursue large projects with high fees and delivered to a limited range of global clients and government agencies. On the downside, this approach results in lost middle-market opportunities, leaving a niche to be filled by smaller regional firms. The firm's market orientation also suffers from having solidified its reputation within a particular consulting domain (e.g., IT consulting); however, this tends to limit the firm in making forays into other domains (e.g., strategy and organization consulting). Organizationally, the one-firm firm approach begins to create a great deal of conformity in consultant behavior as they adhere to the firm's preferred way of doing things.

Fourth Major Crisis: **Need to Enter New Domains and Increase Organizational Flexibility**

The uniformity of the one-firm firm market orientation in Stage IV eventually loses much of its competitive edge because it limits the range of services and restricts flexibility toward clients. The firm's monolithic organization and standardized approach to very large clients begins to inhibit the tailoring of proposals to fit unique client needs. Clients with worldwide operations also need specialized localization assistance. Furthermore, and likely most important, not all clients want a standardized consulting approach where they feel shoehorned into someone else's ill-fitting shoes. These clients have learned that to compete they need to be different from their competitors, not the same.

Another problem involves market limitations caused by the boundaries of the market domain that the firm has established for itself in Stage IV. In order to compete, the largest firms have stayed mainly within their market domains. Thus, many IT firms like KPMG (now BearingPoint) have created themselves as largely IT firms. Or the general management firms like McKinsey and Bain have mainly stayed within the strategy and organization domain.

This is not to say that large consulting firms haven't tried venturing out from their stated domains, but the evidence is that they have not been particularly successful in doing so. Even in these forays, the IT-oriented firms, for example, tend to launch strategy practices with an IT orientation. Clients also see the firm only for its main domain orientation and, therefore, don't consider them as qualified in other domains. Simply trying to become a one-firm firm within one particular domain has been an immense challenge in Stage IV, but becoming successful at it has also created a firm with a limited range of market breadth.

A large overhead structure has also been built up during Stage IV because of the firm's attempts to market and advertise its one-firm firm image as well as to invest in expensive marketing directed at specific clients. Some firms hire a sales force that begins to replace consultants as the principal marketing arm. An expensive office structure has also been created around the world, including complex control and administrative systems, and consultants' salaries have crept up in order to attract and retain a large workforce, numbering at this point in the thousands.

All of this means that fees to clients are high, causing some purchasing resistance, especially during down economic times. Marketplace and economic difficulties are also symptomatic of an even deeper problem in the firm's homogeneous culture. An organizational form of "hardening of the arteries" begins to set in to undermine the firm's effectiveness in the marketplace. A uniform "type" of partner has been developed and molded to fit the firm's universal values; this person is typically one who is loyal and hardworking but probably lacking in creativity and entrepreneurial instinct. And at lower levels, newly recruited, bright, young professionals without a lengthy socialization process behind them begin to feel depersonalized in the sameness of a culture where everyone is expected to behave as one. Many of these employees will stay only long enough to enhance their resumes before making a career jump.

Solutions to this crisis require exploring uncharted waters that are not clear for even the largest consulting firms as they grapple with the relative clumsiness of their large size, overhead costs, distant global reach, and resistant cultures. It remains for these large firms to reinvent themselves to enter a fifth stage. Clearly, they need to reduce their overhead costs, but more important is a need to restore greater flexibility in both their internal practices and their approaches toward clients. But that is not easy.

Making radical changes is difficult because private consulting firms and even public ones typically elect (or express strong sentiments from below) their Managing Partners (CEOs), but they are unlikely to be replaced unless the firm's profits are in serious decline. Even then, hundreds of partners may not vote for or support a reform candidate who might well replace them tomorrow in a radical shakeup. For example, the CEO of Bain & Co., when speaking of the challenges facing McKinsey, said, "It's an open question as to what extent such large, complex multi-country institutions will be able to retain their partnership principles and operate efficiently."[8]

FIFTH STAGE AND RESULTING CRISIS?

Only the very largest consulting firms are beginning to deal with a possible fifth stage. Their efforts will define it for researchers to write about later.

Different routes are currently being pursued: One is to make the large firm feel and act smaller; another is to enter new domains of consulting through acquisitions, including even nonconsulting services; and a third is to create R&D units and separate start-up ventures—and perhaps all three.

The "small is beautiful" approach was related to us by the CEO of a $2 billion consulting firm:

> *We used to grow offices up to eighty or ninety people, but then they would always fall back to about sixty. And so now we make sure that whenever they get too big, we split them apart.*

This spin-off approach is similar to the successful strategy used by the pharmaceutical giant, Johnson & Johnson, which has created over 190 separate companies with different names, many from internal spin-offs. J&J's various company general managers are rewarded for creating new companies and spinning them off as freestanding subsidiaries. Other large consulting firms are now pursuing spin-offs and even new venture strategies with startups, R&D incubators and acquisitions, some of which include Booz Allen's Aestix, CGE&Ys Bios Group and Net-Strike, Hewitt Associate's Sageo, and EDS's Ebreviate.

Another approach is for large firms to use major acquisitions and alliances to reposition themselves outside their established Stage IV domains. For example, one strategy consulting firm in our study, after entering into an alliance with an operations-oriented consulting firm, decided with its new partner to be acquired by a larger information systems software firm. Another example is Mercer Consulting, originally a human resources firm, which has acquired Delta Consulting, a strategy and organization consulting firm, and others.

Our prediction is that the next growth stage will likely involve further consolidation, resulting from major acquisitions and alliances, as key players seek greater scale and diversity of services along the value chain. It seems clear that these firms cannot reach their growth objectives solely through internal reliance on their own capabilities. For example, IT-oriented firms have recently sought growth through adding nonconsulting services like outsourcing and software alliances. However, even these large consulting firms pale in their available capital resources for making acquisitions when compared to the large hardware firms, namely, IBM and HP. We may also see the software giants Microsoft and Cisco move to acquire a large IT consulting firm like Deloitte Consulting. The big IT consulting firms themselves may attempt to acquire a strategy consulting firm like Monitor or specialized software firms like SAP and PeopleSoft.

So this last stage may see current firms being absorbed into a few big megaholding firms composed of several firms ranging from consulting services to nonconsulting enterprises—all positioned somewhere along the value chain. We may finally arrive at the long ago dream of "one-stop-shopping." But that has its own problems that will no doubt emerge.

Today's smaller firms that are still located back in earlier growth stages should continue to prosper. The giants are not likely to compete directly against them because of the relatively small size of projects involved. However, as these small firms become larger, they will become ripe acquisition targets. Their challenge is to prepare for this eventuality by managing effectively through their earlier stages and related growth issues.

DEVELOPMENTAL LEADERSHIP

Developmental leadership depends on a firm's partners being willing to change within themselves if they are also to change their firm. They must possess strong leadership qualities of anticipation, confrontation, and choice. We see the growth of a firm as inseparable from the personal growth of its leadership. Each phase in a firm's life cycle requires key leaders to create a new strategic vision and risk their positions of power and ownership. These partners must continually reevaluate old practices in light of their evolving competitive environment and accept the challenge of introducing new practices and behaviors. Through farsighted acts of leadership and personal change, the firm itself is transformed.

Developmental Perspective

Leaders of firms, if they are to grow their firms effectively, must learn to manage from a developmental perspective. Too often they are quick to blame their firm's problems on market forces, employee mistakes, and bad luck. But today's problems frequently have roots in yesterday's management practices, while the solutions lay hidden in current tensions caused by the pull of the future and the hold of the past; for example, a young partner may want to open a new office but the senior partners prefer to stay put in their current location.

An irony difficult for many firm leaders to understand is that previously successful practices eventually serve to undermine the firm and restrict its growth. Each of the growth stages contains a paradox where the past solution becomes the future problem. For example, Stage I's emphasis on "exploring the market" allows each partner to have a key role and to aid in testing for various market opportunities; however, it also inhibits focused effort and the necessary channeling of resources essential to Stage II. Or there is the paradox of Stage III where we see a shift to diversification that greatly enhances growth but eventually creates a fragmented firm giving poor service to large clients.

In every firm, its leaders need to understand what stage they are in during its growth life cycle. If they do, then they can anticipate better what lies ahead and then prepare for the upcoming crisis and the new management demands of the next stage. For example, in Stage I, it is important for all the partners to understand early that if they "stumble" upon a strong growth market in one of their expertises they may well have to focus on that area if they want to grow, or they will have to opt out of the growth race. Also, during Stage II's intense specialization, the partners need to begin developing future managers who can lead offices and new practices in Stage III. And in the later stages, the senior partners must begin to share ownership with the younger leaders if the firm is to outlive the senior partners' retirements and departures. In any of these instances, the crisis is likely to become severe if the leaders wait too long to take action.

Stopping Growth

Each firm and its leadership must continuously confront the basic underlying strategic choice facing all firms—whether to grow or not. Growth is neither automatic nor assured, nor is it an absolute necessity. However, stopping growth becomes more difficult as the firm develops into its later stages. Getting off the growth path is easier when the firm is small and only the partners' ambitions are at stake. But, as the firm grows larger, a decision to stop growth, or even slow it down, runs the risk of causing high turnover from disappointed employees or the loss of major clients. Also, if the firm has gone public with an IPO, it will have to contend with investors and analysts constantly pressing for improved performance and further growth.

In wanting to stay small, the partners must guard against becoming complacent, which can cause employees to leave or the loss of proposals to more alert competition. They still must find other ways to grow, not in size and geography, but perhaps in the kinds of projects undertaken. One new source of stimulation might be forming a local alliance with other small consulting firms that specialize in different practice areas; that way, they can make referrals to each other and sponsor joint training or even share overhead. Another possibility is to use contract consultants to bid on and secure larger projects than could be undertaken by a small permanent staff, who are usually eager to work with others on larger projects. A number of independent consultants work in major cities. A third possibility is to manage the consulting firm differently, sharing jobs and rotating employees more frequently. It might also grow in profits, but not in employees, by taking on higher margin projects.

Letting Go

Deciding to grow larger implies for many partners a loss of power and control, which is often difficult for them to give up. As a result, many firms become paralyzed by inaction or internal conflict among the partners.

The psychological phenomenon of "letting go" is one of the hardest challenges that any partner will face during his/her professional career. Moving from one stage to another requires one or more partners to let go of something that is highly cherished, whether that be giving up attachment to running a practice area or moving to another city to open a new office, or withdrawing from full-time consulting to assume a top level administrative job in the firm.

At some point, all the founding partners will eventually leave the firm. Some will choose to depart midstream because they don't like what lies ahead. Other partners will choose to stay because they are more flexible and intrigued by the challenge of moving on and growing with the firm. Finally, all the original partners must eventually depart for retirement, leaving the firm in the hands of the new leaders whom they have personally developed and mentored as their successors, thereby assuring the firm's growth into the future.

Notes to the Chapter

[1]*Consulting Magazine* (March 2001).

[2]Larry E. Greiner, "Evolution and Revolution As Organizations Grow," *Harvard Business Review* (November–December, 1972).

[3]We also wish to thank Stephanie Kondik for her assistance in the research phase of this project.

[4] *Business Week* (February 11, 1991): 52–53.

[5] Other studies that identify life cycles in firms include: N. Churchill and V. Lewis, "The Five Stages of Small Business Growth," *Harvard Business Review* (May–June, 1983): 3–12; J. Kimberly and R. Miles, *The Organizational Life-cycle* (San Francisco, CA: Jossey-Bass, 1980); B. Scott, "Stages of Corporate Development," Harvard Business School, Boston, MA, (Unpublished Paper, 1973); L. Greiner, "Evolution and Revolution As Organizations Grow," *Harvard Business Review* (November–December, 1972): 37–46.

[6] For an analysis of the benefits and calculation of economic leverage in firms, see D. Maister, "Balancing the Professional Service Firm," *Sloan Management Review* (Fall 1982): 5–19.

[7] For a detailed discussion of professionals as managers in decentralized structures, see J. Lorsch, "When Professionals Have to Manage," *Harvard Business Review* (July–August, 1987): 78–83.

[8] Jack Sweeney, "Marvin's Shoes, A Tale of Two Firms," *Consulting Magazine* (May 2002): 20.

CHAPTER 16

High-Performance Consulting Firms

Jay W. Lorsch, Harvard Business School

ABOUT THE AUTHOR

Jay W. Lorsch

Jay W. Lorsch is the Louis Kirstein Professor of Human Relations at the Harvard Business School. He is the author of many articles and over a dozen books, including *Aligning the Stars* (2002) and *Pawns or Potentates: The Reality of America's Corporate Boards* (1989). Dr. Lorsch has been a consultant to many companies in the United States and abroad and is currently a director of three companies.

Why do some consulting firms like McKinsey, Bain, and the Boston Consulting Group continue to prosper and survive, while others like the venerable Arthur D. Little decline and eventually disappear? Or why do organizations like Accenture, American Management Systems, or IBM grow successfully as IT consultants, while so many other firms struggle and fail? Whether you are a partner in a large firm or about to hang out your own shingle for the first time, such questions are critically important.

Each firm will obviously find its own way and no doubt appear quite different on the surface. However, the underlying roots of success appear to be the same, whether the firm is new or long established; whether it is large or small. So in this chapter, I shall explain what makes for high-performing consulting firms. The research that underlies my explanation was conducted in successful professional firms of all types, and the findings have direct relevance to most consulting firms, both large and small.[1]

The basic key, as I will explain, is for a firm to accomplish two critical tasks: 1) to create an effective strategy to provide consulting services to clients; and 2) to align its structure, processes, leadership, culture, and people so that they support and reinforce each other and the firm's strategy as the firm grows.

STRATEGY, GOALS, AND PEOPLE SUCCESS FACTORS

Designing Strategy First

Most top managers in any consulting firm would agree that the key to success is having the right strategy and financial model. That is indeed what our research has shown. Success, these managers would say, depends on providing services to chosen clients in a manner that is superior to what other competing firms can offer and is also superior to what clients can do on their own.

Success also depends on providing the given services at a competitive fee and in a cost-effective way so that the firm reaps a healthy profit.

The basic strategy and business model of most successful consulting firms is about as simple as what I have just described, but my research has also shown that is not enough. The key lies in strategy execution, which includes both forming the strategy and making it happen in practice. As in so many business situations, the devil is in the details. For example, just consider the word "strategy." When I speak about a firm's strategy, I am not concerned with advocating some vague visionary plan or simplistic chart on the wall. Rather, I mean the actual and detailed design and content of the firm's strategy, including its market focus, the services to be delivered, financial objectives, and the required behavior of professionals to accomplish certain desired outcomes.

The firm's top management must decide just how they want to compete in specific ways that will allow the firm to win out against equally strong firms. Throughout this effort, a realistic assessment must be made about the firm's capabilities and how these can be channeled into a winning formula—and here I come to the specific goals that need to be set as part of the firm's strategy.

Setting Focused Goals

Strategy is really about goals. What are the firm's goals? Many goals are, of course, financial—the returns the owners hope to achieve on their capital as well as for their personal efforts. But goals can and should include issues of size and durability. How big do the partners want their firm to become? Do they want to build a firm that will endure long after they've retired, or are they intending, at some point, to sell the firm or exit in some other way? On what clients is the firm focusing, and why? How much geography is it planning to cover and why? Should the firm concentrate on one region or strive for national reach or become global in scope? Should the firm become a specialist in one particular service arena, or does it want to offer a broad spectrum of services? And furthermore, what level and type of service does the firm offer to clients?

All of these are valid questions, but the specific answers are frequently different for each firm. What all successful firms have in common is that they have carefully thought through at the partner level their goals and the means to achieve them, and they have made clear choices to focus on certain ones. They don't try to be all things to all clients. For example, Bain and McKinsey each offer their clients a customized study of particular problems. But other firms, such as Accenture, offer a more standardized approach wherein clients know that the same service will be delivered worldwide. Both options clearly are effective for these firms, but they work in large part because their partners have not only chosen a defined strategy built on specific goals but they have communicated them widely to all employees—leading to a broader and deeper understanding about why their respective firms are offering a particular brand of service.

Forging a Strong Strategic Identity

Putting strategy and goals down in detail and on paper with the senior management is only a starting point. Much of this can be accomplished in discussion, but the issue of strategy goes deeper, even within this group of leaders. They must not just say the strategy but believe in and behave like it in their daily leadership behavior. This takes us to the need for creating a strong strategic identity to guide employees, which will be reflected in the behavior of *all* consultants and staff throughout the firm.

Let me explain in more detail what I mean by "strategic identity" because its definition further underscores why consensus around a firm's strategy— and also partner and associate behavior that reflects this consensus—is so important. Strategic identity for a consulting firm is analogous to the personal identity of an individual. It is what the firm wants to become, what it stands for in its beliefs and values, and how it behaves with clients. It gives all of the firm's members a clear sense of who they are and what they should do well in their work. It guides them in making choices about how they deal with and serve clients. It helps them resist the temptation to make a decision for short-term gains or personal recognition—because it is a constant reminder of the greater purpose of their day-to-day work.

A firm's strategic identity is also visible externally. Clients recognize it and use it as a way of judging a firm's capabilities. Competitors recognize it as well. If you consider any of the most successful consulting firms, chances are great that you'll be able to describe the firm's identity to a colleague, and that colleague would use similar descriptors in telling you about the same firm.

Strategic drift, which I mentioned above, blurs this understanding. It confuses the partners' and the clients' understanding of what a firm's core capabilities are. Successful firms thus work hard to preserve and reinforce their strategic identity. They focus on maintaining a strong internal consensus about the firm's strategy. Firm leaders at all levels understand their firm's strategic choices and its resulting identity. They recognize their obligation to not allow strategic drift.

Having a strong and widely shared strategic identity does not imply rigidity. New strategic innovations are not stifled in successful firms. Innovation is encouraged, but the critical "detail" here is that one's colleagues must sanction it as a legitimate experiment that promises to strengthen the firm's strategy and identity.

Creating Consensus and Commitment

Which brings me to another critical "detail." It is not enough for a firm's top leaders and partnership group to agree on a strategy, even one with specific goals and a clear statement of identity. In successful firms, *all* the professionals must reach a strong consensus about these strategic choices and the validity of the firm's business model. Put another way, in the most successful firms, *every* professional member of the firm is in agreement about the firm's future direction and also about the behaviors that are required to keep the firm on track. Next, everyone in the firm must be brought on board and behave the strategy in their daily activities.

Here's why such consensus is critical. Consultants, even those in highly successful firms, are individual operators to a great extent. They spend most of their time working in client locations with a dedicated, but temporary, team of colleagues. Even when they are in their firm's office, they work independently with others on a particular client team. The team leader, whether manager, partner, principal, or director, has wide latitude to make many decisions without checking with a "boss." Nobody is standing over him or her, or rarely is anyone expecting a detailed report on what the team is doing on a daily basis.

Under these autonomous circumstances, it is quite possible for consultants to deviate from their firm's strategic choices. In essence, they may easily choose a path outside the firm's strategy. This "strategic drift" is in constant danger, even in successful consulting firms, and the consequences can be quite harmful. First, the economic model can be undermined. Second, the firm's strategic identity can be weakened, and as a result, the firm can become dangerously fragmented, both internally and in the eyes of clients and other stakeholders.

Building a Galaxy of Stars

Making the right decisions about the firm's strategy and developing a strong consensus that supports this strategic direction is clearly important to high-performance firms. And without firm-wide agreement among the consultants about the kinds of behaviors that will support that strategy, they will likely operate all over the map in determining which clients to attract and serve, as well as how to serve them. But none of these ingredients will work unless the right group of talented and committed people is assembled to lead the firm.

Think about it this way—your firm has this great strategic idea. In theory, it will enable you to do a better job of serving clients than any competitor. But that's "in theory." Here's the rule—*nobody ever built a successful firm on theory alone.* Successful firms are built by attracting and developing outstanding professionals—what I call "stars."[2] By stars I mean professionals who have the necessary skills and knowledge to deliver on the firm's strategy while also providing the firm with the quality of leadership that success requires. Stars are the professionals who are, or are going to be, the most outstanding contributors to the firm.

At the start of this chapter, I mentioned that successful firms deliver superior service to clients in a cost-effective way that allows them to make a healthy profit. Here's another "detail" that turns the business model into reality: In consulting firms—as in any professional firm—*the people you pay are ultimately more important than the people who pay you.* Your strategy may be brilliant, but unless you attract, develop, and keep talented professionals who excel at delivering on your strategy, your firm will never perform up to its potential.

Take a moment to consider "new" or "potential" stars—those professionals who are someday expected to take up the mantel of leadership. Each firm's stars have unique qualities that make them suited to the firm's strategy and organization. And in the highest performing consulting firms, the recruitment and training process is explicitly focused on finding and honing that fit. Two examples from exemplary firms make this point:

1. Bain & Co., a strategy consulting firm, recruits mostly MBAs, as well as a few younger people with bachelor's degrees who are likely to go on to earn an MBA and return later to Bain. These young people are selected not only for their intellect and educational accomplishments, but also because they possess other qualities that fit the "Bain way" of doing things. That is, they seem to be hard workers, team players, and interested in hands-on work with clients, as opposed to being more interested in developing theories, or in taking a more

distant, advisory role. They also appear to have the interpersonal skills necessary to work effectively with clients and have the potential to grow into firm leaders.

2. Accenture, the large IT consulting firm, instead looks for its new talent mainly on undergraduate campuses. Accenture seeks outstanding graduates with bachelor's degrees who have the right combination of intellect and other qualities to learn the Accenture approach to consulting. Once they are hired, they are enrolled in an intensive educational program at the firm's learning center in St. Charles, Illinois. Partners become the teachers in this program.

Where Bain wants most of its young consultants to have an advanced business education coming into the game, Accenture is less concerned about the prior training of its young recruits' education, believing instead that it can supplement raw talent with education in the "Accenture Way" of performing consulting. The point here is not the specifics of each firm's selection requirements, but that each firm has an approach that fits its own unique strategy and organization.

Requiring High Involvement from Partners

Outstanding firms share another detail with regard to recruiting new stars as well: Senior leaders are deeply involved in the process. In fact, in these firms, senior partners are expected to commit substantial amounts of time to the recruiting and selection process. No one can be selected to join one of these firms without having gone through an arduous set of interviews, mostly conducted by partners. Why? First, it is well understood throughout the firm that adding talent—any talent—is not enough. It's the input of the *right* talent that is critical to the firm's success. Second, the experienced partners have an internalized sense of the qualities required of new recruits to succeed. They know potential success when they meet it!

Once a potential "star" joins a successful consulting firm, the investment in his or her development begins in earnest. In some firms, such as the aforementioned Accenture, there is formal education. But in the majority of premier firms, the emphasis is on learning on the job. Young professionals join project teams and work alongside more experienced consultants and under the leadership of partner-level consultants.

Through a variety of such assignments, new recruits learn the craft of consulting as it is practiced in their firm. And again, experienced consultants invest a major amount of time working with these younger consultants. This takes place through teaching and coaching on the job, in explaining to a new recruit why the partner said "this" to the client at a meeting, but not "that." Why the partner pursued a particular client aggressively but cut off negotiations with another potential customer early on. It also involves a careful process of formal performance evaluation. Young people receive extensive feedback, both formal and informal, about how they are doing and how they should think about advancing their careers. In successful firms, this practice of giving and receiving constant feedback is an addiction.

It is important to note that the partners' commitment to training is not a "soft" pledge; rather, at outstanding firms, the clear expectation is that senior partners will be engaged in a very real way in the recruiting process and in the training and development of associates. Partners are held accountable for this responsibility when setting formal performance goals and at the time of compensation review.

Supporting Those Who Leave

Some potential stars, over time, find that they are not suited to the firm that hired them. And some find that they are not suited to a career in consulting. Those who reach this conclusion often do so before one of their superiors tells them they are not suited for the firm or to consulting in general. Because these young consultants have succeeded at everything else they have undertaken—education, extra curricular activities, prior short-term jobs, etc.—"not succeeding" is a new experience for them. But they are generally quick to understand that it is more a matter of "fit" than personal flaws, and they decide to move on.

Successful firms provide a great deal of support to these career changes. They help those leaving to find other jobs that are better suited to their talents, often with clients. They make an effort to ensure that the soon-to-be former employees exit with their egos intact and with positive feelings about the firm. Thus, the firm gains a loyal alumnus, one who may well become an important source of new engagements down the road. Outstanding firms retain contact with and encourage their alumni. McKinsey, for example, has a one-inch thick alumni directory!

To sum up these special characteristics of people development in successful consulting firms, they put in place both the right people and a set of people-oriented systems that are aligned well with both the firm's strategy and the needs of its young talent. As a result, new consultants are motivated to contribute their efforts to the firm, to develop skills that are in alignment with the firm's strategic identity, and to make choices about their futures that will support the firm. At the same time, those who leave the firm do so with positive feelings about the firm and are likely to benefit the firm, in one way or another, over time.

LEADERSHIP AND PARTNERSHIP BEHAVIOR

The Three-Hat Challenge

In the early stages of their careers, stars learn the craft of consulting: how to lead project teams; how to deal with clients; and eventually, how to attract new clients. All of this work can be thought of as "producing." It is the core work of becoming a professional consultant.

But those stars who become proficient at "producing" generally have their eyes set on the "next tier;" they want to become partners. Even though some successful firms are no longer legally partnerships, those associates promoted into key leadership roles, usually with the understanding they have a long-term future with the firm, are referred to as "partners."

At successful firms, the decision to promote someone from associate to partner is undertaken with the utmost care for several reasons. First, the move sends a signal to the rest of the firm, thereby either enhancing or eroding the firm's strategic identity. Second, the promotion brings with it certain challenges that are almost impossible to prepare for in advance. If the soon-to-be former associate is not ready to handle the additional complexity, they will crash and burn quickly.

What are the challenges facing the new leaders? First, in addition to being "producers" (the first hat), they are suddenly expected to be "leaders" (the second hat). On the way to their new positions, they likely exercised some degree of team leadership, although that was integral to their work as consultants. But now they are expected to assume more significant and much broader leadership responsibilities, whether it is for heading up a practice area or a geographic entity or a firm-wide committee.

Suddenly their "free" time, already scarce, is almost nonexistent. Not only are they accountable for the performance of their part of the firm, but they are now among the group of people responsible for developing the young stars, which requires spending considerable time on recruiting, coaching, and evaluation.

And as if that weren't complicated enough, they are also asked to wear a third hat—that of "owner." To some extent this third hat also calls for a shift in psychological focus. It's their firm now. Both their psyches and economic well-being are closely tied to how well the firm does. Further, the ownership hat means they are expected to participate in the governance of the firm. This means serving on firm-wide committees or special task forces or perhaps taking on even greater leadership responsibilities by heading a new practice area or major office.

The "three-hat challenge" is incredibly complex and demanding. Outsiders might ask, "Why do consulting firms organize themselves in this strange way where the leaders are expected not only to lead but also to sell and perform consulting? Why don't these firms follow the advice they give to their clients; that is, to develop a hierarchical management structure where senior executives oversee those who are producing the results?"

The answer lies in the unique characteristics of the consulting business, at least as outstanding firms practice it. One factor is that clients want, even demand, continuous contact with partner-level consultants. Just because a consultant has been asked by the firm to lead a practice area, clients do not want to lose his or her services. Another reason for this curious arrangement of both leading and doing is that the long-term success of the firm depends on close contact with young consultants who must be groomed for future leadership roles.

Developing young people requires, among other things, working directly with them on client projects, and that includes staying "up-to-speed" on the substantive issues that concern young consultants in their work. Another reason is that those who have been elevated to the lofty heights of partnership actually enjoy their consulting work. They joined the firm to be consultants, and they enjoy working with clients, solving their problems, and receiving positive feedback. While they understand the necessity and obligation to play their leadership and owner's role, the act of doing good consulting work is still a great source of motivation, and they are unwilling to give it up!

The three-hat arrangement, with all its attendant problems of time management and the push-pull of personal interest versus firm interest, exists in all outstanding consulting firms. In fact, it exists in all kinds of professional service firms—accounting firms, law firms, and investment banks—for the reasons just cited. How do partners make the three-hat challenge work?

At the partner level, it is impossible to understate the importance of being able to "self-manage." One needs to develop an explicit set of priorities, or what Kotter calls a "personal agenda."[3] It is also necessary to reach out to others in the firm for support. Younger associates and other partners all can help. They can follow up a new client lead or jump in to help a client team. In successful firms, it is generally accepted that to make this type of structure work, it requires a high degree of teamwork from all those involved.

Performance Evaluation and Rewards

Making the three-hat arrangement work also requires the development of a well-executed performance management and career development system at the partner level. In outstanding consulting firms, for example, performance assessment and personal development do not stop when one joins the ranks of the partnership. Partners also receive performance evaluations and suggestions for improving their skills. Usually, these evaluations are conducted either by a more senior partner or by a committee of partners.

In all successful firms, the partners are judged especially on how well they are doing in wearing all three hats. Their performance as a consultant, a leader, and an owner are all part of the evaluation mix. That's not to say that all partners are expected to be equally strong on all dimensions. For sure, some partners excel as rainmakers, while others may be more outstanding as star-makers. Still other partners may make a significant contribution to the firm's governance.

Regardless of where each partner's strengths lie, there are three important points to remember about partner evaluation in high-performing firms:

First, it happens! Partners in outstanding firms are evaluated regularly. Nobody is permitted to rest on his or her laurels—to say, "Well, I've made it, now I can relax."

Second, not all partners are expected to make equal contributions as owners, producers, and leaders. Each partner has his or her own mix of activities and his or her own strengths and weaknesses.

Finally, though each partner is evaluated on how well he or she plays each role, the message is clear to all—you must wear all three hats! Success as a firm requires that the partnership as a whole place a high value on practicing all three roles effectively.

These three points must be strongly reinforced by the firm's compensation system. While the specifics of compensation arrangements differ across successful firms, two commonalities stand out among them. First, pay is used to reinforce the message that wearing all three hats is important. Second, pay arrangements for all partners are tied, to a large extent, to firm-wide results, not simply individual achievement. Whatever other goals the compensation scheme encourages partners to achieve, contribution to firm-wide results is highly rewarded. Being a strong collaborator in helping to build a unified firm is a shared value across all successful firms, and pay is tied to this end.

Participation in Governance

The third hat of owner requires active involvement in the firm's governance process. Because most successful firms are considered to be partnerships, regardless of their legal ownership form, managing the governance process effectively is a significant factor in contributing to a successful firm. Governance in these firms includes decisions about: who is admitted to the partnership; distribution of firm profits and the related question of partner compensation; major strategic questions; and the selection of the firm's leader.

In all high-performing firms, the partners expect to be, and are, involved in all aspects of firm governance. They are expected to step back and, as an owner, consider what is best for the firm. As I have said, too strong a focus on one's personal interests is frowned upon in high-performing firms. Doing what is best for the whole firm and all its partners is the ultimate objective of all governance activities in these firms.

One common goal is to make the partner selection decision on a firm-wide basis. That is, the process is designed to prevent offices or practices from lobbying for their favorite candidates. The intent is to prevent competition from among the firm's various sectors to threaten the firm's overall cohesion and strategic identity. Engaging in politics for oneself or others is frowned upon.

Similarly, the process for selecting a firm's leader may be managed by a committee, but the ultimate decision typically involves all the partners and requires their vote. For example, a representative committee may solicit nominations from among the partners and then interview the possible candidates as well as those who nominated them so as to develop a limited slate of candidates to consider. But again, the goal in successful firms is to minimize conflict and tension between specific practice areas or geographic offices and to select a leader who will have the greatest level of acceptance and support from all partners.

The Managing Director

In a partnership-like environment, the job of taking responsibility for firm-wide leadership is an extremely complex task. What I have found in successful firms is that the managing director operates as if he or she is not a CEO sitting atop a management hierarchy. Rather, these leaders realize they are surrounded by other leaders who are also "owners."

These managing directors do not issue edicts. They lead from *within* the partnership, always striving to build consensus among their fellow owners regarding the firm's direction and governance.

They are on constant guard to ensure that each decision being advocated serves to strengthen the firm's overall strategic identity. They are also on constant guard to make sure that their fellow partners are not simply paying lip service to that identity but are, in fact, behaving in ways that explicitly support it. Often there are real conflicts, given each partner's personal situation. Consider these real examples: A senior partner who is about to retire decides to oppose a decision to invest the firm's resources in developing a new office in Asia, yet another younger partner wants to move to Asia to head-up the office. Similarly, a successful partner interested in the technology sector wants to sign on a client in that field, but the firm as a whole has never agreed to invest in developing that particular sector and expertise.

The managing directors of high-performing firms are exceptional in finding ways to acknowledge and empathize with individual views, while at the same time encouraging colleagues to continue to put the firm's best interests first. It's a tall order—keeping a group of people with largely independent egos in close alignment.

This senior leadership position is a different sort of job from being the CEO of a client company. In many ways, it is more challenging. For the high-performance firms, the managing directors appear to possess a large quotient of what Goleman calls "emotional intelligence,"[4] which includes the capacity to understand one's self and others and to control one's emotions in achieving an effective dialogue with others. They do not sit in their offices and wait for people to come to them; rather, they are in continuous contact with many partners, asking for their views and hearing reactions to controversial decisions. Above all, they are good listeners and questioners.

THE FIRM'S CULTURE: CAUSE AND CONSEQUENCES

At the outset, I emphasized that consultants in high-performance firms typically do not feel constrained by formal roles and that they spend their time working with clients without close supervision from their firm's senior leaders. This means there is always the risk that a consultant will move in directions that are inconsistent with their firm's strategic identity. Temptation is always present in the form of clients who offer more work and money—if only you will do this or that, even when it may be contrary to the firm's strategy.

In the face of such temptation and without the presence of a formal hierarchy or clear policy, it is the strong culture of high-performing firms that keeps everyone singing from the same hymnbook. Culture refers to the set of beliefs members hold about how they are expected to behave and what values they are to share with their fellow consultants.[5] By "strong," I mean that the belief systems are well understood and accepted by all the firm's members.

Consultants on the way up through these firms are inoculated with the values of their firm's culture. When they face the temptation to wander off in new directions, they have been so infused with their firm's culture that they understand that such deviation is unacceptable. My intent is not to imply that new ideas or innovations are impossible in these firms. Quite the contrary! What must happen, though, is new ideas must be acceptable to the partners. A consensus must be developed as to why embarking on a new direction makes sense for the firm.

While many differences exist among firms in their specific beliefs, a number of common themes are evident across successful firms. One is the importance of *focusing relentlessly on clients* and their needs, while simultaneously *building the firm's pool of star talent*. Another is a strong belief in the *importance of working in teams*. Ambitious consultants may exhibit competitive tendencies with their colleagues, but in successful firms not only the leaders but also one's peers frown upon such behavior. Rather, emphasis is placed on working collaboratively in teams.

Another belief shared by successful consulting firms is that the *firm is a unified community*, one entity. It is what Maister has labeled as the "one-firm firm."[6] Connected to this is a strong belief in the importance of *perpetuating the firm for the long term*. The current generation of partners is expected to worry not just about their own well-being but also about building a firm that will be successful for future generations. A final belief characteristic of successful firms is that they are and must function as a *unified partnership*. Decisions must be agreed to and be accepted by the partners. It is their firm, and they are its leaders and ultimate decision makers.

In the successful firms, their leaders preach about culture and its beliefs in their informal and formal talks and speeches. They, too, shape it on a daily basis with their behavior and decisions. They understand that the firm's cultural values must be constantly articulated in words and actions. Not only do they reinforce it, they actively manage it. If they think the beliefs around which the firm is run need to change, they work to develop a consensus among their fellow partners about the need for change. Once agreement is reached, they become vocal advocates of the firm's new beliefs and provide explanations for them.

Overall, a strong culture in successful firms serves to reinforce the alignment of strategy and internal practices with the needs of the firm's professionals. Culture, in this sense, is like the superglue that holds the firm in close alignment. However, unlike real superglue, effective leadership can reduce its "stickiness" if change is needed, allowing the firm to create a new alignment for moving in a new direction.

ALIGNMENT AND FIRM SIZE

The leaders of high-performance firms see their overall responsibility as one of achieving and managing alignment in the firm's different growth stages (see Chapter 15). All other decisions—whether to accept or reject an individual client, where to place resources, which associates to promote to the partnership—are ultimately part of the job of building and sustaining alignment. It is obviously a daunting task in a large, global consulting firm with dozens, or maybe even hundreds, of partners. Yet, leaders of successful firms have been accomplishing this responsibility since the creation of the first major consulting firm fifty years ago. It is a complicated leadership job, but with determination and skill, it gets done.

For those who are involved in leading and building smaller firms, there is good news! While I believe the lessons that I have drawn from the "powerhouses" of consulting and described here have relevance for most firms, I also believe, as I said earlier, that the tasks of leadership are much easier in smaller firms, though nevertheless essential. In small firms, consensus must be achieved among fewer partners. It is possible to get everyone in the same meeting room and to reach joint decisions, whether about strategic direction, partner compensation, or the future of younger professionals. It is also easier to carefully select new talent, to tend to their development, and to shape their careers while simultaneously wearing their producer and owner hats.

Obviously, all this gets more complicated as a consulting firm succeeds and grows in size and complexity. All consultants and all firms should worry about alignment from the moment their first business cards are printed. Alignment is a complicated state that evolves over time and size, and it is a goal to work toward that will never be fully achieved. However, it is easier when you have a clean slate and a small firm. If you start in the wrong direction, making changes later will be much more difficult.

In the end, for all firms, becoming successful requires a mix of strategic, organizational, and leadership attributes that are carefully put in place over the years, while keeping a close eye on alignment. Success cannot be reduced simply to a firm's leadership or its product line or its culture. I have outlined many of the necessary attributes here, as identified in my research on high-performing firms. Still, as firms move into the future, other successful practices will be invented by firms and their leaders and then written about by researchers. It will be interesting to read about high-performance firms ten years from now.

Notes to the Chapter

[1]Jay W. Lorsch and Thomas J. Tierney, *Aligning the Stars: How to Succeed When Professionals Drive Results* (Boston, MA: Harvard Business Press, 2002).

[2]Lorsch and Tierney, op. cit.

[3]John P. Kotter, *The General Managers* (New York: Free Press, 1982).

[4]Daniel Goleman, "What Makes a Leader," *Harvard Business Review* 76, no. 6 (November–December, 1998). Also, Daniel Goleman, *Emotional Intelligence: Why It Can Matter More Than IQ, for Character, Health, and Lifelong Achievement* (New York: Bantam, 1998).

[5]Edgar H. Schein, *Organizational Culture and Leadership* (San Francisco: Jossey-Bass, 1985) and John P. Kotter and James L. Heskett, *Corporate Culture and Performance* (New York: Free Press, 1992) are two books that explore the definition and importance of culture in a broad array of companies.

[6]David H. Maister, *Managing the Professional Service Firm* (New York: Free Press, 1993).

CHAPTER 17

Knowledge Management in Consulting

Thomas H. Davenport, Babson College, and Laurence Prusak, Independent Consultant

ABOUT THE AUTHORS

Thomas H. Davenport

Tom Davenport holds the President's Chair in Information Technology and Management at Babson College, and is an Accenture Fellow. He has also led research centers at Accenture, McKinsey, Ernst & Young, and CSC Index. Dr. Davenport has coauthored or edited ten books and numerous articles on business process reengineering, knowledge management, and enterprise systems.

Laurence Prusak

Larry Prusak is a researcher and consultant living in Lexington, Massachusetts. Over the past twenty-five years, he has worked for five major management consulting firms in a variety of roles. His most recent books include: *What's the Big Idea* (2003), coauthored with Tom Davenport, and *In Good Company* (2001), coauthored with Don Cohen.

Consulting has always been about knowledge. Clients hire and pay high fees to consultants to benefit from their use of leading-edge knowledge. As a result, consulting firms recruit large numbers of knowledgeable graduates from top schools. Once employed, the best firms devote substantial resources to imparting knowledge to their consultants through ongoing education and knowledge management systems.

Many scholars contend that knowledge is represented only in findings derived from systematic research adhering to scientific rules. In consulting, however, a wider definition is typically given to knowledge, including everything from gathered facts about an industry to what went right and wrong on past projects to successful selling methods to analytical models employed by the firm in its consulting practice. All of this information, including facts, perceptions and opinions, is often regarded as useful for the firm and its consultants so they can perform effectively.

Much of this knowledge is accumulated and shared through formal information systems and training programs within the firm, but it is also contained in the heads of consultants and in a firm's cultural heritage, thereby making it necessary for informal interaction among consultants to share their "tacit" knowledge and learn from the experience of others. Frequently, more formal knowledge is created within the firm, sometimes through dedicated research, for wider distribution in books, articles, and on Web sites for access by clients and the general public. All of these many facets of creating and sharing fall under the modern concept of knowledge management as practiced in firms today.

Until the last decade, however, consulting firms were fairly haphazard in dealing with knowledge. Few undertook formal programs to ensure that the knowledge gained in client engagements was documented and distributed. And the creation of new knowledge was often left to individual initiative. In the early 1990s, knowledge management began to advance, with consulting firms among the earliest adopters, especially in structuring and codifying client project experiences.[1] Today, the creation and dissemination of new knowledge, or "thought leadership" as it is often called, has become a key objective for many consulting firms.

Rather we have divided it into two parts, knowledge creating and knowledge sharing, which we believe to be the two most critical aspects of knowledge management. Both are closely related because created knowledge needs to be shared or it isn't useful, and knowledge sharing depends on valuable insights from knowledge creating for it to be effective.

We begin the chapter by framing the reasons for emphasizing the importance of knowledge management in consulting. Then Part I turns to knowledge creating in consulting—an activity that is underinvestigated and underreported for its impact on consulting and management. Then, in the second part, we discuss how knowledge sharing operates within consulting firms to benefit consultants and clients alike. Throughout we examine the roots of each area of focus and then concentrate on describing current practice. In both parts, we focus on three large, well-known consulting firms and what they are doing about knowledge creating and sharing: Accenture, McKinsey, and IBM Global Services. Finally, we conclude with some current and future issues affecting the evolution of knowledge management in general.

Why Knowledge, Why Now?

Why has a shift toward an emphasis on knowledge taken place at this time in consulting? As globalization proceeds at an accelerating pace, businesses in the more economically developed nations are seeking to become more knowledge-based or knowledge-intensive, or even to transform themselves into full-blown knowledge enterprises. They know that many products, and not a few services, can now be made or performed more cheaply in the developing nations. And since capital chases cheaper labor, it becomes difficult to compete on costs with firms employing cheap labor. In addition, the ease and ubiquity of technological communications make the coordination of global work far easier than ever before.

Therefore, many organizations in the developed world have changed their business models to seek profits from selling products and services where the knowledge component is high and cannot be easily reproduced. To maximize their success in these knowledge-oriented businesses, they must draw on the experience and expertise not only of their own employees but also that of outsiders.

This trend explains the rapid growth of the "advice" industry—a sprawling, underreported but substantial piece of the U.S. economy that spans law firms;

investment banks; advertisement, marketing, and public relations firms; some functions of universities such as executive education; and, of course, those original advisors, management consultants. And if the emergence of knowledge-based business drives the consulting industry, it follows that consulting firms—in order to serve their clients in knowledge-oriented industries—must be particularly knowledge-oriented and skilled at managing knowledge.

Consulting firms are immersed in all the issues involving knowledge and its development and management. By the very nature of their work, consulting firms feel the need to acquire or develop various types of knowledge, to codify effectively (or transfer through other means) what they learn, to distribute this knowledge through some mechanisms, and to evaluate the process and the products of this entire operation.

PART I: KNOWLEDGE CREATING IN CONSULTING

Too often we think that academics at business schools are the only creators of business knowledge, but we need to recognize that consultants and researchers at consulting firms have been prominent here as well. In one ranking of the 100 gurus with the most business impact based on several quantitative measures (Web hits using the Google search engine, citation counts, and media mentions), there were thirty-six consultants—second only to the number of academics (fifty) and substantially more than the number of practicing managers (ten) and journalists (four).[2]

Origins of "Thought Leadership"

For a consulting firm to undertake research is not a new idea. In the early 1900s, Frederick Taylor and Frank Gilbreth had a consulting firm on industrial engineering, and they developed research-based benchmarks for how long certain tasks should take to perform. Arthur D. Little, widely regarded as the first professional consulting firm, undertook contract research for clients in a variety of areas. In almost any consulting domain, when aspects of the field are poorly understood, it is reasonable to undertake research.

Research in consulting firms reached a new plane of visibility, however, when Tom Peters and Robert Waterman published their book *In Search of Excellence* in 1982.[3] The two authors were consultants for McKinsey & Company, and they led a research project on "continuously innovative big companies" that was initially sponsored by Siemens, Hewlett-Packard, 3M, and several other companies. The resulting book was an enormous best-seller, and although McKinsey's leadership was initially uncomfortable about giving their firm visibility in a popular book, *Excellence* ushered in the era of "thought leadership." This term is a popular concept in the vernacular of consultants for expressing a firm's or person's capability in creating original ideas for use by clients.

Using this strategy of thought leadership, consulting firms strive to be identified with the latest and most popular thinking about business and management. Their consultants publish articles in practitioner-oriented journals such as *Harvard Business Review*, and they write books that they hope will make business best-seller lists. The goal of this activity, of course, is to persuade clients that a given firm, home to the authors of the publication, has either the best perspective on a particular topic or a reputation for progressive and innovative thinking in general.

By the 1990s, the thought leadership movement became a major force in consulting. Many of the popular management ideas of the decade, including reengineering, knowledge management, e-commerce, enterprise systems, value disciplines, time-based competition, customer relationship management, and many others, were either first put forth or significantly advanced by research and publishing from consulting firms. Many firms handed out books to clients as readily as proposals and copies of PowerPoint presentations. Several firms established their own magazines or practitioner-oriented management journals in order to better control the distribution of their own ideas—*The McKinsey Quarterly*, Booz-Allen's *Strategy and Business*, Accenture's *Outlook*, and Cap Gemini Ernst & Young's *Perspectives on Business Innovation* are notable examples of this phenomenon.

In several cases, the strategy of gaining thought leadership efforts has paid off handsomely. The Index Group (later acquired by CSC) and Ernst & Young (later acquired by Cap Gemini), for example, published research on reengineering in the early days of that movement,[4] and they grew their consulting practices substantially as a result. Several firms (including Accenture and PwC Consulting, now part of IBM) published books, articles, and research reports on enterprise systems, which proved particularly lucrative for systems integration consultants. Early books on e-commerce by McKinsey consultants were also accompanied by success for that firm in e-commerce strategy consulting.

Objectives of Internal Research

Most large consulting firms, including the spin-offs of accounting firms, large strategy firms, and the consulting arms of big IT hardware vendors, now have active research groups and research programs. Smaller firms and solo practitioner firms, usually formed by business academics or gurus, also do some research and publishing of thought leadership issues. The least likely firms to undertake research are medium-sized firms not known for their conceptual bent. Firms with a primary focus on outsourcing (e.g., EDS) have not generally pursued research and thought leadership. However, this may change as outsourcing firms seek to demonstrate through research their deep understanding of the business processes to be outsourced and, thereby, gain a competitive advantage.

Consulting firms want to accomplish two primary objectives when undertaking a research initiative. The first can be characterized as marketing or brand-building; the second involves the development of new services. Marketing-driven research seeks to persuade a broad range of potential clients that a particular firm has the best and most leading-edge ideas in a particular domain. It involves publishing research in prestigious management journals and books so as to enhance both the firm's and the individual consultant's image. The intention is generally that clients will see a particular book or article and then contact the consulting firm for assistance. This contact may lead to a major contract or just to a workshop presentation or informal discussion of the ideas.

To aid in this process, firms often advertise their published works to potential clients—particularly books—in order to increase the likelihood that clients will notice it. Firms also work with publishers to market their books. Firms may also publish excerpts from books or articles in their own magazines and journals. Consultants who author books will go on book tours or speak at conferences about their ideas.

Since brand-building research is primarily aimed at benefiting the firm in general, it does not necessarily require the firm to develop extensive capabilities to deliver the particular service described in the research publication. For example, Bob Thomas of Accenture and Warren Bennis recently published a book entitled *Geeks and Geezers*, a study of leaders under thirty and over seventy.[5] Accenture does not have a leadership development consulting practice, but the firm sponsored and collaborated on the research to improve its brand image and to demonstrate to client executives that it is well-informed about leadership issues. The marketing value of the book was increased by teaming consultant Thomas with academic Bennis, who is a well-known expert on leadership, and by publishing it with the Harvard Business School Press. Accenture sent the book to many senior client executives, and also the firm uses it internally for leadership development—a "fringe benefit" of a marketing-oriented work.

The second major objective of research at consulting firms is to arm its consultants with new ideas for their specific consulting practices. We call this objective "service development," where the aim is to create new services for clients. Research undertaken primarily for service development may also be externally published in books or articles in order to attract clients.

Service development research has different attributes from that designed for marketing purposes. It begins largely with new ideas for internal use, leading then to consultant training and perhaps later to new concepts that can be discussed with clients or used in project presentations. It need not be based on empirical evidence but must only be logical and persuasive. It is more likely to be derived from an analysis of the firm's leading-edge consulting engagements in terms of what worked or didn't work.

When successful, research for service development can lead to a series of client engagements. If a researcher documents the consulting work and the results from it, the service development activity can lead to publishable research that's useful for marketing purposes. Recent best-selling books from consultants at the Gallup Organization—*First, Break All the Rules* and *Now, Discover Your Strengths*—are examples of work arising from client activity; it began as service development and migrated to become effective marketing vehicles.[6]

But service development research is difficult to orchestrate. By the time the research is completed, a variety of other capabilities need to be put in place. Consultants must be trained on how to sell and deliver the work. Marketing materials must be created to persuade clients to buy the service. If the client hears of the idea and wants help implementing it, the organization has to be ready to deliver. The "rollout" activities are similar to those a product-oriented company must perform when introducing a new product.

Attributes of Consulting Research

The research and "thought leadership" that emanates from consulting firms is substantially different from that offered by most business school academics. Whereas academics emphasize testable hypotheses and empirical results, the emphasis of consulting research is on relevance to the daily concerns of managers, new and interesting messages, and easy-to-understand research approaches.

Consulting research is generally much more relevant than rigorous. Clients do not generally demand a high degree of empirical evidence or scientific rigor. Indeed, the presence of statistical models or in-depth discussions of research methods in a consultant's article or book practically guarantees that it will have little impact on practicing managers. Consultants find little utility in confirming someone else's hypothesis or examining a well-understood topic with greater precision or rigor. Rather, the focus is on exploration of "new" and attention-getting ideas.

In 1999, for example, consultant Michael Wolf (then of Booz Allen, now of McKinsey) published a book called *The Entertainment Economy*, which describes how "all consumer businesses are going to have to be partly about entertainment in order to be noticed in the increasingly crowded marketplace."[7] The book supplies no rigorous data to support this hypothesis but is replete with relevant factoids, anecdotes, and percentages. It's an interesting read and surely helped to persuade Booz Allen's clients that their consultants (or at least Wolf) understood the entertainment business and its spillover into other industries. The only problem, of course, is that Wolf didn't necessarily remain at Booz Allen long enough for the firm to reap the returns on its investment in thought leadership.

Consulting research focuses on new and innovative ideas, but little is entirely new in the world of business and management. As one consulting industry researcher puts it, "Knowledge constitutes credible stories about the world."[8] Every idea owes a considerable debt to related ideas that came before. However, for purposes of marketing an idea, it may be desirable at times to emphasize its novelty, or at least the more novel components of the idea. For example, a consultant who writes and speaks about customer relationship management (CRM) might justifiably neglect older ideas, like getting to know the customer, and devote more attention to relatively new tools for increasing sales force productivity. In doing so, the firm creates its specialized version of how to implement "CRM" and perhaps creates a new practice focusing on the sales force.

Since consultants prefer to focus on new and emerging ideas, clients may not be fully aware of them. Therefore, it's often difficult to conduct empirical research on how the ideas have been implemented in real organizations. The only option may be to advance stories of how a particular leading-edge organization has implemented the idea and received benefit from it. It's common, then, for consultants to employ case studies in their research. Most published materials use the case studies as examples, not conclusive proof, of an idea's worth.

Where a business idea already has some recognition in the marketplace, surveys are also frequently employed as a research approach by consulting firms. These are particularly useful in getting press mentions about timely (if not deep) research, e.g., ". . . more than 60 percent said there was no fad this year [for the 2002 Christmas season]."[9] Although such surveys are typically not very rigorous in terms of sampling and analysis, they can be helpful in pointing out that organizations do have a particular problem and in convincing clients that a new approach is needed.

Organizational Approaches to Consulting Research

We know of three different ways to organize research within a firm. Some consulting firms approach research in an *organic* and informal fashion. Nonspecialist, line consultants do research in their spare or non-billable time. Senior consultant/researchers not only publish articles and books but also lead consulting practices in the domains about which they write. This approach typifies—in part at least—McKinsey & Company. At that firm, a senior partner such as Lowell Bryan (author of *Race for the World* and *Bankrupt*[10]) might meet with a client in the morning, review chargeability of consultants in his banking practice in the afternoon, and work on his book at night. At Bain, thought leaders such as Chris Zook (author of *Profit from the Core*[11]) and Darrell Rigby (author of Bain's "Management Tools and Techniques" surveys[12]) are also leaders of consulting practices. This "renaissance" approach to consulting research and publication requires that the firms pursuing it hire and promote talented consultants with exceptional conceptual and writing ability. This strategy is inherently limited, since it is not easy to find consultants who are good at the overall combination of research, writing, client service, and practice management.

Another alternative is to employ *specialist* researchers, often located in a somewhat separate organization, to do research and publishing. For example, in 1994, Ernst & Young's consulting practice (now part of Cap Gemini) formed the Center for Information Technology and Strategy (later renamed the Center for Business Innovation). Ernst & Young located the Center in Boston and hired several individuals to staff it who had done business research in either business schools or consulting firms in the past. The members of this group did not have day-to-day consulting responsibilities or targets for chargeable time. Instead, they were expected to write books, articles, and working papers; to hold workshops for visiting clients; to give presentations at clients and conferences; and to create and manage multi-client research programs. This Center was probably a good investment for the firm, because it pioneered approaches to business process reengineering (*Process Innovation*), knowledge management (*Working Knowledge*), and complexity theory (*Blur*) that clearly differentiated Ernst & Young in the consulting marketplace and brought it additional revenues. However, in late 2002, Cap Gemini Ernst & Young announced that it was closing the Center in a very difficult economic environment for consulting.

Just as many businesses find it difficult to take new products to market that have been developed by a separate organization; consulting firms experience the same difficulty when line consultants don't develop new ideas. A separate organization may create high-quality research, but consultants may not become aware of it or use it in their work. For consultants to employ research, they must either be conceptually oriented to begin with or have an understanding of how to use ideas to sell and deliver consulting work.

A third alternative to organizing research involves the use of external researchers—outsourcing to another organization or more typically to business school professors. For example, the Economist Intelligence Unit has performed research for consulting firms on various topics, but since any EIU reports usually bear their brand name, the marketing benefits for a consulting firm may be minimized.

Contracting with professors for research was widespread in the 1980s but became less popular thereafter for a variety of reasons:

- As firms realized the branding advantages of publishing their own research, they wanted to rely less on publications authored by non-employees;

- Business school professors have limitations on how much work they can do outside of the university (usually one day per week);

- Business school professors often prefer to do and publish research that is more rigorous and less relevant than that preferred by consulting firms;

- The most popular professors had little leftover capacity for new relationships with consulting firms, and exclusive relationships with them became very expensive.

It is still the case that many consulting firms work with individual professors on research projects, and they also coauthor publications with professors. It is rare, however, for a large consulting firm to contract out all aspects of a research initiative to outsiders. During the 1990s, most large consulting firms attempted to build their own internal capabilities rather than outsourcing them to professors or outside research firms.

External Versus Internal Funding for Consulting Research

How is research funded in consulting firms? There are three primary approaches, with the most common one being for the firm itself to absorb the cost. Many consulting firms view research and thought leadership as a necessary investment in marketing and competitive differentiation. They either support the research activities of consultants when they are not engaged in client work, or they pay for the activities of a small number of research specialists, as described in the previous section. To our knowledge, most firms who support research do not attempt to rigorously measure the return on their investment. While no precise expenditure figures are available, we know of several firms that spend between 1 and 2 percent of revenues on research and thought leadership. However, this percentage has been slipping in the current difficult economic times.

Perhaps the second most common approach—though its prevalence varies widely across firms—is to fund research through the contributions of multiple clients. The so-called "multi-client program" has a long history in consulting. We believe it was originally established by the Diebold Group, an IT planning and strategy firm that flourished in the 1970s and 1980s. These research programs offer consulting firms a means not only of financing research but also of producing useful management ideas of high quality.

Multi-client projects are occasionally offered by consulting firms and their research centers; they resemble company-sponsored research centers found in many business schools, such as the Center for Effective Organizations at the University of Southern California. These projects bring together a number of companies that are willing to pay (typically a few tens of thousands of dollars) to jointly explore a particular topic. The program may address a single topic for a specified time period, or it may sponsor research on multiple topics on a continuing basis. For researchers, they provide funding, a set of research sites, and client expectations that useful and stimulating ideas will be produced.

In the 1990s, such topics as the balanced scorecard, value disciplines, business process reengineering, and knowledge management were significantly shaped by multi-client research programs. For example, a research project that led to reengineering was called "Managing Cross-Functional Systems," which was a single topical focus in a ten-year multi-client program at the Index Group (later CSC Index) and Hammer & Company. The specific project on cross-functional systems uncovered several interesting stories about companies who were using IT to redesign cross-functional processes, and this provided the germ that led to the best-sellers *Process Innovation* and *Reengineering the Corporation.*

The final possibility for funding is from individual clients. Most clients of consulting firms, of course, want consulting rather than research. But occasionally clients realize that they don't understand some aspect of their business and competitive environments, and so they commission a research study. McKinsey, for example, researched the causes of problems in rescuing the World Trade Center terrorism victims (as a *pro bono* study). Xerox hired consultant/researchers at Ernst & Young to find examples of how organizations had redesigned their business processes around documents. A regional development organization in Japan hired Accenture to research networked organizations and their implications for how these organizations select their office and plant sites.

Sometimes, research developed for a single client can also be useful for other purposes. At other times, the research is on too narrow a topic to be of more general use. Consultants should strive to be aware of the research conducted for clients and, where possible, attempt to transform it into ideas that are useful for the firm's marketing and service development.

Consultants as Thought Leaders

Consultants are in an ideal position to contribute to knowledge about management—they work on leading edge issues and are exposed to a variety of industries and companies. They are also highly educated; at many firms, even the average management consultant has an MBA from a leading business school; and those who work in consulting R&D groups are often former business school professors with Ph.D.s. Since they make money solving real-world business problems, the research that emerges from them is likely grounded in practice and highly relevant to managers.

These potential generators of knowledge also face constraints. Successful consultants may be too busy serving clients and making money to become a guru. In most firms, the act of doing and publishing research may be tolerated, but only if it doesn't interfere with client work.

Finally, in their zeal to market ideas, consultants may sometimes cross the line into inappropriate business practices. It is clear, for example, that some CSC Index consultants or affiliates inappropriately manipulated the *New York Times* best-selling book list to ensure that their book (*The Discipline of Market Leaders*[13]) made the list.

One consultant whose ideas have helped to benefit Bain is Fred Reichheld with his books, *The Loyalty Effect* and *Loyalty Rules!* [14] These books describe how companies that practice loyalty-based management—to customers, employees, and shareholders—outperform their competitors. Reichheld's role at Bain, however, illustrates some of the difficulties that practicing consultants face when attempting to become experts or gurus. He wrote his first book while leading Bain's consulting practice on loyalty management. He then decided, however, that it was too difficult to do research, write, and speak while remaining a full-time consultant. Reichheld was able to persuade Bain's leaders to create a new half-time role called "Bain Fellow." The job allowed him to produce additional publications, to organize seminars for CEOs on loyalty management, and to speak frequently to audiences on the topic. This role takes him out of the managerial hierarchy of Bain, but it enables him to maintain a mutually beneficial relationship with Bain.

Another type of consultant we label the "academic refugee." These individuals have attributes of both consultant and academic. Most were academics at an early stage in their careers, but they no longer bother much with undergraduate or MBA teaching or committee work. Instead, they've developed organizations—typically quite small—focused around their own reputations. They give presentations to executives, do some high-profile consulting engagements, and write books and articles. Examples of this genre include Stan Davis, Gary Hamel, Michael Hammer, Geoffrey Moore, David Maister, and Alvin Toffler.

Jim Collins, author of the best-selling *Good to Great* and coauthor of *Built to Last*, is another example of a former academic who now runs his own show. As an academic at Stanford Business School, Collins won teaching awards and collaborated with Jerry Porras on the highly successful book *Built to Last*. But he felt that the academic environment wasn't advancing his work:

> The work Jerry Porras and I did on Built to Last *did not fit squarely into the type of research generally favored at Stanford. I've often said, only partly tongue in cheek, that we succeeded largely in spite of Stanford, not because of Stanford. The late John Gardner challenged me to not fall into the trap of "answering questions of increasing irrelevance with increasing precision." So, I decided to become an entrepreneurial professor, rather than a professor of entrepreneurship. I formed my own management research laboratory, where I could work on big-scale research projects on whatever topics interested me. In effect, I became a self-employed professor, endowed my own chair, and granted myself tenure.* [15]

THOUGHT LEADERSHIP AT THREE LARGE CONSULTING FIRMS

Accenture

Accenture, formerly Andersen Consulting, specializes in implementation of information systems for its clients. It also has a large practice involving the outsourcing of IT and other business processes. Most Accenture partners do not engage in research and thought leadership activities, but the company devotes substantial energy to research as a specialist practice.

Accenture has three primary research organizations that carry out the bulk of its research. Technology research is performed by Accenture Technology Labs, the largest of the research groups, which has facilities in Sophia Antipolis in France, Chicago, and Palo Alto. Members of the Labs, most of whom have doctorates in computer science, undertake a variety of activities.

- They conduct research on emerging technologies; the primary technologies currently being explored are sensors, radio frequency identification (RFID) devices, and approaches to generating insights from information;

- A Technology Awareness Group within the Labs educates Accenture personnel about emerging technologies that may become important to the organization's work;

- Researchers develop "demos" of technologies to show clients new technological and business capabilities; one popular recent demo, for example, was the "Automated Medicine Cabinet," which kept track of a consumer's vital signs, reminded him to take his medicine, and presented personalized Internet health information;

- Labs researchers who conduct client workshops and give presentations;

- Some researchers occasionally publish technical papers.

Accenture's London-based Corporate Policy and Affairs organization has a small group that also conducts research. Its specialty is regional and policy studies, which is intended almost exclusively to add to Accenture's image rather than to be used in consulting work. In recent years, the group has performed research on the role of the Internet and electronic commerce in Europe, leadership, entrepreneurship, and how companies can plan for the upturn in the economy. It also works closely with groups that facilitate the exchange of ideas across business and government leaders, such as the World Economic Forum.

The Institute for Strategic Change, based in Cambridge, Massachusetts, is another small group of researchers at Accenture; its mission is primarily to create business innovation and thought leadership, although a large proportion of its research also involves the business application of IT. This group works with clients in workshops and presentations and sometimes produces internally published reports for use by consultants with clients (e.g., a recent series on outsourcing issues). However, its program of external publication distinguishes it within Accenture primarily. Over the past several years, for example, the Institute has published several books (including *Mission Critical*, *The Attention Economy*, *Making Markets*, and *Geeks and Geezers*, all with Harvard Business School Press)[16], and articles in *Harvard Business Review*, *MIT Sloan Management Review*, and *California Management Review*. Institute researchers also publish a large proportion of the articles in Accenture's management journal *Outlook*.

McKinsey

McKinsey is known for a strong program of research, in which line consultants and partners perform most of the research and writing. McKinsey partners have authored numerous books over the past several years, including Lowell Bryan, Ed Michaels, John Hagel (now an independent consultant), Jon Katzenbach (now head of Katzenbach Partners), and others. Since the outstanding success of *In Search of Excellence,* partners and consultants have been encouraged to do research and publish it in external outlets as well as in McKinsey's own journal, *McKinsey Quarterly.*

McKinsey also has a specialized research organization, which employs specialist researcher/consultants. The McKinsey Global Institute is based in Washington, D.C., where its researchers primarily conduct economic studies intended to increase the firm's visibility and enhance its quality image. In recent years, the Institute has completed highly useful research on international variations in service sector productivity, the productivity of capital investment across companies, and the productivity benefits of IT across different industries. The Institute generally releases its results to the business press and publishes articles in the *McKinsey Quarterly.*

McKinsey has also for the past decade hired a relatively small number of researcher/consultant specialists to advance thought leadership in their domains and to inject it into consulting activities with clients. These specialists have included Tom Copeland, a finance expert and author of a leading book on corporate valuation,[17] and Frank Ostroff, author of *The Horizontal Organization.*[18] While these specialists have succeeded in carrying out research and getting it published, it is not always highly rewarded in McKinsey by promotion to partner or senior partner.[19] These rewards mainly go to those who sell the most work and please the most clients.

IBM Global Services

Despite its large size (over $40 billion in services revenues in 2002), IBM Global Services has historically undertaken a relatively small amount of research and thought leadership activity. This may be because of its strong focus on outsourcing and systems integration—areas in which research is less likely to be undertaken than in traditional consulting. A few initiatives are underway, however, and IBM recently announced that it will spend $1 billion (unheard-of numbers in consulting research) to create a new business unit called "On-Demand Innovation Services."[20] The group will seek to provide services from over 200 scientists in IBM's existing research organizations (typically not business researchers, but rather experts in computing, mathematics, materials science, etc.) to clients of IBM's Business Consulting Services.

This move has some precedent. IBM's renowned Watson Labs, for example, did perform early research on "e-business" issues. There are also other sources of e-business research in IBM; in 2000, for instance, the consulting arm of Global Services acquired an e-commerce strategy and research firm called Mainspring. After being acquired by IBM, Mainspring's employees continued to do research and eventually formed the Institute for Business Value, which today focuses on issues related to the economics of information technology. Most of the outputs of this Institute are internally published reports.

Another IBM research group, the Institute for Knowledge-Based Organizations (originally the Institute for Knowledge Management) does research in the area of knowledge and its management within organizations. It has primarily operated as a multi-client program, with annual funding from clients. The Institute has produced a book on managing social capital entitled *In Good Company.*[21] It also produces a regular journal, *Knowledge Directions,* and it has published articles in *Harvard Business Review* and *MIT Sloan Management*

Review. The Institute has recently been restructured to become a sub-unit of the Institute for Business Value.

Other Research-Oriented Firms

Many other consulting organizations produce a considerable body of research, including Bain, Boston Consulting Group, Booz Allen, Deloitte Consulting, Concours Group, Mercer Management Consulting, and others. Despite the current downturn in the consulting marketplace, these firms continue to start and complete research programs and publish results. Little doubt remains that research and thought leadership will continue to flow from these firms. As long as clients seek differentiation and new ideas from their consultants, research will continue to be an important aspect of the industry.

PART II: KNOWLEDGE SHARING IN CONSULTING

Once research from a groundbreaking client engagement is completed and new knowledge has been created, it becomes a proper subject for knowledge sharing. That is, it needs to be codified, distributed, refined, and used like any other piece of knowledge. Knowledge management and creation, then, can form a virtuous cycle. Good knowledge creation provides new content for knowledge sharing, and good knowledge sharing points out specific needs for additional knowledge creation. Certainly the best-managed firms today will have serious initiatives for both knowledge creation and sharing underway.

Recent History of Knowledge Sharing

When the knowledge management movement first gathered steam in the early 1990s, only McKinsey was known for its attempts to manage knowledge in a somewhat formal way. Tom Peters gave his former employer's efforts a huge boost by devoting a chapter to them in his best-selling *Liberation Management*, which, to our knowledge, was the first published discussion of knowledge management in the industry.[22] By the mid-1990s, McKinsey's knowledge manager, Brook Manville, began giving talks at knowledge management conferences. Not wanting to be left behind, other firms quickly followed suit. They either rapidly built new knowledge management systems from scratch, rebranded their former information systems as knowledge systems, or installed various "groupware" systems and called it knowledge management. Soon Accenture (then Andersen Consulting), Ernst & Young, CSC, Booz Allen, Price Waterhouse, Arthur D. Little, and KPMG were all touting their various knowledge systems. Their central message to clients was clear: "By hiring our firm with a state-of-the-art knowledge system, you the client will receive the benefit of gaining access to the whole firm's pool of collective expertise." As one researcher noted, "The firm must show that it is capable of synthesizing its experience and bringing the result to the client. . . . The firm must demonstrate the power of its collective knowledge base."[23]

All major consulting firms now seek to make their own knowledge, in some form or another, available internally as a stimulus to produce new approaches toward clients. After all, as two researchers recently stated, "Consultancies actually derive most, if not all, of their knowledge from client firms."[24] This is really just being efficient with resources. Consulting firms spend a great amount of their resources on human capital development, and making better use of this sunk cost's output makes good business sense. This work can also be seen as making the firms' internal markets for knowledge more efficient, enabling consultant "buyers" and "sellers" to find one another more easily.

A less obvious motivation for firms to embrace knowledge management is that it promotes the value of collaboration within the firm's culture. Consulting firms rely on teams to work together effectively in performing projects, so all internal systems, such as knowledge management, need to support and reinforce teamwork.

Two Approaches to Sharing Knowledge

The roads to sharing knowledge within consulting organizations are varied and many. The knowledge management movement itself is perhaps best seen as a broad collection of policies, practices, and methods that are applied in situation specific ways. Firms pick and choose from a diverse set those elements they feel will best "fit" their organizations. However, at this point in time, we can identify two common emerging "models" of practices that distinguish between firms whose client service offerings lean toward detailed technology work and other firms with less structured strategy and organization work. While some firms try to encompass both these models (e.g., Booz Allen and Accenture), most firms lean in one direction or another.

It's undeniably true that consulting firms whose outputs tend to be more technology focused are more oriented to sharing knowledge that is codified and structured. It may be software code, process designs, or system specifications. Some of this knowledge also takes the form of client or research reports, which can look similar to engineering documents. Another form of codified knowledge common to these firms are methodologies—complex and structured methods for performing such tasks as building or installing a new information system or implementing an enterprise-wide change management program. These methods are usually constructed as "living documents" or "dynamic systems" in that they can be modified by practitioners based on what is learned during an engagement.

In the second model, the more strategy-focused firms reflect a clear difference in comparison to the technology-focused firms. The strategy firms use knowledge sharing systems intended as much to locate an individual with a particular expertise as to locate a document. In one empirical study of knowledge use in a large, global consulting firm, researchers discovered that even though the firm had a large document system, the primary value lay elsewhere: ". . . the use of the database was limited. It was mainly used as a vehicle for finding the right people."[25] The work in strategic consulting is more unstructured and contextual to the client, but knowledge sharing here is just as valuable. For these firms, the most valuable form of sharing is face-to-face (or at least voice-to-voice) meetings, rather than reading a document.

Within all firms, both exchanging documents and meeting face-to-face to share knowledge are key aspects of knowledge management. However, the systems of the technology firms are usually designed to be document focused and are recorded in writing. In contrast, the strategy-oriented firms offer verbal communication links—audio and video connections between consultants—to facilitate discussion and meetings. Interestingly, the integration of face-to-face meetings into knowledge management systems is increasing with the adoption of new technologies. Web-based conferences or "Webinars," for example, are being used in firms to inform and educate consultants on new topics. Some firms, including McKinsey, are capturing video clips of expert consultants and storing them in repositories to augment documents.

KNOWLEDGE SHARING AT THREE LARGE CONSULTING FIRMS

Before proceeding further, we think it useful to provide a snapshot of the ongoing knowledge sharing systems at the same three highly successful firms profiled earlier: IBM, McKinsey, and Accenture. These firms are large, global, and early adopters of knowledge management systems. They are also fairly representative of the two types of firms we have just discussed, with IBM on the technology side, McKinsey on the strategy side, and Accenture attempting to cover both bases.

Accenture

Accenture was an early adopter of knowledge management, creating both its strategy for knowledge creating and sharing and its central repository for knowledge management in the early 1990s. The beginning knowledge management effort at Andersen Consulting (Accenture) was part of its overall business strategy. In 1991, a strategy task force, called "Horizon 2000," was formed to identify how Andersen could continue its strong growth and overall success. One outcome of this effort was called the "Knowledge Exchange Strategy," and the system for implementing it came to be called the Knowledge Xchange system. It was seen as contributing to Andersen's competitive advantage, described in this way in an internal strategy document:

> Our primary program to establish sustainable differentiation in tomorrow's marketplace is the Knowledge Exchange. It is designed to leverage the skills, knowledge, and experience of the individual with the cumulative knowledge and reusable experiences of the global community of Andersen Consulting, connected electronically and culturally. It is the collective empowerment of the individual.[26]

The same strategy document also proposed a new organizational capability within Andersen:

> We will establish "Knowledge Management" as a new function within Andersen Consulting. Key responsibilities will be to ensure the leading edge currency of our knowledge capital, and to keep the Knowledge Exchange demand driven rather than supply driven.

This strategy, accompanied by strong support from the firm's CEO, proved to be largely successful in the eyes of the firm's leadership, helping to support growth throughout the 1990s. The system's success was attributed to three factors: a large number of capable knowledge managers, a knowledge-sharing culture, and a good fit with Accenture's business model.

Accenture's knowledge staff is largely distributed. Each industry group and service line has its own set of knowledge managers. Some are primarily technology-focused; others address content structure and taxonomy issues; while others help to create new content. Although the technology used for knowledge sharing is the same around the firm (originally Lotus Notes and, more recently, a combination of Notes and multiple Web portals), all other approaches to knowledge management vary across the organizational structure. In the recent difficult economic environment for consulting, Accenture has reduced the number of knowledge managers (though there are still more than 300), and some parts of the organization are employing offshore knowledge management services in India and the Philippines.

Employees of Accenture tend to share knowledge readily, rather than hoarding it. New employees are selected, in part, on the basis of their willingness to share what they know. The company has for many years been managed as one global organization with little attention to geographic boundaries. Accenture's earlier roots in Arthur Andersen caused it to be conditioned to Andersen's "one firm" culture that facilitated sharing.[27]

Although the majority of Accenture's work involves some form of IT implementation, it does not subscribe purely to a codification and document-based knowledge management system. Accenture also has a substantial strategy practice (at one point described as second in size to McKinsey in the consulting industry) as well as a variety of process consulting practices that involve CRM and supply-chain management. As a result, the firm makes extensive use of face-to-face contacts at meetings of various types as well as at its educational campus in St. Charles, Illinois. A strong effort is made by Accenture's management to enhance knowledge transfer among locally based social networks and office-based community groups.

Accenture recently was named to the "Most Admired Knowledge Enterprises (MAKE) Hall of Fame" by the research firm Telos for appearing in the MAKE top ten list for five consecutive years. However, it may be difficult for Accenture to maintain its leading role in knowledge management. The growth of both Accenture and the consulting industry have slowed considerably, and as a publicly held firm (Accenture went public in 2001), investments in internal capabilities are subject to the scrutiny of shareholders and investment analysts. The company also faces a difficult transition from Lotus Notes technology to that provided by Microsoft, a joint venture partner of Accenture.

IBM Global Services

Knowledge Management efforts began in IBM Global Services in 1994 as a corporate sponsored reengineering initiative with two major drivers. The first was to supply the knowledge and information for a new services business model being developed within IBM. The service business, although not entirely new to IBM, was growing rapidly and becoming quite complex; it contained four major lines of business: consulting, systems integration, outsourcing, and other IT services. The second driver was a growing and changing workforce composed of new services professionals who had to deliver a consistent set of services worldwide. Their work often took place in non-IBM locations with limited access to the IBM infrastructure. They might have little or no direct access to subject matter experts located elsewhere.

The challenges were immense, as existing systems at IBM were geared to its product hardware and software business. Earlier attempts to improve knowledge sharing had consisted of purely technological initiatives by creating databases as repositories of "knowledge." With little content management or control, these repositories soon became dumping grounds and, as a result, were minimally effective. The new response, under the leadership of CEO Lou

Gerstner, was a more integrated approach addressing various components of the business that needed to change in order to support a knowledge-based business. These components included a combination of company vision, values, management processes, roles and responsibilities, and incentives.

A new knowledge sharing system was created around communities of practice, referred to internally as knowledge networks. The networks had two key goals: establishing a community and collecting and sharing intellectual capital (usually documents and methods) pertaining to a specific knowledge domain, such as SAP implementation. These communities were defined as global communities of consultants stretching across organizational boundaries. Every effort was made to ensure that the core team of each network had representation from each line of business and geography. A standardized database with workflow capabilities was provided to each network.

This decentralized community-based approach proved more effective than the previous centralized repository approach. One benefit is that it eliminated the need to create large staffs to manage content. More importantly, the services professionals were the people best able to review the submissions. Later, as the demands of users overwhelmed the ability of "volunteers" to handle the volume of enquiries, it became necessary to augment the community core teams with a dedicated staff, composed of content managers and knowledge brokers.

Not surprisingly, because of the mobile and dispersed nature of the workforce, technology became the critical enabler to the system. It was not possible to employ any out-of-the-box solutions because the size and complexity of IBM required massive changes in any standardized system. So the firm decided to build from scratch a "Knowledge Web."

As content grew, overload again became a problem, suggesting the possible need for a "central model." However, IBM stayed with its decentralized model of communities, which could establish their own taxonomies (categories, subcategories, and type of documents). The reason was clear—every community had its own shared context and vocabulary. Any formal central taxonomy could scarcely address each individual community's needs. Therefore, while the community spaces all have consistent navigation and layout, the content definition is unique.

Addressing measurements and incentives is also an ongoing effort. Measurements take two forms—activity and survey. Activity-based measurements track such data as the number of users and user activities (e.g., the number of reads, updates, submissions, etc.). This provides insight into participation but doesn't indicate the value to the practitioners or the business itself. Surveys of consultants measure the indirect financial contributions of knowledge, such as time saved, impact on win/loss ratio, etc. Knowledge managers have also tried to document increased revenue from the use of knowledge based on success stories. Additional benefits tend to be more "intangible," such as shorter delivery cycles and increased levels of client satisfaction. These benefits tend to be circulated through "stories" when consultants get together.

IBM Global Services' knowledge management system, like any widely used system, is in continuous evolution. IBM has spent over $60 million on it since its inception. Even in a difficult business environment, knowledge management still has a strong base of support. Its mission has remained steady—to provide consultants with tools, usually in the form of documents and methods, with which to increase the efficiency and effectiveness of their work.

McKinsey & Company

As we mentioned earlier, McKinsey became identified early on with knowledge management, and the firm has striven to keep up with this reputation. It has invested over $85 million in knowledge systems since 1999. One of McKinsey's most frequently stated aims is to bring the firm's collective expertise—widely considered to be a critical resource—to bear on a client's specific issues. However, as McKinsey grew geographically and introduced new practices, its traditional approach of using personal networks to transfer knowledge was no longer so effective. As a result, McKinsey's recent focus on improved knowledge sharing, though small by IBM or Accenture standards, has grown in technological capability.

Three specific themes characterize McKinsey's upgraded approach. The first is using multiple media formats to create "context-rich" documents. These contain audio and video clips that convey an important idea, including explanations and commentary by the persons or groups that developed the idea. These clips are further enhanced by full-text additions and attachments. The firm also conducts knowledge audits within each practice area. A typical audit reviews the practice's codified knowledge, identifies the practice's most important knowledge, and "tags" documents with abstracts as well as metadata about the author(s), publication dates, media formats, and quality indicators. This audit process and the ongoing maintenance associated with it help to identify important sources of tacit knowledge, suggest knowledge development agendas, and create new "families" of documents and experts.

McKinsey also has an extensive network of people who facilitate knowledge sharing at the firm, including extensive knowledge centers in India and in North America. Individuals with formal knowledge sharing roles include "First Alerts" who answer questions, guide consultants to appropriate experts and documents, and generally act as "intelligent switches"; practice experts who are senior consultants with deep experience (e.g., on specific frameworks and processes); and, of course, consulting teams who develop expertise from working with clients. In addition, McKinsey has nearly 1,000 professionals worldwide who provide research support to consultants.

Given its highly matrixed organization, McKinsey is highly dependent on their consultants' goodwill and mutual trust to make this type of knowledge sharing system effective. The firm's output for clients is often in the form of "strategic insights," which are influenced by the knowledge "fusion" produced by individual consultants and teams working on a client issue.

Forthcoming Issues in Knowledge Management

So what does all this tell us about what is going on in knowledge management, from both the creating and sharing perspectives, within consulting firms, and what can we learn from it? We believe that consultants should think carefully about the following issues before changing or undertaking knowledge management strategies.

Commoditization of expertise. As firms put more and more emphasis on embedding their expertise within their client offerings, the risk grows that clients will seek to reduce their costs by just buying "reengineering on a disc" (as one real product was so-called) from a vendor. Some major firms (including Ernst & Young and Arthur Andersen) have experimented with selling knowledge apart from consulting hours, but thus far, clients have shown little interest in these services. Over the long term, however, separating knowledge from individuals can have a deleterious effect on a firm's (or industry's) business and pricing model.

No time or space for reflection. In order for a document or method to be "dynamic" and reflect the current state of practice, practitioners need to be given time and space in which to reflect on their experiences, discuss them in groups, and record them. Asking consultants to do this in some fictional "spare" or downtime gives the message that the activity is not important, and it reduces the quality of the firm's codified knowledge.

Metrics and measures. Without some reliable way to measure a system's real value to its users (rather than just incenting the contributors), knowledge management systems are exposed to the risk of cutbacks or cancellations. When the measures are too simple, they can become counterproductive and lead people to game the system. Unfortunately, we have rarely seen users systematically surveyed or interviewed regarding just how valuable the system's input was to their work.

Knowledge productivity. A common assumption behind firms with technology-based knowledge systems is that knowledge codified is knowledge multiplied. These firms believe that for knowledge to be productive within the firm, it needs to be codified, reproduced, and distributed. This assumption is at best only partly correct. While some forms of knowledge such as methods, systems documentation, and competitive analysis may be easily documented, other forms are much more difficult to structure and codify, such as how to deal with difficult clients or complex situations, how to enter new and unique markets, and coping with cultural intangibles. These issues require critical consulting skills, yet their documentation can easily prove elusive and oversimplified. Knowing what to codify and in what form is a key step in McKinsey's knowledge management design.

Compliance. Systems such as these are dependent on the consultant contributors working voluntarily within the knowledge system. This, in turn, depends on either the goodwill of the contributor or incentives and/or threats from the firm's senior management. However, none of these approaches has proven especially effective in eliciting the desired behaviors that ensure the system's success. An interesting alternative to enterprise-wide compliance is to delegate responsibility for knowledge management to various groups or practice units within the firm—assuming, of course, some general guidelines and system support. Since people usually respond more to immediate peer pressure than a remote hierarchy, this seems like a promising road for gaining compliance with knowledge initiatives.

Embedding Knowledge into Work. Although capturing knowledge in central repositories has many advantages, the task of accessing this stored knowledge usually requires skills different from performing normal consulting work. As such, knowledge sharing is sometimes seen primarily as an activity for specialist knowledge managers. But this is expensive and can create barriers between the knowledge manager and consultant. A more desirable approach is to embed knowledge-related activities into mainstream consulting tasks, such as the planning of engagements, the analysis of client strategies and processes, and the development of client deliverables.

Some firms, such as Cap Gemini Ernst & Young and Accenture, have explored "hybrid" roles on projects called "knowledge champions" or "knowledge stewards." These individuals are responsible for ensuring that knowledge is imported from the rest of the firm to benefit a particular engagement and that new knowledge from the engagement is captured and exported. An even more desirable solution would be to develop a "consultant's workstation" that would make knowledge activities automatic, but despite previous experimentation in professional services[28] and in other industries,[29] such an approach has not been broadly implemented in consulting.

Regardless of the approach a firm takes in dealing with these complexities of knowledge creating and sharing, it remains for senior management to signal its importance to employees. The very act of promoting, funding, and implementing knowledge management approaches and systems sends a clear message throughout the firm that knowledge is highly important and needs to be thought about and worked with in new ways. Without this support, even the best systems will fail. Instead, consultants will proceed as they have in past, "making it up as they go," relying upon previous experiences, rumors and anecdotes, intuition, and gut feelings—all rather poor substitutes for well-documented knowledge.

THE NEXT FEW YEARS

Consulting itself is changing, and the knowledge environment for consulting firms will undoubtedly also change. Today, however, there are conflicting directions. Just as IBM announces a major new focus on consulting knowledge creation by its research scientists, Cap Gemini Ernst & Young closes down its Center for Business Innovation. On the knowledge management front, while many consultants cut back their capabilities for financial reasons or send them "offshore" to lower costs, McKinsey initiates an aggressive new program of knowledge management that will attempt to deliver packaged knowledge directly to clients.

Currently, in the early 2000s, the most economically challenged form of consulting is strategy consulting, which has always been heavily focused on knowledge creating and sharing for their clients. Therefore, it is not surprising that several firms in that industry have recently reduced their expenditures on knowledge. Indeed, whether it is because consultants are investing less in creating new knowledge, or because the down economy is providing infertile ground for new ideas to thrive, the early years of this new century have been notable for a dearth of "thought leadership." After the excesses of e-commerce and "the new economy," the clients for innovative ideas may also have become more skeptical about their worth. We believe that strategy consulting will make a comeback, but it will be only the most knowledge-oriented versions of strategy consulting that will prosper. Clients will remain unwilling to pay large fees for inexperienced consultants and will hire only those firms that can demonstrate superior creation and management of business knowledge.

The form of consulting that has grown recently is outsourcing—initially of clients' IT capabilities and increasingly of transaction—intensive business processes of all types. One reason for this trend is that consulting firms are increasingly turning to public ownership, and outsourcing provides a predictable revenue and earnings stream that is valued by investors and analysts. Yet the knowledge orientation for outsourcing remains unclear. We would imagine that clients for business process outsourcing (BPO) would insist that their outsourcers are highly knowledgeable about the specific processes they propose to operate. Thus far, however, process knowledge has not been a primary issue in the evaluation of BPO providers. Perhaps this trend will develop further as the BPO field matures and becomes more competitive.

Certainly, consulting will remain a competitive field overall in which firms need to differentiate themselves. Over the last several decades, the quality of a firm's people was the primary factor that clients used to differentiate between consulting firms. Over the next few years, we expect that clients will focus not only on people but also upon the quality of a firm's knowledge resources. The best firms will not only be those that hire the best MBAs, but those who have the best processes for creating and sharing new knowledge.

Notes to the Chapter

[1]"The main source of knowledge in consulting is experience from projects." Andreas Werr, "The Internal Creation of Consulting Knowledge: A Question of Structuring Experience" in *Management Consulting,* ed. by Matthias Kipping and Lars Engwall (Oxford, UK: Oxford University Press, 2001): 107.

[2]The list of gurus was compiled for the book by Thomas H. Davenport and Laurence Prusak, *What's the Big Idea: Creating and Capitalizing on the Best Management Approaches* (Boston, MA: Harvard Business School Press, 2003).

[3]Thomas J. Peters and Robert H. Waterman, Jr., *In Search of Excellence* (New York: Harper & Row, 1982).

[4]Thomas H. Davenport, *Process Innovation: Reengineering Work through Information Technology* (Boston, MA: Harvard Business School Press, 1993); Michael Hammer and James Champy, *Reengineering the Corporation* (New York: Harper Business, 1993).

[5]Warren G. Bennis and Robert J. Thomas, *Geeks and Geezers: How Era, Values, and Defining Moments Shape Leaders* (Boston, MA: Harvard Business School Press, 2002).

[6]Marcus Buckingham and Curt Coffin, *First, Break All the Rules: What the World's Greatest Managers Do Differently* (New York: Simon & Schuster, 1999); M. Buckingham and Donald O. Clifton, *Now, Discover Your Strengths* (New York: Free Press, 2001).

[7]Michael J. Wolf, *The Entertainment Economy: How Mega-Media Forces Are Transforming Our Lives* (New York: Times Books, 1999): 17.

[8]Karen Legge, "On Knowledge, Business Consultants, and the Selling of Total Quality Management" in *Critical Consulting,* edited by Timothy Clark and Robin Fincham (Oxford, UK: Blackwell's Publishers, 2002): 75.

[9]"Accenture Survey: It Looks Like a 'Fad-Less' Christmas," press release, December 18, 2002.

[10]Lowell L. Bryan et al, *Race for the World: Strategies to Build a Great Global Firm* (Boston, MA: Harvard Business School Press, 1999); L. Bryan, *Bankrupt: Restoring the Health and Vitality of Our Banking System* (New York: HarperCollins, 1992).

[11]Chris Zook with James Allen, *Profit from the Core: Growth Strategy in an Era of Turbulence* (Boston, MA: Harvard Business School Press, 2001).

[12]See, for example, Darrell Rigby, *Management Tools 2001: An Executive's Guide*, report available from Bain and Company or online through Amazon.com.

[13]Michael Treacy and Fred Wiersema, *The Discipline of Market Leaders* (Somerville, MA: Perseus, 1997).

[14]Frederick F. Reichheld, *The Loyalty Effect* (Boston, MA: Harvard Business School Press, 1996); F. Reichheld, *Loyalty Rules: How Leaders Build Lasting Relationships in the Digital Age* (Boston, MA: Harvard Business School Press, 2001).

[15]Telephone interview with Collins by Tom Davenport, June 2002.

[16]Thomas H. Davenport, *Mission Critical: Realizing the Promise of Enterprise Systems* (Boston, MA: Harvard Business School Press, 2000); T. Davenport and John C. Beck, *The Attention Economy* (Boston, MA: Harvard Business School Press, 2001); Ajit Kambil and Eric van Heck, *Making Markets* (Boston, MA: Harvard Business School Press, 2002); Warren G. Bennis and Robert J. Thomas, *Geeks and Geezers* (Boston, MA: Harvard Business School Press, 2002).

[17]Tom Copeland, Tim Koller, and Jack Murrin, *Valuation: Measuring and Managing the Value of Companies,* 2d edition (Hoboken, NJ: Wiley, 1994).

[18]Frank Ostroff, *The Horizontal Organization* (Oxford University Press, 1999).

[19]Some of the issues with the specialist role at McKinsey are described in Christopher Bartlett, "McKinsey and Co.: Managing Knowledge and Learning," Harvard Business School case study, 1996, case #9-396-357.

[20]Joris Evers, "IBM Research to offer consulting services," IDG News Service, November 20, 2002, online at http://www.idg.net.

[21]Don Cohen and Laurence Prusak, *In Good Company: How Social Capital Makes Organizations Work* (Boston, MA: Harvard Business School Press, 2001).

[22]Tom Peters, *Liberation Management* (New York: Knopf, 1992): 382–396.

[23]Milkos Sarvay, "Knowledge Management and Competition in the Consulting Industry, *California Management Review,* 41, no. 2 (Winter 1999): 97.

[24]Lars Engwall and Matthias Kipping, "Management Consulting as a Knowledge Industry," Kipping and Enwall, op. cit., 68.

[25]Werr, op. cit., 103.

[26]Quotations and discussion of the history and strategy for knowledge management at Andersen Consulting/Accenture taken from Thomas H. Davenport and Morten Hansen, "Knowledge Management at Andersen Consulting," Harvard Business School case study, 1998, case #9-499-032.

[27]The "one-firm" firm is described in David Maister, *Managing the Professional Services Firm* (New York: Free Press, 1993): 303–320.

[28]Robert G. Eccles and Julie Gladstone, "KPMG: The Shadow Partner," Harvard Business School case study, 1991, case #9-492-002.

[29]Thomas H. Davenport and John Glaser, "Just in Time Delivery Comes to Knowledge Management," *Harvard Business Review* (July 2002).

Looking Ahead at Management Consulting

INTRODUCTION

Several major trends in the consulting industry, previously discussed in Chapter 1, are causing major changes. In addition, each chapter in this book has also raised additional questions about the future of consulting in its particular area of concern. In this section, two new concerns are considered that bear significantly on what will happen to management consulting: first, the potential threat and opportunity for online consulting to be conducted over the Internet; and second, the need to establish a stronger "scientific" and intellectual foundation from research to gain a better understanding of the consulting process and validate its outcomes.

Chapter 18, "Will Consulting Go Online?," predicts a greater use of remote consulting in place of traditional face-to-face methods for delivering consulting services. It questions the assumption that "trust" is, as many have argued, the pivotal point in all consulting relationships. Rather, the author argues that trust is relatively unimportant in certain types of projects and in certain stages of a project—such as with IT projects or during the data-gathering stage. The Internet is portrayed as becoming more relevant and usable as a consulting tool in situations where trust is less important. Still, the author does not contend that the Internet will replace face-to-face consulting, but rather that it will become an efficient support tool and thereby strengthen many aspects of consulting.

The lack of scientific evidence to document the claims of consultants about their positive impact on clients' performance is the subject of Chapter 19, "Research on Management Consulting." It is striking how much money is spent on consulting when the decisions to hire a consultant are based largely on hearsay. The authors predict that clients, in the future, are likely to demand more concrete evidence of past success than simply relying on the reputation and pronouncements of the consulting firm. Just as important, it is essential for consultants to learn from research about the latest discoveries affecting the practice of management and the consulting process.

Consulting firms and consultants can and should contribute to new knowledge about management, organizations, and industries. Because of the noticeable lack of research on many aspects of consulting, this chapter raises more questions than it answers about what is known concerning the industry and its value to clients. For example, what is the frequency that the real problems of clients are actually solved by consulting interventions, or what types of interventions are likely to lead to what kinds of results? This chapter also examines the practical problems of performing research on consulting and suggests various ways for overcoming these barriers. The recent increase in publications containing research on consulting is seen as a healthy trend that should be strongly supported by consulting firms, clients, trade associations, and academic researchers.

CHAPTER 18

Will Consulting Go Online?

Fiona Czerniawska, Arkimeda

ABOUT THE AUTHOR

Fiona Czerniawska

Fiona Czerniawska is the founder and managing director of Arkimeda, a research firm focusing on strategic issues in the consulting industry. She is also the Director of the UK Management Consultancies Association's Think Tank. Dr. Czerniawska is the author of numerous books and articles on the consulting industry, including *Management Consulting: What Next?*, *Value-Based Consulting*, and *The Intelligent Client*.

IT consulting has been one of the major sources of growth since World War II. Through constant reinvention, IT-related consultancy has shown itself to be remarkably resilient, offering competitive advantages in good times and cost efficiencies in bad. Even as we have moved from e-business boom to bust, IT budgets cut in one area (large-scale systems implementation) have been increased in others (outsourcing). Yet, despite the importance of technology to their clients, consultants have often been unenthusiastic about adopting it for themselves in their own consulting practices. Looking behind the exquisite facades of many consulting firms, most clients would probably be appalled by the inadequate systems used internally for market planning, financial reporting, and project control.

Nowhere is this paradox more apparent than in the reaction of the consulting industry to the idea of online consulting—which involves the provision of consulting services remotely via the Internet—in contrast to the traditional face-to-face method of delivery to clients on site. First raised in the heady days of the dot.com boom, online consulting currently remains almost wholly confined to limited segments of the consulting market, such as provisions made by firms to convey the latest papers by their consultants on their Web sites.

The aim of this chapter is to evaluate whether online consulting has a future. It looks first at the underlying determinants of the client-consultant relationship, which in turn leads to the basic question of whether consultants are correct in assuming that the consulting process must remain essentially a face-to-face phenomenon. Next, I examine the commonly perceived barriers to online consulting, from both the clients' and consultants' points of view, while arguing that online consulting may not only be able to overcome these hurdles, but that it may even offer positive advantages over conventional consulting in certain areas. Finally, the chapter looks to the future and speculates about the form that online consulting will likely take.

DETERMINANTS OF CONSULTANT-CLIENT RELATIONSHIPS

For years, consultants have assumed that trust is everything in determining the quality of both the client relationship and the outcome of an engagement. This assumption of interpersonal trust makes the relationship highly dependent on face-to-face interaction between consultant and client. Indeed, Maister, Green, and Galford have written an entire book on *The Trusted Advisor*. They contend that a consultant, who is intimately familiar with and trusted by the client, is in a better position to provide advice and deliver the hoped-for results. Presumably, in the authors' view, the trusted advisor is more likely to know how to get things done in the client organization and how to negotiate one's way around political sensitivities. The consulting firm also gains, since it is more likely to win additional work if the client trusts the consultant.

But is trust quite so central? Have we overstated its importance? In my view, the potential of online consulting challenges that assumption, suggesting that, under certain conditions, trust is likely to become less important than other factors and thereby opens up opportunities for online consulting.

Trust and Risk

Central to the decline of trust in the consultant-client relationship is the amount of risk inherent in a consulting project. As Maister et. al. point out: "Trust without risk is like cola without fizz; there isn't much point to it. We don't 'trust' the law of gravity, we assume it. If party A trusts that party B will do something, it means that party B could, in fact, do something different and conceivably might do something different. But because of the trusting relationship, the other party most likely won't do something different." So trust and risk are highly interdependent—that is, if there isn't any risk, we don't need to trust anyone.

Therefore, I contend that as the amount of risk declines in a consulting project, so too will the need to build trust through interpersonal contact between consultant and client. And when this happens, the way is then open for online consulting to serve a useful purpose.

Let's first take a look, though, at what determines risk in a consulting project. Three factors, I believe, are critical: 1) the particular stage of a consulting project from start to finish; 2) the amount of fluidity and face-to-face interaction required by the consulting task itself; and 3) the degree of maturity in the marketplace for the particular consulting service being sold.

Stages of a Consulting Project

Risk is not constant throughout the entire duration of a project. As Exhibit 18.1 shows, risk tends to be highest initially during the sales process when the consulting firm seeks to establish its credibility and responsiveness in the eyes of a potentially skeptical client. Risk is also likely to remain high immediately after the contract is signed, because the consultant and client need to jointly establish the scope and specifications of the work to follow. However, when the project moves to what I call the "development" stage (such as the gathering of data, designing a new business process, building a new IT system, or

Exhibit 18.1	Risk and Stage of Project

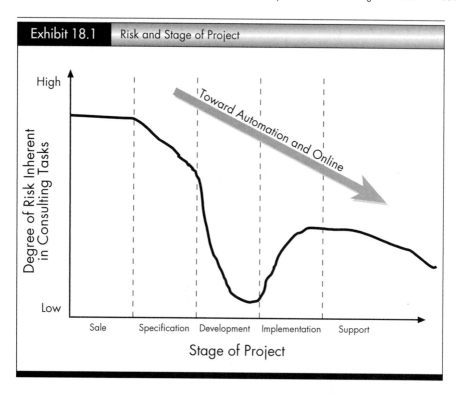

conducting market research), the level of risk begins to fall until toward the end of a project when it rises again as the consultant attempts to influence a reluctant client to take action.

Task Requirements

Besides the evolving stages of a project that affect risk (and therefore the level of trust), another important variable is the nature of the consulting project itself—its task requirements embedded in the type of service being delivered. Exhibit 18.2 portrays requirements stemming from what I call the "fluidity" of the task as it affects the amount of required interaction between consultant and client. The riskiest projects are those where the substantive content is fluid, highly subjective, and the outcomes intangible. Thus, a strategy assignment requires a lot of on-the-feet thinking, or a change management project may only promise initial soft benefits through a training program before enhanced skills lead to higher performance. Less risky is the implementation of a formal and highly programmable IT application. As one can see in Exhibit 18.2, many types of consulting tasks involve less fluidity and less client interaction than others, including market research, employee surveys, and outsourcing.

Of course, every project will vary somewhat in its risk elements; I have placed these types of projects where I see them, but the reader may want to move them about based on personal experience. The point is that a clear difference often exists between projects in their degree of fluidity and hence their level of risk (also meaning trust).

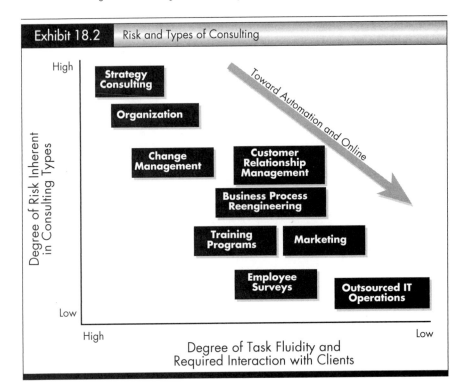

Exhibit 18.2   Risk and Types of Consulting

Consulting projects that are fluid in form and promise to yield intangible results usually require a high degree of interaction where clients need (and want) to become involved in scoping the work, contributing ideas, and validating the conclusions. The greater the amount of required interaction between consultant and client, the greater the possibility for something to go wrong in the relationship, not just right. By contrast, projects that follow a prescribed methodology (especially one where a client is already familiar with its steps and requirements—or the reverse where the client believes him or herself technically unqualified) requires less in the way of client-consultant interaction to perform.

Thus, when required interaction is high, it follows that consultants will need to respond quickly to changing agendas and not be able to control all potential outcomes. Conversely, when interaction is low, consultants can usually follow a set procedure, confident that the expected outcomes are more likely to be realized.

Maturing Market

The final determining factor on level of risk (and hence trust) is the degree of market maturation of a particular consulting service being sold to a client. New and relatively untested services in the market will obviously require more time spent with the client to work out how best to apply the service in practice as well as in convincing stakeholders that there will be a positive return on their investment. In instances of selling a service without a track record, the degree of uncertainty, and consequently, the level of risk, is likely quite high.

As the wider market for a particular consulting service evolves and eventually matures, the level of risk diminishes. More familiar and popular consulting services require a less interactive sales process because clients already believe they are buying a package that appears well received in the market. Those services that contain more structured specifications serve to reduce the pressure on consultants to think on their feet. And when they do interact, the discussion is likely to be more about procedures and factual matters than an interchange of subjective opinions.

A clear example of the market maturation process is demonstrated over the last thirty years in the IT consulting industry, which has shown itself remarkably adept at taking originally interactive consulting services and subsequently automating them. In the late 1980s, business process reengineering (BPR) was a *bona fide* consulting service delivered by teams of consultants working side-by-side with clients in order to streamline organizational processes. As the BPR consulting market has grown rapidly and as more consulting firms have entered that market, this consulting service has rapidly evolved into a structured and standardized methodology that can be applied to many clients. By the end of the decade, this methodology had been codified to such an extent that highly automated BPR software was replacing BPR consulting. In many instances, clients were eventually able to apply the service to themselves without consulting help.

The same pattern holds true if we look at today's rapidly maturing market for Customer Relationship Management (CRM) software. It has passed through its "early adopter" stage in the mid-1990s, requiring much consulting marketing and assistance, to the point where now the IT component of this service is so clear and known that it reduces the subjectivity in marketing the service. In these two cases, the pattern has been set in which "conventional" consulting services transmute into software over time and, hence, reduce the risk inherent to the consultant-client relationship.

LOW RISK GOES ONLINE

Given the many varying levels of risk in consulting, I therefore conclude that trust is only of relative, rather than absolute, importance in the client-consultant relationship. Indeed, we may have historically made a virtue out of trust that is, in practice, only a necessity at certain times in the relationship or on certain types of projects. As I have argued, trust is driven by risk, and not all consulting projects are equally risky at all times. This brings me to the interesting possibility of using online consulting to replace the consultant under conditions of low risk.

Both Exhibits 18.1 and 18.2 indicate opportunities for "automation" under low risk conditions. Thus, the practice area of strategy consulting, which is dependent on considerable client interaction and input, is obviously more difficult to automate than projects with clearly defined procedures and strong elements of standardization, such as in the design and management of the outsourcing of a company's IT operations. Many of the routine tasks for monitoring IT performance can now be handled by computers themselves, but this is not possible in strategy consulting except for limited segments of those projects.

Of course, the majority of consulting services fall somewhere between these two extremes of completely open-ended, subjective projects and highly routinized, objective ones—and every project will have aspects of both within it. For example, the steps for carrying out market research (focus groups, quantitative surveys, etc.) are well-understood and can be implemented without extensive discussion between consultant and client. However, these same parties will require considerable interaction to define the content of the survey and assess the results. While surveys can be done online and quantitative results aggregated through using statistical software, the evaluation of client reactions and feedback is still best obtained by getting everyone together in one room.

Similarly, the tools and techniques for organizational consulting are only effective when deployed within a comparatively fluid framework, capable of reacting to the unique circumstances encountered in each project. However, even in this case, at certain points data can be quickly gathered over the Internet through online surveys of employees, especially for early problem definition, gaining reactions to possible changes, and monitoring the implementation/change process.

As the growing "automation" of certain consulting tasks and services takes place, it will reduce the cost of consulting, which has been an hour-driven profession. This saving can be translated into lower fees—always appreciated by clients but not by consultants. However, perhaps bigger advantages lie in shortening the length of projects and in gaining larger amounts of data from a wider range of people.

CHALLENGING THE BARRIERS TO ONLINE CONSULTING

When one examines why many management consultants believe that client relationships cannot be built or sustained remotely, two types of argument emerge:

- Online consulting has been thought of as something that will appeal mostly to small-scale clients who lack the financial resources to hire traditional, offline consultants. By contrast, its attraction to large-scale organizations is expected to be far more limited because these large firms are less price sensitive.

- Large corporations are also thought to have more complex issues, which will, in turn, require more complex consulting services. By contrast, small businesses are seen as having simpler needs, which can increasingly be met through prepackaged solutions.

In my opinion, both of these assumptions are highly questionable.

The Price Factor

Large organizations may have larger budgets, but for any given project, they are just as likely as small businesses to be interested in keeping the price low. The real problem here relates not to the absolute price an organization pays but to the price relative to other alternatives available, such as online consulting services.

Clients looking to hire consultants have traditionally faced two problems in selecting consultants: First, the scarcity of publicly available pricing information, and second, the inability to compare like-for-like types of consulting. To get around these barriers, clients invite multiple firms to tender proposals for the same project. The Internet could make this bidding process more open and efficient (and there's some small evidence that clients are, indeed, starting to use online auctions as a means for soliciting bids), but can it ever be more than a filtering process, sifting the wheat from the chaff among a variety of consulting firms?

The answer to this question lies in the online/offline price differential. If we assume that it proves significantly cheaper for the consulting to take place remotely rather than turn up in person, then we may see more clients interested in the online route. Of course, the online project would have to be designed very differently from the offline version, which makes like-for-like comparisons difficult. But it all comes down to the ratio of benefits to costs: What client will realistically say no to a proposition that offers them, say, 80 percent of the benefits for 20 percent of the cost?

Commoditization of Knowledge

Clients buying an online consultancy service may get a good deal in price, but will they also receive good service? It's highly possible for consulting firms to provide a useful online consulting service that focuses on clear-cut issues related to consulting, but a yawning chasm still lies between this type of consulting assistance and solving the amorphous problems common to most consulting. Won't a client who takes the online route necessarily have to sacrifice some complexity, both in terms of the problem diagnosis and the proposed solution?

It's an argument that comes down to another differential—not of price, but of intellectual capital. Consulting firms can be roughly segmented according to the ratio of tacit (informal knowledge) to explicit (formal knowledge) on which they depend. Most consulting currently depends on tacit knowledge brought to the client in the heads of the consultants. Thus, a high-end strategy firm will rely on bringing people together to brainstorm a unique and complicated client issue. However, the more a consulting service falls into the explicit and formal knowledge camp (e.g., many IT projects), it may qualify for remote delivery. For example, clients could pay a fee for accessing the consulting firm's Web site to obtain a "package" with specific instructions on how to design a compensation system, along with the firm's recommended "best practices." So far, firms have been giving away for free much of their explicit knowledge in their quarterly journals and on their Web sites.

For firms who rely almost wholly on tacit, informal knowledge, the extent to which their services will or won't be delivered online depends on the extent to which that knowledge stays tacit and informal within the firm. However, I think it will be very difficult to maintain this shadowy position because of three driving forces pushing consulting firms toward making their knowledge more explicit, formal, and public:

1. Clients' need for tangibility. For all the effort that consulting firms have put into marketing in the last decade, the industry's somewhat cloak-and-dagger history continues to haunt it. In particular, clients want reassurance that what they're buying constitutes value for their investment, and if they can't measure the output of a consulting project—as is so often the case—then they look for measurable input to prove its worth. Thus, consulting firms now find themselves having to invest increasingly in developing structured methodologies and tools that can be shown and demonstrated to wary clients. This new knowledge is becoming part of not only the client's domain but the public's as well.

2. Margin erosion. Under ever greater pressure to maintain high margins in what has become a very competitive, price sensitive market, many consulting firms are being forced to reevaluate their business models. These firms are turning increasingly to knowledge management (KM) systems so they can more efficiently pass on their firm's past experience and "best practices" to their current staff; in essence, KM is being used to replace learning by trial-and-error and avoiding the reinvention of old solutions (see Chapter 17, "Knowledge Management in Consulting").

Ironically, this more efficient KM process effectively devalues the content, reducing knowledge to mainly information and, in some cases, to mere factual data. Thus, the more accessible knowledge is to consultants, the less specialized it becomes and the more likely it will eventually become accessible to clients.

Up to now, we have seen consulting firms bringing knowledge to clients, rather than clients to knowledge. In many ways, this practice is inefficient, involving travel, time, and coordination costs in getting consultants to the client's work site. My prediction is that consulting firms will attempt to reduce much of this cost by putting clients in direct touch with the firm's individual gurus via the Internet, wherever they may be located in the world. This is a "pull" rather than "push" approach to marketing and knowledge dissemination. The question is: Will clients pay for it? My hunch is that over time they will get used to it, preferring electronic interaction over the intrusion of consultants in their workplaces.

Even if some elite consulting firms refuse to change and continue to emphasize the delivery of tacit, informal knowledge at the client's site in order to command premium rates, they will not be immune to the need to find other ways to minimize their inefficiencies.

3. Speed to market. Consultants exist to fill gaps in their clients' intellectual capital, gaps that are caused by the client's need to deal with rapid change and high uncertainty in the world economy. Most clients these days are constantly worried that competitors will get to their markets with new products faster than they do. Yet, every time a consulting firm identifies or implements a solution to speed a client to market, it indirectly creates demand among other companies who, while they may not want the same solution, want access to the consultants who invented these new solutions, if only to keep up with the latest fashion. This seems especially true in more mature consulting markets where clients are largely seeking to replicate their competitors' initiatives rather than to be leading-edge and innovative. Thus, consultants face a speed to market problem too and, hence, the future value of the Internet to them.

The intriguing irony is that, while consulting firms have fallen over themselves to come up with end-to-end service packages to provide one-stop panaceas for management's ills, they are more likely to stoke demand than satisfy it. In other words, the faster and more effectively consultants become in plugging the gaps in their clients' intellectual capital, the more these gaps become unfillable elsewhere with other potential clients. And because the cycle reinforces itself, what we may find in the future is that the time available for consultants to visit a client's site will shrink further and further. Moreover, as clients use consultants more and more, clients may become chronically dissatisfied because their gaps in intellectual capital will continue to grow despite consultants' input.

The consulting industry may therefore become a perpetual motion machine, forced to run faster and faster. It will become virtually impossible to complete projects in a reasonable amount of time as consulting firms, bidding for work in an intensely competitive market, try to out do their rivals by shaving time from their diagnosis and implementation efforts through the use of increasingly standardized and programmable services. In this environment, face-to-face contact may become a luxury that few consulting firms or clients can afford. Enter again the Internet and the potential value of online services.

VALUE CHAIN THREAT

The expensive corporate infrastructure that underpins today's typical large consulting firm is facing an identity crisis. After years in which millions of dollars have been expended by consulting firms to open offices, build up brands, and implement knowledge management systems, we still witness many potential clients, even existing ones, remaining unconvinced about the "true" value of consulting. Increasingly, sophisticated clients are asking for proof of its worth in return for the considerable premium they are asked to pay. Moreover, the Enron affair has seriously dented the idea that a big, "branded" consulting firm represents a fool-proof guarantee of quality and integrity.

Disintermediation is occurring in the value chain of the consulting industry, propelled and facilitated partly by skeptical clients and online opportunities. Up to now, the industry has relied on a traditional business model that captures off three advantages—but which is now in danger from disintermediation of the consulting value chain:

1. **Resource network:** The modern consulting firm represents a fast and efficient way of identifying the right expert for the right job. In effect, the value of a consulting firm to its clients lies in its telephone directory. Furthermore, as clients become more global, consulting firms have responded by globalizing their ability to find the right person, irrespective of his or her location.

2. **Quality assurance:** Consulting firms provide implied assurance to clients that the consultants with whom it staffs its teams are appropriately qualified with leading-edge knowledge. The bigger the firm and the more prominent its brand, the greater that assurance is perceived by prospective clients for themselves.

3. **Economies of knowledge:** Consulting firms offer access to superior knowledge bases in many specialized fields. These fields would be prohibitively expensive for clients to invest in and staff independently.

This business model is under threat today because consultants have typically not seen themselves as part of a much wider value chain. This myopic view applies both to the firm's view of itself and to its relationship with other firms and various activities along the value chain. The principal operating unit of even the largest consultancies has been historically one person—the consultant or perhaps a small team, each positioned as a central point in a hub that is supported by a large and expensive fixed-cost infrastructure populated by staff researchers and administrative personnel. The many support functions of a consulting firm today are designed to do just what its name suggests—to support the consultant.

Breaking Down the Chain

The concept of a broader value chain in consulting, however, challenges the traditional model because it sees consultants as only one part of an extended chain, including the many activities of consulting: marketing, advertising, selling, proposing, data-gathering, diagnosing, implementing, communicating, monitoring, and following up; and back in the firm, the various activities of managing, billing, hiring, training, and informing. For consultants, the great majority of them (with the exception of a few senior partners) are focused today on a relatively small segment in this chain; mainly that of diagnosing and implementing. The large mass of consultants have not been particularly involved in any great extent in the other stages. Furthermore, many of these stages, when addressed by the senior partners, are not really within their competence or personal preference for spending their time.

Thus, consulting firms are as ripe for disintermediation today as the insurance industry was five years ago. First is the high probability that much of the back-office support structure for consultants can be outsourced by taking advantage of the Internet and specialized software. This includes a large assortment of activities, such as the marketing and advertising of consulting, recruiting of consultants, training of consultants, maintaining knowledge management systems, billing and paying consultants, arranging travel, following-up with satisfaction surveys, and reselling clients. In one sense, this will be a relief to consulting firms, unloading a lot of costly noncore stuff that gets in the way. However, they will lose some control over these outsourced activities, and that can cause internal disruption and quality problems with clients.

A second and even more threatening possibility is that potential clients now have alternatives for cutting out the consultant and gaining knowledge, services, and information more directly from the Internet, from commissioned studies by market research companies, or from business school professors located miles and even continents away. There are also Web-based consulting services currently available for monitoring consumer buying behavior for a client's products. Most of these services will be widely advertised and available on the Web over time.

As a result, the only area in which consultants continue to hold sway is in their application of human thought to information (in effect, knowledge). But it is questionable how long this will remain unchallenged. Clients will gradually improve their direct access to knowledge, information, and other data; this opportunity will require them to build up their internal expertise to carry out the interpretation of knowledge. We will likely see the growth of internal consultants, company knowledge management systems, and company research centers that may even compete with consultants on their home grounds.

Furthermore, without exclusive ownership of the sources of data and information, consultants will find it harder to sustain client relationships through all stages of the consulting process. For example, the gap between strategy development and implementation has long been a weak link, and many an engagement has failed because it has not been possible to translate a strategic idea into a workable reality. But e-business has probably widened this gap. In the implementation stage, e-business makes it possible for many specialist suppliers to jump in to fill gaps in implementation, making it possible for clients to "do it themselves" without hand-holding by a face-to-face consultant.

THE FUTURE FIRM

Over the next five to ten years, in response to the twin pressures of client demand for greater specialization and the disintegration of the value chain, we are likely to see several changes in consulting firms.

First, all consulting firms will increasingly go online to handle those aspects of projects that can be "automated," as well as acting to outsource much of their back-office operations. Both steps will help to reduce costs and serve clients faster. But from there we are likely to see much variation in the types of consulting firms to emerge, such as:

- Formal alliances will be formed between consulting and nonconsulting firms that will act as resource networks so as to incorporate all types of specialized services.

- Large holding companies will form to make numerous acquisitions of both consulting and nonconsulting firms so as to gain control over more of the value chain.

- Contractor consulting firms will act as project managers to bring together subcontractors from small consulting and nonconsulting firms, as well as independent specialists, to tailor-make services to a particular client.

Future Projects

What might a typical project look like in the future? My hunch is it will look more and more like a studio making a movie. In today's film business, a studio has an option on a particular idea; it discusses it on and off with a small number of executive producers with whom the studio has worked in the past, and at some point decides to make the film. A producer is hired, who, in conjunction with the studio and the executive producer, appoints a director. While the director takes charge of hiring the cast and filming, the producer pulls together the highly complex logistics that go into filmmaking: hiring the crew, finding the locations, building the sets, etc., as well as keeping control of the overall timetable and budget.

The film industry work depends upon a multitude of independent specialists coming together for a short period of time in a creative endeavor involving multiple talents, all with a specific goal of making a film. Some of these specialists play a very specific role and are only involved for a very short period; others, like the director and producers are involved from start to finish. Once the film is completed, the crew disbands.

Although films are created by a number of small companies and freelance specialists, consulting projects operate in marked contrast, tending to be delivered by a single firm with full-time employees. The implication of film-making for consulting is that the studio model may become the future consulting firm as the consulting firm acts as a contractor of services delivered mostly by sub-contractors not owned by the firm. Or to continue with this logic, might it not be possible for clients to act as their own producers and prime contractors, cutting out consultants altogether?

OPPORTUNITIES BEYOND ROTE ONLINE CONSULTING

This chapter puts forward five fundamental reasons why online consulting is likely to become more of a reality in the future:

- The more structured and less interactive the consulting service, the less important trust actually is, and, therefore, the more likely it can be converted into an online and software package.

- The potential price differential offered by lower cost online consulting services versus more expensive offline consulting is likely to become highly attractive to all sizes of potential clients.

- The increasing commoditization of intellectual capital suggests that eventually little genuine difference may exist between the knowledge delivered in face-to-face consulting and that delivered remotely.

- Online services can replace many non-core services of consulting firms.

- Online consulting will improve efficiency in a consulting firm's operating environment where margins are now considerably lower than they were a decade ago.

To date, online's advantages have been confined to limited segments of consulting where interaction (fluidity and intangibility) is low and where trust is relatively unimportant, such as in gathering factual data, market research, and software support. By contrast, consulting work involving problems that are hard to define has continued to be conducted face-to-face, even in those parts of projects where it may not be necessary. While these differences will continue, I predict that more and more activities will become susceptible to online support. To understand how these developments are likely to evolve in the future, let us return to the different phases of a consulting project and the possibilities for online assistance to them (see Exhibit 18.3).

The Sales Cycle

Will it ever be possible to sell consultancy via the Internet? So far, consulting firms have not been particularly astute about using the Internet for marketing. They have treated it mainly as another vehicle for "pushing" their ideas at prospective clients. Most sites emphasize descriptions of the firm's typical solutions to client problems by posting reports, surveys, and methodologies from work they have completed. While clients may be interested in these postings, it also creates an overhead for the client to narrow down from a plethora of available methodologies to the one approach they might want to explore further with the consulting firm.

As any conventional consultant will tell you, an important part of the initial stages of scoping a project for preparation of a proposal is to interview employees in a client organization and then to understand the specifics of the issues raised, whether these be strategic, operational, or technical. These issues are

Exhibit 18.3	Potential Opportunities for Online Consulting	
Sale	Specification	Development and Implementation
Self-diagnosis tool Benchmarking	Online business simulation and systems thinking tools Large-scale employee surveys Self-selection of project participants	"Offshore" delivery, particularly of IT systems and market research Project-specific extranets that enable clients to monitor progress

usually complex because of the number of people involved and their varying perspectives.

However, more success has been found by consulting firms that are operating online with question and answer data-gathering Web sites. For example, one firm asks client employees to submit via email a list of factors falling under the standard categories in a SWOT analysis (strengths, weaknesses, opportunities, and threats). Other firms are posting self-diagnosis tools, which have proved popular with clients (Ernst & Young's online is the most high-profile example). Online consulting may not yet be well designed when it comes to finding and applying the right solution to the right problem, but it is well suited for a prospective client to submit perceptions and opinions and, perhaps, even to engage in self-diagnosis of issues. The self-diagnosis client may also be able to benchmark his or her company against data against other companies. In this way, the client can determine if a real need exists to invite a face-to-face consultant to the client's site for further consultation.

In the future, investing more in diagnostic tools should represent a valuable form of online intellectual capital and competitive advantage for consulting firms plus offer a reduction in marketing expenses. By transferring pre-project diagnostic tools from the consultant (who may have a vested interest in selling a particular solution) to the client, the online client may be able to demonstrate to their own satisfaction that a face-to-face consultant is actually needed. In other words, online self-service diagnosis may offer an advantage over conventional offline relationships where a client may be suspicious, as many are, of a consultant's intent. If the consultant is actually invited to the client's site, their face-to-face dialogue (i.e., trust) may be strengthened by the prework already completed online by the client.

Specification

The act of specifying and agreeing to a consultant's proposal is second only to the sales cycle in terms of dependency on face-to-face interaction. In this process, client needs must be listened to; proposals must be tailored to fit the circumstances; and amendments need to be incorporated. In the wake of highly publicized difficulties with large IT projects, consultants have learned they cannot rely on voluminous specifications in which the minutia of a project take precedence over a single vision of what has to be achieved. Increasingly, they are supplementing face-to-face interaction with interactive ways to involve more people in scoping a potential project, gathering ideas for alternative approaches, and reviewing drafts of proposals. It may even be possible to use the openness of organizational intranets to encourage interested people to volunteer to take part in consulting projects, rather than co-opting the reluctant through a boss's directive.

Development and Implementation

Consulting projects always contain a phase where the consultant goes off to analyze data, reach conclusions, and draw up solutions; this may involve several weeks to customize a software package or a couple of days to brainstorm strategic options. Using intranets as a means of rapidly exchanging information, opinions, and material enables consulting firms to not only cut development costs but to encompass and tap a greater range of ideas and possible solutions.

As consultants reach out to include more people from the client's organization in the consulting process, they become increasingly aware that involving and communicating with these people is as fundamental to their success as the intellectual content of their solutions. Scenario planning, systems thinking, and simulation models are all means through which employees' ideas and reactions can be tested over an intranet, as well as to confirm buy-in before a final decision is taken. Although such techniques can be accomplished via a conventional brainstorming session, the chief disadvantage of doing so is that it is difficult to involve more than a small number of senior people in such a session. Commitment may be solid at the top of the organization to a diagnosis of the issues, but middle and junior managers may feel disenfranchised when not included. Online systems can help to widen the number of people involved, more ideas can be canvassed, provisional ideas can be circulated, and interim results discussed.

During this diagnosis stage, clients often register concern at its "black box" and closed nature, where the analysis is known only to the consultants before being revealed to the client. As a result, the client is unsure about what conclusions are being reached by the consultants operating out of sight. As a result, they are more likely to question its output. Giving clients access to a project-specific intranet allows them to view work-in-progress as well as to keep an eye on timesheets and the overall budget. Although such online systems are comparatively rare in consulting projects, other sectors have set useful precedents; for example, in complex construction projects, site-specific intranets are commonplace for clients, contractors, and subcontractors to update themselves on progress and monitor issues.

ONLINE INTEGRATION, NOT REPLACEMENT

Looking across the online initiatives that are likely to become common over the next five years, my prediction is that there will be a gradual migration of consultancy toward online ways of working. Central to this prediction is my point that the importance of trust between consultant and client varies inversely with the degree of risk involved. When risk is high, trust is important; and when risk is low, trust is less important. Under conditions of low risk and high trust, the Internet and online consulting will find numerous opportunities.

Certain online initiatives are likely to be of more interest to some firms than others, depending on whether internal efficiency or client management is the priority. Internal efficiency has more to do with outsourcing noncore functions on the disintegrating value chain, while client management has more to do with using the Web to gain client access, gather data, and involve client employees in the consulting process.

For consultants within the consulting firm, the Internet facilitates an open and easy exchange of different forms of information by a wide variety of parties. It also offers a faster and more individually controlled alternative to attending endless team meetings and spending wasted time on airplanes. As a way of approaching and involving the client, it offers a new means for making complex collaboration both manageable and profitable. However, trust of another kind may rear its head with a concern for the accuracy of online information—we will see if this is an issue.

The current evolution to new forms of online consulting is quite different from that envisaged in the late 1990s when there was speculation that pure online consulting firms would enter the market and revolutionize it. The threat of such wholesale cannibalization has receded in consulting as it has in other industries; instead, consulting firms are more likely to pick and choose among many more online options that complement and improve their existing *modus operandi*. In the end, consultants may even learn to love technology after all.

References

Baum, B. J. "Ernie: Four Years of Online Consulting," *Consulting to Management*, 11 no.1 (2000): 25–29.

Bloomfield, B. P. and A. Best, "Management Consultants: Systems, Development, Power and the Translation of Problems," *The Sociological Review*, 40 (1992): 532–560.

Bryson, J. R. "Business Service Firms, Service Space and the Management of Change," *Entrepreneurship and Regional Development* (1997): 93–111.

Bryson, J. R. "Spreading the Message: Management Consultants and the Shaping of Economic Geographies in Time and Space," *Knowledge, Space, Economy*, eds. J. R. Bryson et al. London: Routledge, 2000.

Maister, David H., Charles H. Green, Robert M. Galford. *The Trusted Advisor*. New York: Free Press, 2000.

Malecki, E. J. "Creating and Sustaining Competitiveness: Local Knowledge and Economic Geography," *Knowledge, Space, Economy*, eds. J. R. Bryson et al. London: Routledge, 2000.

CHAPTER 19

Research on Management Consulting

Flemming Poulfelt, Copenhagen Business School, and Larry Greiner, USC

Management consulting still remains a profession shrouded in a great deal of mystery, hidden behind private partnerships, client confidences, and proprietary methods. Interestingly, many clients spend millions of dollars each year on consulting, yet their choice of consultants seldom, if ever, depends on scientific evidence supporting the claims of the consultants. Instead, clients use their personal judgment, usually limited to a few people, as they assess a combination of the consultant's proposal, referrals, and "chemistry" with the consultants.

Maybe that is enough, or so it seems to prospective clients, yet if we look at the consulting approaches of various consulting firms, we find that they continue to apply their "preferred" analytical models and intervention methods, most of which are handed down and taught as "gospel" within firms, although these methods have rarely been validated through rigorous scientific inquiry.

In truth, we know very little "scientifically" about the effectiveness of management consulting, even though consultants and their firms are widely touted for their abilities to solve clients' problems. Much of the published information about consulting is largely anecdotal, based more on the personal experiences of consultants, rather than on systematic research. Many critics of the industry now argue that academics and outside commentators need to become more inquisitive and critical about what goes on inside management consulting.[1]

While there are many reasons to argue for more research on consulting, the overriding one is that consulting is a high stakes and expensive profession, which possesses considerable leverage in being able to affect the performance of companies, government agencies, careers, and even economies. Few other organizations possess this same potential for exercising so much power over the fate of others.[2] That potential in itself may explain why there is so little research, since negative results could produce ugly gossip, damage reputations, and diminish sales.

Therefore, the purpose of this chapter, because of the paucity of research about consulting, is to raise far more questions than can be answered about the industry and its efficacy. We will identify what we see to be the future agenda in need of research, coupled with our thoughts about the problems of performing research on consulting and how to overcome these barriers. We hope that our questions and suggestions will help to stimulate and focus future research efforts. For progress to be made, it will take the support and cooperation of all involved parties, consulting firms, clients, academics, and trade associations.

Exhibit 19.1	Consulting Publications over Time				
	Books[1]	Articles[2]	Articles in Peer Journals[2]	Articles[3]	Articles in Scholarly Journals[3]
1960–1970	0	0	0	11	8
1970–1980	3	105	33	39	32
1980–1990	17	563	225	51	29
1990–2000	100	903	457	869	157

Sources: Selected databases at CBS Library.
Note 1) Based on a search at CBS Library
Note 2) Bssed on a search in ABI/Inform
Note 3) Based on a search in Business Source Premier

FUTURE RESEARCH AGENDA

Publications about consulting have been slowly increasing over the past ten years, although the number of refereed journal articles, a measure of actual research, is still relatively small (see Exhibit 19.1). For future research, three obvious and pressing research questions face the consulting profession.

1. What is the frequency that client problems are actually solved by consulting interventions?

2. Even if these problems are solved, is it worth the investment?

3. In explaining the success of consulting efforts, what is the relative contribution of consultants versus other factors in the situation, such as the leadership of client organizations?

In addition to these questions are many other important ones concerning the management of consulting firms, competitive dynamics in the industry, impact of information technology, and the professional development of consultants.

In our view, the future direction of research is likely to focus on eight major streams of inquiry. These eight areas naturally overlap, but here we will address them separately so as to explore them more thoroughly.

• The consulting industry

• Roles, values, and behavior of consultants

• Knowledge creation and knowledge transfer

• Methods and models in consulting

• Impact of technology on consulting

• Client needs and the value of consulting

• Governance and performance of consulting firms

• Professionalism in consulting

The Consulting Industry

Research on the industry is characterized mostly by facts and descriptions about industry demographics, usually performed by consulting associations

(AMCF in the United States, FEACO in Europe, and Zen-Noh-Ren in Japan), as well as by market research firms like Kennedy Information and Alpha Publications. The published data describe trends, types of players, revenues, number of consultants, growth rates, specific markets, structural changes, and other patterns. There are also occasional academic contributions on specific countries and regions; examples include the study of the Scandinavian management consulting markets from 1990[3] and the study of the consultancy field in Western Europe from 1999.[4]

Most striking is the patchwork of available quantitative data, illustrating the weak statistical foundation for understanding the consulting industry. Whereas Coca-Cola and Pepsi routinely reveal precise accounting of their market shares, this is not the case in the consulting industry. One obvious explanation for the lack of transparency is the reluctance among consultancies, especially the private ones, to reveal sensitive information to not only their competition but potential clients. Another reason is that current industry watchers and pundits who gather data are inclined to sell their results because of the premium price commanded by data scarcity. Nevertheless, as more firms go public, the available data will become more common, and this will put pressure on private firms to reveal more about themselves.

Future research on the industry's structure and competitive dynamics needs to address a number of key questions, which include: What is the emerging structure of the industry? Who are the dominant players, and why? Are the top five firms more profitable than the next five? What determines profitability? What firms are declining, and why? Who are the rising stars? What are the dominant practice areas, and how are they changing? Which areas of practice are more profitable? How is the global market evolving? Which firms are doing what internationally? How is the selling process changing? What are the new fee structures? What are the new innovative concepts in the industry? What is the evolving connection between consulting and academe? And what are clients' attitudes toward consulting?

Many of these questions can be answered with simple descriptive statistics from available data and surveys—but much of which requires a lot of digging and cooperation from the firms. An even more intriguing and difficult challenge is to perform research that seeks to establish causality from using statistical analysis. This involves the "why" questions; for example, we need to know if different types of fee structures lead to better or worse results for clients. Are firms that sell integrated solutions more profitable than ones that narrowly specialize? How does innovation take place in the industry; what causes it, and how is it spread within consulting firms and to clients? As some have contended, do high performing clients use consultants more frequently than do lower performing clients? And if so, why isn't consulting reaching the clients who need it the most?

Roles, Values, and Behavior of Consultants

When reviewing the currently available literature in consulting, we find that most of the writing is about the roles and behavior of consultants.[5] This literature has focused on such questions as: What are the different roles played by management consultants when undertaking client assignments? What are the implications of different role patterns? Do certain roles produce better results than others? Do roles and values differ between the major practice areas of consulting, such as IT consultants versus strategy consultants? How can consultants develop the necessary skills and competencies needed to perform various roles? The underlying practical reason for these studies is to find the right kind of consultant for the particular job.

Much of what has been written about consultant roles and behavior is normative—that is, the author's personal opinion dominates what he/she prescribes to be the "best" role to pursue in order to achieve optimum results. These prescriptions, usually appearing in the "how to do it" literature, are often generalized in terms of their "truth" that should be applicable to all consultants in all types of consulting. However, the scientific empirical grounding about what role behaviors actually lead to improved results under what conditions is still quite limited. One study from 1994 developed a "1 + 7" consulting role model based on case stories of consulting assignments illustrating different roles and their underlying competences.[6] Nees and Greiner also describe five consulting roles based on their research; they argue that consultants and even firms cannot play all roles because each role implies different values and behavior. Individuals, through their personalities, gravitate toward certain roles. And firms, because of their focused business strategies, tend to choose a particular line of business approach to clients. The authors identify five different role-types from their research that characterize both individual and firm-wide approaches to consulting: "mental adventurers" (the Rands), "strategic navigators" (the BCGs), "management physicians" (the McKinseys), "system architects" (the Accentures), and "friendly co-pilots (the small independents)."[7] Typologies such as this one need to be studied for how each role behaves with clients and what their strengths and limits are in achieving certain kinds of results.

Knowledge Creation and Knowledge Transfer

Knowledge is the fuel in consulting. It involves both the creation and the sharing of knowledge within consulting firms, as described in Chapter 17. We need to know much more about how knowledge is created in firms and how it is distributed. What is the relative weight and interaction between explicit and tacit knowledge among consultants in their various approaches toward clients, and how are these two different kinds of knowledge developed in firms? A related question involves how knowledge is transferred from consultant to client. Do consultants, in fact, leave knowledge in the client's organization, as they often claim? Or do the consultants take it away with them, as critics often accuse?

A recent study on knowledge sharing in consulting firms found that many firms are still focused on rather simple issues of implementation, such as how to get consultants to use the firm's KM system.[8] The dilemma facing individual consultants concerns how to balance billable hours with time spent on internal knowledge sharing activities. We need to know if firms that invest more in knowledge management systems actually end up performing better than firms with a lower investment in knowledge sharing. How do consulting firms motivate their consultants to use the knowledge system? Are potential clients more attracted to consulting firms that advertise their knowledge capabilities? For those firms that establish internal research centers, we need to find out how they create new knowledge for the firm and if it is worth the investment.

Other knowledge research, primarily conducted in Europe, is related to the creation, dissemination, and the emergence of fads in management practice. We all remember the craze about Japanese management methods and how

| Consulting Insights | **Research Project on Knowledge Sharing** |

What does knowledge sharing in a consulting firm mean in actual practice? What enhances and what impedes knowledge sharing? These questions were explored in a research project involving fifteen consulting firms, including major international consultancies and medium-sized firms located in Denmark. The data were based on semi-structured interviews and meetings with consultants at various levels and partners. The study also included organizational photography. The researcher took about 100 photos per firm, showing parts of the office space and consultants talking with each other in their offices and at meetings, then selected about thirty of these photos and asked a group of consultants to examine them and discuss knowledge sharing in their firm. The point of the photos and free association was to broaden the perspective of the researcher and, thereby, avoid the problem of potential "bias" from only obtaining answers to structured questions posed by the researcher. The findings from the study revealed that knowledge sharing worked best when consultants perceived it as a prerequisite for successful job performance. It also revealed the dilemma that consultants face in choosing between time to share knowledge and giving in to pressure to work on billable projects. The study highlighted the importance of trust between consultants if they are to use knowledge supplied by others. Finally, senior management should "walk the talk" when urging their consultants to engage in knowledge sharing. A seminar was conducted in the final stage of the project involving participants from all the firms to discuss the study's results.

everyone was trying to emulate these practices. Consulting firms in the U.S. even succumbed to this fad by selling their capabilities at installing Japanese management systems. Today, clients want to know about "best practices," as if these practices are applicable to all situations. However, we are concerned that blind conformity to management fashions can represent a threat to the long-term success of organizations, since the adoption of fads follows a different logic than situational analysis and tailor-made solutions. Some examples of research questions are: How do consultants create and use management fads in the selling of consulting? How are popular management concepts created and applied by consultants? What happens to clients who ask for and buy these fads from consultants? Have consultants spread the American way of management to countries where these methods may not be applicable or successful? The EU has sponsored CEMP (Creation of European Management Practice), which is a research project looking into how dissemination of practices takes place across countries. [9]

Methods and Models in Consulting

The "tools" of consulting include the various methods and analytical models that consultants use to understand and solve a client's problem. Often these tools become codified within the culture and ideology of a firm. Each firm develops its unique way of gathering data, favorite models for analyzing data, and certain intervention techniques used in presenting findings and implementing change. They may even recommend certain standardized solution "packages" that they have found useful elsewhere. We need to know more about what the most common methods of inquiry used by firms are and if certain methods are closely tied to certain types of studies. Are, for example, clients who adopt standardized solutions any more or less effective than those who opt for customized solutions?

At the same time, little is known about the effectiveness of various methods, other than what firms tell their clients about past results and what they publish in their firms' brochures and journals. This knowledge gap presents several significant openings for future research. Do certain intervention approaches, such as process facilitation, lead to greater commitment from client employees to change? Under what conditions are certain interventions more effective? Do interventions that reach deeply into the culture of the firm and the values of personnel produce better results, or do they provoke resistance? What should be the contingency rules of thumb for how deep to intervene?[10] Are firms that involve themselves in hands-on implementation more effective than those that believe in "stand off" independence and expert diagnosis? Do the particular methods used for data-gathering, such as interviews or surveys, affect the quality of analysis? Also, research needs to examine how consultants from one national culture attempt to spread and even impose their values on clients from another culture.[11]

The particular methods and models used by consulting firms also have marketing implications. Most major firms are now investing in their own research to create new analytical models that can be published in books and shown to clients. This emphasis on intellectual capital causes us to ask if clients are attracted more to consultants who offer their own models of analysis, such as the *Growth-Share Matrix* developed by BCG or the *7S* model by McKinsey or the *BPR* by Index Systems or the *Value Chain* by Monitor. What types of clients are attracted to more customized solutions, and which ones ask for standardized solutions that have proven successful elsewhere?

Another direction for future research concerns the effects of methods on behavior within the consulting firm itself. Some research evidence suggests that methods and models provide a common language across consultants, which in turn facilitates their ability to persuade and gain legitimacy with clients.[12] Do firms turn to standardized models and methods, not just for clients, but also as a way of indoctrinating their consultants into the firm's culture?

Impact of Technology on Consulting

Information technology is a major force impacting the development of the consulting business. Surprisingly, we cannot find a single research study on the impact and implications of technology on management consulting. For many years, the effects of technology were confined largely to operations consulting, such as in the installation of production systems like just-in-time methods to improve efficiency. However, recent years have seen the impact of information technology broaden out to affect all of consulting in many dramatic ways.

The consulting industry is increasingly being dominated by the IT firms; their service offerings cover a wide range, from e-business strategies to computer software and outsourcing. Chapter 1 points out a strong likelihood that in the future the industry might center around a few mega-technology firms (e.g., IBM Global Services, HP, and perhaps even Microsoft). At stake here are numerous issues open to research, including how consultants will be able to maintain independence when they are also being asked to sell hardware and outsourcing services at the same time, or what the effects are on industry competitiveness, pricing, and innovation from oligarchical consolidation among the firms.

The rapid emergence of e-business and other uses of the Web should be high on any research agenda. Many researchable issues are raised by the deconstruction of the value chain and new openings for specialized consulting firms. This development is clearly shown in Chapter 8 where the face of human resources consulting is changing rapidly because of Web-based opportunities, ranging from the outsourcing of transactions (e.g., payroll) to employee self-service (e.g., cafeteria selection of benefits). Consulting firms now find themselves coping with many new issues about how they will utilize the Web in their consulting for such activities as data gathering, monitoring the progress of projects, knowledge sharing, and involvement of clients in projects.

The role of the consultant will undoubtedly change due to the Web, and we need research to anticipate problems and identify solutions as these adjustments are made. For example, how will consultants balance their traditional expert roles with more facilitation-based approaches made possible by the Web? Consultants will need to acquire greater expertise in IT while at the same time learning how to involve clients in systems design and implementation. Will the consulting firms that develop these combined skills become more desirable to clients and, hence, more profitable?

Consulting firms are now reevaluating and changing their business strategies in order to compete in the IT world. For example, many new alliances are being formed between consulting firms and software vendors, and this will require in-depth research on how well these alliances are being managed. Consulting firms are also confronting serious hiring and training issues with regard to preparing consultants in the use of Web-based technologies. We need studies about how consulting firms are coping internally as they adjust their structures, systems, cultures, training, and hiring to take advantage of the many opportunities opened up by information technology.

Client Needs and the Value of Consulting

The typical rhetoric of consulting firms is "We add value," but the key research question is "Do they?" Bain, for instance, has claimed that their clients outperform the market three to one. One study of consulting's impact published in 1997 indicated a positive effect on the market value of

---

Consulting Insights | **Clients' View of Learning from Consultants**

To gain an understanding of clients' learning from consulting assignments, a study was done in Sweden in 2000. Interviews were conducted with high-level managers from two large Swedish telecom organizations. They all had considerable experience with engaging consultants to assist them in working on large-scale change projects. The interviews lasted one to two hours and were carried out in a semi-structured format, covering positive as well as negative experiences from working with consultants. Special attention was given to the managers' perceived learning during projects. The interviews were taped and transcribed.

The results indicated that learning is seldom discussed or planned for by clients. However, learning does in fact take place during consulting projects. It occurs at an individual level, unique to each person, and comprises mainly tacit knowledge. A not too surprising observation was that many of the managers still adhered to the traditional view of the consultant as a detached expert and not as a "teacher" or colleague who is present to enhance learning within the client organization.

companies, although the study was encumbered with uncertainties about its methodology and a large variance in results.[13] We clearly need more systematic research documenting the effects of consulting. Moreover, these studies need to include more than financial results by examining other variables such as consultant learning from the experience and the quality of knowledge left behind with the client.

In order to evaluate results from consulting interventions, a key objective should be to establish common metrics for measuring success, which is easier said than done. Problems arise with using only the client's financial results, since many factors other than the consultant's actions can affect these numbers. If financial numbers are used, they should be ones that are most directly linked and logically related to the specific interventions. For example, if the goal is plant waste reduction, than that should be the measure, but it should also be compared to waste rates at similar plants in the same company where no interventions are made so as to control for nonconsultant effects. Other outcome indicators of success are pertinent to most consulting projects and worthy of measurement, such as a client's commitment to change and cohesion among the client's top management team. In all of these calculations of "return" on investment, the cost of the consultant's intervention and the expended management time in the change process should be weighed against the results.

Many difficult questions arise concerning the establishment of causality in evaluating how a consulting intervention interacts with certain aspects of a client's situation, such as local leadership, to affect the results. Rarely will the consultant's work be the sole causal element, so contingency theories need to be constructed that describe which interventions work better under what conditions, such as is presented in Chapter 12 for four different intervention strategies.

From the client's perspective, several additional issues for future research pertain to the question of how and why clients hire consultants. Studies in this tradition need to examine both the rational and emotional aspects of consultant selection.[14] For example, if the client hires the consultant only to justify prior decisions already planned by the management, what is the effect on the consultants and the project results? Or if the client is really not serious about major change, as often happens, why are they hiring consultants? The effects of growing sophistication among clients will likely affect how they want to work with consultants; for example, will clients with more MBAs and ex-consultants in their top management expect to become more actively involved in projects, and are these clients likely to purchase consultants who favor and practice methods of client involvement?

Governance and Performance of Consulting Firms

The reluctance of consultants to reveal financial numbers about their practices also suggests that they are rather closed to access by researchers. It is therefore not surprising that few studies of governance structures and management practices in consulting firms have taken place. What constitutes effective management in consulting firms? How do do management practices and organization structures differ between IT firms and strategy firms? Are there certain "best practices," as suggested in Chapter 16, that distinguish high performing firms from others? Do better performers invest more in R&D

and knowledge management? Are they more diversified in their business strategies?

Another set of major research questions relates to the recent decisions of many firms to go public. How does this decision alter the strategy, priorities, and management of firms? For example, will the presence of a board of directors result in more professional CEOs being selected to head these firms, in contrast to the past practice of the partnership electing one of its own? Will publicly listed firms grow faster and become more profitable? Will pressures from the stock market cause public firms to enter nonconsulting markets in order to increase cash flow and profits? Will these public firms be more inclined to "slip" on independence and ethics issues in return for short-term profits?

There are also newer developments impacting firms, such as alliances, outsourcing, and the use of a sales force? How will firms change in their strategies and management when they operate in alliances and cannot fully control their partners? Does the presence of outsourcing compromise the need for independence expected in traditional definitions of consulting? Does the implementation of once frowned upon marketing activities, such as a dedicated sales force and public advertising, increase the performance of firms?

Consulting as a Profession

A continuing issue in consulting lays in the debate about whether it is a profession or not. Some contend that it is not because just about anyone can declare themselves to be a consultant.[15] Still others argue that it is indeed a profession because of the advanced level of expertise and knowledge required to perform effectively. We are inclined toward the latter argument, but it raises numerous research questions about the nature of standards and enforcement.

While many industry leaders and associations have previously attempted to define standards of professionalism for consulting, we need to know more from surveys of consultants about how they personally define standards for their work. Are these standards changing from past definitions? Do these standards vary, for example, between IT consultants and strategy consultants or between senior consultants and junior consultants? And even if we know and can agree on what these standards should be, how can they best be communicated and enforced within the industry and inside firms? Do consultants working for firms with an emphasis on strong codes of ethical conduct actually behave the code on the job? And are firms that rigorously enforce ethical behavior any more or less profitable than firms that do not?

What role do the trade associations, such as IMC and ICMCI, play in setting and enforcing standards? Are "certified" consultants any more professional in their knowledge, attitudes, and behavior than those who are not certified? Some years ago, Marvin Bower from McKinsey & Company, in response to a question regarding the need for certification of consultants, answered in a way that implied that the McKinsey name in itself was sufficient for certification.[16] We need to know if certification by an association makes any difference in the eyes of clients in choosing consulting firms.

A closely related and highly important theme is consultant ethics. Little is known from research about what the common ethical issues are that consultants face and how they can best resolve these issues. Consultants are often exposed to situations characterized by ambiguity where they cannot always apply standard ethical rules. No doubt these ethical challenges will grow in the future as consulting firms expand into nonconsulting activities. Research needs to examine how firms are training their consultants in ethics and then evaluate which training methods are more effective.

ISSUES IN CONDUCTING RESEARCH

As already indicated, it is not an easy task to undertake research on management consulting. The problems are complex, the variables are numerous, and the data are difficult to obtain. Nevertheless, more research must be accomplished if the field is to advance in its effectiveness and professionalism.

In general, we believe an eclectic and open position should be taken by consultants, associations, firms, and scholars toward the philosophy and methods of research used to investigate management consulting. It is important to welcome a broad spectrum of research methodologies, including lab studies, surveys, field studies, and action research. This research may be highly quantitative or mainly qualitative. It can search systematically for causes using numbers or explore qualitatively with interviews and case studies. It can test hypotheses or suggest new ones. It can be carried out by academics or by consultants or both together or even by clients who want to evaluate their investments.

What follows may appear well known to experienced researchers, but we want to highlight three important issues in the conduct of research on consulting that often cause problems: 1) defining the purpose of research; 2) gaining access to consulting firms and their activities; and 3) building collaboration among the involved parties.

Defining the Purpose

The main objective of research is to generate new knowledge through scientific inquiry conducted without prejudice toward the outcomes of a particular study. To date, as we have mentioned, relatively little empirical research has been performed to delve into the mysteries of consulting. Even the available subjective accounts reflect little in the way of systematic research design and data gathering. Anecdotal data from a few consulting experiences, we believe, should not be put forth by consultants as containing the "truth" about certain "best practices" without more empirical verification. This higher standard does not preclude consultants from acting as researchers, but it does assign a special responsibility to them for demonstrating objectivity when making claims about the value of their methods.

Being clear on the purpose of a research study is an essential first step. If the study is to explain causality, such as establishing a link between certain types of interventions (e.g., process versus expert) and financial results, then the study should ideally include a large sample with quantitative data and be accompanied by rigorous statistical analysis. If it is to explore new untapped issues for the purpose of generating new hypotheses and theories, then the use of field research, case studies, and qualitative data from interviews is appropriate (see Chapters 15 and 16 for the results from this research approach).

Clearly, a qualitative approach is more subjective, but it can be extremely useful when the numbers aren't available or as a prelude to generating well-defined hypotheses for verification through additional quantitative research.

Studies about the competitive structure of the consulting industry are more amenable to quantitative research because of the public availability of numerical data. In contrast, studies about the consulting process itself are more likely to be qualitative, based on interviews and observations by the consultant or client. It is possible to perform quantitative studies of supposedly subjective factors by using scalar surveys with numerical responses. Granted, surveys are based on the perception of the respondent, but these results often come closer to reality when clear trends appear across a large sample of survey data.

Gaining Access

Access is a major stumbling block to research studies that attempt to investigate internal practices within consulting firms and to observe the consulting process. Consulting firms are understandably reluctant to be exposed for several reasons, ranging from not wanting to look bad to the potential disruption from the presence of researchers. Nevertheless, we believe there are some useful ways around these problems:

- **Use disguised names.** In most studies, it is not necessary to reveal the actual names of consulting firms, clients, and consultants. Only in studies of industry structure and competition between firms are the names of firms usually essential.

- **Gain support of professional associations.** Some consulting associations may sponsor research and help researchers gain access.

- **Consultants act as surrogate researchers.** Academics can ask consultants to observe what transpires within the consulting firm or in the consulting process and to keep detailed notes. Then the academics can study those notes and work with the consultant in writing up the results.

- **Define the study in ways that meet the consulting firm's needs.** Obviously, the more the firm feels a stake in learning from the study, the more likely they are to grant access.

- **Use anonymous surveys.** Large surveys, with the sponsorship of several consulting firms and associations, can be conducted without asking for the identification of firms, clients, or individual consultants.

- **Go through the client.** Clients may be more open to research that examines the consulting process and documents its effects, since it is their own money that is being expended. Here, clients should request that their consultants permit outside researchers to observe and gather data during the consulting process.

Building Collaboration

Too often academics have defined research in narrow ways useful only to themselves, and then they are puzzled why they are unwelcome by consultants and clients. Furthermore, consultants tend to be wary about the intrusion of researchers and are skeptical about the value of academic research. These differences of opinion between the parties too often hinder the accomplishment of needed research.

The ideal is to create a win-win situation where both scholars and consultants gain from their cooperation. Consulting firms can define what they want to know and then solicit researchers to help them. This approach is more likely to work than academics approaching consulting firms with their own projects in mind. In Europe, an incentive for this type of work is reflected in "The Best Management Practices Award," which highlights outstanding pieces of consulting work performed by consulting firms. This award, and the research behind it, demonstrates the best in analysis, thinking, and cooperation between consultancies and their clients.[17]

Often the only way for academic researchers to gain access is to become consultants themselves, while keeping in mind their secondary role as researchers. Two of the authors in this book, Professors Larry Greiner and Arvind Bhambri, took this approach in one study, resulting in their article, "New CEOs and Strategic Change," which won the McKinsey Prize at the annual 1999 Strategic Management Society Meeting.[18] Similarly, the other author of this chapter, Professor Flemming Poulfelt, teamed with Professor Adrian Payne from Cranfield University to win the Management Consulting Division Award at the Academy of Management Meeting in 1992 for their paper, "Marketing of Management Consulting Firms: Towards a Relationship Marketing Approach."[19] For those working in this way, many industry watchers agree that the combination of both roles is likely to result in higher quality results,[20] and some contend that a "real theoretical breakthrough may come out of in-depth consultative work."

In Exhibit 19.2, we present a model that describes the research approach taken by Greiner and Bhambri for their McKinsey Award paper and subsequent journal article. They began with leads and cues from past consulting to CEOs on strategic change, and then during one of these projects, they kept good notes, gathered both qualitative and quantitative data, and then wrote about their experience afterward within the context of the existing research literature. This process, beginning with a consulting project, can lead to publications in both academic and practitioner journals, as well as to new teaching cases. The circular part of the model is interesting for its synergistic effects in increasing both publications and consulting leads.

MOVING FORWARD

The mystery and secrecy surrounding the consulting profession has not benefited the profession or scholars interested in advancing knowledge about it. However, there seems to be a growing realization among both scholars and consultants that research on consulting is not only a means to develop new insights but provides a way to legitimize the business of consulting in the eyes of an unknowing public. More research projects on consulting are being launched, more papers are being presented at academic and professional conferences, and more books and publications on consulting are being published.

As this chapter has illustrated, the consulting profession has many challenging research issues on its agenda. To move ahead, more active support from the management consulting community (firms and associations) will help to stimulate researchers around the globe. Many scholars are eager to conduct research on consulting because of the industry's impact on clients, education,

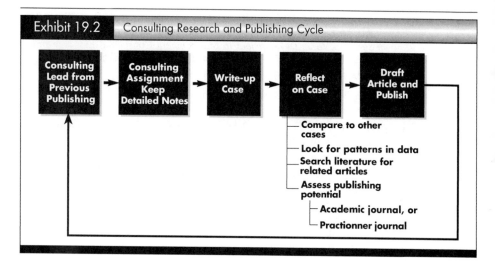

Exhibit 19.2 Consulting Research and Publishing Cycle

Consulting Lead from Previous Publishing → Consulting Assignment Keep Detailed Notes → Write-up Case → Reflect on Case → Draft Article and Publish

- Compare to other cases
- Look for patterns in data
- Search literature for related articles
- Assess publishing potential
  - Academic journal, or
  - Practionner journal

national economies, and management practices. Much can be achieved if consulting firms are willing to allocate some of their resources in time, money, and commitment to future research endeavors.

At the same time, academics need to become more open, sensitive, and collaborative in how they go about the research process. Consulting firms and clients will not stand still in accepting only the researcher's definition of the study methods and questions; rather, the researcher's approach must be carefully tailored to the situation and the goals of all those involved. Everyone affected must see a benefit for themselves. Under these positive conditions, our combined resources and imaginations will likely generate valuable new knowledge about an industry of major importance to many people and institutions.

Notes to the Chapter

[1]"Trimming the Fat—A Survey of Management Consultancy," *The Economist* 22 (March 1997).

[2]J. O'Shea and C. Madigan, *Dangerous Company—The Consulting Powerhouses and the Business They Save and Ruin* (London: NB Publishing, 1997).

[3]P. O. Berg, H. H. Hansen, and F. Poulfelt, *Management Consulting: An Analysis of Unregulated Professional Markets—the Case of the Scandinavian Management Consultants* (Copenhagen: Copenhagen Business School, 1990).

[4]M. Kipping and L. Engwall, *Management Consulting—Emergence and Dynamics of a Knowledge Industry* (Oxford: Oxford University Press, 2002).

[5]S. Tiles, "Understanding the Consultant's Role," *Harvard Business Review*, 39 (1969); E. Schein, *Its Role in Organization Development*, vol. 1 of *Process Consultation* (Reading, MA: Addison-Wesley, 1969); L. E. Greiner and R. O. Metzger, *Consulting to Management*.(Englewood Cliffs, NJ: Prentice-Hall, 1983).

[6]A. Williams and S. Woodward, *The Competitive Consultant* (London: MacMillan, 1994).

[7]D. Nees and L. E. Greiner, "Seeing Behind the Look-A-Like Management Consultants," *Organizational Dynamics* (Winter 1985).

[8]N. Petersen and F. Poulfelt, *Knowledge Management in Action: A Study of Knowledge Management in Management Consultancies,* in ed. A. F. Buono, *Knowledge and Value Development in Management Consulting,* Research on Consulting Series 1, (Greenwich, CT: Information Age Publications Inc., 2002).

[9]Reported in M. Kipping and L. Engwall, (2002).

[10]R. Harrisson, "Understanding Your Organization's Character," *Harvard Business Review* (May–June 1972).

[11]M. Gibson, "Avoiding Intervention Pitfalls in International Consulting," *Journal of Management Consulting* 10, no. 2 (1998): 59–66.

[12]A. Werr, "The Language of Change—the Roles of Methods in the Work of Management Consultants" (Ph.D. dissertation, The Economic Research Institute, Stockholm School of Economics, 1999).

[13]A. L. Solomon, "Do Consultants Really Add Value to Client Firms?" *Business Horizon* (May–June 1997): 67.

[14]T. Clark, *Managing Consultants* (Buckingham: Open University Press, 1995); T. Clark, and G. Salaman, "The Management Guru as Organizational Witchdoctor," *Organization* 3, no. 1 (1996a): 85–107.

[15]P. Kyrö, *The Management Consulting Industry Described by Using the Concept of "Profession"* (Helsinki: University of Helsinki, 1995).

[16]Personal interview in New York with Marvin Bower (1987).

[17]http://www.mca.org.uk (the UK Management Consulting Association) and http://www.danskmanagementraad.dk (the Danish Management Consulting Association).

[18]A. Bhambri and L. Greiner, "New CEOs and Strategic Change Across Industries" (paper presented at Strategic Management Society Conference, Berlin, 1998).

[19]A. Payne and F. Poulfelt, "Marketing of Management Consulting Firms: Towards a Relationship Marketing Approach," (Best Paper Proceedings presented at The Academy of Management Meeting, Las Vegas, NV, 1992).

[20]E. Gummesson, *Qualitative Methods in Management Research* (London: Sage, 1991).

Appendix: Recent Books on Management Consulting

Argyris, C. *Flawed Advice and the Management Trap.* Oxford: Oxford University Press, 2001.

Ashford, Martin. *Con Tricks—The Shadow World of Management Consultancy and How to Make it Work for You.* New York: Simon & Schuster, 1998.

Bellman, Geoffrey M. *The Consultant's Calling.* San Francisco: Jossey-Bass, 2002.

Biech, Elaine. *The Business of Consulting—The Basics and Beyond.* San Francisco: Jossey-Bass/Pfeiffer, 1999.

Biech, Elaine. *The Consultant's Quick Start Guide.* San Francisco: Jossey-Bass/Pfeiffer, 2002.

Biswas, Sugata and Daryl Twitchell. *Management Consulting—A Complete Guide to the Industry,* 2nd ed. New York: John Wiley and Sons, Ltd., 2002

Block, Peter. *Flawless Consulting: A Guide to Getting Your Expertise Used,* 2nd ed. San Francisco: Jossey-Bass Publishing, 1999.

Block, Peter and Andrea Markowitz. *The Flawless Consulting Fieldbook and Companion: A Guide to Understanding Your Expertise.* San Francisco: Joseey-Bass/Pfeiffer, 2000.

Buono, Anthony F., ed. *Current Trends in Management Consulting.* Greenwich: Information Age Publishing, 2001.

Buono, Anthony F., ed. *Developing Knowledge and Value in Management Consulting. Vol. 2, Research in Management Consulting.* Greenwich: Information Age Publishing, 2002.

Carucci, Ron A. and Toby Tetenbaum. *The Value-Creating Consultant—How to Build and Sustain Lasting Client Relationships.* New York: Amacom, 2000.

Clark, Timothy and Robin Fincham. *Critical Consulting—New Perspectives on the Management Advice Industry.* Oxford: Blackwell Publishers, 2002.

Cockman, P., Evans, B. and P. Reynolds. *Consulting for Real People: A Client-Centered Approach for Change Agents and Leaders.* New York: McGraw-Hill, 1999.

Cody, Thomas G. *Management Consulting—A Game Without Chips.* Fitzwilliam, N.H.: Kennedy Information, 2001.

Cohen, William A. *How to Make It Big as a Consultant,* 3rd ed. New York: Amacom, 2001.

Cope, Mick. *The Seven Cs of Consulting—Your Complete Blueprint for Any Consultancy Assignment.* London: Prentice Hall, 2000.

Curnow, Barry and Jonathan Reuvid, eds. *The International Guide to Management Consultancy—The Evolution, Practice and Structure of Management Consultancy Worldwide.* London: Kogan Page, 2001.

Cullen, Sara and Leslie L. Willcocks. Intelligent IT Outsourcing—Eight Building Blocks to Success. Oxford: Butterworth-Heinemann, 2003.

Czerniawska, Fiona. *Management Consultancy in the 21st Century.* London: McMillan Business, 1999.

Czerniawska, Fiona. *Management Consultancy—What Next?* London/Basingstoke: Palgrave Macmillan Press, 2002.

Czerniawska, Fiona. *The Intelligent Client—Managing Your Management Consultant.* London: Hodder & Stoughton Educational Division, 2002.

Czerniawska, Fiona. *Value-Based Consulting.* London/Basingstoke: Palgrave Macmillan, 2002.

Engwall, L. and C. B. Eriksson. *Advising Corporate Superstars.* London: Kings College, 1999.

Ferguson, Michael. *The Rise of Management Consulting in Britain.* Aldershot: Ashgate Publishing Group, 2002.

Fombrun, Charles J. and Mark D. Nevins. *The Advice Business—Essential Tools and Models for Management Consulting.* Upper Saddle River, N. J.: Pearson Higher Education, 2003.

Freedman, Rick. *The eConsultant—Guiding Clients to Net Success.* San Francisco: Jossey-Bass/Pfeiffer, 2001.

Fuller, Gordon W. *Getting Most Out of Your Consultants*. New York: CRC Press, 1999.

Haslebo, Gitte and Kit Sanne Nielsen. *Systems and Meaning—Consulting in Organizations*. London: Karnac Books, 2000.

Hilburt-Davis, Jane W. and Gibb Dyer. *Consulting to Family Businesses—A Practical Guide to Contracting, Assessment, and Implementation*. Chichester: John Wiley and Sons, Ltd, 2003.

Kipping, M. and L. Engwall, eds. *Management Consulting. Emergence and Dynamics of a Knowledge Industry*. Oxford: Oxford University Press, 2002.

Holmes, Andrew. *The Chameleon Consultant—Culturally Intelligent Consultancy*. Aldershot: Gower Publishing, Ltd., 2002.

Holtz, Herman. *The Concise Guide to Becoming an Independent Consultant*. New York: Wiley, 1999.

Holtz, Herman. *Getting Started in Sales Consulting*. New York: John Wiley and Sons, 2000.

Kara, H. and Muir, P. *Commissioning Consultancy—Managing Outside Expertise to Improve Your Services*. Lyme Regis, Dorset: Russell House Publishing, 2003.

Kubr, Milan, ed. *Management Consulting—A Guide to the Profession*. Geneva: ILO, 1998.

Lambert, Tom. *High Income Consulting: How to Build and Market Your Professional Practice*. Nicholas Brealey Publishing, 1997.

Lee, Karen. *Consulting into the Future—the Key Skills*. London: Hodder & Stoughton, 2002.

Maister, David. *True Professionalism*. New York: Free Press, 1997.

Maister, David, Charles Green, and Robert M. Galford. *The Trusted Advisor*. New York: Free Press, 2000.

Maister, David. *Practice What You Preach*. New York: Free Press, 2001.

Meislin, Marcia. *The Internal Consultant*. Menlo Park, CA: CRISP Publications, 1997.

Mooney, Paul. *The Effective Consultant—How to Develop the High Performance Organisation*. Dublin: Oak Tree, 1999.

Nelson, Bob and Peter Economy. *Consulting for Dummies*. New York: IDG Books Worldwide, 1997.

O'Shea, J. and C. Madigan. *Dangerous Company—The Consulting Powerhouses and the Businesses They Save and Ruin*. London: NB Publishing, 1997.

Phillips, Jack. *The Consultant's Scorecard: Tracking Results and Bottom-Line Impact of Consulting Projects*. New York: McGraw-Hill Publishing, 1999.

Pinault, Lewis. *Consulting Demons—Inside the Unscrupulous World of Global Corporate Consulting*. Chichester: Harper Business, 2000.

Prien, Erich P., Jeffery S. Schippmann and Kristin O. Prien. *Individual Assessment—As Practiced in Industry and Consulting*. Mahwah, N.J.: Lawrence Erlbaum Associates, Inc., 2002.

Rasiel, Ethan M. *The McKinsey Way*. New York: McGraw-Hill Publishing, 1999.

Rasiel, Ethan M. and Paul N. Friga. *The McKinsey Mind*. New York: McGraw-Hill Publishing, 2002.

Sadler, Philip, ed. *Management Consultancy—A Handbook for Best Practice*. London: Kogan Page, 1998.

Schaffer, Robert H. *High-Impact Consulting: How Clients and Consultants Can Leverage Rapid Results into Long-Term Gains*. San Francisco: Jossey-Bass, 1997.

Schein, Edgar H. *Process Consultation Revisited—Building the Helping Relationship*. Reading, MA: Addison-Wesley, 1999.

Scott, Beverly. *Consulting on the Inside*. ASTD, 1999.

Scott, M.C. *The Intellect Industry. Profiting and Learning from Professional Services Firms*. New York: Wiley, 1998.

Silberman, Melvin, ed. *The Consultant's Toolkit: High Impact Questionnaires, Activities and How-to Guides for Diagnosing and Solving Client Problems*. New York: McGraw-Hill Trade, 2000.

Sveiby, K.E. *The New Organizational Wealth—Managing and Measuring Knowledge-Based Assets*. San Francisco: Berrett-Koehler, 1997.

Weiss, Alan. *Getting Started in Consulting*. New York: John Wiley & Sons, Inc., 2000.

Weiss, Alan. *The Ultimate Consultant*. San Francisco: Jossey-Bass/Pfeiffer, 2001.

Weiss, Alan. *How to Acquire Clients—powerful Techniques for the Successful Practitioner*. San Francisco: Jossey-Bass/Pfeiffer, 2002.

Weiss, Alan. *Value-Based Fees*. San Francisco: Jossey-Bass/Pfeiffer, 2002.

Werr, Andreas. *The Language of Change—The Roles of Methods in the Work of Management Consultants.* The Economic Research Institute. Stockholm: Stockholm School of Economics, 1999.

Wickhan, Philip A. *Management Consulting.* London: Financial Times, Pitman Publishing, 1999.

Ziegenfuss, James T. *Organization and Management Problem-solving—A Systems and Consulting Approach.* London: Sage Publications, 2002.

Index